The Taiwan Conundrum
in U.S. China Policy

The Taiwan Conundrum in U.S. China Policy

Martin L. Lasater

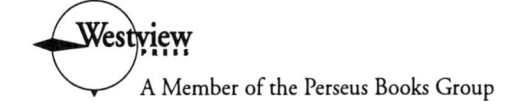

Westview
A Member of the Perseus Books Group

All rights reserved. Printed in the United States of America. No part of this publication may be reproduced or transmitted in any form or by any means, electronic or mechanical, including photocopy, recording, or any information storage and retrieval system, without permission in writing from the publisher.

Copyright © 2000 by Westview Press, A Member of the Perseus Books Group

Published in 2000 in the United States of America by Westview Press, 5500 Central Avenue, Boulder, Colorado 80301-2877, and in the United Kingdom by Westview Press, 12 Hid's Copse Road, Cumnor Hill, Oxford OX2 9JJ

Find us on the World Wide Web at www.westviewpress.com

A CIP catalog record for this book is available from the Library of Congress.
ISBN 0-8133-3696-1

The paper used in this publication meets the requirements of the American National Standard for Permanence of Paper for Printed Library Materials Z39.48-1984.

10 9 8 7 6 5 4 3 2 1

To My Parents

Aubrey and Nanolene Lasater

And My Sisters

Toni and Sandra

Contents

Preface ix

1 American Values in U.S. China Policy 1

2 Congressional Views of China and Taiwan 21

3 U.S. Interests in China and Taiwan 47

4 Strategy and Policy Under Bill Clinton 81

5 U.S. Policy Toward China and Taiwan, 1949–1992 113

6 Clinton's Policy Toward China and Taiwan:
  The Formative Years, 1993–1994 155

7 Clinton's Policy Toward China and Taiwan:
  The Lee Teng-hui Visit and Repercussions 193

8 Clinton's Policy Toward China and Taiwan:
  The Military Crisis and Its Aftermath 241

9 Conclusion: The Jiang-Clinton Summits and Beyond 275

Bibliography 313
About the Book and the Author 317
Index 319

Preface

The central theme of this book is that the ambiguity which characterizes U.S. policy toward Taiwan should continue. Although this ambiguity creates uncertainty when dealing with the Taiwan issue, ambiguity is a proven method of handling the Taiwan conundrum in Sino-American relations: how to maintain friendly, unofficial ties with the people of Taiwan while pursuing the strategically important goal of integrating China into the global community as a cooperative partner of the United States rather than a hostile competitor or foe. In the pages that follow, the argument is made that U.S. values, interests, strategies, and policies—as well as institutional checks-and-balances in the American political system—dictate that the current U.S. "dual-track" approach of engagement with the PRC and support of Taiwan should remain in place, unless and until circumstances arise which compel a fundamental shift in U.S. policy. It is further argued that, while the PRC, Taiwan, the United States, and the international environment are undergoing significant evolution, the trends at present do not justify the high costs of changing U.S. policy. Nor will they, in all likelihood, justify a change for the next several years.

The fact that Taiwan remains a central—even explosive—issue in Sino-American relations, fifty years after the founding the People's Republic of China in October 1949 and twenty years after the establishment of U.S.-PRC diplomatic relations in January 1979, proves that the fate of Taiwan is a matter of great importance to both China and the United States. Although Taiwan at times has been a convenient point of contention between Beijing and Washington—enabling both sides to vent their frustrations while maintaining a dialogue—the importance of Taiwan transcends that utility, although its exact importance is not easy to define and escapes consensus.

For many Chinese, Taiwan is lost Chinese territory which must be recovered if China is to regain its rightful place as the central power of Asia. The recovery of Taiwan is a reflection of national pride, an issue of sovereignty, a matter of strategic significance to China's security, a critical determinant of China's potential as a superpower. From this perspective, a future for Taiwan other than as part of China is unacceptable. Any effort to separate Taiwan from China, whether originating on Taiwan itself or from foreign countries such as the United States or Japan, must be opposed by all means necessary. If Chinese leaders are to be taken at their word, China would be willing to set back its economic modernization and to risk war with the United States to ensure that Taiwan remains part of China. In all likelihood, China would fight over Taiwan because of Chinese values and because of China's interests in Taiwan, although not all American analysts agree with this assessment.

For the people of Taiwan, 98 percent of whom are of Han Chinese ancestry, the future of their home is of vital concern. But what that future should be—or perhaps more appropriately can be—is a subject of intense disagreement. The so-called "mainlanders," those who came to Taiwan after 1945 and their descendants (roughly 14 percent of the population), are far more attached to the idea of a united China than the so-called "Taiwanese" (84 percent of the population), whose ancestors moved to Taiwan much earlier and who lived under Japanese rule cut off from China from 1895 to 1945 as a result of Tokyo's victory in the 1894–1895 Sino-Japanese War. The majority of Taiwanese, now largely in control of Taiwan's democratic political institutions, seem to favor autonomy from mainland China—if not outright independence as a separate nation-state. The younger generations, many of whom are the product of mixed mainlander-Taiwanese marriages and most of whom consider Taiwan their home but view relations with China as necessary or inevitable, fall into various categories of views regarding the future relationship of Taiwan with mainland China. As far as can be determined by election results and repeated polls, the majority of Taiwan residents are pragmatic, preferring to enjoy the stability and prosperity of the status quo in the Taiwan Strait, whereby Taiwan enjoys de facto autonomy, and leaving to the future the determination of Taiwan's political ties with China. Since virtually no one on Taiwan wants to become part of China as long as its central government is controlled by the Chinese Communist Party (CCP), the principle of Taiwan's self-determination is not well received in Beijing. Increasingly, the PRC views developments on Taiwan—particularly efforts by the Republic of China under President Lee Teng-hui to broaden Taiwan's international presence—as threatening the fundamental principle of Taiwan being part of China. Lee's most recent contribution—the concept that all Taiwan residents, regardless of provincial origin, are "new Taiwanese"—is seen by the PRC as yet another example of Lee's traitorous attempts to divide the motherland.

For Americans, the issue of Taiwan is more complex—albeit equally visceral to many. There is no consensus in the United States over the future of Taiwan, in large measure because Taiwan is far away from Peoria and, for those interested, the Taiwan issue is replete with conflicting values and interests. To a great many "average" Americans—hard to define numbers or percentages here—Taiwan is a separate country, clearly distinguished from what is still widely referred to as "Communist China." The idea that Taiwan should be forced against its will to become part of Communist China is viewed as being un-American, although not necessarily worth fighting to prevent. Among Americans with greater interest in foreign policy and China policy in particular, the Taiwan issue is a constant reminder of the volatility of domestic and international politics.

This lesson was brought home once again in the 1995–1996 Taiwan Strait crisis, when, for a short while, PRC missiles flew over Taiwan and PRC and U.S. fleets eyed each other warily near Taiwan waters. In large part, the crisis was precipitated by Lee Teng-hui's unofficial visit to the United States in June 1995, a trip seen by

Preface xi

many in Beijing as proof of U.S. complicity in Lee's strategy of gaining international support for an independent Taiwan. The possibility of a future military conflict between China and the United States over Taiwan prompted renewed debate among China specialists over an appropriate U.S. policy toward Taiwan. The existing policy—still in place since the 1950s—was designed to ensure that the resolution of the Taiwan issue would be achieved peacefully between the two sides of the Taiwan Strait.

Various viewpoints emerged or solidified in these policy debates, with consensus on two fundamental points: China was becoming a much stronger power and Taiwan increasingly looked as if it were leaning in the direction of independence. Some expressed the view that China was an emerging threat to U.S. interests and that American support for Taiwan should be strengthened; others felt U.S. relations with the PRC should be improved at almost any cost to avoid a future Sino-American conflict over Taiwan; others believed the United States should support the principle of self-determination for Taiwan; others thought that Washington should signal clearly its opposition to Taiwan independence; still others argued that U.S. policy should be continued with only minor adjustments to restrain precipitous actions by both Taiwan and China and to encourage their dialogue. Generally speaking, current and former administration officials were inclined to hold the last viewpoint, whereas Members of Congress, academic specialists, and media observers fell into all categories.

Regardless of which side one took in the debate, it was recognized that critical questions had been raised about the foundations on which U.S. policies toward China and Taiwan were built. For example:

1. To what extent is the emerging power of China a threat to U.S. interests in Asia or the Western Pacific? Is it inevitable that the United States and the PRC will confront each other as China seeks to expand its sphere of influence and as the United States seeks to maintain its forward military presence and a favorable balance of power in the region? What is the likelihood of China continuing its reforms and thereby becoming more open economically, politically, and socially? Would a democratic China pose less of a potential threat to U.S. interests than a China remaining under the political control of the Chinese Communist Party? Is it possible for the United States both to engage China and to prepare for a potential future struggle with Beijing? Does the nature of future Sino-American relations necessarily influence U.S. policy toward Taiwan? If so, how?

2. Would U.S. accommodation over Taiwan lead to significantly improved U.S.-PRC ties, thereby serving American strategic interests in avoiding an adversarial relationship with China? Would U.S. interests in areas such as nonproliferation, balanced trade, and human rights be advanced as well?

3. Over the medium and long term, are the forces of independence on Taiwan stronger than those seeking to preserve the status quo or eventually to unify with the mainland? Are the centripetal forces of cross-Taiwan Strait economic ties and Chinese cultural affiliation stronger than the centrifugal forces of self-determina-

tion and separate national identity on Taiwan? What is the probability of the people of Taiwan formally exercising their right of self-determination through a referendum on their relationship with the mainland? How would China and the United States react to the results of that referendum? How likely is the Democratic Progressive Party (DPP) to replace the Kuomintang (KMT) as the ruling party on Taiwan? How should the United States treat a democratically-elected DPP government? If in charge of the central government on Taiwan, would the DPP declare Taiwan an independent nation? Should the United States intervene militarily on Taiwan's behalf if the PRC uses force to prevent Taiwan from becoming an independent country?

4. Should the United States more actively support a particular outcome of the Taiwan issue? How would U.S. interests be affected if China were united, if it were divided into two Chinas, if the status quo in the Taiwan Strait were perpetuated indefinitely, or if Taiwan became an independent country? How likely is each of these scenarios? Is a consensus on a preferred outcome of the Taiwan issue a possibility in the United States?

5. Has U.S. policy under President Bill Clinton drifted toward supporting Taiwan's reunification with China? To what extent should the United States pressure Taipei to enter into cross-Straits negotiations? Is it possible for the United States to avoid at least indirect involvement in these negotiations in view of Clinton's "three-no's" promises to Beijing that the United States would not support an independent Taiwan, would not support Taiwan's entrance into the United Nations, and would not support a two-Chinas policy or one China, one Taiwan policy—thereby limiting Taiwan's political options—and his policy of supporting Taiwan's defense through arms sales and, in March 1996, deployment of U.S. aircraft carrier battle groups to the Taiwan region—thereby limiting Beijing's military options?

6. What guidelines should govern future U.S. arms sales to Taiwan? Which should take precedence in U.S. arms sales policy: the Taiwan Relations Act or the August 17 communiqué? Should the United States adjust downward its arms sales to encourage Taiwan to be more accommodating to Beijing? In what way should Taiwan be more accommodating: to simply sit down and talk, to discuss sensitive political issues, to accept the one country, two systems formula for reunification?

7. What U.S. interest (or value) would justify American forces being asked to fight the People's Liberation Army (PLA) in defense of Taiwan? What is the probability of the United States becoming involved in a war between China and Taiwan, regardless of the circumstances precipitating the conflict? Given the nature of the American decision-making process, is it possible to forecast U.S. intervention beforehand?

8. Should the U.S. commitment to defend Taiwan be more explicit? Is the time-honored U.S. policy of ambiguity toward Taiwan's defense still appropriate in view of recent changes in the PRC and Taiwan? Does "tactical ambiguity and strategic

clarity" now characterize U.S. security policy toward Taiwan? Does "creative ambiguity" still have a role in U.S. policy toward Taiwan?

9. To what extent is Taiwan defensible without U.S. military intervention? Are the scenarios of PRC invasion or blockade of Taiwan the most likely or serious threats faced by Taipei? Should the United States include Taiwan in its theater missile defense plans for East Asia? Should the United States sell Taiwan submarines to counter the PRC naval threat? Should the United States seek to maintain a military balance in the Taiwan Strait; if so, how?

10. To what extent should the United States support Taiwan's role in international organizations? Is an increased official presence for Taiwan in the international community more likely to fan the desire for independence on the island or to give the government and people of Taiwan the confidence and self-respect necessary to negotiate sensitive political issues with Beijing?

The pages that follow provide the background necessary to address these difficult questions. The major factors that influence American policy toward the Taiwan issue in U.S. China relations are discussed in a policy-oriented approach, reflecting a concern about what is possible in the American political context. Within this context, perceptions often are as important as fact; values as important as *Realpolitik* calculations; editorial opinion and media coverage as influential as the analysis of China specialists and foreign policy experts; and the views of Congress as important to policy as guidelines issued by the White House, the State Department, and the Pentagon.

Perceptions, history, facts, values, *Realpolitik* considerations, media opinion, expert analysis, congressional legislation, policy guidelines from the administration—all have influential roles in determining U.S. policy toward Taiwan, particularly in areas receiving a great deal of public attention, as issues related to China are prone to be. To a great extent, it is the complex interaction between these influences that make U.S. policy toward Taiwan and China so controversial and contradictory, yet also resistant to change. U.S. policy toward these Chinese societies likely will remain so characterized for some time to come. But this is not necessarily a weakness. Indeed, it is a reflection of strength in the American political system: an ability to meld divergent influences into a set of policies which, while not hierarchical or consistent, nonetheless serve the wide range of U.S. interests in China, Taiwan, and their future relationship.

A word on the book's organization is in order. Chapters 1-3 present the conundrum of Taiwan in U.S. China policy in the context of American values, the role of Congress, and U.S. interests and national strategy. Chapter 1 examines a wide sampling of American newspaper editorials surrounding certain significant events in Sino-American relations. The purpose of this chapter is to identify the values the American public most often associates with Taiwan and China, and how the public evaluates U.S. policy toward these Chinese societies. Chapter 2 looks at the role of Congress in U.S. policy toward Taiwan and China, with special emphasis on legislation introduced with wide bipartisan support in both Houses of

Congress to indicate congressional concerns over U.S. policy. Chapter 3 identifies the most important U.S. interests in China and Taiwan, as these have been defined by recent administrations.

Chapters 4-8 examine the Taiwan policy conundrum—as well as the conundrum of China policy itself—as these evolved during the Clinton presidency. Chapter 4 provides an overview of U.S. strategy and policy under President Clinton, with consideration given to the global and regional context in which U.S. policy toward China and Taiwan is formulated. Chapter 5 summarizes U.S. policy toward both China and Taiwan through the end of 1992. Chapters 6 through 8 focus on the critical period of 1993-1996 in U.S. policy toward China and Taiwan, with emphasis on the formative years of Clinton's policy (Chapter 6), the disruptions caused by the visit of President Lee Teng-hui (Chapter 7), and the confrontations in the Taiwan Strait (Chapter 8). Generally chronological in order, these chapters document the many twists and turns characteristic of U.S. relations with China and Taiwan. The 1995-1996 period is given special attention because the crisis over Taiwan during this period provides an excellent case study demonstrating why the Taiwan issue is so difficult for the United States to resolve in its relationship with China.

The concluding Chapter 9 discusses renewed Sino-American efforts to construct a strategic partnership after 1996, as reflected in the Jiang Zemin-Bill Clinton summits of 1997 and 1998. The second round of high-level talks between Koo Chen-fu of Taiwan and Wang Daohan of mainland China in 1998 also is examined as evidence of resumed dialogue across the Taiwan Strait, in spite of wide differences between the two sides in their visions of Taiwan's future. Chapter 9 concludes with answers to the policy questions cited earlier in this Preface, hopefully stimulating further study on what promises to be one of the most intractable foreign policy issues still facing the United States at the turn of the century: the role of Taiwan in U.S. China policy.

Finally, let me take this opportunity to thank Dr. Alfred D. Wilhem, Jr., of the Atlantic Council of the United States for his support during the research and writing phase of this book. The contents of the study, however, solely reflect the views of the author and are not intended to represent the views of the Atlantic Council.

Martin L. Lasater
Washington, D.C.
June 1999

1

American Values in U.S. China Policy

One of the reasons the Taiwan issue is a conundrum in U.S. China policy is that American views of Taiwan are shaped not only by perceptions of U.S. national interest but also by moral convictions held by individuals. These convictions play an important role in decision making, whether by a parent of an adolescent teen or the commander-in-chief of U.S. armed forces. Since absolute truth is hard to come by in any of life's situations, an individual's moral beliefs help to create a hierarchy of values which make decisions easier if not necessarily more correct. In real life, especially in complicated circumstances, pure reason is insufficient if only because all the facts are not known; some judgment has to be made, and that judgment is influenced not only by reason but by peer pressure, bureaucratic or job politics, and by values—personal sentiments of what is right or wrong, justified or unjustified, appropriate or inappropriate. The fact that these values often differ between individuals and circumstances, and are difficult to quantify, does not negate their key role in complex decision making. Shared values are important in establishing trust between individuals and between nation-states. A person's character does matter, whether it be in the trust shared by a handshake over the sale of a neighbor's car or the credibility of a national leader promising his foreign counterpart to deliver on some vital matter of state.

Values shared by the nation's citizens are national values, and it is these which often characterize a nation in the eyes of other countries and in the retelling of history. The United States will be remembered as a superpower in the twentieth century, but also remembered for its democracy and support of freedom. Without these national values, the United States would be another of history's great powers, enjoying its moment of glory. But with these values, the United States will leave an enduring legacy of uplifting mankind from servant of the state under authoritarian rule to a dignified individual responsible not only for his own behavior but also for the affairs of state through freely elected representatives.

In the case of Taiwan, the values held by the American people have greatly influenced their assessment of the appropriateness of U.S. policy. This assessment is not necessarily the key factor in an individual's approval or disapproval of a certain policy, but it is an important component of his or her evaluation; sometimes it can be decisive.

This chapter attempts to define American values as they relate to U.S. policy toward the Taiwan issue in Sino-American relations. The approach is to assume that the nation's editorial pages reflect these values. What follows, then, is a summary of editorial views of certain highly publicized events surrounding Taiwan, China, and U.S. policy toward these societies. These events include the death of Republic of China President Chiang Ching-kuo in January 1988, the death of People's Republic of China leader Deng Xiaoping in February 1997, the visit of PRC President Jiang Zemin to the United States in October 1997, and the visit of U.S. President Bill Clinton to China in June 1998. The objective is to find editorial comments about Taiwan, China, and U.S. China-Taiwan policy that give insight into American values as they are used to evaluate developments on both sides of the Taiwan Strait and U.S. policy.

Following the review of editorials, a concluding section will consider the morality of state often used by foreign policy analysts and China experts to evaluate U.S. policy. As will be seen, there frequently is a contradiction between American values and the morality of the state: one of the many dimensions of the Taiwan conundrum.

Editorial Views

Passing of Chiang Ching-kuo

Insight into American values as they relate specifically to Taiwan can be found in newspaper editorials appearing shortly after the death of ROC President Chiang Ching-kuo on January 13, 1988. Perhaps more than any other individual, Chiang helped to move Taiwan from an authoritarian state ruled by mainlanders in the Kuomintang to a democratic state in which opposition parties freely compete with the KMT for power and in which the Taiwanese dominate decision making. The passing of Chiang Ching-kuo ended the era of Chiang family leadership of the ROC and the KMT, making possible the rise of President Lee Teng-hui, scheduled to remain in office through the year 2000 when new presidential elections will be held.

In the two-week period between January 13 and January 26, 1988, an informal survey of twenty-four editorials and columns found reference to Chiang Ching-kuo in the following terms:[1] liberalizing Taiwan society, lifting martial law, opening the economy, democratization, expanding freedom, political reform, allowing opposition political parties, relaxing restraints on newspapers, easing restrictions on travel

American Values in U.S. China Policy 3

to the mainland by residents of Taiwan, moving forward on constitutional democratic development, integrating Taiwanese into the government and ruling party, overseeing Taiwan's flourishing market economy, freeing political prisoners, being firmly anti-communist and a faithful ally of the United States, showing flexibility in dealing with Beijing, allowing trade with the mainland, putting into place the succession of Lee Teng-hui to the ROC presidency, ushering in a new era of civil rights and political participation, being a champion of free enterprise and democracy, upholding the principle that democracy was the best argument against communism, resisting the temptation to build a dynasty, helping to make Taiwan into a bastion of capitalism, producing one of the world's fastest rates of economic growth, being a force for moderation in ROC foreign affairs, being a modest man and informal leader, helping to make Taiwan into one of the strongest countries—militarily and economically—in the Far East.

The accomplishments of President Chiang Ching-kuo that received the most praise from American editorials were achievements that reflected cherished values of the American people: freedom, democracy, a free press, the right to organize opposition political parties and to criticize the government, the right to travel abroad, a stable and prosperous economy, free enterprise and capitalism, anti-communism, modest but effective leadership, friendship with the United States, moderate and liberal policies, and the avoidance of a family dynasty. The major concern expressed by these editorials was whether his successor Lee Teng-hui would be able to continue and expand the political reforms initiated by Chiang. Most of the editorials were strongly in favor of continued American support of Taiwan and hopeful that Taiwan's democracy and free enterprise would one day take hold on the mainland.

Passing of Deng Xiaoping

American values toward China were reflected in editorials written on the occasion of the death of Deng Xiaoping on February 19, 1997. A Chinese leader very familiar to Americans since his January 1979 visit to the United States, Deng helped to move China from the straightjacket of Mao Zedong Thought to the modern economic powerhouse of China today. In a review of twenty-four newspaper editorials written February 20–24, 1997, many comments expressed both praise and criticism for Deng and the People's Republic of China.[2] These editorials described Deng as: modernizing a great country, being a reformer of substantial achievement but leaving much undone, opening up China economically, maintaining the Communist Party's unchallenged political control, introducing market reforms, lifting millions of Chinese out of abject poverty, encouraging participation in local government, crushing without reserve any political dissidence, normalizing and stabilizing relations with the United States, leaving the future of China in an uncertain state, abolishing lifetime tenure of party leaders, remaking

China economically and politically, succeeding with economic reform but failing to reform politically, making China both a more assertive and a more responsible member of the international community, authorizing the Tiananmen Square crackdown, leaving a legacy stained by relentless persecution of democracy campaigners, being the reformer as well as the unambiguous repressor, insisting on the primacy of centralized decision making, abusing human rights, being a pragmatist, opening a xenophobic and isolated China to the world, making China's economy an irresistible magnet for Western capital, placing highest value on political stability, maintaining a dictatorship, introducing socialism with Chinese characteristics (i.e., coupling economic reforms and bustling consumerism with central planning and tight political control), being a totalitarian leader with little regard for basic freedoms of expression, forever linked with the crushing of China's nascent democracy movement in 1989, giving responsibility to China's peasants for their economic production and profits, making China into a world power, embodying much that was evil and foul but also bringing astonishing economic change to China, maintaining fierce loyalty and devotion to the tenets of communism, giving the Chinese people economic freedom but denying them political freedom, refusing to give China the rule of law, preserving the absolute power of the Chinese Communist Party, being the liberator of the economy but the monster of Tiananmen Square, feeding the people and freeing the market but keeping the body politic in chains, setting in motion the peaceful transfer of Hong Kong, being one of history's great economic liberators but also one of its major political tyrants, being leader of an economic paradox: state ownership, private property, central planning, competitive markets, political dictatorship, and limited social and cultural freedom, becoming the Great Pragmatist and the Communist Party's most revolutionary revolutionary, embracing the free market not because he agreed with Adam Smith or for moral sentiments but out of a desire to reinforce the Communist Party's power, being remembered not as a good man but as one of China's greatest leaders, wedding totalitarianism to elements of capitalism, leaving unanswered the question of what kind of China the United States and its allies in Asia will face in the future, being remembered by Americans as the Chinese leader who presented the United States with some of its greatest opportunities and some of its greatest problems, being remembered by history as the man who brought China to the doorstep of the modern world and as a killer and unwavering enemy of political and personal freedom, leaving behind a Chinese society with a frayed social fabric and non-existent civil society, and leaving uncertainty over whether the Taiwan issue can be settled peacefully.

It is clear from this survey of editorial opinion that Americans viewed the legacy of Deng Xiaoping—and China itself—with mixed feelings. There was genuine feeling of friendship toward the Chinese people; deep respect for the rapid modernization of China; clear acknowledgment of China's size and potential power; and abiding dislike and distrust of the Chinese Communist Party and the PRC government. A frequent comment seen in these editorials was that the United States should continue to engage China and encourage its reforms, but also to keep in mind that China's future is uncertain, requiring preparation for a wide range of eventualities.

As reflected in the editorials, Americans highly valued Deng's pragmatism—i.e., his willingness to reject blind adherence to socialism and to experiment with and adopt certain capitalist methods of productivity; his decision to open China to the outside, especially Western, world; his efforts to normalize and bring stability to Sino-American relations; and his historic role in modernizing China and bringing it into the councils of great powers. On the other hand, Americans faulted Deng's totalitarian instincts: his insistence on the political primacy of the Chinese Communist Party; his persecution of political dissent; his repression of basic freedoms and human rights; and his holding on to power until his death with no certainty of a smooth succession. Perhaps of greatest concern to editors was the uncertainty left by Deng's passing: Would China's new leaders continue his economic reforms? Would they eventually liberalize China's political system? Would a stronger China become a future threat to the United States and its allies? What policy should the United States follow toward the PRC in view of its uncertain future?

Many of these evaluations of Taiwan and China remained true through the end of 1998. This could be seen in editorial comments surrounding the exchange of state visits by Presidents Jiang Zemin and Bill Clinton in 1997 and 1998. In part, the state visits were intended by both governments to end the distrust in Sino-American relations that had existed since the June 1989 Tiananmen Square incident and to remedy the frosty relations brought about by President Lee Teng-hui's visit to the United States in June 1995 and the subsequent U.S.-PRC quasi-military confrontation in waters near Taiwan in March 1996. The goal of the state visits was to usher in a new era in Sino-American relations, referred to as "constructive strategic partnership" between the two countries.

The editorials commenting on the Jiang-Clinton summits reflected a deep American concern with both values and interests in U.S. policy toward China and Taiwan, and they demonstrated a conviction that while U.S. interests dictated continued engagement with China, American values dictated a continued close relationship with Taiwan. Because of their direct reference to many current issues in U.S. policy toward Taiwan and China, some of the editorial comments are quoted at length below.

State Visit of Jiang Zemin

In a review of fifteen editorials on PRC President Jiang Zemin's state visit to the United States, which took place October 26 through November 3, 1997, the following comments on U.S.-PRC relations and the Taiwan issue could be found.[3]

China today is hurtling down the capitalist road. Only the ruling party is still communist, and the party bosses in power operate like robber barons . . . The American betting is that China's turn down the capitalist road will not strengthen socialism and will eventually break down the system of oppression that has ruled China since 1949. (*Boston Globe*, October 24, 1997)

There is no shortage of sources of friction between the world's lone superpower and its most rapidly emerging potential rival . . . There is a long-term question of whether the emerging Chinese superpower, led as ever by a Communist dictatorship, is gathering strength in order to challenge both America's standing in Asia and the world and the democratic values Americans associate with their world leadership . . . Mr. Clinton argues for continued engagement despite these tensions, acknowledging long-term risks but arguing that China can evolve differently—as a cooperative superpower with a gradually liberalizing political system . . . This is a policy of some coherence, and Mr. Clinton has enhanced its credibility in the past couple of years by firmly pursuing the maintenance of a strong U.S. presence in Asia such as by sending aircraft carriers to the Taiwan straits . . . The United States intends to counterbalance China's growing strength now and in the future . . . The administration's zigzag course to its current policy and suspicions of its susceptibility to pressure from commercial interests will continue to provoke anxiety about its ability to maintain a steadfast policy of engagement without appeasement . . . Most Americans will recoil if Mr. Clinton does not accord sufficient weight to the thousands of prisoners of conscience suffering in Mr. Jiang's gulag. (*Washington Post*, October 26, 1997)

The reality is that China is the world's most populous country, most rapidly developing military power and most rapidly expanding economy. Its capacity for disturbing the peace is immense . . . These are the reasons why Washington needs a mature working relationship and candid communication with Beijing . . . Engagement is needed not as a reward for any supposed niceness on China's part but because of China's importance in all spheres and the dangers inherent in a bad relationship. (*Baltimore Sun*, October 26, 1997)

It's not just that Americans are disgusted by Chinese human rights abuses, including forced abortions, slave labor, orphans allowed to starve to death and ethnic cleansing in Tibet. These atrocities must inevitably impact on relations between our countries. How can a state that treats its own people so brutally be trusted to keep its international commitments? (*Boston Sunday Herald*, October 26, 1997)

Jiang stresses that China and the United States share a common responsibility to build a strong and stable relationship in the 21st Century. The big question is whether the Chinese leader truly believes that his country and the United States share the responsibility equally. If he does, then Jiang can prove it by taking positive steps during his first sojourn in this country to address the issues weighing most heavily on Sino-American relations—nuclear proliferation, human rights, trade and Taiwan. (*Chicago Tribune*, October 26, 1997)

American Values in U.S. China Policy 7

Clear understanding is fundamental to building a deeper, more viable Sino-American relationship. In particular, we hope Jiang will appreciate that the American demonstrations of concern for human rights are not artificial annoyances engineered by politicians, but sincere expressions. (*Honolulu Advertiser*, October 26, 1997)

Many Americans, including President Clinton, have come to the conclusion that China is too big to isolate and too important to ignore . . . For most Americans, even for proponents of a policy of engagement, this summit is not an occasion to declare Tiananmen history nor to forget Mr. Wei Jingsheng and his compatriots. (*Washington Post*, October 28, 1997)

Not since the end of the Cold War has a foreign policy issue ignited passions the way U.S.-Sino relations have . . . In a certain sense, our China debate is as much about American values as it is about China. Communist China stands for many things abhorrent to Americans, who are among the few true champions of human and religious rights on the planet. Americans feel strongly that U.S. foreign policy must have a moral component and become testy when the politics of pragmatism prevail . . . China is no longer needed as a necessary strategic counterbalance to the Soviet Union . . . The real trick here is to find a balanced position that serves the interest of human rights, trade and American national security. (*Washington Times*, October 29, 1997)

The United States has a policy of engagement that includes a growing economic relationship as well as cultivating a mutually beneficial strategic relationship. The administration is therefore correct to be concerned about China's place in the international community as well as our bilateral relationship. But human rights has fallen to the bottom of the American agenda not because it is less important today that it has ever been, but because the Clinton administration wants it that way. (*Washington Times*, October 29, 1997)

Jiang's message to his hosts is something like this: We have no intention of adopting anything approximating Western-style democratic values. But we'll keep building on our economic relationship with you as long as you don't get too nosy about how we run our country . . . In our relations with most other governments, our commitment to democratic values complements our economic and security interests. China should not be a huge exception to that rule. By combining good business with deft diplomacy, Washington can ensure that our expanding economic ties serve the larger purpose of helping to transform China into a more open society and a more trustworthy member of the world community. (*St. Petersburg Times*, October 30, 1997)

Bill Clinton looks to China for his place in history . . . China's treatment of its own citizens is for Americans the most sensitive aspect of the entire relationship . . . The two countries cannot develop a normal relationship until China modifies its repressive policies . . . Mr. Jiang did not use the summit conference to renounce the use of force in reuniting Taiwan with the mainland . . . Though China's promises on nuclear proliferation may be shaky, Clinton otherwise did a good job of affirming American democratic values while promoting its strategic and commercial interests. (*New York Times*, October 30, 1997)

There's been a lot of disagreement and frustration within U.S. policy circles over just how to deal with this large, complicated country ... Congressional efforts are notable in searching for things the U.S. can do to assert its principles and interests without the self-destructive symbolism of trade sanctions or isolation. (*Wall Street Journal*, October 31, 1997)

Jiang Zemin's comments before and during his visit to the Liberty Bell and Independence Hall in Philadelphia have shown no understanding of or sympathy for the values they commemorate ... China, with one-fourth of the world's population and a rapidly growing economy, is too big to ignore—and that's true whether or not you accept the administration's thesis that trade and diplomatic engagement are likely to promote political openness inside China ... This relationship will continue to make Americans uncomfortable, because in the end human rights are not just one strand—as the administration maintains—among many in a complex bilateral relationship. Human rights is shorthand for the wretched condition of political dissent and unimpeded religious practice and freedom of speech in China. Until this situation changes all summits will have this same kind of asymmetry that will color whatever progress may be made. (*Washington Post*, October 31, 1997)

These editorial comments, and many like them, reflect the ambivalence most Americans feel about the PRC and Washington's relations with Beijing. There is a sense of the historic importance of Sino-American relations, yet also deep uncertainty about the future of the relationship. A common view is that the United States is faced with unprecedented challenges and opportunities by the emergence of China as a global power. Most Americans see little alternative to a policy of continued engagement with the PRC, but there is almost universal insistence that the search for engagement should not lead to appeasement on critical issues of importance to the American people, such as trade, proliferation, human rights, and Taiwan. It is important to note that engagement with China is not sought for engagement's sake alone, but rather as a foreign policy instrument both to deal pragmatically with Beijing on substantive matters and to effect positive change in China toward greater political and economic openness. There is little or no inclination on the part of the American people to sacrifice American values to preserve Sino-American relations. Indeed, the insistence that American values must play a key role in U.S. foreign policy toward China and Taiwan was very apparent in editorials commenting on Jiang's visit. This insistence was reflected as well in editorials reviewing President Clinton's state visit to China from June 25 through July 3, 1998.

American Values in U.S. China Policy

State Visit of Bill Clinton

President Clinton's trip to China, the first by an American president since George Bush's state visit in February 1989, was a major effort by the administration to move Sino-American relations beyond Tiananmen into a new era of cooperation on a broad front. The fact that President Clinton chose to reaffirm the "three no's" in Shanghai ("We don't support independence for Taiwan; or two Chinas; or one Taiwan, one China. And we don't believe that Taiwan should be a member in any organization for which statehood is a requirement") ensured that many American editorials would address U.S. policy toward both China and Taiwan. Once again, the editorials reflected the important role Americans place on values in their assessments of U.S. policy. The following are some of the comments found in eighteen sampled editorials from the June 21–July 6, 1998, period:[4]

> What is disquieting about Mr. Clinton's China policy is not that he is pursuing a policy of engagement but that the engagement too often is on China's terms . . . Mr. Clinton should not trumpet "real progress" in a human rights record where no such progress exists. (*Washington Post*, June 23, 1998)

> One reason for Jiang's efforts to cultivate the United States is that after years of trying to deal with Taiwan directly, he has apparently come to the conclusion that the road to reunification with the breakaway Chinese province of 21 million people leads through Washington . . . China expects that Washington will begin to pressure Taiwan to engage in reunification talks with China. Already, a string of former U.S. officials, including former defense secretary William J. Perry, have journeyed to Taiwan with a blunt message: If you declare formal independence, the United States might not be there to protect you from China's response. (*Washington Post*, June 23, 1998)

> Bill Clinton's trip to China—the first presidential visit since 1989—marks another step in rebuilding U.S.-Sino relations, sharply shaken nine years ago when the Chinese regime turned its tanks and guns on pro-democracy demonstrators in Tiananmen Square . . . The president must stand firm publicly and privately on American principles regarding human rights, trade and arms nonproliferation. (*Los Angeles Times*, June 24, 1998)

> No matter how much the matter has been discussed here at home, Americans undoubtedly found it troubling to watch their president in Tiananmen Square march alongside Chinese President Jiang Zemin, inspecting troops from the People's Liberation Army. (*Washington Times*, June 29, 1998)

> The claims of new [Sino-American] friendship have caused extreme nervousness in Japan, Taiwan, India and the other surrounding democracies with which the United States really does share values and really should be strengthening its partnership. (*Washington Post*, June 30, 1998)

The weekend's unprecedented human rights debate between President Clinton and Chinese President Jiang Zemin put their summit on the right side of history . . . Clinton raised the issues of religious freedom and Tibet at the news conference and endorsed "universal rights" in his speech at Beijing University. (*Los Angeles Times*, June 30, 1998)

The most touchy issue facing President Clinton and Chinese President Jiang Zemin was undoubtedly the status of the Republic of China on Taiwan . . . This time, the Chinese would have liked the United States to denounce the idea of Taiwanese "independence" and Taiwan's aspirations to participate in the United Nations, none of which are for us to do. At least Mr. Clinton had self-preservation instinct enough not to go along; he would have faced an avalanche of congressional denunciation at home . . . It is not for the United States to dictate the terms of negotiations between mainland China and Taiwan—not beyond encouraging discussion and demanding that the use of force be renounced by the PRC . . . The first precondition has to be keeping Taiwan secure and able to decide its own fate. And that's where the United States comes in. (*Washington Times*, June 30, 1998)

The signs of unexpected openness may be the most encouraging development of the Clinton visit . . . China for the most part remains a repressive dictatorship. But modest liberalizing changes have been under way for much of the last year. (*New York Times*, July 1, 1998)

The outlines of a deal are beginning to emerge. China gives President Clinton air time for his speech. Mr. Clinton says what China wants to hear on Taiwan. Then, in classic Clinton fashion, the White House tries to have things both ways, denying that U.S. policy has changed when in fact it has, and not for the better . . . Recently officials of the Clinton administration have explicitly adopted a "three no's" formula much more pleasing to the Communist Chinese: no support for one Taiwan-one China; no support for Taiwan independence; no support for Taiwan membership in international organizations such as the United Nations. Now Mr. Clinton has given that policy a presidential stamp of approval—and on Chinese soil, to boot. Why does it matter? Because Taiwan's 21 million people have forged a prosperous democracy over the past decades. There is no justification for the United States to oppose their right eventually to determine their own future . . . Mr. Clinton is trading away the human rights of Taiwan's 21 million people and sending an unfortunate signal to other democracies that might hope to rely on U.S. moral support . . . Mr. Clinton has sided with the dictators against the democrats. To pretend this is no change only heightens the offense. (*Washington Post*, July 2, 1998)

Just when we were giving President Clinton credit for sounding the right notes in China, he managed to turn his visit into a fiasco after all. His kowtowing to China's "three no's" over Taiwan is likely to set off a cycle of reactions and counterreactions that ultimately will damage rather than improve Sino-American relations . . . President Jiang got his number one priority, Mr. Clinton carving the next slice of salami toward the Chinese goal of getting the U.S. to coerce Taiwan to join China, or alternatively to stand aside while China invades . . . The issue of Taiwanese membership in international organizations is especially ridiculous . . . The world's remaining superpower should be acting to curb this ongoing farce, not entrench it . . . Congress, historically supportive of Taiwan and already restive over its foreign-policy prerogatives, will resist Mr. Clinton's unilateral change in long-standing American policy . . . Taiwan is now plainly a democratic nation, and has every right to determine its own future. In the end, the U.S. will not resist this principle, whatever Mr. Clinton said in Shanghai this week. (*Wall Street Journal*, July 2, 1998)

Now is the time for renewed American assurances that Taiwan always will have the military resources to deter mischief and direct assault. The U.S. cannot impose a so-called solution to the fundamental disagreements between Beijing and Taipei, but it must avoid encouraging Beijing's relentless campaign to isolate and destroy Taiwan. (*Richmond Times-Dispatch*, July 2, 1998)

The warm feelings and positive comment generated by President Clinton's China trip were eclipsed momentarily this week when the American leader responded to a Chinese professor's question about Taiwan. The president simply repeated longstanding U.S. policy: one China, and no independent Taiwan . . . More, perhaps, than any other issue, Taiwan's future underscores the complexities of U.S.-Chinese relations . . . U.S.-Taiwan ties, though altered by the shift to a one-China policy, remain strong. Washington is not about to forsake Taiwan's freedom-loving people. The president's open statement of an understood policy aside, Taiwan has powerful supporters in the American government. Military aid for the island will continue . . . But a strengthening relationship with China hinges on adherence to the no-independent-Taiwan formulation. Is there any way out of the contradictions inherent in this policy? The answer lies more with Beijing than Washington . . . Allowing people freedom to develop culturally, intellectually, and economically is the greatest assurance of stability . . . Hong Kong is the immediate test case . . . Tibet, another sensitive issue, could become a second test case . . . If China passes such tests, the time could come when Taiwan might consider reunification with a democratizing mainland. Until then, no one, least of all the United States, should force the issue. (*Christian Science Monitor*, July 2, 1998)

Ultimately, the point is not that a visiting U.S. president can speak and worship freely in China, but that Chinese citizens can. (*Christian Science Monitor*, July 3, 1998)

The question is whether it is possible to pursue a "strategic partnership" between the United States and China of the intensity displayed over the past nine days without jeopardizing U.S. relations with our long-standing allies in East Asia. It would be nothing less than disastrous were the Clinton administration to sacrifice the post-World War II U.S. role as guarantor of peace in the Pacific region in pursuit of closer ties with Beijing. It must not be allowed to happen . . . At best, a policy such as the one Mr. Clinton is pursuing, one that seeks to draw China into a system of international regimes and organizations, would have to be carefully calibrated to take into account real conflicts of interest and values between our two countries. But it would also have to focus on nurturing our relationships with China's neighbors, so as to provide regional counterweights to its growing power. The fact is you just don't do that by neglecting and snubbing your old friends. (*Washington Times*, July 6, 1998)

These editorial comments on the Jiang-Clinton summits clearly indicated that Americans tend to evaluate U.S. China policy from both moral and national interest perspectives. From the moral point of view, there was great concern over the status of political liberalization in China, human rights, Tibet, and the possibility of the Clinton administration sacrificing the security of Taiwan in order to further Sino-American relations. From the national interest perspective, these commentators were strongly in favor of U.S. engagement with China, but insisted upon hard bargaining with the Chinese over issues such as proliferation and trade. They also favored a strong American military force in the Western Pacific and an alliance structure sufficient to counterbalance the rising power of China. Many observers pointed out that the most difficult and sensitive issue facing the United States and China was Taiwan. None of the editorials recommended that Washington pressure Taipei into negotiating reunification with Beijing or suggested abandoning U.S. support for the island's security. There was in fact a great deal of criticism of President Clinton's enunciation of the "three no's" in Shanghai, not so much because his statement signaled a change in U.S. policy, but because it was unseemly for an American president to attempt to place limits on Taiwan's self-determination. The fact that Clinton made his comments in a communist country intent to absorb Taiwan added insult to injury in the minds of many of these editors.

A Different Kind of Morality

Far removed from the values expressed by American editors are the *Realpolitik* rationales used by many foreign policy experts to evaluate U.S. policy toward Taiwan and China. It is not that practioners of *Realpolitik* are less moral than other Americans, it is that they are convinced that the moral guidelines used by individuals in their personal lives cannot be used to guide the state. National leaders are concerned with the survival of the state and with the manipulation of power. Hence, to some but certainly not all students of international politics, individual morality is far different from state morality, and American values are not appropriate lens through which to view or judge American foreign policy.

In keeping with state morality but in contrast to the editorial views discussed above—and presumably the views of the American public at large—there is a perception among some American China specialists and foreign policy experts that Taiwan is (1) insignificant when compared to China, (2) an irritant in Sino-American relations, (3) a problem that must be managed by the United States to ensure that Sino-American relations are not disrupted, and (4) a potentially explosive issue that must be defused to prevent a future U.S.-PRC war. Rather than insisting on balance between American values and national interests in U.S. policy toward China and Taiwan, the thrust of policy recommendations from these specialists is that U.S. support for Taiwan should be reduced in order (a) to foreclose Taiwan's option of declaring independence, (b) to encourage cross-Strait negotiations to resolve the Taiwan issue sooner rather than later, and (c) to gain Chinese cooperation on matters of greater importance to the United States such as proliferation, trade, and peace and security in Asia. In their calculations of what is in the national interest, the role of American values such as freedom and self-determination is assumed to be of minor importance when compared to larger interests in avoiding conflict in the Taiwan Strait and encouraging the peaceful integration of China into the international community.

The higher value of state morality is conflict avoidance, not individual freedom or self-determination, or so argue many of these experts. In the case of Taiwan, conflict avoidance would spare the American, Chinese, and Taiwanese people the pain and suffering sure to result from war. The value of conflict avoidance contrasts sharply with values cited earlier which stress the right of the people of Taiwan to have freedom and to determine their own future through democratic means. If conflict avoidance is the higher value, then one can reasonable argue that the United States should make additional concessions to the PRC over Taiwan. If freedom and democracy are the higher values, then one can reasonably argue that the United States should support Taiwan in its confrontation with the communist government of the PRC.

For the most part, Americans want balance in U.S. China policy: few want to abandon Taiwan to a communist takeover, few want to isolate or contain the PRC, few want to take Taiwan away from China, and few want to fight China over Taiwan. The conundrum of the Taiwan issue is how to define a balanced policy in a political environment in which there is no consensus on a hierarchy of values by which to determine and judge that policy. Absent a consensus, either balance must be pursued as a public policy goal or foreign policy has to be conducted in secret, away from the scrutiny of Congress and the media. Although secret diplomacy in China policy has been attempted by many administrations—usually to the detriment of Taiwan—in the end nothing remains a secret for long in Washington and attempts are always made to restore balance in U.S. policy toward the two Chinese societies.

One of the classic statements of American callousness toward Taiwan was Richard Holbrooke's comment in 1980: "The strategic relationship with China, not Taiwan, is the main issue, with global and historic importance. That it has been submerged under the Taiwan issue only illustrates anew that trivia can command center stage while great issues wait in the wings."[5] Most foreign policy professionals who recommend reduced support for Taiwan are less abrasive in their comments, justifying their recommendations on the grounds of serving the national interest by improving relations with China or avoiding a future war over Taiwan.

Although these recommendations were heard frequently during earlier debates over China policy, many resurfaced with new intensity in the aftermath of the 1996 military standoff in the Taiwan Strait. At that time there was deep concern expressed in foreign policy salons that developments on Taiwan could lead to further confrontations between the United States and China.[6] There was, for example, some anger over the way in which President Lee Teng-hui's visit to Cornell University was facilitated through the heavy lobbying of Congress. It was felt that Taiwan had pushed the envelope of acceptable behavior and had precipitated the downturn in Sino-American relations during 1995–1996. Some attempted to use the John Huang–Mark Middleton–James Wood controversy over fund raising in Taiwan for Clinton's re-election campaign to undermine Taiwan's moral authority. Still others observed that Taiwan was inextricably linked to one of the most important strategic issues in East Asia: how to ensure the smooth integration of China into the Asian-Pacific community. It was argued that if President Clinton wanted to focus on this issue as his presidential *coup de maître*, he would find it necessary to encourage mainland-Taiwan reconciliation in order to reassure Beijing of America's intentions not to separate Taiwan from China. The president might even find it necessary, it was argued, to apply some pressure on Taipei to be more accommodating in its dealings with the PRC. Other analysts believed that Jiang Zemin truly wanted to improve Sino-American relations but was constrained by hardliners in the government and military who believed the United States secretly supported Taiwan independence to divide and weaken China. To advance the goal of a strategic partnership, some American concessions over Taiwan might be necessary and justified. Almost all of those holding the above views were convinced that the ROC government under Lee Teng-hui was deliberately moving Taiwan further away from the one-China principle, seeking de facto if not de jure independence from China, a direction the PRC had pledged to oppose by force if necessary.

The subtleties of language here should not obscure the essential point. The perception of some American, and certainly most PRC scholars, was that President Lee Teng-hui was leading Taiwan—whether known as the Republic of China or Republic of Taiwan—into a nation-state status of being separate from mainland Chinese territory. It was believed that this "two Chinas" or "one China, one Taiwan" situation would not be tolerated by Beijing, nor any strong Chinese government for that matter, because of the fundamental Chinese interest in a united China, including Taiwan. Thus, if the policy direction of the Lee government continued, the possibility of force being used by Beijing to prevent Taiwan independence was thought to be high. Although not committed to Taiwan's defense by treaty, the United States had been intimately involved in Taiwan's security since the outbreak of the Korean War in June 1950, and the Taiwan Relations Act provided ample legal and political justification for U.S. military intervention in case of a PRC attack. In view of these perceptions—Taiwan's leaning more toward independence, Beijing's willingness to use force to prevent that from occurring, and the high probability of U.S. military intervention in a future Taiwan Strait crisis—there was growing concern that something had to be done to avoid placing the United States in the uncomfortable dilemma of having to choose either to fight China or abandon Taiwan.

There had been repeated unsuccessful efforts by the United States to convince Beijing to renounce the use of force as a means of resolving the Taiwan issue. This Beijing refused to do, insisting upon its right as a sovereign nation to defend its territorial integrity. After the 1995–1996 crisis, the emphasis shifted somewhat from Beijing to Taipei. There were increased calls by some American foreign policy specialists for the Clinton administration to apply pressure on Taiwan to renounce independence as an option. It was reasoned that the PRC would not attack Taiwan if the principal justification for Beijing to use force—i.e., Taiwan's move toward independence—would be removed. This in turn would nullify the most likely scenario for a future Sino-American war—a conflict in the Taiwan Strait into which the United States would be drawn—and U.S. interests in peace and stability in the Western Pacific would be served.

It was recognized that opposing Taiwan independence would deny the people of Taiwan their right of self-determination and that it would run counter to the U.S. goal of supporting market democracies in their competition with communist countries. It was reasoned, however, that the U.S. interest in avoiding a conflict with China was more important in this instance. Upon weighing the pros and cons inherent in this choice, several influential American foreign policy experts concluded that it would be better to prevent Taiwan independence now than to fight China in the future. According to former defense official Chas Freeman, one way to do this was to place limits on future arms sales to Taiwan:

> For the first time since the 1950s, there is a real danger that decisions in Taipei, not just Beijing, could ignite a conflict in the Taiwan Strait. The United States, as well as both Chinese parties, would be a loser in any such conflict, whether American forces joined it or not. U.S. policy can no longer hope to deter war exclusively by keeping Beijing at bay. The United States must also discourage decisions and actions by Taipei that could leave Beijing with little choice but to react militarily. . . .
> The rising military tensions in the Taiwan Strait also call for a reevaluation of arms sales to Taiwan. . . . U.S. arms sales to Taiwan no longer work to boost Taipei's confidence that it can work out its differences with Beijing. Instead, they bolster the view that Taiwan can go its own way . . . . And as the United States considers further arms sales to Taiwan, it should weigh their impact on Taipei's intentions and behavior as well as Beijing's.[7]

Another argument along these lines was presented by Joseph Nye, former assistant secretary of defense for international security affairs in the Clinton administration.[8] Nye argued that the United States should clarify its policy toward Taiwan by making clear that: (a) U.S. policy was "one China"—i.e., Taiwan is part of China; (b) Washington would not recognize or defend an independent Taiwan;

and (c) the United States would not accept the use of force in the Taiwan Strait under any circumstances. To make the package acceptable to all parties, Nye suggested Beijing should (a) allow Taipei more international breathing space, if Taiwan rejected the idea of declaring independence; and (b) expand its "one country, two systems" approach to national unification to "one country, three systems" to accommodate the unique circumstances of the mainland, Hong Kong, and Taiwan. Taipei, according to Nye, should (a) forswear any steps toward independence; (b) intensify cross-Strait dialogue; and (c) increase its flows of investment and people-to-people exchanges across the Taiwan Strait. Nye dismissed the Taiwan people's "alleged right to 'self-determination'" as being neither legal nor moral.

Taking the argument a step further, some American scholars concluded that Taiwan's eventual unification with China would be in the U.S. interests and that, therefore, the United States should actively support unification once the process of democratization takes hold on the mainland and guarantees for a continuation of Taiwan's way of life are in place. This point was argued, for example, by Lynn White, a respected China specialist from Princeton University.[9] White believed the United States should make clear to both Beijing and Taipei that the unification of China, with verifiable guarantees of Taiwan's current system for several decades, was an American objective. The basis of his argument was that economic reform in China would likely lead to political reform and that political reform on the mainland was far more important to U.S. national interests than Taiwanese self-determination. White argued that if a more liberalized China in the future would offer Taiwan very favorable terms, including the continuation of its current system for many decades and assurances of the nonuse of force barring attempted independence, then the United States should openly support China's unification. White was convinced that Taiwan might secure better terms sooner rather than later, since the PRC's position might harden once it gains the means to bring about unification by force.

The visit of a high-level, quasi-official U.S. delegation led by former Secretary of Defense William J. Perry to both the PRC and Taiwan in January 1998 was designed in part to warn Taipei not to move in the direction of independence but rather to begin discussions with Beijing as a step toward resolving their differences.[10] Making it clear that they were speaking with backing from the Clinton administration, the delegation included former Chairman of the Joint Chiefs of Staff General John Shalikashvili, former national security adviser Brent Scowcroft, and Ashton Carter, former assistant secretary of defense for international security policy. The group was sponsored by Harvard University and the National Committee on U.S.-China Relations. According to Carter, the delegation was acting as a catalyst for Washington to improve its relations with the PRC, particularly in the area of security cooperation, where the Chinese People's Liberation Army (PLA) had been slow to embrace American initiatives.

One of the delegation's main purposes was to open an informal back channel of communications between Taiwan and mainland China, a so-called "track-2" approach used successfully in other difficult international situations. Before visiting Taipei, the Perry delegation urged PRC leaders to resume economic, cultural, and trade talks with Taiwan. The delegation spent three days in Taiwan, meeting various high-ranking officials and opposition political leaders. Because Perry and General Shalikashvili were close to President Clinton and were instrumental in the U.S. decision to deploy aircraft carrier battle groups to the Taiwan area early in 1996, ROC officials and political observers paid close attention to what they had to say.

The delegation told Taiwan that the PRC was willing to hold unconditional talks on economic, cultural, and trade issues. But ominously, Perry warned Taiwan's political leaders that they should not count on U.S. military help if they declared independence and the mainland attacked them as a result. Perry said he told DPP leaders Hsu Hsin-liang and Chen Shui-bian, possible presidential candidates for the 2000 elections: "There is a possibility that they could be in power one day. I just wanted them to understand that independence could be a catastrophe and if they thought that the U.S. would bail them out, they were wrong."[11] The public warnings given by the Perry delegation, apparently made with Clinton administration approval, went far beyond previous statements of U.S. intentions in regards to the circumstances under which the United States would intervene militarily in the event of a PRC attack against Taiwan. Nor, as will be seen in the next chapter, did the Perry warning necessarily accord with the Taiwan Relations Act or congressional understanding.

Nonetheless, the combined message of articles such as those written by Freeman, Nye, and White, of warnings such as those conveyed by the Perry delegation, and of statements by Clinton on the "three no's" in Shanghai was clear: the Clinton administration could not be counted on to protect Taiwan if Taipei declared independence. This message was conveyed to Taipei for at least five reasons: first, to restrain the Lee Teng-hui government from provocative international behavior; second, to deny to Taiwan its independence option, thereby removing the most likely cause of war in the Taiwan Strait; third, to lower the probability of a future Sino-American military confrontation over Taiwan; fourth, to encourage Taipei and Beijing to begin in earnest the difficult negotiations leading to an eventual resolution of the future relationship of Taiwan and the mainland; and fifth, to advance the Sino-American strategic partnership by calming PRC concerns over Taiwan.

What is important to note at this stage of the book is that there are several different kinds of values influencing American policy toward Taiwan and China. To some Americans, the United States should protect and help the market democracy of Taiwan in its decades-long competition with the People's Republic of China. To other Americans, the United States should avoid a conflict with China over Taiwan because of the potentially horrendous costs involved. Both groups of

Americans are convinced that their policy recommendations—including support for Taiwan's right of self-determination on the one hand and curtailment of Taiwan's right of self-determination on the other—would serve the best interests of the United States. Taiwan is a conundrum in U.S. policy because it touches so many core values, a dilemma made even more difficult because the different values often lead to contradictory policy prescriptions.

Conclusion

The editorials reviewed in this chapter provide anecdotal evidence of the values held by the majority of Americans as they viewed Taiwan and China between 1988 and 1998. Americans tended to judge these societies by the degree to which they reflected American values such as freedom, democracy, respect for human rights, free enterprise, capitalism, and the rule of law. Far-sightedness, efficiency, hard work, and pragmatism were greatly respected. Totalitarianism and communism were disliked immensely, while inclinations toward friendship and openness toward the United States were much appreciated. According to this criteria of values, Taiwan was viewed quite favorably by the American public. The view of China was more complex: great praise for market reforms and severe criticism for the communist party and its repression of dissent. There was also a great deal of uncertainty about China's future. Overall, little sympathy existed in the public at large to change U.S. policies of friendship and support for Taiwan or engagement with the PRC. A balance in Washington's relations with Taipei and Beijing was preferred, with the understanding that diplomatic relations were maintained with the PRC and nondiplomatic relations were maintained with Taiwan.

The editorials reviewing the Jiang-Clinton summits in 1997 and 1998 confirmed broad American approval of U.S. engagement with China, both for the practical necessity of dealing with the emerging power of China as well as in the expectation that, over time, China's openness to the United States would help encourage political reforms—or at minimum the ending of CCP monopoly on political power. At the same time, it was clear that Americans wanted to counterbalance the rising power of China through existing alliances and strong military forces in the Pacific. Equally important to the American public was continued U.S. support of Taiwan, in spite of PRC objections. Efforts to compromise Taiwan's security or international standing as a means of improving Washington's relations with Beijing were deemed highly inappropriate.

In short, the American public applied two major standards to U.S. policy toward China and Taiwan: pragmatism and idealism. The need to deal with China as a major power was accepted as was the need to support Taiwan because of shared values and loyalty between old friends. The American people expected both of these elements, one based on utility and the other on traditional American values, to be represented in U.S. policy toward China and Taiwan.

In contrast were the views of some China specialists and foreign policy experts, using models of state morality, who argued that Washington should reduce its support of Taiwan to gain PRC cooperation in a strategic partnership with the United States or to avoid a future Sino-American war. Some of these individuals suggested that Washington curtail arms sales or take other steps to pressure Taipei into early unification talks with Beijing. Recommendations such as these were often justified on the grounds that China was larger and more powerful than Taiwan and that, therefore, U.S. interests in closer ties with China were more important than U.S. interests in Taiwan. These *Realpolitik* suggestions were not new, but they gained added momentum following the 1995–1996 crisis in the Taiwan Strait.

Neither the highly individualist values of the American people nor the calculations of *Realpolitik* advocates exercise control over U.S. policy toward Taiwan and China. Both schools of thought are strongly reflected in U.S. policy, and there exists a constantly shifting balance between the two schools on many specific issues in Sino-American relations. This tension between "right and might" is one of the major reasons why the Taiwan issue has become such a conundrum in U.S. China policy. But there are many other aspects of the conundrum, including, as discussed in the next chapter, the unique role of Congress in the formulation and implementation of U.S. policy toward Taiwan and China.

Notes

1. Editorials from *Wall Street Journal*, January 15, 1988; *Honolulu Star-Bulletin*, January 13, 1988; *San Francisco Examiner*, January 14, 1988; *Houston Chronicle*, January 14, 1988; *Atlanta Journal*, January 14, 1988; *Journal of Commerce*, January 14, 1988; *Birmingham Post-Herald*, January 15, 1988; *Rocky Mountain News*, January 15, 1988; *New York City Tribune*, January 15, 1988; *Globe & Mail*, January 15, 1988; *Deseret News*, January 15, 1988; *Cleveland Plain Dealer*, January 16, 1988; *Baltimore Sun*, January 16, 1988; *Dallas Morning News*, January 16, 1988; *Newsday*, January 16, 1988; *Washington Post*, January 17, 1988; *Los Angeles Times*, January 17, 1988; *New York Times*, January 18, 1988; *Washington Times*, January 18, 1988; *Mobile Register*, January 18, 1988; *Chicago Tribune*, January 20, 1988; *Palm Beach Post*, January 20, 1988; *Richmond Times-Dispatch*, January 21, 1988; and *Indianapolis Star*, January 26, 1988.

2. Editorials from *Washington Post*, February 20, 1997; *Wall Street Journal*, February 20 and February 24, 1997; *New York Times*, February 20, 1997; *Los Angeles Times*, February 20, 1997; *Chicago Tribune*, February 20, 1997; *Boston Globe*, February 20, 1997; *Houston Chronicle*, February 20, 1997; *New York Post*, February 20, 1997; *Miami Herald*, February 20, 1997; *Boston Herald*, February 20, 1997; *Times-Picayune*, February 20, 1997; *Baltimore Sun*, February 20, 1997; *Seattle Times*, February 20, 1997; *Richmond Times-Dispatch*, February 20, 1997; *Washington Times*, February 20, 1997; *Oregonian*, February 20, 1997; *Honolulu Star-Bulletin*, February 20, 1997; *Dallas Morning News*, February 21, 1997; *St. Louis Post-Dispatch*, February 21, 1997; *Atlanta Constitution*, February 21, 1997;

Kansas City Star, February 21, 1997; *Seattle Post-Intelligencer*, February 21, 1997; and *Union Leader* February 24, 1997.

3. Editorials from *Washington Post*, October 26, 28, and 31, 1997; *New York Times*, October 30, 1997; *Wall Street Journal*, October 31, 1997; *Washington Times*, October 23, 28, and 29, 1997; *Baltimore Sun*, October 26, 1997; *Boston Globe*, October 24, 1997; *Boston Sunday Herald*, October 26, 1997; *Chicago Tribune*, October 26, 1997; *Honolulu Advertiser*, October 26, 1997; and *St. Petersburg Times*, October 30, 1997.

4. Editorials from *Washington Times*, June 21, 29, 30, and July 6, 1998; *Washington Post*, June 23, 25, 30, and July 2, 1998; *Wall Street Journal*, June 30 and July 2, 1998; *Richmond Times-Dispatch*, July 2, 1998; *Los Angeles Times*, June 24 and 30, 1998; *New York Times*, June 25, July 1 and 2, 1998; and *Christian Science Monitor*, July 2 and 3, 1998.

5. Richard Holbrooke, "Reagan's Foreign Policy: Steady As She Goes," *Asian Wall Street Journal*, April 8, 1980, p. 4. Holbrooke was assistant secretary of state for East Asia and the Pacific in the administration of President Jimmy Carter.

6. The following summary of concerns about developments on Taiwan came from several closed-door workshops in which the author participated during 1996–1997, mostly in the Washington, D.C., area.

7. Chas. W. Freeman, Jr., "Preventing War in the Taiwan Strait: Restraining Taiwan—and Beijing," *Foreign Affairs* 77, 4, (July/August 1998), pp. 10-11.

8. Joseph S. Nye, Jr., "A Taiwan Deal," *Washington Post*, March 18, 1998, p. C7.

9. Lynn T. White, "Taiwan's China Problem: After a Decade or Two, Can There Be a Solution?" (Washington, DC: SAIS Policy Forum Series, December 1998).

10. For an analysis of the Perry visit and the reasons for the mission, see *Washington Post*, February 21, 1998, p. A16.

11. Ibid.

2

Congressional Views of China and Taiwan

Just as differences between American values and the morality of the state contribute to the Taiwan conundrum in U.S. China policy—by forming various standards by which policy is judged to be appropriate or effective—so too is that conundrum made more difficult by major differences in the institutional perspectives of the administration and the Congress. This chapter examines the role of Congress in the formulation and evaluation of U.S. policy toward China and Taiwan. The first section provides an overview of the many pieces of legislation dealing with China and Taiwan introduced by Members of Congress in recent years, while the second part of the chapter offers several examples of Congress at work: how the legislative branch actually affects policy adopted by the executive branch.

The significant differences in perception from Capitol Hill and from the White House and Foggy Bottom—coupled with the inability of one branch of government to dominate China policy—make it extremely difficult to find and sustain a governmental consensus on the Taiwan issue. This has been especially true in the post-Cold War period, when perceptions of Taiwan and China within the U.S. government vary tremendously. A major element of the Taiwan conundrum, therefore, is the inability of Congress and the administration to agree on the proper way to handle Taiwan within the context of U.S. China relations.

Although the executive branch of the U.S. government has primary responsibility for the conduct of foreign affairs, the American system of checks-and-balances makes it very difficult indeed for any administration to sustain an unpopular foreign policy. This is particularly true in cases such as China and Taiwan, where public attention frequently is focused in a highly politicized atmosphere. Policies toward Taiwan and China are subject to many influences. The American people at large, the media, scholars and experts, interest groups, businesses, and Congress and its staff routinely examine and judge the effectiveness and the moral correctness of U.S. China-Taiwan policies. Whereas the executive branch tends to determine policy on the basis of official assessments of the national interest—a subject examined in the next chapter—the appropriateness of those policies is judged by non-bureaucrats both from a value-based perspective and from personal opinion as to what is in the national interest.

The fact that Taiwan is identified with American values such as democracy and free enterprise, whereas the PRC is viewed much more ambiguously because it embodies both economic reform and communist rule, has an important influence on American judgments of the appropriateness of U.S. policies toward Taiwan and China. China's size and potential power, as well as the appealing possibility of its eventually shedding the communist system and adopting a more liberal government, ensure American support for continued engagement with the PRC. On the other hand, strong support exists for a policy of continued friendship with Taiwan. Because of this support for parallel policies, there is great sensitivity in the American body politic over balance and fairness in U.S. policies toward China and Taiwan. While various administrations have attempted to establish a strategic partnership with China since the early 1970s, the public's demand for balance in China-Taiwan policy has worked to protect Taiwan. In this effort to find balance and fairness, the U.S. Congress has played an especially important role since 1979 to ensure that the executive branch did not harm the people of Taiwan—and U.S. interests in Taiwan—in its enthusiasm to advance ties with Beijing.

Congressional Influence on China Policy

Congress can exert enormous influence over American foreign policy: it declares war, pays the bills, authorizes extended use of force, approves personnel appointments, passes laws, commands the ear of the media and the public, holds hearings. Congress is especially active on issues which are viewed as being important to the national interest and which are highly visible due to their controversial nature. This certainly has been the case with policy toward China and Taiwan, as various administrations and congresses have argued and maneuvered for decades to place their imprint on U.S. relations with the two sides of the Taiwan Strait. At times, both branches of government have tried to gain control over China policy, but this has proved impossible for more than a short time. Consequently, there is persistent compromise and confrontation on that policy, with honest efforts on the part of many to find a consensus and determined efforts on the part of some to keep the poles far apart. As a result, the contradictions that exist in U.S. policy toward Taiwan and China are perpetuated from year to year, making the Taiwan conundrum ever more complex. But—and this is important to remember—those who seek to solve the conundrum are far fewer than those who wish to see it continue for the time being. The Taiwan conundrum exists because the complexities and dilemmas of the Taiwan issue are less harmful to American interests than currently available solutions. By being closely aligned with American values and enjoying the strong support of most Members of Congress, Taiwan has managed to survive quite nicely in the dynamic environment of Washington, where multitudes of perceptions and interests compete for attention and resources.

The most striking example of congressional involvement in policy toward Taiwan is the 1979 Taiwan Relations Act (S. 245/H.R. 2479), passed both Houses of Congress by more than two-thirds vote in late March and signed into law by President Jimmy Carter on April 10, 1979, as P. L. 96-98. Much has been written on the TRA and its legislative background, so there is no need to belabor the point that this was a unique piece of legislation designed to remedy what Congress felt were inadequacies in President Carter's proposals to handle Taiwan affairs in the post-normalization period.[1] The policy guidelines found in the TRA will be discussed in Chapter 5, but it should be noted here that Congress was especially concerned that Taiwan's security needs be met, an issue which has surfaced repeatedly since 1979.

Since the enactment of the TRA, Congress has frequently revisited Taiwan policy, usually to monitor administration activities through hearings but occasionally to force some revision in existing policy. Each year Members of Congress express their views on U.S. policy toward Taiwan and China in numerous bills and resolutions. In recent years, for example, the 103rd Congress (1993-1994) considered thirty-four bills dealing with Taiwan and eighty-eight bills dealing with the People's Republic of China; the 104th Congress (1995-1996) considered thirty-eight separate bills concerned with Taiwan and ninety-six bills concerned with China; and the 105th Congress (1997-1998) considered forty-eight bills dealing with Taiwan and 129 bills dealing with the PRC.[2]

Usually, bills introduced in Congress dealing with Taiwan are favorable or supportive, while bills dealing with China are critical. In the case of Taiwan, for example, recent bills through 1998 introduced in the House or Senate have called for Taiwan's membership in the United Nations and other international organizations, higher-level contacts between American and Taiwan officials, more U.S. arms sales for the island's defense, American involvement in the defense of Taiwan in case of PRC attack, more liberal policies allowing high-ranking Taiwan officials to visit the United States in private capacities, amendments to the Taiwan Relations Act to make it more supportive of Taiwan's security, congratulations on the occasion of democratic progress on Taiwan or for meritorious service by Taiwan representatives or officials, and presidential reaffirmations of U.S. support for Taiwan or caution so as not to compromise Taiwan's interests in dealing with the PRC.

Bills concerning China reflect the ambivalence the American public feels about the PRC; often the bills are unfavorable. Recent bills through 1998, for example, called for the promotion of human rights in China, conditions attached to most-favored-nation (MFN) trading status, the denial of MFN, purchases of wheat and other American products to redress China's trade surplus with the United States, opposition to China's hosting prestigious events such as the Olympics in the year 2000, ending Chinese repression of Tibet, curtailment of Chinese imports made by prison labor, prohibitions on the exports of satellites to be launched by China, barring U.S. funds to international organizations supporting China's population control program, the establishment of a "Radio Free Asia" to broadcast to China, support of the development and growth of democratic institutions in China, improving U.S. ties with Tibet, China to follow nonproliferation guidelines and condemnation for perceived violations, release of prisoners of conscience or those imprisoned for religious beliefs, redress of intellectual property rights violations, approval of fisheries and other mutually beneficial treaties and agreements, peace and stability in the South China Sea, disapproval of the arrest of well-known Chinese activists such as Harry Wu and Wei Jingsheng, restricting imports of products made by the People's Liberation Army, China's entrance into the World Trade Organization, expressing concern about the future of Hong Kong after its reversion to Chinese sovereignty in June 1997, working with Chinese authorities to account for American missing-in-action, approval of agreements between the United States and China on the control of illicit narcotics, disapproval of the practice of harvesting and transplanting organs for profit from executed prisoners, guidelines for the president to follow in his state visit to China in June 1998, probes of illegal political contributions and fundraising activities, monitoring of Chinese intelligence activities in the United States, investigation of various immigration and visa matters relating to China and Hong Kong, prohibition of export of certain high-tech equipment to China, expressions of the sense of Congress on the state visit of President Jiang Zemin in October 1997, guidelines for overall U.S. policy with China, encouragement of China to integrate with the world economy and to enter into a strategic working relationship with the United States, and extension of permanent MFN trading status to China.

Most of these bills were introduced by a small number of congressmen or senators, and most never made it beyond committee review. Some, however, received considerable backing throughout the Congress both in terms of cosponsorship and, in some cases, passage or inclusion in larger bills signed into law by the president. Bills concerning Taiwan and China that received wide support in the 103rd, 104th, or 105th congresses included the following:

103rd Congress (1993-1994)

S. Res. 148 expressing the sense of the Senate that the United Nations should be encouraged to permit representatives of Taiwan to participate fully in its activities. Sponsored by Sen. Simon and passed the Senate on June 10, 1994.

S. Res. 261 commending Ambassador Mou-shih Ding, representative of the Taipei Economic and Cultural Representative Office in Washington, D.C. Sponsored by Sen. Murkowski and passed by the Senate on September 20, 1994.

S. Res. 270 expressing the sense of the Senate concerning U.S. relations with Taiwan. Sponsored by Sen. Murkowski, the resolution passed the Senate on October 5, 1994.

H. Res. 188 expressing the sense of the House of Representatives that the Olympics in the Year 2000 should not be held in Beijing or elsewhere in the People's Republic of China. Sponsored by Rep. Lantos and passed by the House on July 26, 1993, by a vote of 287-99.

H. Res. 509 providing for consideration of a joint resolution and a bill relating to most-favored-nation treatment for the People's Republic of China. Sponsored by Rep. Bonior and passed by the House on August 9, 1994.

H. R. 4590 providing conditions for renewing nondiscriminatory (most-favored-nation) treatment for the People's Republic of China. Sponsored by Rep. Pelosi and passed by the House on August 9, 1994.

104th Congress (1995-1996)

S. J. Res. 43 expressing the sense of Congress regarding Wei Jingsheng; Gedhum Choekyi Nyima, the next Panchen Lama of Tibet; and the human rights practices of the Government of the People's Republic of China. Sponsored by Sen. Helms and passed by the Senate on December 13, 1995.

S. Res. 97 expressing the sense of the Senate with respect to peace and stability in the South China Sea. Sponsored by Sen. Thomas, passing the Senate on June 22, 1995.

S. Res. 148 expressing the sense of the Senate regarding the arrest of Harry Wu by the Government of the People's Republic of China. Sponsored by Sen. Helms, passing the Senate on June 30, 1995.

S. Res. 169 expressing the sense of the Senate welcoming His Holiness the Dalai Lama on his visit to the United States. Sponsored by Sen. Thomas and passed by the Senate on September 8, 1995.

S. Res. 271 expressing the sense of the Senate with regard to the international obligation of the People's Republic of China to allow an elected legislature in Hong Kong after June 30, 1997, and for other purposes. Sponsored by Sen. Helms, passing the Senate on June 28, 1996.

H. Con. Res. 53 expressing the sense of the Congress regarding a private visit by President Lee Teng-hui of the Republic of China on Taiwan to the United States. Sponsored by Rep. Lantos, passed the House on May 2, 1995, by a vote of 396-0, and passed by the Senate on May 9, 1995, by a vote of 97-1.

H. J. Res. 96 disapproving the extension of nondiscriminatory treatment (most-favored-nation treatment) to the products of the People's Republic of China. Sponsored by Rep. Wolf, passing the House on July 20, 1995, by a vote of 321-107.

H. Con. Res. 117 concerning writer, political philosopher, human rights advocate, and Nobel Peace Prize nominee Wei Jingsheng. Sponsored by Rep. C. Smith, passing the House on December 12, 1995, by a vote of 409-0.

H. Con. Res. 148 expressing the sense of Congress that the United States is committed to the military stability of the Taiwan Strait and United States military forces should defend Taiwan in the event of invasion, missile attack, or blockade by the People's Republic of China. Sponsored by Rep. Cox, passed the House on March 19, 1996, by a vote of 369-14, and passed by the Senate on March 21, 1996, by a vote of 97-0.

H. Con. Res. 154 congratulating the Republic of China on Taiwan on the occasion of its first Presidential democratic election. Sponsored by Rep. Funderburk and passed by the House on May 21, 1996.

H. Res. 178 calling upon the People's Republic of China to release U.S. citizen Harry Wu unconditionally and to provide for an accounting of his arrest and detention. Sponsored by Rep. C. Smith and passing the House on June 29, 1995.

H. Res. 193 providing for consideration of a bill establishing United States policy toward China and a joint resolution relating to most-favored-nation treatment for the People's Republic of China. Sponsored by Rep. Solomon and passed by the House on July 20, 1995.

H. Con. Res. 212 endorsing the adoption by the European Parliament of a resolution supporting the Republic of China on Taiwan's efforts at joining the community of nations. Sponsored by Rep. Solomon, passing the House on September 24, 1996.

H. Res. 461 regarding U.S. concerns with human rights abuse, nuclear and chemical weapons proliferation, illegal weapons trading, military intimidation of Taiwan, and trade violations by the People's Republic of China and the People's Liberation Army, and directing the committees of jurisdiction to commence hearings and report appropriate legislation. Sponsored by Rep. Cox and passed by the House on July 27, 1996, by a vote of 411-7.

H. R. 2058 establishing United States policy toward China. Sponsored by Rep. Bereuter and passed by the House on July 20, 1995, by a vote of 416-10.

105th Congress (1997-1998)

S. Res. 19 expressing the sense of the Senate regarding United States opposition to the prison sentence of Tibetan ethnomusicologist Ngawang Choephel by the Government of the People's Republic of China. Sponsored by Sen. Moynihan, passing the Senate on March 11, 1997.

S. Con. Res. 103 expressing the sense of the Congress in support of the recommendations of the International Commission of Jurists on Tibet and on United States policy with regard to Tibet. Sponsored by Sen. Moynihan and passing the Senate on September 17, 1998.

S. Res. 105 expressing the sense of the Senate that the people of the United States wish the people of Hong Kong good fortune as they embark on their historic transition of sovereignty from Great Britain to the People's Republic of China. Sponsored by Sen. Lott and passing the Senate on June 27, 1997.

S. Con. Res. 107 affirming U.S. commitments under the Taiwan Relations Act. Sponsored by Sen. Lott and passed by the Senate on July 10, 1998, by a vote of 92-0.

S. Res. 125 commending Dr. Jason C. Hu, Representative of the Taipei Economic and Cultural Representative Office in the United States. Sponsored by Sen. Murkowski, passing the Senate on September 24, 1997.

S. Res. 187 expressing the sense of the Senate regarding the human rights situation in the People's Republic of China. Sponsored by Sen. Mack and passed by the Senate on March 12, 1998, by a vote of 95-5.

S. Res. 244 expressing the sense of the Senate on the ninth anniversary of the massacre of pro-democracy demonstrators on Tiananmen Square by military forces acting under orders from the Government of the People's Republic of China. Sponsored by Sen. Collins, passing the Senate on June 5, 1998.

H. Res. 188 urging the executive branch to take action regarding the acquisition by Iran of (Chinese exported) C-802 cruise missiles. Sponsored by Rep. Gilman and passed by the House on November 6, 1997, by a vote of 414-8.

H. Con. Res. 270 acknowledging the positive role of Taiwan in the current Asian financial crisis and affirming the support of the American people for peace and stability on the Taiwan Strait and security for Taiwan's democracy. Sponsored by Rep. Solomon and passed by the House on June 10, 1998, by a vote of 411-0.

H. Con. Res. 285 expressing the sense of Congress that the President of the United States should reconsider his decision to be formally received in Tiananmen Square by the Government of the People's Republic of China. Sponsored by Rep. Armey and passed by the House on June 4, 1998, by a vote of 305-116.

H. Con. Res. 301 affirming the United States commitment to Taiwan. Sponsored by Rep. DeLay, passing the House on July 20, 1998, by a vote of 390-1.

H. Con. Res. 334 relating to Taiwan's participation in the World Health Organization. Sponsored by Rep. Solomon and passed by the House on October 10, 1998, by a vote of 418-0.

H. Res. 364 urging the introduction and passage of a resolution on the human rights situation in the People's Republic of China at the 54th Session of the United Nations

Commission on Human Rights. Sponsored by Rep. Smith, passing the House on March 17, 1998, by a vote of 397-0.

H. Res. 463 establishing the Select Committee on U.S. National Security and Military/Commercial Concerns With the People's Republic of China. Sponsored by Rep. Solomon and passed by the House on June 18, 1998, by a vote of 409-10.

H. R. 697 prohibiting the use of United States funds to provide for the participation of certain Chinese officials in international conferences, programs, and activities and to provide that certain Chinese officials shall be ineligible to receive visas and excluded from admission to the United States. Sponsored by Rep. Gilman and passed the House on November 6, 1997, by a vote of 366-54.

H. R. 750 supporting the autonomous governance of Hong Kong after its reversion to the People's Republic of China. Sponsored by Rep. Bereuter, passing the House on March 11, 1997, by a vote of 416-1.

H. R. 2195 providing for certain measures to increase monitoring of products of the People's Republic of China that are made with forced labor. Sponsored by Rep. C. Smith, passing the House on November 5, 1997, by a vote of 419-2.

H. R. 2232 providing for increased international broadcasting activities to China. Sponsored by Rep. Royce and passed by the House on November 9, 1997, by a vote of 401-21.

H. R. 2358 providing for improved monitoring of human rights violations in the People's Republic of China. Sponsored by Rep. Ros-Lehtmen, passing the House on November 5, 1997, by a vote of 416-5.

H. R. 2386 implementing the provisions of the Taiwan Relations Act concerning the stability and security of Taiwan and United States cooperation with Taiwan on the development and acquisition of defensive military articles (short titled "U.S.-Taiwan Anti-Ballistic Missile Defense Cooperation Act). Sponsored by Rep. Hunter and passed by the House on November 6, 1997, by a vote of 301-116.

H. R. 2570 condemning those officials of the Chinese Communist Party, the Government of the People's Republic of China, and other persons who are involved in the enforcement of forced abortions by preventing such persons from entering or remaining in the United States. Sponsored by Rep. Fowler and passed by the House on November 6, 1997, by a vote of 415-1.

H. R. 2605 requiring the United States to oppose the making of concessional loans by international financial institutions to any entity in the People's Republic of China. Sponsored by Rep. Solomon and passed by the House on November 6, 1997, by a vote of 354-59.

H. R. 2647 ensuring that commercial activities of the People's Liberation Army of China or any Communist Chinese military company in the United States are monitored and are subject to the authorities under the International Emergency Economic Powers Act. Sponsored by Rep. Fowler, passing the House on November 7, 1997, by a vote of 408-10.

The fact that these bills received such large support in the Congress makes it clear that Congress as a body is very supportive of Taiwan and very critical of certain policies and actions of China. It should also be noted that these congressional views are not the product of partisan politics. During the 105th Congress, for example, there were fifty-five members of the GOP in the Senate and forty-five Democrats; in the House there were 228 Republicans, 206 Democrats, and one independent. The very lopsided vote on many issues related to Taiwan and China during the 105th Congress— e.g., S. Con. Res. 107, S. Res. 187, H. Res. 188, H. Con. Res. 270, H. Con. Res. 301, H. Con. Res. 334, H. Res. 364, H. Res. 463, H. R. 750, H. R. 2195, H. R. 2358, H. R. 2570, and H. R. 2647—is convincing evidence that Congress is remarkably nonpartisan in its evaluation of U.S. policy toward Taipei and Beijing. Nor can congressional support for Taiwan or opposition to certain activities of the PRC be explained along a liberal-conservative continuum. As an institution, the Congress—like the editorial staff of national newspapers and the public opinion they reflect—is strongly in favor of Taiwan because of its accomplishments as a market democracy and strongly opposed to aspects of PRC behavior which offend American values and harm U.S. interests. The idea that such widespread congressional support for Taiwan can be purchased through lobbying or campaign contributions is simply ludicrous.

More so than the administration, the Congress serves as the conscience of American China policy, bringing value judgments as well as assessments of national interest into the calculation of policies toward Taiwan and China. The check-and-balance system of the U.S. government and institutional tension between the executive and legislative branches help to ensure that U.S. policy is reflective of both the values and interests of the American people. The system is far from perfect, but it usually prevents the abuse of power by any one individual, institution, or branch of government, and to date it has preserved a degree of balance in U.S. policy toward Taiwan and China.

Many congressional resolutions express the "sense of Congress" and are non-binding on the administration. These can have great influence, however, on specific administrative decisions relating to Taiwan and China, particularly if the resolutions are supported by expressions of public concern over the issue. Congressional influence can be further enhanced when the threat exists for binding legislation if the administration does not acquiesce to the wishes of Congress. The work of Congress and its influence on U.S. policy can be seen in the following three examples from the 1993–1995 period: the 1993–1994 Murkowski amendment to the Taiwan Relations Act, the 1994 Taiwan Policy Review, and the 1995 issuance of a tourist visa to ROC President Lee Teng-hui.

There are several important lessons to note from these examples. First, Congress is very concerned with U.S. policy toward Taiwan and China, and it takes seriously its self-delegated responsibilities to see that the administration does not sacrifice Taiwan's interests in the pursuit of improved Sino-American relations. Second, Congress exercises great influence over U.S. policy toward Taiwan and China whenever it chooses to exert its power. Third—and this is important in the context of the Taiwan conundrum—the deep involvement of Congress in the Taiwan issue precludes any possibility of the administration forging a deal with Beijing that would undermine Taiwan's security or the self-determination of Taiwan's residents. Fourth, Congress is the primary force in the U.S. government arguing for improved relations with Taiwan, not necessarily for diplomatic recognition or for Taiwan independence, but for proper balance in a dual-track policy of official relations with China and friendly ties with Taiwan. Above all: Congress is not searching for ways to solve the Taiwan issue; it is trying to ensure that Taiwan survives as a market democracy, even while U.S.-PRC relations move forward.

Murkowski Amendment to the TRA

Congress can express its views through non-binding resolutions or, as in the case of the TRA, through major, stand-alone legislation enacted into law. A more common method of passing substantive policy directives, however, is to attach amendments to major authorization or appropriation legislation, which the president must sign into law if he or she wants authorization for administration projects or funding for the government. An excellent example of how this is done—as well as an illustrative lesson on the interaction between Congress and the administration over Taiwan policy—is the Murkowski amendment to the Taiwan Relations Act.

In July 1993 the Senate Foreign Relations Committee adopted by a vote of 20-0 an amendment to the Taiwan Relations Act introduced by Senator Frank Murkowski. The amendment stated that the arms sales provisions of the TRA would supersede provisions of the August 17, 1982, Sino-American joint communiqué agreed to by the Reagan administration. The TRA stated that arms sales to Taiwan would be based on U.S. determination of the security needs of Taiwan, whereas the August 17 communiqué placed limits on the qualitative and quantitative levels of future weapons sold to Taiwan, if the PRC continued its policy of seeking reunification through peaceful means.[3]

As mentioned earlier, security has been one of the major concerns of Congress in U.S. policy toward Taiwan. In trying to reconcile the August 17 communiqué with the TRA, the State Department explained to Congress that the TRA, as law of the land, took legal precedence over the communiqué. State Department legal adviser Davis R. Robinson said in September 1982: "[The communiqué] is not an international agreement and thus imposes no obligations on either party under international law. Its status under domestic law is that of a statement by the President of a policy which he intends to pursue. . . . The Taiwan Relations Act is and will remain the law of the land unless amended by Congress. Nothing in the joint communiqué obligates the President to act in a manner contrary to the Act or, conversely, disables him from fulfilling his responsibilities under it."[4]

Over time, however, the August 17 communiqué did have a negative impact on Taiwan's security since the amount of arms annually sold to Taipei was reduced by an average of about $20 million. The so-called "Taiwan bucket" for U.S. arms sales was reduced from a 1982 high of $820 million to a level of about $580 million in 1993. Although the United States found ways to circumvent some of the communiqué's restrictions—e.g., the sale of U.S. defense technology to enable Taiwan to manufacture its own advanced weapons and the replacement of obsolete ROC military equipment with newer models—by the early 1990s the Taiwan bucket had shrunk to what many in the Congress considered dangerously low levels. Moreover, advanced U.S. arms sales were vital to Taiwan's continued security, since Taiwan could not manufacture some of the essential weapons needed for its defense, such as modern air defense fighters. The problem of Taiwan's growing defense obsolescence became even more apparent after the collapse of the Soviet Union in August 1991, when Moscow began to offer advanced Russian weapons systems to the PRC at fire sale prices. President Bush's decision in September 1992 to sell Taiwan 150 F-16s was in large measure designed to remedy these deficiencies in Taiwan's defense, but the decision was widely seen as a violation of the August 17 communiqué, which had become one of the foundations of Sino-American relations.

Senator Murkowski intended to do away with the Taiwan bucket altogether by establishing through explicit legislation the TRA's legal precedence over the August 17 communiqué in arms sales decisions. This would have profound implications, since the communiqué promised a gradual U.S. reduction of arms sales to the island—as long as Beijing pursued peaceful reunification—whereas the TRA tied the level of arms sales to Taiwan's security requirements, a key component of which was the PLA's capabilities to use force in the Taiwan Strait. Under TRA guidelines, Taiwan would be eligible to receive higher levels of arms sales as the PLA modernized.

The Senate Foreign Relations Committee approved Murkowski's plan and the Senate as a whole included the Murkowski amendment in the Senate version of the FY 1994-1995 State Department Authorization Bill. No such provision was contained in the House version of the bill, however. When the two Houses of Congress met in conference in April 1994 to work out the differences in their respective versions, a non-binding sense of Congress substitute for the Murkowski amendment was adopted in Section 531 of the State Department Authorization Bill. Section 531 read:

In view of the self-defense needs of Taiwan, the Congress makes the following declarations:
(1) Sections 2 and 3 of the Taiwan Relations Act are reaffirmed.
(2) Section 3 of the Taiwan Relations Act take primacy over statements of United States policy, including communiqués, regulations, directives, and policies based thereon.
(3) In assessing the extent to which the People's Republic of China is pursuing its "fundamental policy" to strive peacefully to resolve the Taiwan issue, the United States should take into account both the capabilities and intentions of the People's Republic of China.
(4) The President should on a regular basis assess changes in the capabilities and intentions of the People's Republic of China and consider whether it is appropriate to adjust arms sales to Taiwan accordingly.

The conference committee explained its intentions in writing Section 531 in the conference report accompanying the revised State Department Authorization Bill:

With this provision, the committee of conference expresses its continued concern for the security of Taiwan. It reaffirms the commitments made in the Taiwan Relations Act (TRA) to enable Taiwan to maintain a sufficient self-defense capability. Among the policy statements over which Sections 3(b) of the TRA takes precedence is the communiqué concluded between the United States and the People's Republic of China on August 17, 1982.

The congressional statement reflects concern on the part of the committee of conference over the effect of stability in the Asia-Pacific region of China's military modernization, its increased military spending, and its territorial claims. If the President, in consultation with the Congress as provided in Section 3(b) of the TRA, finds that PRC capabilities and intentions have increased the threat to Taiwan, then a compensating adjustment in the transfer of defense articles and services to Taiwan should be seriously considered. Pursuant to the TRA, U.S. policy on arms sales to Taiwan should be based on Taiwan's defense needs and be formulated jointly by the Congress and the President.

The Taiwan Relations Act is explicit that the nature and quantity of defensive articles and defensive services to be transferred to Taiwan shall be based solely upon the judgment of the President and Congress of the needs of Taiwan, in accordance with procedures established by law. Consequently, the transfer of particular defense articles and services—such as advanced ballistic missile defense systems and conventionally powered coastal patrol submarines—should be based on Taiwan's needs and not on arbitrary principles, such as prohibiting the incorporation of U.S. equipment on defensive platforms produced by other nations or the exclusion of entire classes of defensive weapons. The committee of conference calls on the Executive Branch to streamline and rationalize the procedures for implementation of U.S. policy concerning arms sales to Taiwan.

The conference bill, H.R. 2333, was passed by both Houses of Congress in late April 1994 and signed into law by President Clinton on April 30, 1994, as P. L. 103-236. In addition to the arms sales provision, the new law contained language urging high-level U.S. official visits to Taiwan and U.S. support for Taiwan in multilateral organizations. Thus, in 1994 Congress passed laws approved by the president supporting not only increased arms sales to Taiwan but also allowing high-level exchange visits between American and Taiwan officials.

The negative reaction of the administration to the Murkowski amendment illustrates the differing perspectives of the executive and legislative branches on U.S. policy toward Taiwan. The White House, and especially the State Department, tried from the outset to block the Murkowski amendment, warning the Senate Foreign Relations Committee that the amendment would set U.S.-China relations back twenty years. One official explained the August 17 communiqué actually was a "cover [for arms sales to Taiwan], so as not to provoke China's wrath. . . . We're afraid to change this."[5] There was some validity to this argument, but the official's statement also revealed a fundamental difference in congressional and administration views of the Taiwan issue in Sino-American relations. Whereas Congress was concerned that Taiwan's security was being undermined gradually by U.S. arms sales policy—thus necessitating an adjustment by Congress through legislation—the foreign policy bureaucracy did not want to change the ground rules for handling arms sales because it feared jeopardizing U.S. diplomatic relations with China. The State Department preferred maximum flexibility and ambiguity in U.S. policy rather than to operate under an environment of clear legal precedence of the TRA over the communiqués, an environment which would make management of Sino-American relations more difficult.

State Department official Strobe Talbott wrote a March 8, 1994, letter to Senator Claiborne Pell, Chairman of the Senate Foreign Relations Committee, urging that the Congress delete the amendment during the Senate-House conference on H.R. 2333, saying the change was "essential to the Administration's ability to support the final bill." Talbott wrote: "In particular, section 706 of the Senate bill [the Murkowski amendment], regarding the Taiwan Relations Act, would seriously undermine the foundation of the peace and stability we have helped create in the Taiwan Strait over the last fourteen years. It is critical to the Administration that the conference committee adopt a conference report that does not include this section."

When the final version of the amendment was passed in any case and signed into law by President Clinton, the State Department said the non-binding language in the conference report would not change U.S. policy toward Taiwan or China.[6] Nonetheless, to assuage congressional concerns over Taiwan's security, Secretary of State Warren Christopher reaffirmed the TRA's legal precedence over the August 17 communiqué in a private letter to Senator Murkowski. His letter also promised to streamline the process of approving arms sales to Taiwan.[7] One immediate effect of Clinton signing the bill was the sale to Taiwan of advanced U.S. naval electronic equipment for the six new *LaFayette* frigates Taipei recently had purchased from France.

As the events surrounding the Murkowski amendment indicate, Congress diligently monitors key aspects of U.S. policy toward Taiwan, particularly arms sales and other elements critical to Taiwan's security. There is much less concern in the Congress than in the administration over possible PRC reaction. Congress insists that balance be maintained in U.S. policy toward Taiwan and China, whereas the executive branch routinely prefers to maintain a low-key approach to Taiwan to avoid offending PRC sensitivities. Congress is interested in balance and fairness in U.S. policy toward Taiwan and China, while the administration is concerned with managing U.S. relations with both Chinese sides without crisis. These institutional differences are not likely to change in the foreseeable future, thus ensuring that the Taiwan conundrum will continue.

Another excellent example of congressional efforts to ensure balance in U.S. policy toward Taiwan and China can be found in the events leading to the Taiwan Policy Review announced by the administration in September 1994.

Taiwan Policy Review

Following the termination of diplomatic relations with the Republic of China on January 1, 1979, the United States became very conservative in extending visas to high-ranking officials from Taiwan. This was done mainly to avoid angering Beijing, which tended to become apoplectic when confronted with the possibility of even slight improvement in Washington's treatment of Taipei. These severe restrictions on official travelers from Taiwan were reflected, for instance, in a controversial decision by the State Department in May 1994, refusing to allow President Lee Teng-hui to stay overnight in Honolulu or Los Angeles en route to a state visit in Latin America.[8] Instead, he was permitted a ninety-minute refueling stop in Honolulu and was invited to a brief reception in a spartan airport lounge. Angered at the treatment, Lee refused to leave his plane. There he was visited briefly by Natale Bellocchi, chairman of the American Institute in Taiwan (AIT), the private corporation established by Congress in the TRA to manage U.S. relations with Taiwan in the aftermath of derecognition. Many Members of Congress were outraged at the treatment accorded Lee, prompting them to criticize Secretary of State Warren Christopher and to invite President Lee to visit their own states. The State Department's hypersensitivity to China contrasted sharply to the willingness of many Southeast Asian leaders to meet socially with Lee and Prime Minister Lien Chan, as occurred for example during their trips to Malaysia and Singapore in December 1993–January 1994 and to the Philippines, Indonesia, and Thailand in February 1994.[9]

Throughout the 1993–1994 period, there was widespread feeling in the Congress that the administration was needlessly compromising American values in dealing with Taiwan. To Congress, it made little sense to deny American hospitality to the democratic leader of Taiwan in order to pursue friendly relations with communist leaders in Beijing who persistently defied the United States on issues such as proliferation, trade, and human rights. Irritation over the State

Department's humiliation of President Lee prompted Members of Congress to introduce a host of bills to mandate change in U.S. Taiwan policy through legislation.

Examples of legislation introduced in the 103rd Congress (1993-1994) to force the administration to adjust its Taiwan policy included:[10] H. R. 763, introduced by Congressman Philip Crane in February 1993, calling for the establishment of free trade areas with Pacific Rim countries, including Taiwan; S. 1467, introduced by Senator Claiborne Pell in September 1993, calling for high-level official exchanges between the United States and Taiwan; and S. Con. Res. 20, introduced by Senator Joseph Lieberman in March 1993, expressing the sense of Congress that Taiwan should be represented in the United Nations and other international organizations. Resolutions similar to S. Con. Res.20 were introduced by Congressman Gerald Solomon (H. Con. Res. 148), Senator Alfonse D'Amato (S. Con. Res. 45), and Senator Paul Simon (S. Res. 148).

In addition to these and other resolutions, Congress held hearings on various aspects of U.S. policy toward Taiwan. On July 15, 1994, for example, two subcommittees of the U.S. House of Representatives held a joint hearing to consider Taiwan's participation in the United Nations.[11] The Subcommittee on International Security, International Organizations and Human Rights and the Subcommittee on Asia and the Pacific of the House Foreign Affairs Committee heard testimony generally in favor of Taiwan joining the United Nations. The subcommittees were considering two House resolutions on the issue. One, offered by Representative Gerald Solomon, called for a seat in the United Nations for the Republic of China on Taiwan, while the other, offered by Representative Robert Torricelli, called for Taiwan's representation at the U.N. but not specifically for a seat in the international organization. At the time of the hearing, Torricelli's resolution had sixty-five cosponsors in the House.

Ten members of the two subcommittees spoke in favor of Taiwan's increased role in international affairs and membership in the U.N. Representative Tom Lantos, chairman of the subcommittee on international security and organizations, said: "Taiwan's exclusion [from the U.N.] cannot be justified in terms of international law as Taiwan more than meets the traditional criteria of statehood. Nor would granting Taiwan U.N. representation in any way prejudice the resolution of Taiwan's ultimate status. . . . The two Germanys reunited, although both had seats in the U.N., and so could mainland China and Taiwan at some future date, if that were the wish of both nations." Representative Gary Ackerman, chairman of the subcommittee on Asia and the Pacific, said Taiwan's future was inextricably linked to U.S. interests in Asia and that Taiwan could play an important role in the U.N. He commented: "We must face reality. And that reality is that Taiwan is an economic goliath and the interrelationship and interdependency between the community of nations and Taiwan will only grow more important as time goes on."

Hearings and comments such as these were common on Capitol Hill. The bills and hearings were indicative of a trend in the Congress toward more vocal and active support for Taiwan, a momentum seen in the Murkowski amendment discussed earlier. For the most part, this trend was based on bipartisan congressional perceptions that American policy had not evolved sufficiently to take into account the tremendous economic and political strides made on Taiwan. In the view of Congress, the administration was far too sensitive to PRC complaints and not adequately tuned to American values—in this case, the emergence of a true market democracy on Taiwan. Although the Clinton administration initially resisted moves by Congress to mandate changes in its Taiwan policy, and managed to thwart many of the more intrusive congressional initiatives, congressional pressure could not be ignored. Gradually, growing congressional and media support for Taiwan began to influence the administration's views on Taiwan policy.

In July 1994 the Clinton administration concluded a year-long interagency review of U.S. policy toward Taiwan.[12] The review was one of several initiated by the president to examine various aspects of American foreign policy. The Taiwan policy review was at first assigned a low priority because no change was deemed necessary. By mid-1994, however, several factors had forced some adjustment in policy toward Taiwan. These factors included: widespread public anger at the State Department's refusal to allow President Lee in May 1994 to rest in the United States; a rapidly expanding movement in the Congress to legislate better treatment of Taiwan; overwhelming American public approval of Taiwan's democratization; business demands to make it easier to deal with Taiwan; and popular opinion that Clinton was leaning too much in Beijing's favor (in spite of human rights violations, missile sales, and the PLA's modernization) while ignoring the significant progress Taiwan had made politically and economically.

The results of the Taiwan Policy Review were announced on September 7, 1994, in a background briefing given to reporters by a senior State Department official.[13] The official said President Clinton had authorized certain "refinements" in policy toward Taiwan to better serve America's increasingly extensive and complicated interests in Taiwan, while at the same time preserving the U.S. one-China policy and unofficial relations with Taiwan. "There is only one China," the official said, "and Taiwan is a part of China." He noted that U.S. policy toward China and Taiwan was designed to help maintain stability in Asia, but that the policy remained a delicate balancing act.

One of the "refinements" was designed to allow more effective meetings between U.S. and Taiwan officials. The administration was "willing to establish under the AIT auspices, a sub-cabinet economic dialogue with Taiwan. We will permit high-level U.S. government officials of economic and technical agencies to visit Taiwan. . . . All such meetings and visits will be focused sharply on solving practical problems and doing business. They carry with them no implication that we consider the relationship to be official and should not be interpreted by anyone as being so." He explained that top-level U.S. officials having no economic, commercial, or technical portfolio would not be allowed to visit Taiwan. Similarly,

Taiwan's top leadership—including its president and vice president—would not be issued permits to visit the United States. However, to avoid embarrassments such as that occasioned by Lee Teng-hui's stop-over in Hawaii, Taiwan's leaders would be allowed "to transit the United States when necessary." Exchange visits by cabinet-level officials with economic, commercial, or technical portfolios would be considered on a case-by-case basis: "We don't rule anything out." Senior Taiwan officials would be able to meet with undersecretary-level U.S. officials in the State and Defense departments in unofficial settings, while high-level economic and trade officials from Taiwan would be able to meet with the leadership of U.S. economic, commercial, and technical agencies in official settings.

The official said the U.S. government acknowledged that Taiwan had a legitimate role to play in international organizations such as APEC (Asia-Pacific Economic Cooperation) and GATT and that it was in the general interests of the world community that Taiwan's voice be heard in some additional international organizations. However, the United States would not support Taiwan's entry into the United Nations. Taiwan could change the name of its representative office in Washington, D.C., from "Coordination Council for North American Affairs" to "Taipei Economic and Cultural Representative Office in the United States." As mandated by the Taiwan Relations Act, the United States would continue to provide equipment for Taiwan's self-defense, while at the same time adhering to the August 17 communiqué.

Most Members of Congress thought the adjustments announced in the policy review were cosmetic. Senator Paul Simon called the policy refinements "official pettiness," commenting: "We continue to give Taiwan the cold shoulder. . . . Taiwan has a multiparty system, free elections, and a free press—the things we profess to champion—while we continue to cuddle up to the mainland government, whose dictatorship permits none of these." Senator Hank Brown said the administration's policy treated "one of our closest democratic allies in the Pacific worse that we treat North Korea, Cuba, or Libya. . . . The policy does not even recognize Taiwan as a political entity. . . . It is a tragic mistake to treat corrupt dictators better than democratic allies." Senator Frank Murkowski said, "the administration should have taken bolder and more substantive steps to recognize the more mature relationships between the U.S. and Taiwan. The people and the government of Taiwan should be rewarded for their tremendous strides toward building a free and prosperous country."[14]

The comments of these and other legislators indicated, once again, that congressional and administration views differed considerably on how Taiwan should be treated in U.S. policy. The criticism of Congress was not so much directed at the administration's strategy of engagement with China or a challenge to the unofficial nature of U.S. ties with Taiwan, as it was a reflection of a collective sense of injustice being perpetuated against Taiwan by an administration too focused on developing cooperative relations with Beijing. As a body, the Congress shared the view of the nation's editors that U.S. policy toward Taiwan and China should be balanced, that U.S. policy should reflect both American values and U.S. interests, and that U.S. policy should include better treatment of Taiwan and its people by the administration. The growing congressional discontent with the Clinton administration over its Taiwan policy became even more obvious in the debate over whether Lee Teng-hui should be granted a visa to deliver a lecture at Cornell University in June 1995.

Lee Teng-hui's Trip to the United States

President Lee's visit to the United States in June 1995 was a major turning point in Sino-American relations during the Clinton administration. Prior to that event, while U.S. relations with China were strained in many areas such as proliferation, trade, and human rights, the triangular relationship between Washington, Beijing, and Taipei was being managed with moderate success by the administration through its strategy of comprehensive engagement—a strategy made viable by similar engagement strategies pursued by China and Taiwan. China's sharply negative reaction to Lee's visit caused U.S.-China and China-Taiwan relations to spiral downward for more than two years, and even brought the three sides to the brink of a military confrontation in early 1996 in waters near Taiwan. Sino-American relations did not return to normal until mid-1997, when President Jiang Zemin paid a state visit to the United States, while cross-Strait relations did not turn around until the Koo-Wang talks in the fall of 1998.

In early March 1995, Cornell University, from which President Lee Teng-hui received his doctorate in agricultural economics in 1968, invited Lee to deliver the Olin Lecture at an alumni reunion to be held June 9–11 of that year. The ROC government thereupon requested a visa for Lee from the U.S. government, despite the fact that the Taiwan leader previously had been denied a visa to receive an honorary degree from Cornell. The second request for a visa came over the advice of some in Taiwan, who felt the eventual cost to Taipei in terms of its relations with Washington and Beijing might prove too great.

As noted above, the Clinton administration adjusted its policy toward Taiwan in September 1994 to allow some high-level visits by ROC officials. Top Taiwan leaders, however, were only allowed transit visas. In keeping with these guidelines, the State Department initially ruled out the possibility of a visa being extended to Lee to visit Cornell, arguing that it was inconsistent with the one-China policy of the United States. Already angry over the State Department's refusal a year earlier to allow Lee to rest in a hotel while refueling in Hawaii, Members of Congress introduced several resolutions urging President Clinton to allow the Taiwan president to attend the Cornell ceremony. Senator Frank Murkowski, who sponsored one such resolution, noted that Taiwan had ended martial law, allowed a free press, and legalized opposition political parties. "Rather that rewarding Taiwan for these great strides, it remains the policy of the Clinton administration to deny entry into the United States to the democratic leader of Asia's oldest republic, in effect treating Taiwan like an international pariah."[15]

Congressional hostility toward administration policy intensified when Clinton allowed visits to Washington by Palestinian leader Yasser Arafat and Sinn Fein party leader Gerry Adams. There was also intense lobbying of Congress on behalf of the Lee visit, largely orchestrated by the Washington firm of Cassidy & Associates, which had received a three-year $4.5 million contract from a KMT-controlled organization to lobby on Taiwan's behalf.[16]

For its part, China voiced strong opposition to Lee's visit, viewing it—correctly—as part of Taipei's strategy to expand its international presence through "pragmatic diplomacy." At the time, Beijing was also battling efforts by Taiwan to rejoin the United Nations, an endeavor finding some support in the U.S. Congress. House Speaker Newt Gingrich, for example, was vocal in calling for Taiwan's readmittance to the U.N. on the grounds that the organization was intended to be a universal institution. Concerned that Taipei's efforts to expand its international political presence might further delay China's unification under terms favorable to the PRC, Beijing sought to isolate the ROC wherever possible from the global community. Beijing, for instance, even opposed Taiwan's hosting the 2002 Asian Games in the port of Kaohsiung.[17]

Unlike the State Department, Congress was largely insulated from China's protests—and disinclined to listen to Beijing in any case. On May 2, 1995, the House of Representatives rejected State Department counsel and unanimously passed a resolution by a vote of 396-0 expressing the sense of Congress that President Clinton should allow Lee Teng-hui to make a private visit to the United States. H. Con. Res. 53, titled "Expressing the Sense of Congress Regarding a Visit by the President of the Republic of China on Taiwan," said in part: "Resolved by the House of Representative (the Senate concurring), that it is the sense of Congress that the President should promptly indicate that the United States will welcome a private visit by President Lee Teng-hui to his alma mater, Cornell University, and will welcome a transit stop by President Lee in Anchorage, Alaska, to attend the USA-ROC Economic Council Conference." A week later, the Senate passed an almost identical resolution (S. Con. Res. 9) by a vote of 97-1. Congressional sponsors of these bills warned the administration that if it did not invite Lee to visit the United States, Congress would pass mandatory legislation to that effect.

American public opinion also was strongly in favor of allowing Lee's visit. A sharply worded editorial in the *Washington Post* in May 1995 captured the general mood:

> The State Department contends that admitting President Lee would "unavoidably be seen" by Beijing as "removing an essential element of unofficiality" from U.S.-Taiwan relations. Excluding him is unavoidably being seen by Congress and many American citizens as removing an essential element of principle from American foreign policy.... The State Department embarrasses the country by barring the

leader of the part of the Chinese people who already enjoy much democracy and are expert in free-market ways.[18]

China angrily denounced the congressional resolutions, warning that "Lee's visit to the United States, under whatever name or form or whatever pretext, is bound to entail serious consequences."[19] Secretary of State Warren Christopher and other top administration officials repeatedly assured Beijing that the trip would not happen.[20] Later, Christopher would explain that he tried to warn the Chinese that congressional support for Lee's visit might be a factor in the president's eventual decision. He said en route to Brunei in late July 1995: "I think it's well understood I did try to signal to Foreign Minister Qian Qichen the very strong congressional attitudes that existed with respect to Lee. If I was unable to do so or not articulate enough to let him know of that risk, I hope he now understands better the basis on which the visit was made."[21]

Faced with mounting pressure from Congress and the media in favor of Lee's visit, and also cognizant of a move underway in Congress to pass bills containing dozens of mandated changes in foreign policy—initiatives that would attempt to place more control over foreign affairs into the hands of Congress—President Clinton decided to allow Lee to make a six-day private visit to the United States. The decision was announced in a State Department news briefing on May 22:[22]

> President Clinton has decided to permit Lee Teng-hui to make a private visit to the United States in June for the express purpose of participating in an alumni reunion event at Cornell University, as a distinguished alumnus. This action follows a revision of administration guidelines to permit occasional private visits by senior leaders of Taiwan, including President Lee. President Lee will visit the U.S. in a strictly private capacity and will not undertake any official activities.
>
> It is important to reiterate that this is not an official visit. The granting of a visa in this case is consistent with U.S. policy of maintaining only unofficial relations with Taiwan. It does not convey any change in our relations with or policies toward the People's Republic of China, with which we maintain official relations and recognize as the sole legal government of China. We will continue to abide by the three communiqués that form the basis of our relations with China. The United States also acknowledges the Chinese position that there is but one China, and Taiwan is a part of China.
>
> Americans treasure the rights of freedom of speech and freedom of travel and believe others should enjoy these privileges as well. This sentiment clearly motivated the Congress, in its recent actions, to support overwhelmingly permitting Mr. Lee to return to Cornell, his alma mater.
>
> Secretary of State Christopher has indicated that our relationship with China and Taiwan will continue to be governed by the three joint communiqués with the People's Republic of China and the Taiwan Relations Act. It is also Secretary Christopher's view that this decision to permit a private visit does not in any way reflect a change in the fundamental nature of U.S. relations with Taiwan. We continue to maintain unofficial economic and cultural relations with Taiwan.

The PRC was furious with Clinton's decision to permit the Lee visit, particularly in view of previous assurances from Secretary Christopher and other officials that no such visit would be approved. The PRC Foreign Ministry said: "The Chinese government and people express grave indignation and lodge a strong protest with the U.S. government over the announcement." The invitation was "an extremely serious act of brazenly creating two Chinas or 'one China, one Taiwan,' that damages China's sovereignty and undermines its cause for peaceful reunification." The statement warned, "If the United States maintains this erroneous situation . . . it will inevitably bring serious harm to Sino-U.S. relations, and all the consequences will be the responsibility of the U.S. government."[23]

In addition to its formal protests, the Chinese government abruptly cut short the visit to the United States of PLA Air Force Chief of Staff Yu Zhenwu and canceled the visit of State Counselor Li Guixian. A few days later, the visit of Defense Minister Chi Haotian was postponed. Chinese consultations with U.S. officials responsible for nuclear cooperation and controlling the spread of missile technology also were postponed. Since these areas of dialogue were a key element of U.S. security policy toward China, the Chinese clearly were signaling that they intended to link future strategic cooperation with Washington to U.S. policy toward Taiwan—a tactic used in the past on arms sales issues.[24]

Somewhat surprised by the intensity of PRC protests, Assistant Secretary of State Winston Lord commented to reporters: "Beijing has overreacted in terms of the significance" of the Lee trip, because "we made it very clear it does not change our unofficial ties with Taiwan or any other aspect of our policy."[25] The State Department worked hard to keep Lee's visit strictly unofficial: limitations were placed on the number of people accompanying Lee, pressure was applied to Cornell to keep his public appearances to a minimum, and press conferences for the ROC president were canceled.

President Lee was in the United States from June 7 through June 10, with stopovers in Los Angeles, Cornell University in Ithaca, New York, and Anchorage, Alaska. The ROC government officially described the trip as an attempt to find "the international space that we need for our survival and development."[26] Lee's personal popularity soared back home, an important factor in light of the forthcoming presidential elections in March 1996, although there was some apprehension about the possible long-term negative effects the trip might have on Taiwan's relations with both the United States and China.

While in the United States, Lee explained that the ROC did not seek the independence of Taiwan but rather the unification of a democratic China. He told the Cornell audience: "We believe that mutual respect will gradually lead to the peaceful reunification of China under a system of democracy, freedom and equitable distribution of wealth."[27] Lee emphasized in a private breakfast with Taiwanese-Americans at Cornell: "The Republic of China (Taiwan) is definitely not a part of the People's Republic of China, and neither is it a province of that country."[28] As President Lee was leaving the United States from Anchorage on June

11, ROC government spokesman Jason Hu linked his country's expectations for unification with Taiwan's desire for wider international recognition: "We will try to make [Beijing] understand that the more we become accepted in the international community, it will give us confidence in dealing with them."[29]

Despite Lee's stated commitment to a unified China and the State Department's efforts at damage control, PRC spokesmen condemned the United States for "dishonoring the international commitment" made to China in the three joint communiqués, saying the United States lied about calling the visit unofficial. A signed editorial in Xinhua warned: "The issue of Taiwan is as explosive as a barrel of gunpowder. It is extremely dangerous to warm it up, no matter whether the warming is done by the U.S. or by [Lee Teng-hui]." The editorial said U.S. motives were to keep China weak and divided: "Contrary to what the U.S. government has said, the United States is extremely nervous and irritated about China's insisting on developing socialism and becoming more powerful day by day. The reason that the U.S. chose this dangerous act of encouraging and supporting the independence of Taiwan is that it thinks China is weak and cannot afford to give up the economic exchanges and trade it has with the U.S., so that it will be forced to make a concession in this case."[30]

As has often been the case, the United States was caught in the middle of the dispute between the PRC and ROC. Beijing was intent upon isolating Taiwan to force it into political negotiations; any effort by Taipei to expand its international representation threatened that strategy. From the PRC point of view, Lee's trip to the United States could open a pandora's box of other nations extending similar invitations. Indeed, a few days after Lee's return from the United States, ROC Premier Lien Chan departed for Europe, meeting his Czech counterpart Vaclav Klaus and with President Vaclav Havel. Perhaps most important, the granting of a visa to Lee also precipitated a power struggle inside the CCP itself, with hardliners using the occasion to push aside the moderates in the government responsible for policy toward Taiwan and the United States. At least until the March 1996 military showdown with the United States in the Taiwan Strait, these hardliners exerted considerable influence on PRC policy, in part explaining the bellicosity of PRC attitudes toward Washington and Taipei during this period. At the same time, the moderate-hardliner polarity should not be overstated, since the PRC leadership had evolved a consensus that policy toward Taiwan must incorporate both a carrot and a stick. The Lee visit necessitated that the coercive element of PRC policy come to the fore, at least temporarily.[31]

The United States, as Taiwan's most important international friend, stood to bear much of the heat of that coercive diplomacy. Taiwan, on the other hand, felt it had little to lose. Deprived of all but a handful of diplomatic ties, Taipei had no recourse but to use informal visits by its high-ranking officials as a means of breaking out of its diplomatic isolation and finding "breathing space" in the international community. Lee's trip, and that of Lien Chan to Europe and others similar in nature, were part of the so-called Lee Doctrine, a pragmatic, flexible approach through which Taiwan acted independently without declaring independence, recognized the PRC government and asked for reciprocity, and constantly sought to expand Taipei's role in world affairs.[32]

As Taiwan's traditional friend and as leader of the global community of market democracies, it was inevitable that Taiwan would seek to expand its presence in the United States. Further, with the strong backing of the Congress, the media, and a large portion of the American public, Taiwan could be fairly optimistic that its efforts to obtain a visa for President Lee would succeed—despite the opposition of the State Department and hesitancy on the part of the White House.

The Lee trip resulted in a significant downturn in U.S. relations with China. It also precipitated a military crisis in the Taiwan Strait and added credibility to those Americans warning of a possible future war between China and the United States over Taiwan. What is important to note in this chapter, however, is that Congress was willing to confront both the White House and the PRC over Taiwan policy, in spite of the cost. As demonstrated by the numerous bills and resolutions supporting Taiwan in the aftermath of Lee's visit, Congress remains adamant in its insistence that U.S. policy toward Taiwan and China be balanced and fair. Despite repeated attempts by the Clinton administration to manage the Taiwan issue in a way inoffensive to the PRC, Congress often forces policy changes designed to strengthen U.S. support of Taiwan. This pattern of congressional intervention in Taiwan policy continued through the end of 1998, and there is no indication that it will cease during the 106th Congress.

Conclusion

As demonstrated repeatedly since the 1979 enactment of the Taiwan Relations Act, Congress intends to monitor U.S. China-Taiwan policy and to intervene in that policy when Members perceive that Taiwan is being short-changed in Sino-American relations. The role of Congress, therefore, is a highly important element of the Taiwan conundrum in U.S. China policy.

Several general observations about congressional views of Taiwan and China can be noted. First, Congress is far more critical of the PRC and more friendly toward Taiwan than is the administration, which tends to pay greater heed to Beijing. Second, Congress is extremely vigilant over administration policies and behavior toward Taiwan. Third, Congress wants, expects, and demands to play a central role in U.S. policy toward these two Chinese nations. Fourth, Taiwan enjoys enormous support in the Congress, as reflected in key votes on highly visible developments in the Taiwan Strait. Fifth, although the composition of Congress has changed over the years, its attitude toward Taiwan and China and its involvement in controversial aspects of U.S. policy toward Taiwan and China have remained fairly consistent, enjoying broad support among both Democrats and Republicans, liberals and conservatives. Sixth, in the case of Taiwan, Congress is especially concerned over matters dealing with the island's security and its democratic institutions; in the case of China, Congress is especially concerned over trade, human rights, military aggression, proliferation, and PRC policies toward Tibet, Hong Kong, and Taiwan. Seventh, whereas Congress as a whole does not pay too much attention to the day-to-day implementation of U.S. policy toward China and Taiwan (leaving these matters to relevant committees and subcommittees), there is close attention paid to the overall policy followed by the administration in these areas. Eighth, once congressional concern is aroused over some aspect of U.S. policy toward Taiwan and China, then momentum quickly builds that can apply intense pressure on the executive branch for some specific action. And ninth, Congress has many instruments through which to influence U.S. policy toward China and Taiwan—including amendments to major legislation such as defense and foreign operations appropriations—and the Congress does not hesitate to use these instruments to exercise its power.

Although many Members of Congress are experts in national security and foreign policy, as a body Congress often reflects American values, counterbalancing the more *Realpolitik* orientation found frequently in the executive branch of the U.S. government. In this role, Congress has ensured over the last two decades that U.S. relations with China do not damage Taiwan too severely or eclipse too completely U.S. interests in Taiwan. The formulation, implementation, and oversight of U.S. policy toward China and Taiwan is a classic example of the American system of checks-and-balances. Since oversight is its constitutional responsibility, the Congress will continue to be deeply involved in the Taiwan issue.

As a result, not only does the Taiwan issue present a conundrum in U.S. policy in terms of the many, sometimes conflicting, values involved, there also is the conundrum of how to design a policy supported not only within the administration, but also within the Congress—which, as we have seen, often views policy toward Taiwan and China from quite a different perspective. To date, no solution to the Taiwan issue in Sino-American relations has been found that enjoys a consensus among both the administration and the Congress. This disagreement reflects not only institutional differences in perspective, but it also strongly suggests that the timing and circumstances for a solution to the Taiwan issue are not yet in sight. In this sense, a resolution of the Taiwan conundrum is premature; Taiwan will continue to be a conundrum for the foreseeable future, but that is not necessarily a bad thing since the course of China has not yet been set and the people of Taiwan have not yet decided their preferred future relationship with China.

The complexities of the Taiwan issue become further apparent in the next chapter, when we consider how U.S. interests are involved in China and Taiwan and how perceptions of those interests dramatically influence American policy choices.

Notes

1. See especially Lester L. Wolff and David L. Simon, *Legislative History of the Taiwan Relations Act: An Analytic Compilation with Documents on Subsequent Developments* (Jamaica, NY: American Association for Chinese Studies, 1982). Also see Louis W. Koenig, ed., *Congress, the Presidency, and the Taiwan Relations Act* (New York: Praeger, 1985); William B. Bader and Jeffrey T. Bergner, eds., *The Taiwan Relations Act: A Decade of Implementation* (Indianapolis, IN: Hudson Institute, 1989); Ramon H. Myers, ed., *A Unique Relationship: The United States and the Republic of China under the Taiwan Relations Act* (Stanford, CA: Hoover Institution Press, 1989); and appropriate sections in Stephen P. Gibert and William M. Carpenter, eds., *America and Island China: A Documentary History* (Lanham, MD: University Press of America, 1989). In addition, congressional hearings are held fairly frequently, most of the records of which are printed by the Government Printing Office (GPO). The most important of these hearings probably is U.S. Congress, Senate, Committee on Foreign Relations, *Taiwan: Hearings on S. 245*, February 5, 6, 7, 8, 21, and 22, 1979 (Washington, DC: GPO, 1979).
2. According to the Thomas search engine of the Library of Congress using the terms "Taiwan" and "China" in the legislative history of the 103rd, 104th, and 105th congresses.
3. See the August 18, 1982, testimony of Assistant Secretary of State John Holdridge in U.S. Congress, House of Representatives, Committee on Foreign Affairs, *China-Taiwan: United States Policy* (Washington, DC: GPO, 1982), pp. 2-29.
4. Prepared statement of Davis R. Robinson, Legal Adviser, Department of State, given before U.S. Congress, Senate, Committee on the Judiciary, Subcommittee on Separation of Powers, September 27, 1982, pp. 1-2, ms.
5. *Far Eastern Economic Review*, August 5, 1993, p. 15.
6. On May 16, 1994, the State Department reiterated that the various Taiwan provisions in P. L. 103-236 would not alter U.S. policy and practice toward Taiwan. See Robert G. Sutter, "Taiwan: Recent Developments and U.S. Policy Choices," Library of Congress, Congressional Research Service *Issue Brief*, No. IB94006 (updated May 26, 1994), p. 12.
7. Statement of Senator Murkowski before the U.S. Senate on May 3, 1994, as provided by the Senator's office.
8. For an account of the May 4, 1994, incident and its repercussions, see James Mann, "Between China and the U.S.," *Washington Post*, January 10, 1999, p. C1; and his book, *About Face: A History of America's Curious Relationship with China, from Nixon to Clinton* (New York: Knopf, 1999).
9. *Far Eastern Economic Review*, June 9, 1994, p. 18.
10. For a discussion of the role of Congress in the Taiwan issue in the 1993-1994 period, see Robert G. Sutter, "Taiwan: Recent Developments and U.S. Policy Choices." See also his more recent study, *U.S. Policy toward China: An Introduction to the Role of Interest Groups* (Lanham, MD: Rowman & Littlefield Publishers, 1998).
11. The proceedings of the congressional hearing were summarized in a CNA (China News Agency) report filed from Washington, D.C., July 15, 1994.
12. For background factors influencing the Taiwan Policy Review, see James Mann, "U.S. May Ease Limits on Ties with Taiwan," *Los Angeles Times*, July 6, 1994, p. 1.
13. The official's remarks are taken from a CNA report from Washington, D.C., September 7, 1994. For a brief, formal explanation of the policy adjustments, see

"Statement of Assistant Secretary Winston Lord, Senate Foreign Relations Committee, Hearing on Taiwan Policy," September 27, 1994, ms.

14. *New York Times*, September 8, 1994, p. A5; *Washington Post*, September 8, 1994, p. A10; CNA report from Washington, D.C., September 8, 1994.

15. Reuters report from Washington, D.C., March 6, 1995.

16. James Mann, "Between China and the United States," *Washington Post*, January 10, 1999, p. C1.

17. UPI report from Beijing, March 23, 1995.

18. "A Visa for Taiwan's President," *Washington Post*, May 10, 199⌐, p. A24.

19. UPI report from Beijing, May 11, 1995.

20. See *Wall Street Journal*, July 14, 1995, p. A8.

21. Reuters report from Andersen Air Force Base on Guam, July 31, 1995.

22. "Daily Press Briefing" (Washington, DC: U.S. Department of State, Office of the Spokesman, May 22, 1995).

23. Reuters report from Beijing, May 23, 1995.

24. See, for example, the author's *The Taiwan Issue in Sino-American Strategic Cooperation* (Boulder, CO: Westview, 1984) for a discussion of China's linkage of strategic cooperation with the United States to U.S. arms sales to Taiwan in the cases of the FX fighter issue of 1981 and the August 17, 1982, communiqué.

25. Reuters report from Washington D.C., May 30, 1995.

26. Reuters report from Ithaca, NY, June 9, 1995.

27. Associated Press report from Ithaca, NY, June 9, 1995.

28. Quoted by Jason Hu, ROC government spokesman, in Reuters report from Ithaca, NY, June 9, 1995.

29. Reuters report from Anchorage, Alaska, June 11, 1995.

30. See, for example, AP report from Beijing, June 1, 1995; UPI report from Beijing, June 9, 1995; Reuters report from Beijing, June 9, 1995.

31. See You Ji, "Missile Diplomacy and PRC Domestic Politics," in Greg Austin, ed., *Missile Diplomacy and Taiwan's Future: Innovations in Politics and Military Power* (Canberra: Australian National University, 1998), pp. 29-55.

32. See Lorna Hahn, "Kowtow: The State Department's Bow to Beijing," *Washington Post*, March 31, 1995, p. A31.

3

U.S. Interests in China and Taiwan

It is difficult to devise a policy toward Taiwan that embodies an appropriate balance between realism and idealism and one that gains a consensus of support within both the administration and the Congress. There also is difficulty in defining a policy that serves the various U.S. interests involved with the Taiwan issue. In fact, there is disagreement over the definition of those interests, with some specialists arguing, for example, that Taiwan has no geostrategic importance to the United States and other experts insisting that, because of the maritime nature of U.S. Asia-Pacific strategy, Taiwan should be kept out of the hands of potential enemies of the United States.

The calculation of U.S. interests in Taiwan is further complicated by the island's unique relationship with China and by the nature of Sino-American relations, which, from the outset of normalization, have centered around strategic considerations. Hence, U.S. interests in Taiwan are almost always considered in the context of U.S. interests in China and in the Asian Pacific in general.

Making the calculation even more difficult is the fact that Japan and several Southeast Asian countries have important economic and security interests in Taiwan. In the case of Japan, Washington must take those interests into account because of the central role Tokyo plays in U.S. security, political, and economic policies toward Asia. Moreover, there is throughout Southeast Asia a residual fear of an aggressive China. Since the United States views its ties with the Association of Southeast Asian Nations (ASEAN) as an important pillar of American influence in Asia, Washington must seriously consider their security concerns. Many Southeast Asian states view U.S. security ties to Taiwan as a bellwether of American commitment to maintain a forward presence in the Western Pacific—a vital counterbalance to the growing power of China. In other words, consideration of U.S. interests in Taiwan reach far beyond the shores of that island; Taiwan is intricately linked with many other U.S. bilateral and regional interests.

There is also a persistent problem in the theory of national interests, which are defined in a highly subjective manner, particularly in American political culture where every concerned citizen freely speculates on what is the national interest. Although each administration defines the national interests for its term in office—and there is great continuity in most of those definitions from administration to administration—even these carefully formulated statements of security, political, economic, and other interests sometimes contradict each other and often pull in different policy directions. The endless debates over human rights interests versus commercial interests in U.S. most-favored-nation (MFN) trading status for China is a case in point. Thus, what is or is not in the national interest is subject to honest disagreement even among foreign policy specialists and political scientists.

Despite these theoretical problems, as a matter of practicality, most policy analysts and policymakers conceptualize, rationalize, and justify their policy prescriptions in terms of the national interest. It is almost impossible to consider foreign policy without reference to the national interest. But, it should be noted, these interests can be used to justify policies quite different in their purpose and execution. For example, the justification frequently given for engagement with China is to encourage that country to adopt more liberal economic and political policies; at the same time, it is sometimes argued that to ensure the success of engaging China the United States should reduce its support of Taiwan, which already practices those liberal economic and political policies. Policies toward Taiwan, and the interests used to justify those policies, are filled with such contradictions: hence, the need for ambiguity and hence the Taiwan conundrum.

While acknowledging the problems inherent in defining national interests as a basis for U.S. policy toward Taiwan and China, those various interests must be explored to understand the Taiwan conundrum in U.S. China policy. One of the best places to start is to consider briefly how Asians view the importance of Taiwan, particularly from the Chinese perspective of Taipei and Beijing. Thereafter, several sections of this chapter will define U.S. interests in increasing detail, concluding with a discussion of American interests as expressed in the strategies and policies of the Reagan and Bush administrations, particularly toward East Asia.

Overview of Chinese and Asian Interests in Taiwan

From the point of view of the Republic of China and the people on Taiwan, the fate of their island is of vital interest: a matter of survival of the ROC government and the KMT's historical legacy and a matter of preservation of the lives and well-being of the Taiwanese people. On a national level, there is no higher interest than this; and the fact that the PRC is determined to incorporate Taiwan as an integral part of a China controlled by a communist government presents an ever-present and serious threat to the survival of the ROC on Taiwan. As long as the government and people of Taiwan have the will to survive as a democracy and as an entity separate from communist-dominated China, they will use every means necessary to retain control of Taiwan. In all likelihood, the ROC government and the residents of Taiwan will fight before accepting an unwanted imposition of control from the PRC. This determination to survive does not rule out the possibility of some future, mutually acceptable arrangement between Taipei and Beijing. Indeed, in this author's view such an arrangement is likely over time—if peace and stability can be maintained in the Taiwan Strait—because the economic and cultural links between Taiwan and the mainland are very strong and because Taiwan is too close to the Chinese mainland to remain politically separate.

From Beijing's perspective, the future of Taiwan is a central domestic and international issue, touching core Chinese interests such as territorial integrity, sovereignty, nationalism, and relations with the United States. Taiwan is important to the PRC because of (a) the island's geographic location off China's eastern coast; (b) Taiwan's status as unrecovered Chinese territory; (c) the political challenge posed by the KMT and DPP to the CCP; (d) Taiwan's potential as a base of operations for powers hostile to China; (e) international perceptions of Beijing's prestige and power, which are linked to a great extent to the future status of Taiwan; (f) Taiwan's existing and potential contribution to the mainland's modernization; (g) the role Taiwan plays in CCP politics either as a unifying force under nationalism or as a divisive factor splitting party leaders; and (h) Taiwan's value as a lightning rod in Sino-American relations.

Because so many Chinese interests are tied to Taiwan, it is unlikely that the PRC—or any strong mainland Chinese government for that matter—will abandon its claim that Taiwan is Chinese territory, drop its insistence that the resolution of the Taiwan issue is an internal Chinese affair, or promise that force will not be used against Taiwan in the event the island seeks independence or foreign powers seek to control Taiwan. On the other hand, the nature of China's interests in Taiwan do not dictate that reunification has to take place within a short period of time or according to an existing formula such as "one country, two systems." The critical Chinese interests in Taiwan are threefold: (1) the island must remain part of Chinese territory; (2) no foreign power can occupy Taiwan or use it as a base to threaten Chinese security; and (3) the KMT must not use Taiwan to subvert CCP power on the mainland. As long as the United States does not threaten these fundamental interests, then China can tolerate unofficial U.S. relations with Taiwan.

PRC interests in Taiwan leave Beijing with considerable flexibility in dealing with both Taipei and Washington. The fundamental point on which there probably is no compromise is the principle that Taiwan is part of China. How "China" is defined remains the major point of political contention between Beijing and Taipei. Until Beijing and Taipei can resolve their fundamental differences over what comprises "China," the Taiwan conundrum in U.S. China policy will in all likelihood continue.

It should be noted in passing that Taiwan is important to other Asian countries as well. Japan, for example, sees Taiwan as a valuable trading partner, a key destination of Japanese investment, a security gateway to the southern approaches to Japan, a guardian of vital sea lanes to Southeast Asia and the Middle East, and a key factor in Sino-Japanese relations. A prevalent view in Japan is that Taiwan falls under regional security concerns in the U.S.-Japan defense alliance. In the 1997 Guidelines for U.S.-Japan Defense Cooperation, for instance, Tokyo pledged to cooperate with Washington "in situations in areas surrounding Japan." Defined as a situational rather than a geographic concept, Chief Cabinet Secretary and top Japanese government spokesman Seiroku Kajiyama nonetheless explicitly stated in August 1997 that Taiwan was covered by the guidelines, explaining "we have strong anxieties over a possible military liberation of Taiwan by mainland China."[1] To date, the Japanese government has refused to endorse the "three-no's" policy enunciated by President Clinton in Shanghai in 1998. During President Jiang Zemin's state visit to Japan in late November 1998, for example, Japanese Prime Minister Keizo Obuchi would only say, "There is no change in our policy on Taiwan that Japan will not support Taiwan's independence."[2]

The Philippines also see Taiwan as being important to their security interests, controlling access to northern Luzon and the Luzon Strait choke point, as well as being a major player in territorial disputes in the South China Sea. The Philippines, as well as most other Southeast Asian countries, consider Taiwan a valuable trading partner and vital source of capital investment. In addition, most countries in the Asia Pacific view Taiwan as being a crucial factor in China's future national power. A united China would be far more able to leverage its interests vis-à-vis its neighbors than a divided China. In view of China's potential hegemony in the South China Sea and the constant possibility of yet another military crisis in the Taiwan Strait, most Southeast Asian states, like Japan, view favorably the American involvement with Taiwan's security: it is seen as an indicator of the credibility of the American commitment to their own security. Perhaps most importantly, U.S. actions with respect to Taiwan are taken as a signal of American determination to continue to play its essential balancing role in East Asia and the Pacific, ensuring that no hegemon threatens regional peace and stability.

Overview of U.S. Interests in Taiwan

Unlike China, where most U.S. interests are determined by the sheer size and power of the PRC, U.S. interests in Taiwan are more normal in the sense that America has security, political, economic, and cultural interests in most countries of the world. Taiwan is a fairly large island of 14,000 square miles (roughly the size of West Virginia); it has a population of 21.8 billion, a 1997 GDP of $284.8 billion, per capita income in that year of $13,130, a global trade of $236.5 billion in 1997, a large defense establishment relative to the size of the nation, the capability to produce nuclear weapons and limited-range surface-to-surface missiles, diplomatic recognition from twenty-eight governments, and no membership in the United Nations.[3] Under circumstances other than Taiwan being involved with China, the United States no doubt would have friendly, close diplomatic relations with Taiwan.

U.S. interests in Taiwan are many and diverse.[4] First, the United States has an interest in Taiwan because the future of Taiwan and its people are critical issues in Sino-American relations. No true partnership between China and the United States is possible until the Taiwan issue is resolved to the satisfaction of all parties involved: the PRC, the ROC government, the Taiwanese people, and the United States. As President Jiang Zemin said during his state visit to the United States in October 1997: "The question of Taiwan has always been the most important and the most sensitive issue in Sino-American relations."[5] Since Taiwan is considered by Beijing to be a central issue in Sino-American relations, how the Taiwan issue is handled can have substantial influence on Beijing's behavior domestically and internationally.

Second, the United States has an interest in the security of Taiwan. Taiwan is one of the few issues over which Washington and Beijing might one day go to war. However, U.S. support for Taiwan's security is an important factor in American credibility in Asia. This is especially true in the post-Cold War period when many Asian nations doubt whether the United States has the will to remain the "balance wheel" of Asia. The U.S. role in Taiwan's security is closely watched in the Asian Pacific as a crucial test of Washington's willingness to counterbalance China and to sustain a commitment to the region as a whole.

Third, the United States has interest in Taiwan because Taiwan is a highly volatile issue in American domestic politics. As discussed earlier, American values are deeply involved with U.S. policy toward Taiwan and China, and the Congress—with a perspective often differing from that of the administration—maintains close vigilance over all aspects of U.S. policy toward both sides of the Taiwan Strait. No change in U.S. policy toward either Taiwan or China can be contemplated without careful consideration of its impact on American domestic audiences.

Fourth, the United States has interests in Taiwan because of the island's influence on China's domestic and foreign policies. Taiwan firms have invested more than $30 billion in 45,000 enterprises on the mainland, and China is Taiwan's second largest market after the United States.[6] Moreover, Beijing's leaders know they must liberalize their economic, social, and political policies if the people of Taiwan are ever to be attracted to the prospects of unification. Thus, although the Taiwan issue can be a disruptive force in Sino-American relations and can adversely affect the hardline-moderate balance of power in mainland politics, Taiwan also can play a moderating role on developments on the mainland.

Fifth, the United States has economic interests in Taiwan. One of Asia's "four tigers" or "four little dragons"—the others being South Korea, Hong Kong, and

Singapore—Taiwan in 1997 was the seventh largest trading partner of the United States ($32.6 billion exported to the U.S. and $20.4 billion imported from the U.S.) and the fourteenth and fifteenth largest exporter and importer, respectively, in the world. Taiwan also is a key strategic partner for U.S. corporations seeking to do business with China, and in 1996 the stock of U.S. foreign direct investment in Taiwan was $4.5 billion.[7] In addition, Taiwan is a major source of capital investments to regions of importance to U.S. foreign policy, such as Southeast Asia, Latin America, Africa, and the Pacific island states. Taiwan's economy was one of the very few in Asia not undermined during the financial crisis which began in 1997.[8]

Sixth, the United States has interests in Taiwan because it is an excellent model of market democracy in Asia. Taiwan has a reputation as an economic miracle based on free enterprise and capitalism. Equally important, Taiwan since the mid-1980s has become a model for democracy in Asia, particularly in a Chinese cultural context. It is widely viewed as a highly successful model in the peaceful transformation of an authoritarian state into a democracy. In December 1998, for example, Taiwan held its ninth major election since multiparty democracy was implemented in 1987. In that election the Kuomintang received 46.4 percent of the total votes (including independents, who received over 9.4 percent) and 51.2 percent of the votes cast for parties (of which eleven competed). The largest opposition party, the Democratic Progressive Party, won 29.5 percent of the total vote and 32.6 percent of party votes. In the 225-member legislature elected in 1998, the KMT won 123 seats, the DPP 70 seats, the New Party 11 seats, the Taiwan Independence Party 1 seat, and others 20 seats. Many observers viewed the election as a victory for the moderate policies of the KMT, since the DPP ran on a highly ethnic platform ("Vote for the Taiwanese, not for the Chinese" was the motto of defeated DPP mayor Chen Shui-bian) and on a party platform calling for Taiwan independence.[9] The essential point is that Taiwan today is a well-established member of the community of market democracies, and U.S. support and encouragement since 1950 has helped Taiwan to achieve that goal.

Seventh, the United States has interests in Taiwan because the government and people of the island consider themselves to be friends and allies of the American people. This tradition of close U.S.-ROC ties harkens back to before World War II, and it has continued unbroken to this day, despite the 1949 retreat of the Nationalist to Taiwan and the 1979 severance of diplomatic ties between Washington and Taipei. The personal, educational, and cultural ties between the people of the United States and Taiwan are among the most extensive in the world, perhaps one explanation for the support shown to Taiwan by American editorials reviewed in Chapter 1.

Eighth, the United States *may* have a strategic interest in Taiwan, especially if the PRC becomes more threatening to U.S. interests in the future. Whether China will become such a threat is unknown and highly controversial. Two prevalent viewpoints are those of Richard Bernstein and Ross Munro, who argue that China almost inevitably will confront America in East Asia, and those of Andrew Nathan and Robert Ross, who consider China to be less outward looking and more defense oriented.[10] Since China's future policy direction is not known—other than the high probability that it will increase its strength and its capabilities to challenge the United States in Asia—the goal of U.S. engagement (i.e., the assumption that wider contacts with the United States will inevitably undermine the monopolistic power of the CCP and lead to more moderate PRC policies at home and abroad) may or may not prove successful. If engagement is successful, then U.S. interests in a "dual-track" approach to China and Taiwan will diminish considerably; if engagement is unsuccessful, then U.S. interests in a divided China might increase substantially. Since Taiwan could be a critical factor in Beijing's power projection capabilities, until China's future course is determined, the United States has strategic interests in Taiwan. This is not justification to divide China or to stand in the way of Taipei-Beijing rapprochement, but simply a precautionary consideration that should weigh against any premature U.S. effort to push Taiwan into the arms of the mainland. But this point is controversial: yet another aspect of the conundrum Taiwan presents to U.S. policy.

A ninth *possible* U.S. interest is in the geostrategic location of Taiwan. Few Americans any longer look at Taiwan an "unsinkable aircraft carrier," but many PRC analysts highly value Taiwan's geostrategic importance. One Chinese author argued that U.S., Japan, and other foreign involvement in Taiwan was "driven by deep-rooted geostrategic considerations."[11] Lu Junyuan outlined three aspects of China's geostrategic interest in Taiwan: security for the mainland, control of strategic links between north and south China, and the development of China's naval power. Because Taiwan "is an inseparable part of China and has extraordinary significance for China's national security . . . national reunification must be achieved to protect China's fundamental interests." If Chinese strategists place such value on Taiwan as a shield against a potential U.S. threat, then perhaps under conditions of a Chinese threat, Taiwan has potential geostrategic importance to the United States.

From this brief overview of U.S. interests in Taiwan, two main observations can be drawn. First, considered on its own merits separate from China, Taiwan qualifies as an independent state in which the United States would have normal and friendly state-to-state interests: Taiwan is a functioning democracy; it has a thriving free-market economy; its people have a decent and improving standard of living; they enjoy basic human rights and freedoms much like Americans; Taiwan and its people are friendly toward the United States; Taiwan is a cooperative member of the community of market democracies; it has a history of alliance with the United States in times of crisis. In short, Taiwan has done very little to deserve its outcast status in the world.

A second observation is that it is difficult to consider U.S. interests in Taiwan on their own merits; rather, U.S. interests in Taiwan are inexorably linked with U.S. interests in China and in Taiwan's relationship with mainland China. When the China factor is considered, U.S. interests in Taiwan are much more complicated and controversial. For example, Americans who view China as an emerging threat to U.S. interests tend to see Taiwan as a strategic asset the United States should preserve, or at least not push away into the arms of Beijing. Those who view China as evolving toward potential market democracy see Taiwan either as a model and inducement for greater openness on the mainland or as an obstacle to Chinese reforms because its separation fans the flames of ultranationalism in China. Because of the wide (and sometimes controversial) range of U.S. interests in Taiwan, there is a broad spectrum of opinion as to what U.S. policy toward Taiwan should be, a spectrum which ranges, for instance, from curtailment of arms sales to pressure Taipei to enter into early unification talks with Beijing to increased arms sales to ensure that Taiwan is able to exercise its right of self-determination.

Much of the conundrum Taiwan presents to U.S. policy is due to differing interpretations of U.S. interests in Taiwan as it relates to China. This conundrum is made more difficult by the fact that Taiwan, on its own merits, deserves to be treated as a friendly nation by the United States. How to manage the Taiwan issue provokes intense debate among U.S. foreign policy experts—who generally focus on China—but popular support for Taiwan remains strong among Americans because of Taiwan's accomplishments and its democracy. The combination of popular support, the protective role assumed by Congress, and the wide range of U.S. interests in Taiwan ensures that it would be politically very difficult for any administration to implement policies openly harmful to Taiwan—even if the justification were improved relations with China. Indeed, from the grassroots and congressional levels of the American body politic, there is frequent pressure to improve U.S. ties with Taiwan. This pressure has been resisted by successive administrations concerned over the negative impact on U.S. interests in China, discussed in the next section. As a result of these differing views of U.S. interests in Taiwan and China, there is continuous tension between those who are willing to make concessions over Taiwan to further U.S. interests in China and those who seek to strengthen U.S. ties with Taiwan even at the cost of alienating the PRC. In the middle are those, including the author, who believe U.S. policy can serve both sets of interests by continuing to pursue a dual-track approach of maintaining official relations with the PRC and friendly unofficial ties with Taiwan, and by ensuring that the Taiwan issue is settled peacefully by both Chinese sides. As will be seen in later chapters, the pendulum of policy has swung back and forth with changes in circumstances since 1979, but the dual-track approach anchored during the first term of the Reagan administration has to date been the point of equilibrium.

Overview of U.S. Interests in China

The United States has a wide range of interests in China, but perhaps the most important stem from the fact the China is one of the world's great powers, a civilization with roots extending back at least 3,500 years. China has a total area of about 3.7 million square miles (roughly the size of the United States), a population of 1.22 billion, a 1997 GDP of around $890 billion, a global trade in that year of $324 billion, the largest military establishment in the world, a substantial nuclear weapons and ballistic missile capability, diplomatic recognition of 156 countries, and a permanent seat on the U.N. Security Council.[12] Barring a foreign policy of isolationism in the United States, there is simply no way the United States can function in the modern global community without dealing extensively with China. Among the many interests the United States has in China, the following are especially important.

First, the United States has a strategic interest in China. Since the end of the Cold War, Sino-American relations have become pivotal in international politics. China can play a constructive or destabilizing role in many regions of the world, especially in the Middle East, Central Asia, South Asia, Southeast Asia, and Northeast Asia. Because China is a Permanent Member of the U.N. Security Council, it has an influential voice in virtually all multilateral issues facing the United States. Developments on the Korean peninsula and the Indian subcontinent are especially important strategic issues being discussed by Washington and Beijing due to their potential for rapid escalation of conflict and even the use of weapons of mass destruction. U.S. strategic interests also are served by intelligence cooperation between various Chinese and American agencies, particularly as it relates to countries bordering the PRC. Perhaps the most important long-term strategic issues between the United States and the PRC, however, are (1) how China is to be accommodated in the emerging new world order, (2) what role China will play in that new international order, and (3) how China will fit in the evolving security architecture in the Western Pacific.

Second, the United States has security interests in China. There are a wide range of interests here, including a multitude of nonproliferation issues involving China herself (e.g., nuclear cooperation with Iran, assisting unsafeguarded nuclear facilities in Pakistan, implementing strict nuclear export controls, joining the Non-Proliferation Treaty exporters' committee, ratifying the chemical weapons convention, and implementing controls on the export of items of potential use in chemical and biological weapons of mass destruction). Other security interests the United States has in China included the direction of the modernization of the People's Liberation Army, transparency of Chinese intentions and capabilities, and the future military posture of the PRC. China's refusal to rule out the use of force to achieve unification with Taiwan is also related to U.S. security interests in peace and stability in the Western Pacific. The growing cooperation between the U.S. military and the PLA—part of the U.S. strategy of comprehensive engagement with China—is a reflection of this wide range of American security interests in the PRC.

Third, the United States has many political interests in China. These range from the practical necessity of dealing with Beijing across the whole spectrum of international issues, including Taiwan, to the hope—some might say prayer—that

American engagement with the PRC will someday help evolve that country into a market democracy. The United States certainly has an ideological interest in seeing China move beyond its communist government. There are domestic political interests involved in U.S. policy toward China as well. A consensus on U.S. policy toward Taiwan and China would be impossible if engagement were not in place. Most Americans are no more interested in ignoring, isolating, or containing China than they are in ignoring, isolating, or containing Taiwan.

Fourth, the United States has enormous economic interests in China. Overall, the U.S. trade deficit with the Pacific Rim in 1997 was $126.5 billion; of this amount, the trade deficit with Japan was $55.7 billion and the overall deficit with China was $48.7 billion. U.S. merchandise exports to China in 1997 were $12.8 billion, while U.S. imports from China were $62.6 billion; U.S. services exports to China were $3.1 billion and services imports from China were $2.0 billion. In 1997 China was the fourteenth largest export market for the United States, and the value of U.S. foreign direct investment in China in 1996 was $2.9 billion.[13] The United States has great interests in the reduction of China's trade surplus with the United States, which if allowed to continue expanding will soon be more than Japan's. Many factors are involved in that surplus, however, including the shift of export industries to China from Asia's newly industrialized nations (including Taiwan), China's restrictive import policies, and the huge American demand for inexpensive labor-intensive goods. Other U.S. economic interests in China include the PRC's integration into the global economic and trading systems and increased access for American goods and services in the Chinese market. A fundamental U.S. economic interest in China is the expectation that as more market-oriented reforms are adopted by Chinese leaders, not only will the Chinese people benefit from an improved standard of living but also many of the restrictions on their daily lives will be lifted by the Chinese Communist Party. A basic assumption of U.S. engagement policy is that economic openness and reform will lead inevitably to political openness and reform: faith or science, only time will tell—but a worthy risk since democracies historically seem almost never to fight one another.

Fifth, the United States has several cultural and humanitarian interests in China. These include the highly publicized goal of improving human rights conditions in the PRC, but also include a wide range of scientific, cultural, and educational exchanges meant to improve the quality of life of both the Chinese and the American people. Issues in the area of human rights include the persecution of political dissidents and religious leaders, forced labor by prisoners, late-term forced abortions as part of China's draconian population control program, and the treatment of Tibet, its people, and its cultural institutions. In this broad area of cultural and humanitarian interests could also be included U.S. interests in cooperating with China in the enforcement of crime and drug trafficking regulations, protection of the environment, and the development of new sources of energy.

Clearly, the broad scope of U.S. interests in China dictate a complete range of interaction between the United States and the PRC. This would be true if the Taiwan issue did not exist, and it is true despite the existence of Taiwan. Even though the Taiwan issue frequently is pointed to by the Chinese as being the single most important issue in Sino-American relations, there are a host of other controversial issues between the United States and China. The issues of proliferation, trade, human rights, Tibet, the role of the PLA, political and economic reform in China—to name a few—would exist if Taiwan were to disappear completely from the radar screen of Beijing and Washington. Just as U.S. engagement with China is necessary because of China's size and potential power, so U.S. disagreement with China is inevitable due to China's growing power, its communist government, and its historical tendency to be the dominant power in Asia. These realities are independent of the Taiwan issue.

One point deserving emphasis is that engaging China is not an end in itself but rather a means to an end. As will be shown in the next several chapters, the end is the U.S. goal of China evolving into a more responsible and cooperative member of the international community. Eventually, the United States wants China to become a full-fledged member of the community of market democracies. While these are long-term and rather idealistic goals, they have been consistent U.S. goals for much of the twentieth century. These goals have gained added urgency in the late 1990s, as China has become much stronger and better able to pursue its own domestic and international agenda. If history is any guide, the United States will continue to pursue a goal of transforming China, and China will continue to define its own role in global and regional affairs—attempting always to be free from outside interference.

Perhaps the greatest danger for a future Sino-American confrontation comes from fundamental differences in American and Chinese goals. The Taiwan issue may be a possible spark for such a confrontation, but the removal of the issue would not end the possibility of a Sino-American conflict in the future. Nor should it necessarily be assumed that Sino-American relations will normally be peaceful. Many in Beijing, and some in the United States, believe it is in the U.S. interest to keep China weak—a perception that could undermine whatever trust and goodwill remain between the two countries.

How U.S. Interests Would Be Harmed in a Taiwan-China Conflict

One of the fundamental U.S. objectives in East Asia is the maintenance of peace and stability in the Taiwan Strait. This is usually expressed in terms of U.S. concern that the resolution of the Taiwan issue be peaceful. The harm to U.S. interests resulting from a conflict in the Taiwan Strait is essential to understand, and ironically it provides rationale for two nearly opposite prescriptions for U.S. policy: the need to protect Taiwan and the need to make concessions over Taiwan.

The prevailing U.S. interest in the first case would be protection of market democracies from communist attack. The determining interest in the second instance would be the avoidance of a Sino-American war. Regardless of one's policy preference, a war in the Taiwan Strait would probably have the following negative consequences:

First, there is high probability the war could not be confined to the Taiwan Strait area. Taiwan's war-fighting strategy is to expand the conflict as widely and as rapidly as possible to maximize damage to the PRC. Thus, in addition to heavy destruction on Taiwan, Chinese ports between Shanghai and Hong Kong might have facilities damaged by ROC air and naval forces. The commercial interests of all countries trading with Taiwan and China would be harmed. The economies of both China and Taiwan would be severely damaged. There is a strong possibility that Taiwan's market democracy might be destroyed and that the economic reforms instituted by Beijing over the past decade might be seriously jeopardized.

Second, the likely use of PRC submarines to blockade Taiwan would pose a danger to all shipping in transit through the Bashi Channel, Luzon Strait, and Taiwan Strait. These are choke points through which flow a huge quantity of ocean cargo moving between Northeast Asia and ports in southern China, Southeast Asia, South Asia, and the Middle East. Submarine identification of friend, foe, or neutral is enormously difficult in heavy traffic on the high seas. Similarly, most air traffic from the United States and Northeast Asia into southern China, Taiwan, and Southeast Asia would be disrupted due to hostilities around Taiwan.

Third, a war involving the two Chinese sides would harm the economies of most Asian countries. Both Taiwan and China are vital export and import markets for Asian nations, and Taiwan is a vital source of investment capital. Since economic growth is a key factor in political stability in most Asian countries—witness the political chaos in Indonesia following the recent Asian financial crisis—the negative consequences of a war in the Taiwan Strait could extend beyond the economic sphere into areas of political and social stability. As demonstrated by the Asian contagion, the economies of the region are far more vulnerable than previously thought.

Fourth, a conflict involving China and Taiwan would generate deep security concerns throughout Asia. Most countries in the region harbor distrust of long-term Chinese ambitions. A war in the Taiwan Strait could lead to a major arms buildup in the region, especially in Japan. Since many Asian countries possess the technology, industrial capability, and financial resources to develop modern weapons, a war in the Taiwan Strait might create an unprecedented arms race and major proliferation problems for the United States.

Fifth, war in the Taiwan Strait would immediately focus world attention on the U.S. response. Since the United States has a long history of defending Taiwan against PRC attack, Asian countries would carefully evaluate the U.S. action in terms of their own security relationship with the United States. If not handled correctly, a major crisis in the Taiwan Strait would challenge, and perhaps threaten, the entire web of the U.S. security architecture in Asia.

Sixth, because of the TRA and close U.S.-Taiwan security ties, a war between Beijing and Taipei could escalate into a major regional conflict involving China and the United States. This is true regardless of the causes of the mainland-Taiwan war, since pressure for U.S. intervention would be immediate and intense from the Congress, the media, and possibly the general public observing Taiwan under PRC attack on the evening news and CNN. It goes without saying that a major conflict between the United States and the PRC would be enormously damaging to both American and Chinese interests.

Seventh, a war in the Taiwan Strait would probably remove the positive role Taiwan has played in economic reform on the mainland. U.S. long-term interests in a strong, modern, stable, and cooperative China have been well served by the moderating influence Taiwan generally exerts on PRC economic policy. The 1994 Hong Kong Agreement between Beijing and London contained many guarantees for the Hong Kong people because Deng Xiaoping and other PRC leaders wanted to prove to Taiwan (and Western audiences) that unification with mainland China would not be a catastrophe under the "one country, two systems" formula. The implementation of the joint agreement has been spotty at times, but Beijing still hopes to bring Taiwan into the embrace of the motherland through carrots rather than sticks. Also, there is a close linkage between Taiwanese investments in China and the modernization of the PRC economy. The opening of China's economy, in turn, has had a slow but steady liberalizing effect on Chinese politics and human rights behavior. These moderating trends have been encouraged and supported by Taiwan. If the Taiwan factor is removed, then the incentives for Beijing to continue its liberalization process might be weakened.

Eighth, a war in the Taiwan Strait would in all likelihood destroy all prospects for a domestic consensus on U.S. China policy. The emotions of those arguing for U.S. intervention and those arguing against would surely split the body politic in ways reminiscent of the cast for blame in the aftermath of the "loss" of China in 1949. The preservation of friendly U.S. ties with Taiwan gives the administration the political flexibility necessary to maintain its strategy of engagement with China, despite the many serious policy differences that exist between Washington and Beijing.

Ninth, a war in the Taiwan Strait might upset the regional balance of power in East Asia. Historically, U.S. strategy in the Western Pacific has centered on the maintenance of a favorable balance of power, an essential element of which is the prevention or counterbalancing of any rival regional hegemon. During the first decades of the Cold War, Taiwan played an important role as a forward base for American forces, serving as a key link in the chain of containment around communism in Asia. After Sino-American rapprochement in 1979, Taiwan's importance in the regional balance of power diminished; but Taiwan retains some geostrategic relevance in the post-Cold War era in terms of China. If Taiwan were seized by the PRC in a conflict, China would be well-positioned to challenge the United States as the major power in the Western Pacific. If China lost Taiwan in the conflict, then China's political stability might be undermined, or Beijing might turn to much more hostile relations toward the United States. Simply put, no one knows the long-term effects of a conflict in the Taiwan Strait; but, whichever side wins, the results could be damaging to U.S. regional interests.

Even if the United States avoided a war with China by allowing, for example, the PRC to take over Taiwan by force or to intimidate it into an unwanted accommodation, or even if the United States pressured Taiwan into surrendering to Beijing, the balance of power in East Asia would be changed in ways harmful to U.S. interests. American credibility, influence, and prestige would be diminished greatly, while that of China would be increased correspondingly. Having access to Taiwan's military ports, airfields, infrastructure, production capabilities, foreign exchange reserves, and investment capital would tremendously expand PRC national power. Moreover, such a victory over Taiwan might encourage Beijing to use a similar mixture of force and politics to gain advantage in other regional issues. These concerns—despite PRC public assurances that it does not pose a threat to any of its neighbors—are the principal reason most Asian countries want the United States to remain in the region as a strategic balance to China. Asian countries must deal with China and maintain diplomatic relations with Beijing, but they do not want to see the PRC use force against Taiwan and they are not anxious to see China unified under a communist central government. For their own interests, they prefer a balance of power in the region, and that balance is best maintained by an American military presence in the Western Pacific and the status quo in the Taiwan Strait.

U.S. interests in Taiwan and China are indeed broad, but they also must be considered in the context of larger U.S. interests on global and regional levels. The next section will examine these interests from the perspective of U.S. strategy and policy through the end of the Bush administration.

U.S. Strategy and Policy Toward Asia

Traditionally, the United States has defined its interests in Asia in terms of security, trade, and cultural expansion.[14] After the 1898 Spanish-American War, the United States became interested in maintaining a balance of power in the region. Militarily, this was accomplished through the expansion of American naval power and the acquisition of possessions in the Pacific such as the Philippines and Hawaii, both of which gave the United States a forward military presence in the Western Pacific. Politically and economically, the United States attempted to maintain a balance of power through the "open door" commercial policy enunciated by Secretary of State John Hay around the turn of the century. The element of idealism in American foreign policy toward Asia was noticeable as well, particularly in popular support given the American missionary movement in China and, more officially, in the attempt of President Woodrow Wilson to craft a better world order. During periods of threat from a rival hegemon—Japan during the 1930s and the 1940s and the Soviet Union during the Cold War—the United States built up its military forces to protect its interests in the Pacific. Isolationism was considered by the American people at various times but then rejected in favor of a strong forward presence. All of these elements of early U.S. strategy and policy toward Asia—interests in security, trade, and cultural expansion; seeking to maintain a favorable balance of power in the Western Pacific through an integrated military, diplomatic, and economic strategy; and a goal of establishing a new world order in which Asian nations would play an important role—are reflected in U.S. strategy and policy today.

By the end of the Second World War, the United States had adopted three further characteristics of its long-term strategy and policy toward Asia: the willingness to wage total war to defeat an Asian enemy; the tendency to form and lead coalitions of like-minded countries to serve common interests; and the use of American national power to create international institutions and systemic frameworks that served U.S. interests in stability, peace, self-determination, and prosperity.

During the Cold War, the United States viewed Asia primarily in terms of the global grand strategy of containment, especially directed toward the Soviet Union and during the 1950s and 1960s toward the newly formed People's Republic of China. During the 1970s, however, a number of developments altered U.S. policy toward Asia. The U.S. disengagement from Indochina, rapprochement with China, the oil shocks early in the decade, and international economic developments changed the U.S. approach from one of maintaining military predominance to one much more concerned with economic policies. In response to regional economic problems, momentum built toward greater economic cooperation in the Pacific, and an era of recognized economic interdependence among Pacific Rim countries was born. At first, the United States was somewhat reluctant to participant in multilateral Asia-Pacific economic cooperation processes. But by the end of the 1980s, the United States had embraced the goal of creating a regional community of market democracies as a grand strategy serving all aspects of U.S. interests in Asia.

Asian nations experienced rapid economic growth during the 1980s, mostly through market incentives. Economic interdependence between the United States and Asia increased significantly. Also during this decade, there were strong movements toward democracy in many authoritarian states, including Taiwan, South Korea, and the Philippines. Regional political trends seemed firmly in the direction of democracy. To the consternation of many Asian leaders who preferred the "Asian way," American values and popular culture became very much in vogue. In many ways, the much heralded Pacific Century actually reflected the era of Pax Americana.[15]

Strategy and Policy Under President Reagan

By the time Ronald Reagan became president in 1981, a strong continuity existed in U.S. interests, strategy, and policy toward the Asian Pacific. For over a century U.S. interests had concentrated on security, trade, and the export of American values, particular democracy and the free market. The priority of these interests had changed at various times but the interests themselves had been consistent. There had also evolved a set of fairly consistent characteristics of U.S. Asian policy: concern with maintaining a favorable balance of power; a strong U.S. military presence forward deployed in the region; active American private sector trade and investment in Asia; U.S. political leadership in the region; attempts during times of peace to create a new international order built on American ideals; a generally friendly (if sometimes superior) attitude toward all Asian countries save those few identified as threats; an emphasis on maintaining free access to Asian markets; a strong element of cultural imperialism; efforts by U.S. government officials to counter tendencies toward isolationism among the American public; a strong sense of realism, as reflected in American military power in the Western Pacific; a firm conviction that U.S. interests could be served over the long term by the promotion of American values and their adoption by Asian peoples; and a tendency to use coalitions and multilateral institutions as tools of American foreign policy.

The principal U.S. strategy in the Western Pacific was the maintenance of a favorable balance of power in which the United States was predominant. The favored method of achieving this balance was a combination of military strength in the littorals of Asia stronger than that of any rival; a strong economy serving as an essential source of investment capital, markets, and technologically advanced goods and services; political leadership seeking to protect American interests through the building of coalitions for security and for economic integration; and encouragement for the liberalization of Asian economic, social, and political institutions.

When President Reagan first assumed office, his priority was protecting U.S. security from a perceived growing threat from the Soviet Union—a threat the incoming Republican administration said had been allowed to build because of weakness and misperception on the part of the Democratic administration of Jimmy Carter. Under Reagan, American interests in trade and culture were operative in U.S. strategy and policy, but priority was given to security concerns. U.S. national security objectives for the East Asian and Pacific region reflected these priorities. According to the Fiscal Year 1984 Posture Statement of the Secretary of Defense, these objectives were to maintain the security of essential sea lanes and to protect U.S. interests in the region; maintain the capability to fulfill U.S. treaty commitments to the Pacific and East Asia; prevent the Soviet Union, North Korea, and Vietnam from interfering in the affairs of others; support the stability and independence of friendly countries; and build toward a durable strategic relationship with the People's Republic of China.[16]

The U.S. objective of building a durable strategic relationship with the PRC to help counter the Soviet Union was as important to the highly anti-communist President Reagan as it had been to his predecessors, Jimmy Carter, Gerald Ford, and Richard Nixon. As explained by Reagan in his statement accompanying the August 17, 1982, U.S.-PRC Joint Communiqué: "Building a strong and lasting friendship with China has been an important foreign policy goal of four consecutive American administrations. Such a relationship is vital to our long-term national security interests and contributes to stability in East Asia. It is in the national interests of the United States that this important strategic relationship be advanced."[17] In early 1993 Paul Wolfowitz, Assistant Secretary of State for Asian and Pacific Affairs, listed several U.S. interests served by cooperative relations with Beijing:

> We no longer have to plan and spend to confront a Chinese threat; our parallel interests in containing the Soviet Union have been repeatedly reaffirmed and we are in fundamental agreement that the Soviets remain the principal threat to peace in the world; we have common interests in containing not only Vietnamese aggression in Southeast Asia and encouraging a peaceful settlement of the Kampuchean [Cambodian] problem based on Khmer self-determination, but also in resisting Soviet aggression in Afghanistan; we are able to maintain a useful dialogue with China on a wide range of important international problems of common concern; China has developed constructive regional policies and cooperative relations with our Asian allies; China has developed increasingly strong ties to the western-oriented international economic system; trade and investment opportunities for American business have grown tremendously; despite problems, East Asia has emerged as one of the more stable and prosperous regions of the world, with China playing an increasingly responsible regional role.[18]

While focused primarily on the strategic imperative of Sino-American cooperation against the mutual Soviet threat, the United States under the Reagan administration also began to see other fruits of engagement with China: namely, cooperation on regional affairs, expanded economic opportunities, and enhanced peace and stability in the Asia-Pacific region as a whole. During the subsequent Bush administration, however, the strategic and political underpinnings of Sino-American relations were suddenly and unexpectedly shaken by the collapse of the Soviet Union and the slaughter at Tiananmen Square.

Strategy and Policy Under President Bush

President George Bush, who served as vice president under Ronald Reagan, entered office in 1989 with every expectation of continuing his predecessor's highly successful policies toward Asia. Two developments early in the Bush administration, however, completely changed the security and political environment for the United States: the implosion of the Soviet Union in the 1989-1991 period and the near breakdown in normal Sino-American relations after the Tiananmen Square events of June 1989.[19] The first development dramatically lowered the Soviet threat to U.S. security interests, while the second poisoned the friendly atmosphere of U.S.-PRC relations. The net result of these developments was the collapse of the global bipolar system dominated by Washington and Moscow and the Asian strategic triangle dominated by Washington, Moscow, and Beijing. In a remarkably short period of time, the comfort President Bush might have felt in policy continuity with his predecessor was replaced by the uncertainty of trying to forge new policies to cope with a radically changed strategic environment in Asia.

New World Order. One of the most important U.S. strategic visions to come out of this period was the "new world order," a growing community of market democracies led by the United States and tied together by universally applicable American values. Bush described his vision (actually, an on-again, off-again American theme since Wilson) in May 1989: "What is it that we want to see? It is a growing community of democracies anchoring international peace and stability, and a dynamic free-market system generating prosperity and progress on a global scale. The economic foundation of this new era is the proven success of the free market—and nurturing that foundation are the values rooted in freedom and democracy."[20]

The president did not have a blueprint for the new world order, but he did not envision some supernational structure or institution that would manage global affairs. Nor did he believe in the surrendering of national sovereignty or forfeiting of national interests. Rather, he said, the new world order referred to "new ways of working with other nations to deter aggression and to achieve stability, to achieve prosperity and, above all, to achieve peace." Most importantly, the new world order was based on a shared commitment of nations to a common set of principles. These principles included "peaceful settlements of disputes, solidarity against aggression, reduced and controlled arsenals, and just treatment of all peoples." The new world order "gains its mission and shape not just from shared interests, but from shared ideals." And, according to the president, "the ideals that have spawned new freedoms throughout the world have received their boldest and clearest expression in [the United States]. . . . What makes us American is our allegiance to an idea that all people everywhere must be free."[21]

To achieve this new world order based on American ideals, Bush suggested that a grand strategy of integration replace the grand strategy of containment: "The grand strategy of the West during the postwar period has been based on the concept of containment: checking the Soviet Union's expansionist aims, in the hope that the Soviet system itself would one day be forced to confront its internal contradictions. The ferment in the Soviet Union today affirms the wisdom of this strategy. And now we have a precious opportunity to move beyond containment. . . . Our [present] goal—integrating the Soviet Union into the community of nations—is every bit as ambitious as containment was at its time. And it holds tremendous promise for international stability."[22]

As will be noted in greater detail in Chapter 5, the PRC criticized Bush's vision of the new world order, seeing immediately that the new U.S. strategy of integration—originally spoken of in reference to the Soviet Union—could equally be applied to China. In essence, the strategy underlying the new world order was the opposite from the Cold War strategy of containment. Containment sought to isolate potential enemies of the United States from the world community; integration sought to bring former and potential enemies into an emerging world community of market democracies. Both strategies were intended to undermine ideologically hostile regimes, although by different means.

In the post-Cold War world, the Bush and later Clinton administrations did not see China as a strategic partner against the Russians, nor as a direct threat to U.S. interests, but rather as a potential candidate for transformation into a respected member of the community of market democracies. Even the crisis of Tiananmen did not fundamentally alter the perception of China as a society in transition from authoritarianism. As will be explained later, in the aftermath of Tiananmen, the Bush strategy toward China was one of engagement as the best means to bring about the desired change in the PRC.

There were other elements in Bush post-Cold War strategies that should be noted here, particularly the concepts of collective engagement, the military strategy of regional contingencies, the idea of a "new partnership" in Asia, and the role of the United States as the "balance wheel" of the Asian Pacific.

Collective Engagement. Collective engagement was perceived by the administration as a way of preserving U.S. global leadership in an era of American weariness from shouldering the burden of four decades of Cold War. After the collapse of the Soviet Union, most Americans wanted their leaders to focus less on foreign affairs and more on the economy and domestic issues such as education, crime, drugs, care for the elderly, and affordable housing.

The case for collective engagement was made by Secretary of State James Baker in a speech before the Chicago Council on Foreign Relations in April 1992.[23] The secretary noted that the United States had been called upon to lead the world into a peaceful new order following the first and second world wars. The United States decided to stay out of world affairs after World War I, but the disasters of isolationism had cost the country dearly during the Second World War. After World War II, the United States led a forty-year struggle against the communist threat, a struggle which ended with the collapse of the Soviet Union in 1991. Baker recalled that U.S. decisions to implement the Marshall Plan, to create NATO, and to support democracy in Japan were very controversial at the time. The American people were willing to pay the price of these policies, however, because they understood that containing the Soviet Union was not adequate. The United States had to transform its World War II enemies into democratic friends and allies. The result was a "zone of peace and prosperity" in the world.

Baker said the end of the Cold War had brought a third summons for the United States to assume global leadership, this time to win a "democratic peace" for the whole world. The Bush administration wanted to help shape the post-Cold War order by extending the "zone of peace and prosperity" across Russia and Eurasia. "Our idea is to replace the dangerous period of the Cold War with a democratic peace—a peace built on the twin pillars of political and economic freedom. . . . Shared democratic values can ensure an enduring and stable peace in a way that balance of terror never could, [since] democracies do not go to war with each other."

The administration would build a democratic peace by pursuing a policy of American leadership called "collective engagement." Based on U.S. leadership in collaboration with its friends and allies, collective engagement had the strategic objective of enlarging the community of market democracies. Collaboration often would occur through international institutions such as the United Nations; however, "the moving force of collective engagement is American leadership, drawing on the common values and common interests shared by the democratic community of nations." U.S. leadership was the "catalyst" in driving forward the expansion of the democratic community since "the world trusts us with power . . . they trust us to do what's right." When necessary, the United States would act alone "to truly lead or serve our national interests."

Bill Clinton adopted much of his predecessor's vision of a new world order and his foreign policy of collective engagement—reborn as Clinton's national strategy of "engagement and enlargement." The terminology may have been a little different, but both Bush and Clinton pursued goals quintessentially American: using U.S. influence and power to create a favorable world order dominated by democratic governments and free market economies.

Regional Contingencies. Another key concept relevant to Bush's new world order was the military strategy of regional contingencies. The sudden termination of the Soviet threat necessitated a complete reexamination of U.S. military strategy. The first stage of this process was completed in 1992, when the Pentagon announced that in the post-Cold War period the United States would change its national security strategy from preparation to fight a global war with Moscow to preparation to fight nearly simultaneously in two regional conflicts anywhere in the world. The forces required to implement the new regional contingencies strategy were organized in a so-called Base Force. This new strategy was explained in detail in the unclassified version of the 1992 Joint Military Net Assessment (JMNA) prepared by the Joint Chiefs of Staff.[24]

The 1992 JMNA said the primary threat to the United States in the post-Cold War period was "instability and being unprepared to handle a crisis or war that no one predicted or expected." The growing complexity of the world's security environment made it "increasingly difficult to predict the circumstances under which U.S. military power might be employed." In the new period, the United States would continue to deploy forward-based forces to deter traditional threats such as North Korea, but "new planning will be focused primarily on regional contingencies where specific threats are unknown and uncertain." For planning purposes, the Joint Chiefs of Staff used a surprise North Korean attack against South Korea and an aggressor, such as Iraq or Iran, threatening U.S. interests in Southwest Asia. The Base Force necessary to respond to these nearly simultaneous regional contingencies would include the following elements by the year 2000: Strategic forces comprising B-52H, B-1B, and B-2 bombers; 550 ballistic missiles; and 18 nuclear ballistic missile submarines; Army forces comprising 12 active divisions, 6 reserve divisions, and 2 cadre divisions; Navy forces comprising 450 ships, including 12 aircraft carrier battle groups; 11 active air wings; and 2 reserve air wings; Marine Corps comprising 2.5 active Marine Expeditionary Forces and 1 reserve division and wing; and Air forces comprising 15.25 active fighter wing equivalents (FWEs) and 11.25 reserve FWEs.

According to the Joint Chiefs, "the Base Force is capable of resolving quickly—with low risk—only one major regional crisis at a time. For two crises occurring close together, the United States would have to employ economy of force and sequential operations and make strategic choices. The risk to US objectives in either case is no more than moderate, but there is little margin for unfavorable circumstances."

Thus, the Bush administration not only changed U.S. national strategy from containment to integration (expanding the community of market democracies through collective engagement), it also changed U.S. national military strategy from preparing to fight a global war against the Soviet Union to one of preparing to fight two major regional conflicts. China was viewed as a potential member of the new community, and it was not considered a threat to U.S. interests in the regional contingencies strategy. (Although in most Korean War game scenarios, the PRC always played a prominent and uncertain role.) As in the case of collective engagement, the Clinton administration's "bottom-up review" retained most elements of the regional contingencies strategy but with fewer forces. A similar continuity of strategy and policy could be found in the two administrations in terms of the U.S. approach to the Asian Pacific region and bilaterally with China.

New Partnership in Asia. As its basic strategy toward Asia, the Bush administration sought to create a "new partnership" in the Pacific in which the United States would continue to provide leadership but in a closer, more equal, and expanded coalition of market democracies. The president outlined his strategic and foreign policy goals toward Asia in a speech to the Asia Society in New York in November 1991.[25] Bush said the United States was deeply committed to the Asia-Pacific because of the region's growing importance to U.S. interests, particularly in the area of economics. While the United States would remain large and powerful in the region, it would seek to deepen relationships with Asian nations on the basis of true partnership in order to build strong foundations of democracy and freedom.

Three areas were of paramount concern to the United States in Asia: security, democracy, and trade. In the area of security, Bush noted that the United States had built a diverse pattern of political and strategic relationships in the region, custom-made for each country and subregion. These provided a strong foundation for future security. Both peace in the region and defense of U.S. interests could be advanced through these flexible military arrangements already in place in Asia. The most important of these was the U.S. security relationship with Japan.

According to President Bush, the key sources of instability in the region were North Korea, China, and other states resisting the global movement toward political pluralism and contributing to the proliferation of dangerous weapons. The greatest immediate threat to regional peace was North Korea's suspected nuclear weapons program. China was a special case because it was important to the United States in several areas.

In terms of U.S. concerns with democracy in Asia, the president noted that democracy had swept across much of the region, with the exception of Burma, China, North Korea, and Vietnam. Bush said, "the United States will support democracy wherever it can, understanding that nations adopt political freedom in their own ways in manners consistent with their histories and cultures." As its long-term strategic goal in Asia, Bush said the United States was seeking to build "a commonwealth of freedom" in the region.

In terms of trade, the president highlighted examples of increased cooperation between Pacific Rim nations in multilateral frameworks such as the Uruguay Round of the GATT talks and the Asia-Pacific Economic Cooperation (APEC) process. (APEC was established in November 1989 by regional governments to promote free trade and investment in the Pacific Basin.) The president also noted that technology, especially mass communication, would play an increasingly important role as a tool to sweep away totalitarianism and advance freedom.

At about the same time President Bush was speaking to the Asia Society, Secretary of State James Baker was explaining the administration's ideas about a new post-Cold War architecture in Asia.[26] In a speech given in Tokyo in November 1991, Baker said the overall structure of U.S. engagement in the Pacific could be envisioned as a

> fan spread wide, with its base in North America and radiating westward. Its central support is the alliance and partnership between the United States and Japan. To the north, one spoke represents our alliance with the Republic of Korea. To the south, another line extends to our ASEAN colleagues. Further south, a spoke reaches to Australia.... Connecting these spokes is the fabric of shared economic interests now given form by the Asia-Pacific Economic Cooperation (APEC) process. Within this flexible construct, new political and economic ties offer additional support for cooperative actions by groups of Pacific nations. Over time, we should strive to draw China and the Soviet Union or the Russian republic closer to this system.

In an important nod in the direction of increased multilateralism, Baker said U.S. bilateral security relations in the region were essential, but the administration believed they could be supplemented by multilateral approaches: "In the future, our bilateral security ties will continue to provide geopolitical balance, enable us to serve as an honest broker, and reassure against uncertainty. But multilateral actions may also supplement these bilateral ties." One example was the Cambodian peace process [under the auspices of the United Nations Transitional Authority in Cambodia]. Multilateral security forums might also discuss disputed islands in the South China Sea and security dangers on the Korean peninsula. However, he cautioned that at this stage of the post-Cold War era, "an overly structured approach" to multilateral cooperation would not work.

Baker also noted that economic dynamism was the major distinguishing quality of East Asia. The growing "intra-Asian and trans-Pacific trade and investment provide the broad common interests on which to build the Pacific community." The secretary noted that U.S. support for the APEC process was "as much a hallmark of our engagement in the region as are our security ties."

The enduring sense of community which the United States wished to build in Asia had not only security and economic elements, but also a foundation of common values. "Without such a foundation, alliances and other ties will not have resilience, since relations based solely on realpolitik can fracture as circumstances change." These common values included universal concerns for human dignity, individual welfare, and freedom of thought and expression. Baker emphasized the need for continued progress in democracy and human rights, and he called upon friends and allies to work with the United States for "the promotion of political as well as economic reform in the few remaining Marxist-Leninist states in Asia."

Specifically in regards to China, Baker said "great uncertainty still clouds our relations." The June 1989 Tiananmen Square episode "shattered the bipartisan consensus in the U.S.—carefully constructed over two decades—for engagement with China. Rebuilding that consensus is proving to be a daunting task." Nonetheless, "China casts a long shadow in Asia and beyond" and thus warranted close attention. "China is in a time of transition" with its future yet to be decided. Meanwhile, the United States would move ahead with its agenda, secure improvements where possible, and "create the context for managing the change that will come some day."

Virtually all of these elements of the Bush administration's approach to Asia—maintaining strong bilateral ties while encouraging gradual multilateralism in the region; emphasis on U.S. interests in security, trade, and the promotion of democracy and human rights; continued American leadership while working toward a new partnership in Asia; and engagement with China despite future uncertainties—were adopted by the Clinton administration in its grand strategy of building a "new Pacific community."

Balance Wheel of Asia. Another continuity in the Bush and Clinton approaches to Asia was the articulation of U.S. strategy and policy toward the region in terms of a "balance wheel," that is, the essential and unique role played by the United States in maintaining "balance" in the Asia Pacific. This was not seen as a traditional balance of power strategy by the Pentagon, but rather more benignly as an effort by the United States to ensure the continuation of regional security and stability, thereby allowing the dynamic processes of economic liberalization and political evolution to continue without interference from regional or outside hegemons. Call it an enlightened balance of power strategy.

Assistant Secretary of State for East Asian and Pacific Affairs Richard Solomon explained the balance wheel strategy in a February 1990 statement before the House Foreign Affairs subcommittee on Asia and the Pacific.[27] Solomon said the U.S. goal was to create "a new partnership in the Pacific" in which "the U.S. role, as the dynamic balancer in Asia, is crucial to regional—and global—stability in the 1990s." According to Solomon, "For four decades, the United States has been the central unifying hub of a network of bilateral security relationships in the Pacific. We are the dynamic balancer, the buffer force, and the ultimate security guarantor in a region of great political, cultural, and historical diversity." A new strategic environment was unfolding in Asia with the emergence of new power centers in Japan, China, and India. At the same time, the region had the world's largest armies standing in an uneasy coexistence. Solomon warned, "Any diminishing of the credibility of the U.S. forward deployed deterrent would only produce an increase in regional tensions, with other powers tempted to fill any perceived gaps. For the foreseeable future, we—and most nations in the region—view the United States as the irreplaceable balancing wheel. No other power is viewed as an acceptable substitute for our critical stabilizing role."

The role of the United States as the balance wheel of Asia was described more completely in a 1990 Defense Department report entitled *A Strategic Framework for the Asian Pacific Rim: Looking Toward the 21st Century*.[28] The report was the first of four East Asia strategic initiative reports published through 1998, referred to as EASI-I (published in 1990), EASI-II (1992), EASI-III (1995), and EASI-IV (1998). EASI-I argued that in spite of the reduced Soviet threat in Asia (the collapse of the Soviet Union occurred fifteen months later in August 1991), U.S. interests in the region remained similar to those of the past: protecting the United States from attack; supporting U.S. global deterrence policy; preserving U.S. political and economic access to the region; maintaining the balance of power to prevent the rise of any regional hegemony; strengthening the Western orientation of Asian nations; fostering the growth of democracy and human rights; deterring nuclear proliferation; and ensuring freedom of navigation.

Because of the historical continuity of these interests, the basic elements of U.S. security strategy toward Asia also remained valid: forward deployed forces, overseas bases, and bilateral security arrangements. To protect its interests, the United States would need to preserve both peacetime and wartime deterrent and warfighting capabilities in the Pacific. Given the continuity in U.S. interests and strategy, and the continued need for deterrence and warfighting capabilities in Asia, the report concluded that the existing U.S. military presence in the region should remain largely intact, although some reductions, mostly in ground forces, could take place to reflect the improved international climate and to help reduce the U.S. budget deficit. The U.S. military adjustments would occur in three phases through the end of the century. In Phase I (1990-1993) an initial reduction of 14,000-15,000 personnel out of some 135,000 U.S. troops forward deployed in the Pacific would take place. Phase II (1993-1995) and Phase III (1995-2000) adjustments would depend on security situations prevailing at the time. By the end of Phase III in the year 2000, the United States would have a sustainable (then undefined but later set at about 100,000 personnel) presence in the region. In terms of forward deployment, American troops would remain in Japan over the long term with few changes while U.S. forces in Korea would be kept at a minimum level necessary to deter North Korean aggression.

The Defense Department described its role in the Western Pacific as that of "regional balancer, honest broker, and ultimate security guarantor."[29] Another phrase used to describe the role of the U.S. military in Asia was an "irreplaceable balance wheel." The EASI-I report said the key phrase describing the mission of the U.S. military in Asia in the post-containment period was a "central stabilizing role." Other officials used the terms "regional balancer, honest broker, and arbiter" to describe the military's role.[30]

Under the EASI plan, the United States sought to preserve a favorable balance of power in Asia by: (1) maintaining a strong forward deployed military force in the region for the purposes of deterrence and, if need be, early military response to a crisis; (2) coordinating policies with other Asian Pacific nations through bilateral and multilateral channels to minimize conflict and to maximize regional stability and prosperity; and (3) attempting to play the role of "honest broker" to help resolve problems between the Asian nations themselves.

In February 1991 the Department of Defense sent a brief report to the Congress stating that the 1990 *Strategic Framework* study had been well-received by Asian nations and was being implemented according to schedule.[31] The following year the Pentagon submitted a second full report on its Asia-Pacific strategy.[32] EASI-II took into consideration the collapse of the Soviet Union in August 1991 and the Philippine Senate's refusal to ratify a new treaty negotiated in July 1991 extending continued basing rights to the United States. The new report observed that with the end of the Cold War, "the United States' regional roles, which had been secondary in our strategic calculus, have now assumed primary importance in our security engagement in the Pacific theater." The report noted that during the postwar period, the United States was the predominant power in the Asia-Pacific region. Consequently, U.S. national security objectives "centered on defending American territory as far forward as possible, global containment of the Soviet Union, and protecting friends and allies." U.S. military strategy, dictated largely by the distances involved in transiting the Pacific Ocean, was "to forward deploy forces to permanent base infrastructures, primarily in Japan, Korea and Southeast Asia" and to complement that presence "through the development of a range of bilateral security arrangements."

According to EASI-II, "this approach worked well because of the diverse threat perceptions, disparate cultures, histories, political systems, and levels of economic development among our friends in the region." In particular, the U.S. forward based presence has underpinned stability in East Asia and helped secure its economic dynamism. Moreover, the forward presence "has made the U.S. the key regional balancer, contributed to regional stability, enhanced U.S. diplomatic influence, and contributed to an environment conducive to the growth of U.S. economic interests." The report emphasized, "maintaining a credible security presence is an important element in our effort to build a sense of Asia-Pacific community vital to the post-Cold War international system now taking place."

Rather than specifying threats to U.S. interests in Asia in the post-Cold War period, EASI-II noted several potential sources of instability that the United States had to be prepared to meet. These sources of instability included:

- North Korea, particularly its "quest for a nuclear weapons capability" and uncertainties surrounding the pending political transition from Kim Il-sung to Kim Jung-il
- the remaining communist states of Asia, which "will change, but it is difficult to predict whether the process will proceed peacefully or violently"
- the PRC, where "politics will almost certainly be volatile as Deng Xiaoping and the current octogenarian leaders pass from the scene"
- Taiwan, whose future relationship with mainland China is uncertain
- Cambodia, which still confronts the danger of the Khmer Rouge
- The Philippines, which continues to be threatened by terrorism and insurgency from the communist New People's Army
- Spratly Islands, whose territory and waters are claimed by China, Taiwan, Vietnam, the Philippines, Malaysia, and Brunei
- Burma, under a military dictatorship which refuses to recognize the results of the 1990 elections and tends to ignore narcotics activities within its borders
- proliferation, particularly missile exports from North Korea and China and the North Korean nuclear weapons program.

To met these and other potential regional crises, the EASI-II report said the United States would maintain its military forward presence in the Asia-Pacific as "an essential element of our global military posture." According to the report, these forward deployed forces ensured a rapid and flexible crisis response capability; contributed to regional stability; discouraged the emergence of a regional hegemony; enhanced the U.S. ability to influence a wide spectrum of important issues in the region; enabled significant economy of force by reducing the number of U.S. forces required to meet national security objectives; overcame the handicaps of time and distance presented by the vast Pacific Ocean; and demonstrated to friends, allies, and potential enemies a tangible, visible U.S. interest in the security of the entire region.

Since Japan continued "to be America's key Pacific ally and the cornerstone of U.S. forward deployed defense strategy in the Asia-Pacific region," the Japanese archipelago afforded "U.S. forward deployed forces geostrategically crucial naval, air and ground bases on the periphery of the Asian land mass." U.S. military forces based in Japan contributed to the security of Japan and were "well located for rapid deployment to virtually any trouble spot in the region." Consequently, the United States considered the presence of U.S. forces in Japan to be permanent.[33] U.S. forward deployed forces in Korea, intended primarily to deter a North Korean attack, would remain in South Korea "as long as the Korean people and government want us to stay and threats to peace and stability remain." With the loss of its bases in the Philippines, EASI-II said the United States was shifting its force posture in Southeast Asia from having a large permanent presence to having a forward presence accommodated by wider access agreements with several regional countries.

Of the 109,440 troop strength in Western Pacific at the end of the Bush administration, 45,227 were in Japan (1,978 Army; 6,498 shore-based Navy; 21,511 Marines; 15,440 Air Force); 37,413 were in South Korea (27,000 Army; 400 shore-based Navy; 500 Marines; 9,513 Air Force); 1,000 troops were being redeployed in the region from the Philippines; and 25,800 were afloat or otherwise forward deployed. According to the 1992 JMNA,

> Forward-presence forces [in the Pacific] will be principally maritime, with half our projected carrier and amphibious force oriented toward this area, including one forward-deployed CVBG [aircraft carrier battle group] and one MEF [Marine Expeditionary Force]. We plan to keep one CVBG and one ARG [amphibious readiness group] homeported in Japan and have developed new forward-basing options not dependent on our former bases in the Republic of the Philippines. The improving military capability of South Korea has enabled our Army forces to be trimmed to less than a division. Air forces can be reduced to two or three FWEs [Fighter Wing Equivalents] in Korea and Japan. The pace of the reductions is gauged to shifting to a supporting role in Korea and modulated by North Korea's actions and nuclear cooperation. In addition, we retain forces in both Alaska and Hawaii. . . . Crisis response forces focused on the Pacific region include forces in Hawaii, Alaska, and CONUS [continental United States]. These include one [Army] division (reinforced), one FWE, and five CVBGs.

Thus, according to post-Cold War plans formulated by the Bush administration, the United States would deploy through the end of the century about half of its aircraft carrier battle groups and nearly two-thirds of its Marine forces to the Pacific, as well as substantial air forces. These military deployments reflected a substantial U.S. commitment to Asian security and were designed to protect growing American interests in the Asian Pacific. With minor adjustments, these deployments continued under the administration of President Clinton. Despite Tiananmen and the hardening of PRC domestic policies for a time, China was not considered a threat to U.S. interests, although it did represent a potential source of instability under several possible conditions, including the use of force in the Taiwan Strait. For the most part, the Pentagon planned for a Chinese contingency quietly, hoping that engagement would result in China eventually changing in a direction more favorable to U.S. interests.

Conclusion

Part of the conundrum of the Taiwan issue in U.S. China policy is the complexity of weighing the various American interests in Taiwan and China. U.S. foreign policy and national security strategy traditionally have been concerned with security, trade, and the promotion of American values, including democracy and free enterprise. These concerns have been consistent on global, regional, and bilateral levels of U.S. strategy and policy, and these interests have been relevant to Washington's dealings with both Taiwan and China. There are potential conflicts, however, between the U.S. interest in protecting Taiwan's existing market democracy and the U.S. interest in securing China's cooperation on regional security and other issues. Moreover, a long-term American goal is to see democracy and free enterprise take hold in mainland China. One aspect of the Taiwan conundrum is that too much U.S. support for Taiwan might bring to power hardliners in China who want to slow down reform, while too much U.S. emphasis on political and economic reform on the mainland (to the neglect of Taiwan) might jeopardize the market democracy already existing in the ROC.

The characteristic blending of pragmatic and idealistic interests in American foreign policy also contributes to the conundrum in U.S. China-Taiwan policy. Often this centers on such policy trade-offs as balancing the promotion of human rights in China and the expansion of American commercial interests, or balancing continued support for Taiwan and the desire for strategic partnership with China.

At various times, different priorities have been placed on enduring U.S. interests such as security, trade, and the promotion of American values. Security concerns, for example, dominated U.S. strategy and policy during much of the 1930s through 1980s, a long period of international tension encompassing both the Second World War and the Cold War. In an attempt to bring coherent vision to American foreign policy in the post-Cold War era, President Bush expressed support for a "new world order" in which American ideals of freedom, democracy, justice, and rule by law would prevail in the international system—a vision continued by President Clinton in his goal of enlarging the community of market democracies. Both presidential visions, however, were heavily dependent on the strength of the U.S. economy and the power of the U.S. armed forces.

Unlike in Europe, where U.S. policies had focused heavily on the Soviet threat and therefore required considerable change after the Cold War, American strategy and policy toward Asia remained largely in place after the Soviet demise. The East Asian strategic initiative, for example, preserved U.S. strategy and policy toward Asia, while reducing U.S. forces by about 25 percent. This continuity reflected the fact that U.S. interests in the Pacific had changed very little with the passing of the Cold War. For the most part, the EASI reports provided a new justification for continued U.S. forward deployed forces, now stressing the preservation of a regional balance of power rather than containing a specific threat. The U.S. strategy toward Asia became a "new partnership," the idea being that an expanded community of market democracies in the region would best serve the complete spectrum of U.S. interests in Asia, including continued American leadership.

As will be seen in the next chapter, these basic strategic concepts were adopted by the Clinton administration in the grand strategy of the enlargement of the community of market democracies, a part of which was the creation of a "new Pacific community." These global and regional grand strategies, reflecting the unique blend of American idealism and pragmatism in U.S. foreign policy, coupled with Washington's decentralized system of decision making and propensity to use massive amounts of force in regional conflicts, made the United States appear unpredictable and dangerous in the eyes of many Chinese leaders. Chapter 5 records PRC criticism of Bush's new world order and China's alternative vision of a new international order in which each nation would be left to decide its own national policies, free from the U.S. model.

It is important to note here that both the Bush and Clinton administrations defined U.S. interests, goals, and strategies in the post-Cold War period in a very consistent manner. Despite some changes in phraseology, the U.S. strategy essentially was one of engagement with all countries, except a few rouge or terrorist states, and enlargement of the community of market democracies. The U.S. policy of engagement with China was part of the U.S. grand strategy of engagement and enlargement. The U.S. goal of engagement with China was to change China in the direction of more open markets and greater political liberalization. The United States wanted to enlarge the community of market democracies by integrating China into that community.

Because of its size and power, China played a major role in assessments of U.S. national security strategy in the post-Cold War period. Generally, it was identified as a potential regional peer about which the United States should be concerned, but mostly over the long term. China was not seen as an immediate threat to the United States; indeed, it was viewed optimistically as a future market democracy. At the same time, however, China was recognized as a potential threat with tremendous and growing national power, a strong sense of nationalism, and a keenly felt need to exercise a leadership role in Asia.

These two somewhat contradictory views of China—potential market democracy and potential regional threat—coexisted in the minds of U.S. government officials and foreign policy experts. In general, however, most everyone was willing to give China a chance to fulfill the more optimistic vision. Still, as early as the Bush administration, several areas of potential conflict of interest with China could be identified. For example:

- The fundamental U.S. goal of expanding the community of market democracies ran counter to China's stated intention of retaining socialism with Chinese characteristics, i.e., the preservation of the Chinese Communist Party's dominance of the political system even while the Chinese economy became more liberal.
- The basic requirement of U.S. leadership to promote and defend the community of market democracies ran counter to the PRC desire to have a true multipolar international system in which the United States was only one of several major powers, including China. China rejected American leadership on global and regional levels.
- In adopting its strategy of engagement and enlargement, the United States relied on various coalitions and international institutions to protect its interests. From China's point of view, these were instruments of American foreign policy designed in part to contain the growing power of China.
- The United States openly pointed to China as a nation it would like to see become more democratic and capitalist. Since this was a stated U.S. goal, it was difficult for China to know which motivation was operative in a given policy emitting from Washington: was the United States seeking to deal with the PRC from a pragmatic point of view, or was the United States seeking to use its contacts with the PRC to manipulate China's future?
- The United States stated its intention to use military force in cases where its vital or important interests were threatened. Although China did not directly threaten the United States, there were areas of importance to both countries where their interests might collide, particularly Taiwan and potentially the South China Sea. Of special concern to China was the American tendency to use force to protect or defend its ideals and principles, even when no direct threat to U.S. security interests existed.
- Washington viewed the proliferation of weapons of mass destruction as being a threat to U.S. security interests. China not only possessed and continued to produce such weapons for its own use but also exported some weapons and WMD technology to countries viewed as unfriendly or unstable by the United States.
- The United States stressed the need to have balanced and fair trade with its major trading partners. China's surplus with the United States was growing rapidly, soon to become the world's second-largest after that of Japan. Moreover, some of China's trade practices were viewed as being unfair by Washington.

- The United States placed high priority on respect for human rights. Especially after Tiananmen, China was pointed to as one of the world's greatest violators of the human rights of its citizens, the object of intense criticism by many Americans and of sanctions by Washington.
- Although China was not specifically identified as a threat to U.S. interests, it was identified as a nation under close scrutiny because of its national power and the uncertainty surrounding its future.

Overall, there was a qualitative and quantitative difference in U.S. interests in Taiwan and China. Because of its national power and growing international prestige, Beijing could either be of great help to the United States in resolving international problems or it could be of great hindrance, making the management and resolution of many issues difficult if not impossible. The U.S. strategy of engagement presumed that constructive dialogue with the PRC was preferable to a policy of containment and confrontation, and that, indeed, over time the very process of engagement with the United States might help transform China into a more politically liberal, market-oriented country, cooperating with the United States and its Asian neighbors to bring stability and prosperity to the region.

The United States also had many interests in Taiwan, but—barring an American decision to pursue hostile relations with China—the more important of these interests were: (a) the preservation of peace in the Taiwan Strait; (b) the preservation of Taiwan's market economy and its model of peaceful transition from authoritarian rule to democracy; (c) Taiwan's proven friendship and commitment to American values and interests; (d) the hope that Taiwan's democratic, free market alternative to communism might one day be adopted by China; and (e) an unarticulated "wild card" value as a hedge against worst-case scenarios involving the mainland. Thus, while China was seen to be more strategically important than Taiwan, Taiwan had both a moral advantage and some strategic value as model and hedge in regards to China. In the American political context, this ensured that U.S. interests in Taiwan would not easily be sacrificed for U.S. interests in China, especially in an environment of there being no major threat compelling Sino-American strategic cooperation such as existed during the 1970s and 1980s.

The Taiwan conundrum in U.S. China policy became more complex under President Clinton, whose strategy and policy will be examined in the next chapter.

Notes

1. TV comment translated by the Foreign Broadcast Information Service (FBIS) in *Daily Report: East Asia*, August 17, 1997.

2. *Washington Post*, November 27, 1998, p. A1.

3. Details summarized from "Background Notes: Taiwan" (Washington, DC: Department of State, October 1998).

4. For a detailed discussion of U.S. interests, see the author's *U.S. Interests in the New Taiwan* (Boulder, CO: Westview, 1993).

5. C-SPAN recording of President Jiang Zemin's speech in Washington, D.C., October 30, 1997, at a luncheon cosponsored by the American-China Society and the Asia Society, among other groups.

6. *Washington Post*, December 4, 1998, p. A31.

7. For U.S. trade figures, see *USTR: 1998 National Trade Estimates: Taiwan* (Washington, DC: Office of the U.S. Trade Representative, 1998).

8. For a description of the Asian financial crisis and its impact throughout the region, see Karl D. Jackson, ed., *Asian Contagion: The Causes and Consequences of a Financial Crisis* (Boulder, CO: Westview, 1999).

9. See, for example, *Washington Post*, December 6, 1998, p. A31. For a complete report on the election, see *Free China Review*, December 11, 1998, p. 1.

10. Richard Bernstein and Ross H. Munro, *The Coming Conflict with China* (New York: Knopf, 1997); Andrew J. Nathan and Robert Ross, *The Great Wall and the Empty Fortress: China's Search for Security* (New York: Norton, 1997).

11. Lu Junyuan, "Taiwan's Geostrategic Value Makes Reunification Essential," *Taiwan Yanjiu*, March 20, 1996, translated by the Foreign Broadcast Information Service in *Daily Report: China*, March 20, 1996. Hereafter cited as *FBIS-China*.

12. Summarized from "Background Notes: China" (Washington, DC: Department of State, October 1998).

13. For U.S. trade statistics, see *USTR: 1998 National Trade Estimate: People's Republic of China* (Washington, DC: Office of the U.S. Trade Representative, 1998).

14. Akira Iriye, "The American Experience in East Asia," in Mary Brown Bullock and Robert S. Litwak, eds., *The United States and the Pacific Basin: Changing Economic and Security Relationships* (Washington, DC: Woodrow Wilson Center Press, 1991), pp. 13-29.

15. See Mark Borthwick, *Pacific Century: The Emergence of Modern Pacific Asia* (Boulder, CO: Westview, 1992).

16. U.S. Department of Defense, *Annual Report to the Congress, Fiscal Year 1984* (Washington, DC: U.S. Government Printing Office, 1983).

17. "Statement by President Reagan, August 17, 1982," *American Foreign Policy Documents, 1982* (Washington, DC: Department of State Publications, U.S. Government Printing Office, Document 496, p. 1040). This and other important policy documents relating to China and Taiwan can be found in Stephen P. Gilbert and William M. Carpenter, *America and Island China: A Documentary History* (Lanham, MD: University Press of America, 1989).

18. Prepared statement of Paul Wolfowitz, "Sino-American Relations Eleven Years After the Shanghai Communiqué," given before U.S. Congress, House of Representatives, Committee on Foreign Affairs, Subcommittee on Asian and Pacific Affairs, February 28, 1983, ms.

19. Richard H. Solomon, "Who Will Shape the Emerging Structure of East Asia?" in Michael Mandelbaum, ed., *The Strategic Quadrangle: Russia, China, Japan, and the United States in East Asia* (New York: Council on Foreign Relations, 1994), p. 199.

20. George Bush, "Security Strategy for the 1990s," Department of State *Current Policy* 1178 (May 1989).

21. George Bush, "Address by the President to the Air University" (Washington, DC: The White House, Office of the Press Secretary, April 13, 1991).

22. George Bush, "Security Strategy for the 1990s."
23. James A. Baker III, "A Summons to Leadership," *Dispatch* (Washington, DC: Department of State Bureau of Public Affairs, 1992).
24. U.S. Department of Defense, *1992 Joint Military Net Assessment* (Washington, DC: Joint Chiefs of Staff, August 1992).
25. George Bush, "Remarks by the President to the Asia Society" (Washington, DC: White House Office of the Press Secretary, November 12, 1991).
26. James A. Baker, III, "The U.S. and Japan: Global Partners in a Pacific Community" (Tokyo: U.S. Department of State, Office of the Assistant Secretary/Spokesman, November 11, 1991).
27. Richard H. Solomon, "Sustaining the Dynamic Balance in East Asia and the Pacific," *Current Policy* 1255 (Washington, DC: Department of State Bureau of Public Affairs, February 1990).
28. U.S. Department of Defense, *A Strategic Framework for the Asian Pacific Rim: Looking Toward the 21st Century* (Washington, DC: Office of the Assistant Secretary of Defense for International Security Affairs, April 1990). The report was a requirement contained in the FY 1990 Defense Authorization Act.
29. See "Statement of Paul Wolfowitz, Under Secretary of Defense for Policy before the Senate Armed Services Committee," April 19, 1990, pp. 8-9, ms.
30. Richard H. Solomon, "Asian Security in the 1990s: Integration in Economics, Diversity in Defense," *Dispatch* 1, 10 (Washington, DC: U.S. Department of State, Bureau of Public Affairs, 1990), p. 4.
31. U.S. Department of Defense, *A Strategic Framework for the Asian Pacific Rim: Looking Toward the 21st Century: A Report to Congress* (Washington, DC: Department of Defense, February 28, 1991).
32. U.S. Department of Defense, *A Strategic Framework for the Asian Pacific Rim: Report to Congress 1992* (Washington, DC: Department of Defense, 1992).
33. Not mentioned in the report, but certainly considered by Pentagon planners, was the desire of most Asian countries—including China—for the United States to keep Japan's military defensively oriented. A postwar U.S. strategic goal was to ensure that Japan did not again become a threat in the Pacific.

4

Strategy and Policy Under Bill Clinton

Although personally fond of Taiwan and committed to its defense in the event of a PRC attack, President Bill Clinton set into motion strategies and policies that greatly complicated the Taiwan issue. The principal reason for this was the growing perception of China as a strategically important country in the post-Cold War era. During the Cold War, China derived its strategic importance from the U.S.-PRC-USSR strategic triangle. When the Cold War ended with the unexpected collapse of the Soviet Union, China lost much of its strategic importance in U.S. security. During the Bush administration, American views of China were largely colored by images of Tiananmen Square. The Clinton administration, at first highly critical of the PRC for human rights violations, proliferation, and trade improprieties, soon came to regard Beijing as an essential partner in the creation of a new Pacific community, an extension of Clinton's grand strategy of enlarging the community of market democracies.

Even though Taiwan for some time had been a member of that community, the allure of drawing China into membership dwarfed Taiwan's importance. This seductive vision—combined with the practical necessity of dealing with such a large and powerful nation—resulted in a gradual shift in perceptions on the part of many U.S. officials and observers. By the end of 1998, Taiwan increasingly had come to be seen as something of a "problem" standing in the way of a strategic partnership with China. While supportive of Taiwan's defense in case of blatant PRC aggression and supportive of Taiwan's democratization, many in Washington were not supportive of trends on Taiwan pushing the island toward greater autonomy. Nor did these observers approve of Lee Teng-hui's unceasing efforts to push for Taiwan's wider participation in the international community. These expressions of democratic choice on Taiwan caused great anxiety in Beijing and thus were considered counterproductive to the U.S. goal of encouraging China to play a constructive role in global and regional affairs.

The best way to understand this evolving perception is to see how China fit into U.S. global and regional strategy under Clinton. In this larger perspective of national interests, Taiwan could do little to compete with China in the eyes of an ambitious administration. However, as will be seen in subsequent chapters, the PRC was not nearly as cooperative as many in the administration had hoped.

National Strategy: Engagement and Enlargement

From the outset of his administration, President Clinton's foreign policy was one of American engagement in the world. His strategy of engagement had three main objectives: the restructuring of U.S. military forces to reduce the cost of defense to the American people; cooperation with U.S. allies to encourage the spread and consolidation of democracy and free markets worldwide; and reestablishment of American economic leadership to stimulate global growth and prosperity. The three objectives reflected traditional U.S. interests in security, trade, and the promotion of democratic values and institutions; and the strategy itself was similar to the collective engagement of the Bush administration. One major difference between the Clinton and Bush strategies was the higher priority placed on the economic aspect of U.S. foreign policy under Clinton.

Secretary of State-designate Warren Christopher referred to the three objectives of engagement during his confirmation hearings before the Senate Foreign Relations Committee in January 1993, calling them the "three pillars" of economic growth, military strength, and support for democracy.[1] He further explained the "three pillars" in a speech to the Chicago Council on Foreign Relations in March 1993.[2] He said foreign policy should first and foremost serve the economic needs of the United States. The U.S. government should ensure that foreign markets are open to American goods, services, and investments; and it should press other wealthy nations to do their part to stimulate global economic growth. Second, the armed forces of the United States should be "more agile, mobile, flexible and smart," even while they were being reduced and their budgets shrunk. Third, democracy and respect for human rights should be encouraged abroad, since "history has shown that a world of more democracies is a safer world."

The close connection between economic growth, security, and encouragement of democracy created problems of prioritization for the new administration. By appearing to pursue all three foreign policy objectives simultaneously, the articulation of a coherent national security strategy was made difficult. Moreover, the administration wanted to retain U.S. leadership in the world but to reduce defense and foreign affairs expenditures. This created a dilemma for the administration: how to maintain U.S. influence in global affairs and thereby serve U.S. interests in trade, security, and democracy, while at the same time shrinking resources committed to overseas activities. When in May 1993 a top State Department official told reporters in a background briefing that the Clinton administration would focus primarily on domestic economic issues and redefine "the extent of its commitment commensurate with those realities," an impression was created that Washington was retreating from its global leadership.[3] Quickly countering this perception, Secretary Christopher said in a speech later that month at the University of Minnesota: "The need for American leadership is undiminished. The United States stands prepared to act decisively to protect our interests wherever and whenever necessary. When it is necessary, we will act unilaterally. . . . Where collective responses are more appropriate, we will lead in mobilizing responses. . . . But make no mistake: we will lead."[4]

One of the first efforts by the administration to formulate a coherent foreign policy strategy came from U.S. Ambassador to the United Nations Madeleine K. Albright. She told the Senate in early June 1993 that the administration's approach to Somalia and other difficult Third World crises was an "assertive multilateralism." She explained that the strategy was meant to address the central security issue of the day: how to respond to global situations that required American involvement but that did not directly threaten U.S. interests.[5] Assertive multilateralism implied that the United States would exert its leadership through multilateral channels such as the United Nations to achieve American foreign policy goals and objectives. The types of U.N. action the administration said it would support included humanitarian relief in the case of civil strife or natural disasters, countering threats to democratically elected governments, containing situations where a local conflict might spread to a regional conflagration, and deterring threats to international security.[6]

Assertive multilateralism quickly became discredited as a strategy in the wake of U.S. frustrations in attempting to support U.N. peacekeeping operations in Bosnia and Somalia. However, the essential rationale of the strategy—using multilateral means to serve U.S. interests—remained in place throughout the administration. The problem with the strategy was that, absence an immediate, common threat, other countries did not always accept U.S. leadership. In the U.N. Security Council, Washington found it could nearly always count on the support of London, but frequent opposition came from Moscow, Beijing, and Paris. The United States all too often found itself in a situation where it had to use American troops and other resources in situations where there was not a clear justification for the expenditures based on U.S. interests.

In September 1993 national security adviser Anthony Lake announced at Johns Hopkins University that the United States would adopt a new strategy of "enlargement" to replace the Cold War strategy of containment.[7] This concept of "enlargement," together with the earlier concept of "engagement," became U.S. national security strategy through the end of 1998. Lake's explanation of the national strategy remains one of the best and deserves close review.

In his speech, Lake said U.S. engagement in international affairs throughout the twentieth century was "animated both by calculations of power and by this belief: to the extent democracy and market economics hold sway in other nations, our own nation will be more secure, prosperous and influential, while the broader world will be more humane and peaceful." The essence of U.S. foreign policy was this: "we must promote democracy and market economics in the world—because it protects our interests and security; and because it reflects values that are both American and universal." During the Cold War, the United States contained a global threat to market democracies. Now, Lake explained, "the successor to a doctrine of containment must be a strategy of enlargement—enlargement of the world's free community of market democracies."

There were four components to the strategy of enlargement. First, "we should strengthen the community of major market democracies—including our own—which constitutes the core from which enlargement is proceeding." In this, "renewal starts at home," since Americans must be strong domestically before they have the will or capacity to engage in commitments abroad. In addition, the United States must renew "the bonds among our key democratic allies," especially Europe, Canada, and Japan.

The second imperative of the strategy of enlargement "must be to help democracy and markets expand and survive in other places where we have the strongest security concerns and where we can make the greatest difference." He explained: "This is not a democratic crusade; it is a pragmatic commitment to see freedom take hold where it will help us most." In terms of priorities, "we must target our effort to assist states that affect our strategic interests, such as those with large economies, critical locations, nuclear weapons or the potential to generate refugee flows into our own nation or into key friends and allies." Further, "we must focus our efforts where we have the most leverage. And our efforts must be demand-driven—they must focus on nations whose people are pushing for reform or have already secured it." In this regard, "pursuing enlargement in the Asian Pacific" was of strategic importance to the United States.

The third element of the strategy of enlargement was "to minimize the ability of states outside the circle of democracies and markets to threaten it." Lake observed that "democracy and market economics have always been subversive ideas to those who rule without consent." Consequently, "we should expect the advance of democracy and markets to trigger forceful reactions from those whose power is not popularly derived." In cases of "backlash states," U.S. policy must be "to isolate them diplomatically, militarily, economically and technologically" and, if they pursue policies that "directly threaten our people, our forces, or our vital interests, we clearly must be prepared to strike back decisively and unilaterally.... We must always maintain the military power necessary to deter, or if necessary defeat, aggression by these regimes."

While the United States cannot impose democracy on regimes that appear to be leaning toward liberalization, it can "help steer some of them down that path, while providing penalties that raise the costs of repression and aggressive behavior." China, according to Lake, was one of these borderline states: "It is in the interest of both our nations for China to continue its economic liberalization while respecting the human rights of its people and international norms regarding weapons sales. . . . We seek a stronger relationship with China that reflects both our values and our interests."

The fourth component of the U.S. strategy of enlargement "involves our humanitarian goals, which play an important supporting role in our efforts to expand democracy and markets." Public pressure may drive U.S. humanitarian engagement, but other more pragmatic factors must be considered as well, such as "cost; feasibility; the permanence of the improvement our assistance will bring; the willingness of regional and international bodies to do their part; and the likelihood that our actions will generate broader security benefits for the people and the region in question." Lake said that these practical considerations "suggest there will be relatively few intra-national ethnic conflicts that justify our military intervention."

The Clinton administration formally defined its national security strategy as one of "engagement and enlargement" in White House national security strategy statements beginning in July 1994.[8] As defined in the May 1997 national strategy statement, the fundamental U.S. interests were protection of the lives and safety of Americans; maintenance of the sovereignty of the United States, with its values, institutions and territory intact; and provision for the prosperity of the nation and its people.[9]

In his preface to the documents, President Clinton described engagement and enlargement as "a new national security strategy for this new era," a strategy that reflected both "America's interests and our values." The strategy was "based on enlarging the community of market democracies while deterring and containing a range of threats to our nation, our allies and our interests." Three components comprised the strategy: (1) efforts to enhance U.S. security by maintaining a strong defense capability and promoting cooperative security measures; (2) efforts to open foreign markets and spur global economic growth; and (3) efforts to promote democracy abroad.

East Asia was described as a region of growing importance for U.S. security and prosperity: "nowhere are the strands of our three-pronged strategy more intertwined, nor is the need for continued U.S. engagement more evident. Now more than ever, security, open markets and democracy go hand in hand in our approach to this dynamic region." According to the White House statements, "President Clinton envisions an integrated strategy—a New Pacific Community—which links security requirements with economic realities and our concern for democracy and human rights."

The May 1997 national security strategy statement referred specifically to the PRC, saying: "We must pursue a deeper dialogue with China. An isolated, inward-looking China is not good for America or the world. A China playing its rightful role as a responsible and active member of the international community is. . . . Engaging China is the best way to work on common challenges such as ending nuclear testing—and to deal frankly with fundamental differences such as human rights."

In an excellent summary of the goals of American national security strategy, the document said:

> We week to create conditions in the world where our interests are rarely threatened, and when they are, we have effective means of addressing those threats. In general, we seek a world in which no critical region is dominated by a power hostile to the United States and regions of greatest importance to the U.S. are stable and at peace. We seek a climate where the global economy and open trade are growing, where democratic norms and respect for human rights are increasingly accepted and where terrorism, drug trafficking and international crime do not undermine stability and peaceful relations. And we seek a world where the spread of nuclear, chemical, biological and other potentially destabilizing technologies is minimized, and the international community is willing and able to prevent or respond to calamitous events. This vision of the world is also one in which the United States has close cooperative relations with the world's most influential countries and has the ability to influence the policies and actions of those who can affect our national well-being.

The 1997 document noted that there were three categories of threats to U.S. goals and national security interests: regional or state-centered threats, transnational threats, and threats from weapons of mass destruction. Since the United States could not defeat these threats alone, "a central thrust of our strategy is to adapt our security relationships with key nations around the world to combat these threats to common interests." In addition to building effective coalitions, the United States would continue to strengthen its capabilities to more effectively lead international responses and to be able to act alone where necessary.

A key part of the strategy was "shaping the international environment to prevent or deter threats." Efforts to shape the international environment were carried out through diplomacy, international assistance, arms control, nonproliferation activities, and military activities. As an example of military activities relevant to China, the document noted: "With countries that are neither staunch friends nor known foes, military cooperation often serves as a positive means of engagement, building security relationships today in an effort to keep these countries from becoming adversaries tomorrow."

The White House document defined three categories of interests: (1) Vital interests were "those of broad, overriding importance to the survival, safety and vitality of our nation. Among these are the physical security of our territory and that of our allies, the safety of our citizens, and our economic well-being." The United States would do whatever was necessary to defend these interests. (2) Important national interests were those that "do not affect our national survival, but they do affect our national well-being and the character of the world in which we live. In such cases, we will use our resources to advance these interests insofar as the costs and risks are commensurate with the interests at stake." (3) Humanitarian interests came into play "in the event of natural or manmade disasters or gross violations of human rights." In these situations, the United States might act "because our values demand it"; however, U.S. armed forces would be employed only under limited conditions.

Promoting prosperity was another core objective of U.S. national security policy. In regards to China, the national strategy document said, "The emergence of a politically stable, economically open and secure China is in America's interest. Our focus will be on integrating China into the market-based world economic system. An important part of this process will be opening China's highly protected market through lower border barriers and removal of distorting restraints on economic activity."

The promotion of democracy was also a core objective of Clinton's national security plan. Specifically, the United States would help democratic and free market institutions in countries making the transition to freedom from authoritarian systems, gain wider international support and adherence to universal human rights and democratic principles, and provide humanitarian assistance to alleviate human suffering. The document stated: "Supporting the global movement toward democracy requires a pragmatic and long-term effort focused on both values and institutions. Our goal is a broadening of the community of market democracies, and strengthened international non-governmental movements committed to human rights and democratization."

In relating these documents to the Taiwan conundrum in U.S. China policy, several points should be noted. First, China was frequently mentioned in the context of U.S. national strategy whereas Taiwan was not—an indication of the relative importance of the two Chinese sides from the point of view of the administration. Second, references to China were made in varied contexts, ranging from the need to improve its human rights, to gain its cooperation on non-proliferation issues, to integrate China into the global market. This reflected acknowledgment of the complexity of dealing with China, as well as recognition of the many problems in Sino-American relations. Third, cooperation with China was seen as being important, and perhaps essential, to achieving the goals of Clinton's national security strategy. Fourth, although China's strategic importance had been downgraded as a result of the end of the Cold War, Clinton gave China renewed strategic importance by recognizing it as an essential member of the new world order. And fifth, because of the importance of China in U.S. strategy, and the importance China placed on Taiwan, some in the administration—and certainly many of its academic supporters—came to regard Taiwan as an irritant or spoiler in Sino-American relations.

This sense of Taiwan being an obstacle to the realization of cooperative relations with Beijing was not new; indeed, it had been a perception held by some Americans almost from the outset of the Cold War. What changed during the Clinton administration was the basis of China's importance to U.S. strategy. During the later phases of the Cold War, China was seen as an essential strategic partner to counter the Soviet Union; during Clinton's administration, China was seen as an essential strategic partner to build a new world order. The Taiwan issue was believed by some officials and analysts to be the main factor preventing Sino-American strategic partnership in both instances.

National Military Strategies

President Clinton's strategic concepts and foreign policy principles were translated into defense strategy in a comprehensive "bottom-up" review of U.S. security requirements completed by the Pentagon in the fall of 1993 and in the Quadrennial Defense Review of May 1997. The October 1993 *Report on the Bottom-Up Review* said that the most striking change in the U.S. security environment since the end of the Cold War was "in the nature of the danger to our interests."[10] Previously, the greatest danger to the United States was a global threat from massive Soviet nuclear and conventional forces. Now the threat was more diffuse and included such dangers as the spread of nuclear, biological, and chemical weapons of mass destruction; aggression by major regional powers or ethnic and religious conflict in regions of strategic importance to the United States; the potential failure of democratic reform in the former Soviet Union and the reemergence of authoritarian regimes hostile to the United States; and the potential failure to build a strong and growing U.S. economy.

The report said the United States had an historic opportunity in the post-Cold War period to shape the new world order in ways favorable to American long-term interests. Specifically, the United States could enlarge "the community of nations, guided by a common commitment to democratic principles, free-market economics, and the rule of law." Other opportunities included the expansion of security partnerships with friendly nations, the improvement of regional deterrence, and the protection of U.S. security with fewer resources.

According to the Pentagon, the U.S. grand strategy resulting from these considerations was "a strategy of engagement, prevention, and partnership." (Elsewhere in the document it was called a "strategy of engagement [with] two characteristics: prevention and partnership.") The United States had to pursue a strategy of political, economic, and military engagement in the world to protect and advance its enduring goals. Such a strategy would help would avoid "the risks of global instability and imbalance that could accompany a precipitous U.S. withdrawal from security commitments" and it would help "shape the international environment in ways needed to protect and advance U.S. objectives over the longer term and to prevent threats to our interests from arising." The strategy of engagement

> advocates preventing threats to our interests by promoting democracy, economic growth and free markets, human dignity, and the peaceful resolution of conflict, giving first priority to regions critical to our interests. Our new strategy will also pursue an international partnership for freedom, prosperity, and peace. To succeed,

this partnership will require the contributions of our allies and will depend on our ability to establish fair and equitable political, economic, and military relationships with them.

To achieve its strategic objective, the United States had to build "a coalition of democracies." Fortunately, "the common values and objectives of democratic nations provide a basis for cooperation across a broad spectrum of policy areas, from deterrence and defense against aggression to the promotion of individual and minority rights." Making the most of this "commonality of values and interests" was in the U.S. strategic interest and required the United States to expand and adapt "mechanisms to facilitate policy coordination and cooperation among democracies." Sustaining cooperation among allies necessitated "a continued willingness on the part of the United States to act as a security partner and leader" in regions such as Europe, East Asia, the Near East, and Southwest Asia. At the same time, however, ways had to be found "to sustain our leadership at lower cost." To do this, the United States had to make clear to its allies "the linkages between a sustained U.S. commitment to their security on the one hand, and their actions in such areas as trade policy, technology transfer, and participation in multinational security operations on the other." Yet another key aspect of U.S. coalition strategy was to encourage "the spread of democratic values and institutions" into new areas such as the former Soviet empire.

U.S. defense strategy was defined in terms of appropriate U.S. responses to the major dangers of the post-Cold War era. Most notably, these dangers included the proliferation of weapons of mass destruction, regional conflicts of various kinds, threats to newly democratic states, and threats to the American economy. The Pentagon was primarily concerned with the dangers of proliferation and regional conflicts.

In terms of proliferation, "the acquisition of nuclear weapons by a regional aggressor would pose very serious challenges" to the United States. North Korea, Iraq, and Iran were specifically mentioned as examples of potentially hostile nations pursuing nuclear weapons programs, as well as possessing other weapons of mass destruction (WMD), such as chemical and biological weapons, and advanced means for their delivery. The U.S. strategy to meet this threat involved several dimensions: nonproliferation efforts were designed to prevent the spread of WMD through diplomatic means such as strengthening and widening participation in the Nuclear Non-Proliferation Treaty, implementing the Chemical Weapons Convention and the Missile Technology Control Regime, and negotiating nuclear testing limitations; maintaining the capability for nuclear retaliation against "those who might contemplate the use of weapons of mass destruction"; improving ways to counter proliferation, "such as active and passive defenses against nuclear, biological, and chemical weapons and their delivery systems"; and developing military counterproliferation capabilities "to deter, prevent, or defend against the use of WMD if our nonproliferation efforts fail."

The danger of regional conflicts came from several sources: "large-scale aggression; smaller conflicts; internal strife caused by ethnic, tribal, or religious animosities; state-sponsored terrorism; subversion of friendly governments; insurgencies; and drug trafficking." Each threatened U.S. interests to varying degrees. Specific regional dangers mentioned by the bottom-up review included the possibility of war on the Korean peninsula, efforts by Iraq or Iran to dominate the Persian Gulf region, the continuing civil war in Croatia and Bosnia, struggles in central or eastern Europe, state-sponsored terrorism executed in the United States, and drug trafficking in Latin America. The U.S. strategy to address these varied dangers was "a multifaceted strategy based on defeating aggressors in major regional conflicts, maintaining overseas presence to deter conflicts and provide regional stability, and conducting smaller-scale intervention operations, such as peace enforcement, peacekeeping, humanitarian assistance, and disaster relief to further U.S. interests and objectives."

The defense review said the size of U.S. armed forces necessary to implement the grand strategy of engagement and enlargement would be based on the scenarios of a North Korean attack against South Korea and a remilitarized Iraqi attack against Kuwait and Saudi Arabia. The U.S. force structure in place by the year 1999 should include Army forces of 10 active divisions and 5+ reserve divisions; Navy forces of 11 active aircraft carriers, 1 reserve/training aircraft carrier, 45-55 attack submarines, and 346 ships; Air forces of 13 active fighter wings, 7 reserve fighter wings, and up to 184 bombers (B-52H, B-1, B-2); Marine forces of 3 Marine Expeditionary Forces, comprising 174,000 active personnel and 42,000 reserve personnel; and Strategic nuclear forces of 18 ballistic missile submarines; up to 94 B-52H bombers, 20 B-1 bombers, and 500 single-warhead Minuteman III ICBMs (by 2003).

The most important ground-based presence would remain in Europe and Northeast Asia, with the United States maintaining about 100,000 troops in both theaters. In Northeast Asia the United States would freeze troop levels in South Korea due to the continuing threat from North Korea at about one Army division (comprised of two brigades) and one wing of Air Force fighters. On Okinawa the United States would continue to station a Marine Expeditionary Force and an Army special forces battalion. In Japan the United States would homeport the aircraft carrier *Independence*, the amphibious assault ship *Belleau Wood*, and their support ships. One and one-half wings of Air Force fighters would be stationed in Japan and Okinawa, and the U.S. Seventh Fleet would routinely patrol the Western Pacific.

The Bottom-Up Review stated that the recommended force structure would enable the United States "to carry forward with confidence our strategy of being able to fight and win two major regional conflicts nearly simultaneously." It would not, however, provide adequate forces to maintain overseas presence and to conduct peacekeeping operations during a period of fighting two major regional conflicts. Moreover, the key to the "force's ability to carry out its strategy are a series of critical force enhancements" in areas such as "additional prepositioning of brigade sets of equipment, increased stocks of antiarmor precision-guided munitions, more early-arriving naval air power, and other initiatives."

These forces were slightly smaller than the Bush administration's Base Force, with a "peace dividend" of about $91 billion in savings through fiscal year 1999. There were continued disagreements both in and out of government over whether the proposed reduction in U.S. forces would enable the United States actually to fight two major regional conflicts nearly simultaneously. Debate over the required size, composition, and mission of the armed forces continued throughout the Clinton administration, necessitating another review of U.S. military strategy in 1997.

In May of that year the Department of Defense released the *Report of the Quadrennial Defense Review* (QDR).[11] The QDR attempted to assess American security needs from 1997 to 2015. Essentially, this period would be one of "strategic opportunity" in which many in the world would see the United States "as the security partner of choice." On the other hand, the world would remain "a dangerous and highly uncertain place" in which the United States would likely face a number of significant challenges to its security. The QDR identified five probable categories of security challenges:

1. A variety of regional dangers existed, including "the threat of coercion and large-scale, cross-border aggression against U.S. allies and friends in key regions by hostile states with significant military power," such as Iraq, Iran, and North Korea; the emergence of one or more aspiring regional powers that have both "the desire and the means to challenge U.S. interests militarily"; and "failed or failing states may create instability, internal conflict, and humanitarian crises" within regions where the United States had vital or important interests.
2. "The flow of sensitive information and . . . the spread of advanced technologies that can have military or terrorist uses . . . could destabilize some regions and increase the number of potential adversaries with significant military capabilities." Areas of special concern included "the spread of nuclear, biological, and chemical (NBC) weapons and their means of delivery; information warfare capabilities; advanced conventional weapons; stealth capabilities; unmanned aerial vehicles; and capabilities to access, or deny access to, space."
3. Transnational dangers would continue from terrorists, drug trafficking, international criminal elements, and uncontrolled flows of migrants.
4. An increased danger from "asymmetric attacks," that is, attacks against areas of U.S. vulnerability such as dependence on space-based assets and computers and the open nature of American society. These vulnerabilities made sabotage and terrorism viable options for both large and small-scale adversaries.

5. Various "wild card" scenarios could threaten U.S. security interests. Examples of such threats included the overthrow of friendly governments by hostile forces, the emergence of unforeseen technological threats, and the loss of critical facilities and lines of communications.

The QDR thought it unlikely there would be a "global peer competitor" able to challenge the United States around the world by 2015. It was also unlikely there would be a regional power or coalition of powers able to muster the conventional or nuclear weapons necessary to defeat American armed forces, "once the full military potential of the United States is mobilized and deployed to the region of conflict." According to the study, the United States was expected to remain the world's only superpower throughout the 1997–2015 period. Beyond 2015, however, "there is the possibility that a regional great power or global peer competitor may emerge." Russia and China were the most likely competitors, although "their respective futures are quite uncertain." In regards to China, the QDR said:

> China has the potential to become a major military power in Asia. The United States will continue to engage China, seeking to foster cooperation in areas where our interests overlap and influence it to make a positive contribution to regional stability and act as a responsible member of the international community. China is likely to continue to face a number of internal challenges, including the further development of its economic infrastructure and the tension between a modern market economy and authoritarian political system, that may slow the pace of its military modernization. Moreover, China's efforts to modernize its forces and improve its power-projection capabilities will not go unnoticed, likely spurring concerns from others in the region.

The QDR noted that the fundamental goals of the United States were enduring: "to maintain the sovereignty, political freedom, and independence of the United States, with its values, institutions, and territory intact; to protect the lives and personal safety of Americans, both at home and abroad; and to provide for the well-being and prosperity of the nation and its people." To achieve these basic goals in an increasingly interdependent world, the United States was required to foster an international environment in which critical regions are stable, at peace, and free from domination by hostile powers; the global economy and free trade are growing; democratic norms and respect for human rights are widely accepted; the spread of nuclear, biological, and chemical and other potentially destabilizing technologies is minimized; the international community is willing and able to prevent and, if necessary, respond to calamitous events; and the United States plays a leadership role in the international community, working closely and cooperatively with nations that share its values and goals, and influencing those that can affect U.S. national well-being.

According to the QDR, the best strategy to achieve these goals and the preferred international environment was engagement, a strategy between the opposite sides

Strategy and Policy Under Bill Clinton

of the spectrum of isolationism and the world's policeman. Thus, the essence of U.S. strategy until the year 2015 will be "to help shape the international security environment in ways favorable to U.S. interests, respond to the full spectrum of crises when directed, and prepare now to meet the challenges of an uncertain future." Among the missions the U.S. military could perform in shaping the international environment were promoting regional stability, preventing or reducing conflicts and threats, and deterring aggression and coercion. Missions involved in responding to the full spectrum of crises included deterring aggression and coercion in crisis, conducting smaller-scale contingency operations, and fighting and winning major theater wars. Preparing now for a uncertain future required that the U.S. military pursue a focused modernization effort, exploit the "Revolution in Military Affairs" and the "Revolution in Business Affairs," and prepare insurance policies for various "wild cards" that could emerge between now and 2015.[12]

To implement the U.S. strategy outlined in the QDR, certain military capabilities would be required. These included a balanced mix of overseas presence and power projection forces; quality people at all levels; a globally vigilant intelligence system to provide early strategic warning and timely battlefield information; an effective and secure global communications system; superiority in space; control of the seas and airspace; and robust and effective strategic lift capabilities.

To address the challenges presented by the strategy of "shaping, responding, and preparing," the QDR recommended a defense posture designed "to meet our requirements to shape and respond in the near term, while at the same time transforming U.S. combat capabilities and support structures to shape and respond in the face of future challenges." The resulting U.S. force structure would be as follows by the year 2015:

- Army. There will be 10 active divisions from FY 1997 until 2015. Reserve personnel will decrease from 582,000 in FY 1997 to 530,000 at the end of the QDR.
- Navy. There will be a total of 12 aircraft carriers between FY 1997 and 2015, with 11 active and 1 reserve. Similarly, there will be 10 active air wings and 1 reserve air wing throughout the period, as well as 12 amphibious ready groups through 2015. The number of attack submarines will decrease from 73 to 50, and the number of surface combatants will decrease from 128 to 116.
- Air Force. Active fighter wings will decrease slightly from 13 in FY 1997 to more than 12 at the end of the QDR. Reserve fighter wings will increase from 7 to 8 during the same period. Reserve air defense squadrons will decrease from 10 to 4, and the total number of bombers will decrease from 202 to 187.
- Marine Corps. The number of Marine Expeditionary Forces will remain at 3 throughout the FY 1997 to 2015 period.

- Nuclear forces. U.S. nuclear forces would remain at START I levels until START II was ratified by the Russian Duma and START III negotiations were completed. American nuclear forces would remain at 18 Trident SSBNs, 50 Peacekeeper missiles, 500 Minuteman III missiles, 71 B-52H bombers, and 21 B-2 bombers.

Under the QDR plan, the United States would maintain roughly 100,000 military personnel forward deployed in both Europe and in the Asia-Pacific region. According to the 1997 report: "This force structure gives us an effective capability to conduct a wide range of smaller-scale contingency operations, to redeploy from smaller-scale contingency operations to a major theater war, and in concert with regional allies, to deter and, if necessary, defeat large-scale aggression in two theaters in overlapping time frames. In the event of two nearly simultaneous major theater wars, certain specialized, high-leverage units or unique assets that the United States fields in limited numbers . . . would very likely 'swing' or be redeployed from one theater of conflict to another."

As reflected in the QDR and other national security documents, the United States intended to remain as the world's sole superpower through at least 2015. Despite reductions in the size of its military, the United States would continue to modernize its armed forces to ensure their superiority over any combination of competitors. No global or regional peer to the United States was believed likely to emerge for at least two decades. It was clear that the United States would continue to pursue its global interests and to play a leadership role in global and regional affairs. It could be predicted with a high degree of certainty that the United States would react with force if it perceived its interests as being threatened almost anywhere in the world. The likelihood of the United States retreating into isolationism—or even to reduce its treaty commitments to nations such as Japan and South Korea—was extremely small. At the same time, however, limitations on American resources suggested the probability of the United States seeking to become the world's policeman was also small. Moreover, despite the global reach of self-declared U.S. interests, there was a troubling possibility of overextension of the resources available to protect those interests.

Under the Clinton administration, therefore, the United States would maintain its superpower status and role of regional leader in the Asian Pacific. At the same time, however, Chinese power was seen as increasing to the point where it might challenge the United States sometime in the early twenty-first century. The United States continued to view two of its most fundamental security interests as being the maintenance of a favorable balance of power in the Asian Pacific and the prevention of the rise of any threatening regional hegemon. If China sought to establish itself as the preeminent power of Asia, these U.S. security interests would be directly challenged. The national strategy documents produced during the Clinton administration gave every indication that such a challenge would be met by the United States.

In this context of expanding big power rivalry in the Western Pacific, the danger existed that the Taiwan issue—always there and always volatile—might become a spark for a Sino-American military confrontation. The best way to counter this, the Clinton administration concluded, was to integrate China as a full-fledged great power into regional and global politics. But the cost of such integration was greater sensitivity on the part of Washington to Beijing's concerns over Taiwan. In a policy environment in which emphasis was placed on engaging and integrating China, Taiwan increasingly came to be viewed as more of a hindrance to China's cooperation than as a political-economic model for Beijing to emulate. Almost inevitably, the search was on for a resolution of the Taiwan issue that would further U.S. interests in a more cooperative China. The approaches of Freeman, Perry, and Nye, summarized earlier in Chapter 1, are but a few examples of attempts at resolution from well-meaning and highly respected former Clinton administration officials.

The next section will examine President Clinton's Asian Pacific strategy, especially his goal to create a new Pacific community as part of the global U.S. strategy of engagement and enlargement. The United States invited China to be an active member of the new Pacific community, not as a way to appease Beijing, but as part of a long-term strategy to shape the international environment to reduce the possibility of a future Sino-American conflict. And once again, the Taiwan issue was seen by some as standing in the way of this larger U.S. strategic objective.

Regional Strategy: The New Pacific Community

During his confirmation hearings before the Senate Foreign Relations Committee in March 1993, Winston Lord, former U.S. Ambassador to China and appointed by President Clinton as his assistant secretary of state for East Asian and Pacific affairs, stated that the administration's policy toward Asia would center around the strategy of building a "new Pacific community."[13] He pointed to ten goals that would guide U.S. policy, and these general goals remained consistent through the end of 1998:

1. Forging a revitalized global partnership with Japan that reflected a more mature balance of responsibilities.
2. Erasing the nuclear threat and moving toward peaceful reconciliation on the Korean peninsula.
3. Restoring firm foundations for cooperation with China while pursuing greater political openness and economic reform.
4. Deepening ties with the Association of Southeast Asian Nations (ASEAN) as it broadened its membership and scope.
5. Obtaining the fullest possible accounting of U.S. missing in action as Washington moved to normalize relations with Vietnam.

6. Securing a peaceful, independent, and democratic Cambodia.
7. Strengthening the Asia Pacific Economic Cooperation (APEC) process as the cornerstone of economic cooperation in the Pacific.
8. Developing multilateral forums for security consultations while maintaining U.S. alliances.
9. Spurring regional cooperation on global challenges like the environment, refugees, health, narcotics, nonproliferation, and arms sales.
10. Promoting democracy and human rights.

Lord noted that in the aftermath of the Cold War, economics increasingly supplanted military considerations in the U.S. foreign policy agenda: "More than ever our national security depends on our economic strength. With domestic renewal now America's highest priority, trade and investment are critical. And no region is more central for American economic interests than the world's most dynamic one—Asia." By the time Clinton assumed office in 1991, the Asia-Pacific region was the world's largest consumer market and the biggest export market for the United States. According to Lord, U.S. economic policy toward Asia would focus on four areas: increasing American competitiveness; completing successfully the Uruguay Round of GATT; opening large Asian markets such as Japan and China; and increasing regional cooperation through vehicles such as APEC.

Security continued to be a U.S. concern in Asia. Lord noted, "by virtue of history and geography the United States is the one major power in Asia not viewed as a threat." Furthermore, "virtually every country [in Asia] wants us to maintain our security presence." Since Asian countries tended to view a regional balance of power as essential to their security, a perception stemming from centuries of interaction with their neighbors, Lord said, "a precipitous American military withdrawal would magnify these concerns" and possibly result in "escalating arms races and future confrontations that could threaten U.S. interests."

One new element in U.S. security policy toward Asia was Clinton's emphasis on support for multilateral security discussions, particularly centered in Southeast Asia and Northeast Asia. Lord observed: "Asia is not Europe. We do not envisage a formal CSCE-type [Conference on Security and Cooperation in Europe] structure. But it is time to step up regional discussions on future security issues. We are open-minded on the arenas."

The promotion of democracy was one of President Clinton's "central pillars" of foreign policy. Lord said the United States would not seek to impose the American model on Asian nations, as "each nation must find its own way in its own cultural and historical contexts. But universal principles of freedom and human rights belong to all, the peoples of Asia no less than others." Accordingly, the administration would deal pragmatically with authoritarian governments such as China, but at the same time it would press universal principles and whenever possible work with others to expand freedom.

Strategy and Policy Under Bill Clinton 97

In addition to traditional American concerns with economic prosperity, security, and the promotion of democratic values, Lord pointed to several global issues that were of concern to the United States in Asia. These included the proliferation of dangerous weapons in countries such as North Korea; the high rate of population growth in Asia; severe environmental problems in the region; the potential of major refugee migrations; and the traffic in narcotics, especially from Burma and neighboring countries.

Lord said the Clinton administration would follow a carefully nuanced policy toward China, balancing the PRC's importance as a major country with its continued abuse of human rights and pursuit of certain policies inimical to U.S. interests. Specifically, the administration would

- be guided by the three Sino-American communiqués of 1972, 1979, and 1982
- leave China and Taiwan alone to work out their future relationship, insisting only that the process be peaceful
- not challenge the principle of there being only "one China"
- continue to build unofficial relations with Taiwan based on the 1979 Taiwan Relations Act
- make clear the U.S. humanitarian and commercial stakes in the future of Hong Kong, scheduled to revert to Chinese sovereignty in 1997.

A more complete explanation of what he had in mind in building a new Pacific community was given by the president himself in trips to Japan and Korea in July 1993. In a speech at Waseda University in Tokyo on July 7, Clinton said the new Pacific community would rest upon five building blocks: (1) "a revived partnership between the United States and Japan"; (2) "progress toward more open economies and greater trade"; (3) "support for democracy"; (4) "the firm and continuing commitment of the United States to maintain its treaty alliances"; and (5) the U.S. commitment to maintain "its forward military presence in Japan and Korea and throughout this region."[14] Clinton explained the economic aspects of the new Pacific community and his support for democracy at Waseda University. He discussed security policy before the Korean National Assembly in Seoul on July 10.

In his Waseda speech Clinton noted that Asian imports of $2 trillion were creating "a tripolar world, driven by the Americas, by Europe, and by Asia." Because of the economic growth of the region, Asia was increasing in importance to the United States. To build the new Pacific community, the first economic priority was "to create a new and stronger partnership between the United States and Japan," neither of which "could thrive without the other." The U.S. relationship with Japan would continue to be "the centerpiece of our policy toward the Pacific community," but it did require further opening of Japan's markets. "What the

United States seeks," the president said, "is not managed trade or so-called trade by the numbers, but better results from better rules of trade."

A second economic building bloc for the new Pacific community was "a more open regional and global economy." This meant resistance against protectionist pressures, the successful completion of the Uruguay Round of the GATT negotiations, and the reduction of regional trade barriers. The president suggested an Asian-Pacific free trade area might eventually emerge, noting that "the most promising economic forum we have for debating a lot of these issues in the new Pacific community is the Organization for Asian-Pacific Economic Cooperation, APEC."

The third priority in building a new Pacific community was "to support the wave of democratic reform sweeping across this region." The president said, "It is not Western urging or Western imperialism, but the aspiration of Asian peoples themselves that explain the growing number of democracies and democratic movements in this region. . . . Each of our Pacific nations must pursue progress while maintaining the best of their unique cultures. But there is no cultural justification for torture or tyranny. We refuse to let repression cloak itself in moral relativism. For democracy and human rights are not Occidental yearnings; they are universal yearnings."

President Clinton outlined the fundamentals of security for the new Pacific community in his address to the Korean National Assembly on July 10.[15] Noting that in Asia "security comes first," Clinton assured his audience that the United States intended to remain actively engaged in the region. U.S. engagement and leadership were "the best way for us to deter regional aggression, perpetuate the region's robust economic growth, and secure our own maritime and other interests." There were four security priorities for the new Pacific community: (1) a continued U.S. military commitment to the region, (2) stronger efforts to combat the proliferation of weapons of mass destruction, (3) new regional dialogues on common security challenges, and (4) support for democracy and more open societies throughout the region.

"The bedrock of America's security role in the Asian Pacific," Clinton said, "must be a continued military presence." Reaffirming U.S. bilateral security agreements with Korea, Japan, Australia, the Philippines, and Thailand, the president said these agreements "enable the U.S. Armed Forces to maintain a substantial forward presence. At the same time they have enabled Asia to focus less energy on an arms race and more energy on the peaceful race toward economic development and opportunity for the peoples of this region."

The second security priority for the new Pacific community was "to combat the spread of weapons of mass destruction and their means of delivery." Clinton said the most dangerous threat to Asian security was nuclear proliferation, with North Korea's nuclear program the prime example. North Korea's "indiscriminate" sale of SCUD missiles was cited in particular. In addition, the United States had serious concerns "about China's compliance with international standards against missile proliferation."

The third security priority for the new Pacific community was "to develop multiple new arrangements to meet multiple threats and opportunities." He described these arrangements as "overlapping plates of armor individually providing protection and together covering the full body of our common security concerns." Examples of these new arrangements included groups of nations confronting immediate problems such as North Korea's nuclear program; U.N. peacekeeping operations such as those in Cambodia; and confidence-building measures. Another example was new regional security dialogues. Washington would support the ASEAN post-ministerial conference and a Northeast Asian security forum. In addition, regional economic organizations like APEC could also play a role in easing regional tensions. The goal of all these efforts, the president said, was "to integrate, not isolate, the region's powers."

The fourth security priority in the new Pacific community was democratic progress: "Ultimately, the guarantee of our security must rest in the character and the intentions of the region's nations themselves. That is why our final security priority must be to support the spread of democracy throughout the Asian Pacific. Democracies not only are more likely to meet the needs and respect the rights of their people, they also make better neighbors. They do not wage war on each other, practice terrorism, generate refugees or traffic in drugs and outlaw weapons. They make more reliable partners in trade and in the kind of dialogues we announced today."

A few days later, these same economic, security, and political goals were further explained by Secretary of State Warren Christopher at the annual ASEAN Post-Ministerial Conference held in Singapore. During these meetings, the secretary said the United States wanted to include both China and Russia in expanded security dialogue in the Asian Pacific to help define a new regional balance of power.[16]

China and the New Pacific Community

Whatever one may think of Clinton's grand strategy for a new Pacific community, one thing is clear and of great relevance for this study: China played a central role. For example, as will become clear in subsequent chapters:

- China became, especially after the 1995–1996 crisis in the Taiwan Strait, a critical issue in the redefinition of the U.S.-Japan defense alliance, the centerpiece of American security architecture in the Asian Pacific.
- Opening China's market became a primary goal of U.S. trade policy.
- China was widely perceived in the administration as being both a major obstacle to and a leading candidate for the expansion of the community of market democracies in Asia.

- For its part, China increasingly came to view the U.S. system of security treaties and alliances in Asia as being aimed at the containment of PRC power.
- Many PLA leaders concluded that the U.S. military presence in the Western Pacific was a threat to Chinese security and an outdated remnant of Western hegemony within China's legitimate sphere of influence.

In essence, China posed a major contradiction in Clinton's strategy for the new Pacific community: Beijing's cooperation was required for continued peace and stability in the Western Pacific; yet, other than North Korea, China was the only significant state threatening U.S. interests in the Asian Pacific. To bridge the gap between these two views of China, the administration looked to the engagement argument—that is, increased contact with the PRC will moderate Chinese behavior and help make China a responsible, cooperative member of the international community. Eventually, China might even become a market economy and more democratic, thereby reducing the Chinese threat since democracies do not go to war with each other. The alternative policy, the administration argued, was to treat China as an enemy, an approach which surely would result in China becoming an enemy. Because of the high stakes involved, virtually everyone was willing to give engagement a chance; but it was a cobbled policy built on hope, unattractive alternatives, and unproven assumptions. Under the Clinton administration, China, like Taiwan, became a major conundrum in U.S. policy.

One of the early successes of the new administration was greater integration of Asia-Pacific economies. The instrument chosen by the Clinton administration to advance this objective was the Asia-Pacific Economic Cooperation (APEC) forum, established in November 1989 to promote free trade and investment in the Pacific Basin. The United States was chairman of APEC in 1993, hosting its fifth annual ministerial meeting in Seattle in November of that year. During the Seattle meeting, Mexico and Papua New Guinea were added to the membership, then comprising Australia, New Zealand, the six ASEAN states, Japan, South Korea, China, Taiwan (designated as Chinese Taipei), Hong Kong, Canada, and the United States. The Clinton administration placed high priority on APEC because of the economic importance of its members to the U.S. economy. In 1992, U.S. trade with APEC constituted 54 percent of U.S. global trade, compared to 24 percent with Europe and the former Soviet Union.[17] By 1997, U.S. trade with APEC totaled $955.9 billion, about 65 percent of total U.S. trade; U.S. exports to and imports from APEC had increased about 70 percent since 1990.[18]

Clinton explained his support of APEC in Seattle on November 19, 1993, tying together U.S. security and economic interests.[19] U.S. security, he said, "depends upon enlarging the world's community of market democracies because democracies are more peaceful and constructive partners." He explained that APEC's mission was "to help build connections among economies to promote economic growth." Immediately following the APEC ministerial conference, the president hosted the first-ever meeting of Asian-Pacific leaders on nearby Blake Island. Chinese leader Jiang Zemin attended but Lee Teng-hui could only send a personal representative. Although no substantive agreements were reached, APEC leaders reached a consensus vision of the Asian-Pacific community and initiated an annual summit meeting. The president explained the consensus in this way: "We've agreed that the Asian Pacific region should be a united one, not divided. We've agreed that our economic policies should be opened, not closed. . . . [W]e're helping the Asian Pacific to become a genuine community; not a formal, legal structure, but rather a community of shared interests, shared goals and shared commitment to mutual beneficial cooperation."[20]

In November 1994 in Bogor, Indonesia, APEC leaders announced their "commitment to complete the achievement of our goal of free and open trade and investment in Asia Pacific no later than the year 2020." Because of the differing levels of economic development, APEC industrialized countries would achieve this goal "no later than the year 2010 and developing economies no later than the year 2020."[21]

Clinton's support for APEC demonstrated the close linkage between economic, political, security, and ideological elements of U.S. policy toward Asia in the post-Cold War period. Through a strategy of integration—creating "a common identity rooted in a common purpose"—the administration sought build a sense of community in the Asian Pacific which would further all U.S. interests in the region. Clinton did not attend APEC summits in 1995 and 1998 due to crises abroad and at home, but the APEC process highlighted the fact that a "new web of human and commercial relationships" were being formed in the Pacific and that "growing interdependence within the region is producing shared goals and aspirations and fostering a spirit of common purpose and of community among APEC members."[22] Still, as reflected in the November 1998 APEC meeting in Kuala Lumpur—held under the dark clouds of the Asian financial contagion and Prime Minister Mahathir Mohamad's domestic political difficulties—the goal of economic integration would have problems advancing during times of crisis.

In terms of the respective roles of Taiwan and China in APEC, the ROC was one of the strongest and most open economies in all of Asia, yet it was unable—due to PRC objections—to have membership in its own name (referred to instead as "Chinese Taipei") and its president was denied access to APEC leaders' meetings. China, on the other hand, was also one of Asia's strongest economies but one of its most closed as well. The PRC, however, enjoyed full membership in APEC as "China" and its president routinely participated in the organization's summits. The United States did not oppose these arrangements.

Statements on Regional Policy

The relationship between Clinton's strategy toward the Asian Pacific and perceptions of China's importance could be seen in numerous policy statements by

U.S. government officials through the end of 1998. A few of these statements can be noted to illustrate the point.

The 1994 posture statement of Admiral Charles R. Larson, Commander in Chief, U.S. Pacific Forces (USCINCPAC) provided a useful summary of U.S. security interests and theater military strategy in the Asian Pacific.[23] Admiral Larson defined the U.S. theater military strategy of cooperative engagement as one that "aggressively employs the available means: forces, assets, funds, and programs; in three principal ways: forward presence, strong alliances, and crisis response; to achieve the desired ends of: engagement and participation in peace, deterrence and cooperation in crisis, and unilateral or multilateral victory in conflict." He said, "If we must fight to protect our national interest, then we'll use the necessary force to achieve swift, decisive victory. But it's better to act with friends and allies as partners with a common stake in regional security; and it's best to prevent crises from arising by promoting cooperation and engagement."

In this strategy, U.S. bilateral security relations with key countries were critical, notably relations with Japan, South Korea, and China. In the case of Japan the U.S. bilateral security relationship would remain "the cornerstone of U.S. security policy in the Asia-Pacific region." In the case of South Korea, the continued U.S. military presence in that country was seen as "the single most visible indicator of U.S. commitment to the security of Korea and the long-term stability of Northeast Asia." And in the case of China, the U.S. military wanted to ensure that Beijing would not think of the United States as an enemy. Larson explained the Pentagon's perception on this crucial issue:

> China is at an historic crossroads. A stable, prosperous China which adheres to international standards of human rights and weapons proliferation is good for the region and for the world. We sincerely hope and expect that China will continue to make progress in that direction. At the same time, China faces potentially serious internal challenges, any of which could derail China's progress.
>
> We want a China that does not seek to impose hegemony or exclude the United States from the region. China and the United States have many areas of common interest upon which to build a much stronger relationship. The United States actively supports China's full integration into the international community. We want a China that freely accepts its full range of international responsibilities with respect to human rights, nuclear proliferation safeguards, and environment protection.
>
> China remains intransigent regarding regional issues it sees as bearing on sovereignty. China declares its claims in the South China Sea non-negotiable while denying that others might have a legitimate basis for their claims. Beijing refuses to forswear the use of force regarding Taiwan's future. The United States does not take sides in the various territorial and historical disputes along China's borders. However, we do have significant interests involved. The use of force to resolve these disputes would be highly destabilizing to the region.
>
> In the military arena, China continues to increase the pace and scope of its military modernization program. China's military is not a near-term threat to the United States. However, we do recognize the concerns of many regional nations about the

power projection components of China's military modernization program. We seek sufficient transparency in China's strategic planning and procurement processes to reassure China's neighbors and ourselves that Beijing's military modernization program is limited to legitimate defensive needs and is peaceful in intent.

In the final analysis, I believe the best approach to dealing with China's continuing progress in the political, economic, and military arenas is to engage Beijing in a dialogue aimed at fostering cooperation and avoiding the development of a peer competitor in Asia.

These observations on U.S. security policy were restated in greater detail in the February 1995 release of a third major report in the East Asian strategic initiative series.[24] EASI-III described the U.S. military presence in Asia through the year 2000 as vital to the region's political stability and economic development: "Security is like oxygen: you do not tend to notice it until you begin to lose it. The American security presence has helped provide this 'oxygen' for East Asian development. . . . For the security and prosperity of today to be maintained for the next twenty years, the United States must remain engaged in Asia, committed to peace in the region, and dedicated to strengthening alliances and friendships."[25] The report emphasized that U.S. interests in the region were mutually-reinforcing: "security is necessary for economic growth, security and growth make it more likely that human rights will be honored and democracy will emerge, and democratization makes international conflict less likely because democracies are unlikely to fight one another."

EASI-III noted that the United States intended to pursue several security objectives in the Asian Pacific:

- work with allies and friends to refocus U.S. security relations on new post-Cold War challenges
- strengthen the U.S. bilateral partnership with Japan which serves as the basic mechanism through which the two countries work together to promote regional and global security
- maintain the strong U.S. defense commitment to and ties with the Republic of Korea to deter aggression and preserve peace on the Korean peninsula
- work closely with Australia to pursue the numerous security objectives shared by the two allies
- engage China and support its constructive integration into the international community, including participation in global efforts to limit proliferation of weapons of mass destruction and foster transparency in its defense policy and military activities
- fully implement the Agreed Framework on North Korea's nuclear program while standing ready to respond if North Korea does not meet its obligations or threatens U.S. allies [26]

- work with Russia to develop mutually advantageous approaches that enhance regional stability
- contribute to maintaining peace in the Taiwan Strait
- work with ASEAN and others to explore new cooperative security approaches through the ASEAN Regional Forum[27]
- encourage creation of a sub-regional security dialogue in Northeast Asia
- support efforts by countries in the region to strengthen democracy
- seek the fullest possible accounting of those missing in action from U.S. wars fought in Asia
- prevent the proliferation of weapons of mass destruction
- stem the flow of narcotics.

The report noted that Asia's prosperity and stability were "vital to America's economic health and to the world's security." The U.S. military presence in the region "guarantees the security of sea lanes vital to the flow of Middle East oil, serves to deter armed conflict in the region, and promotes regional cooperation." Most importantly, the U.S. military presence "denies political or economic control of the Asia-Pacific region by a rival, hostile power or coalition of powers, preventing any such group from having command over the vast resources, enormous wealth, and advanced technology of the Asia-Pacific region."

The Pentagon argued that the United States could ill afford a power vacuum in the Asian Pacific and that its continued military presence would ensure that this did not happen.

> If the United States does not provide the central, visible, stabilizing force in the Asia and Pacific region, it is quite possible that another nation might—but not necessarily in a way that meets America's fundamental interests and those of our friends and allies.... If the American presence in Asia were removed, the security of Asia would be imperiled, with consequences for Asia and America alike. Our ability to affect the course of events would be constrained, our markets and our interests would be jeopardized. To benefit from the growth and prosperity of the Asia-Pacific region, the United States must remain fully engaged economically, diplomatically, and militarily.

The need for engagement with China was addressed. The EASI-III report noted that "the rapid growth in China's material strength has raised the importance of China in the Asian security equation." It is "essential for peace, stability, and economic growth in the Asia-Pacific region that China is stable and continues to develop friendly relations with its neighbors." Observing that China's real growth in defense expenditures over the past five years exceeded 40 percent and that the PLA was modernizing its forces across the spectrum of conventional and strategic programs, the Pentagon said:

> China's military posture and development have a great impact on the expectations and behavior of other states in the region. Although China's leaders insist their

military build-up is defensive and commensurate with China's overall economic growth, others in the region cannot be certain of China's intention, particularly in this period of leadership transition. China's military modernization effort is in an early stage, and its long-term goals are unclear. Moreover, it has territorial disputes with several neighboring states. Absent a better understanding of China's plans, capabilities and intentions, other Asian nations may feel a need to respond to China's growing military power. This will be particularly true as China modernizes its strategic forces, naval assets and other forces capable of power projection. The United States and China's neighbors would welcome greater transparency in China's defense programs, strategy and doctrine. [The United States] is enhancing its military dialogue with China in order to promote better mutual understanding, as well as greater transparency and trust.

The report identified several regional issues of security concern to the United States. These included North Korea, Cambodia, territorial disputes, Taiwan, and proliferation. In terms of the Taiwan issue, the report said simply: "Peace in the Taiwan Strait has been the long-standing goal of our policy toward Taiwan. United States arms sales to Taiwan are designed to serve this end. We welcome the growing dialogue between Taipei and Beijing and applaud actions on both sides which increase the possibility of a peaceful resolution of the situation in the Taiwan Strait."

Assistant Secretary Winston Lord provided a valuable overview of U.S. policy toward the Asian Pacific in two presentations in January 1995.[28] These statements confirmed the continuity of administration strategy and policy. In terms of the U.S. goal of security in Asia, Lord said, "Virtually every nation in the region wants us to remain engaged for strategic balance. . . . It is in our interest to do so—to maintain stability, to support our economic interests, and to bolster our diplomatic position."

Key strategic bilateral relationships were maintained with Japan, China, Russia, and Vietnam. In regards to China, Lord said relations were crucial due to the PRC's size, nuclear power, and destiny to become a global economic power. "Our strategic goal is to help integrate the Middle Kingdom into the international community, to encourage it to accept both the benefits and the obligations that come with interdependence and cooperation." He noted that while modest success had been gained in securing China's cooperation on certain issues—international peacekeeping, the North Korean nuclear issue, missile exports, narcotics, alien smuggling and regional security dialogues—there remained important "differences over the sensitive issue of Taiwan, human rights and trade."

Looking to the future, Lord pointed to "the contours of commonality [that] are surfacing in the Pacific." Despite the region's diversity and its many challenges, the administration believed a sense of community was developing in the Pacific. This process of integration was being achieved through trade, telecommunications, transportation, and contact between regional business people, as well as the strengthening of regional governmental institutions such as APEC and the ASEAN

Regional Forum (ARF). Lord said the administration wanted to be part of and to help shape the emerging community of Asian-Pacific nations.

Assistant Secretary of Defense for International Security Affairs Joseph Nye discussed U.S. strategy for East Asia in a speech in San Francisco in March 29, 1995.[29] He described U.S. security strategy for Asia as resting on three pillars: "our alliances, in particular with Japan, the Republic of Korea and Australia; our forward military presence; and our participation in multilateral dialogue." Nye said the essential U.S. interests in Asia were stability, American influence, deterrence of threats, countering aggression, protection of sea lanes for commerce, and counterproliferation.

Nye said one of the key security issues was China's emergence in global affairs. The ISA director noted that "how we work with China over the near term will set the course for the region over the long term." The PRC's "rapid growth in material strength had raised the importance of China in the Asian security equation." The Clinton administration believed "our best prospects for positively influencing its emergence as a global power lie in encouraging trends already under way in China—such as the movement toward a market economy and greater participation in the international economic system. Our policy of comprehensive engagement with China, including military contacts, has the best chance of ensuring we achieve this objective." Nye explained U.S. strategy was not to treat China as an enemy but to work with it as if it were a cooperative major power: "to cast China as an enemy would risk creating a self-fulfilling prophecy. Instead the U.S. has chosen to engage China."

Secretary of Defense William J. Perry addressed U.S. strategy and policy toward the Asian Pacific in two speeches in September and October 1995.[30] He argued before the Japan Society in New York on September 12 that the United States had to continue its postwar strategy of maintaining a strong military presence in the region and firm alliances. "If we were to withdraw our military forces from the region . . . countries will be forced to rethink their needs, with building up defense structures at or near the top of the list. Rapid growth of military structures, plus historic animosities, would be a volatile mix that could quickly destabilize the region, destroying the foundations of economic prosperity and dramatically increasing the risk of regional conflict." This would have serious consequences for U.S. interests, particularly since the U.S. and East Asian economies has become so interdependent. "The best way to prevent or deter conflict is for the U.S. to remain fully engaged in its leadership role by maintaining our forward presence, reinforcing alliances, developing bilateral and multilateral relationships and by developing dialogues that promote confidence- and security-building measures."

In an anecdote Perry disclosed one of the principal reasons why the Clinton administration adhered so tenaciously to its policy of engagement with China. During the Korean nuclear crisis, Perry was in China visiting the PRC minister of defense. On a Monday he told PLA leaders that the United States viewed the North Korean program "as a serious danger to regional security." The Chinese side agreed. Perry told the Chinese leadership that he "thought the North Koreans were about to go ahead with reprocessing the nuclear fuel, and I asked them to use their influence with the North Koreans." The following day, the DPRK agreed to halt its program and met the U.S. terms. Perry said, "It is not clear to me what specific influence the Chinese had. What is clear to me is that on this and other important security issues, China sees our two sets of interests as compatible."

On October 26, 1995, Secretary Perry told the Council on Korean Security Studies in Washington, D.C., that four principal elements comprised U.S. strategy toward the Asian Pacific:

1. A strong military presence. The United States planned to keep about 100,000 troops forward deployed "to provide a security umbrella for the entire region."
2. Promotion of multilateral initiatives to reduce tensions. Participation in joint military training exercises and in joint peacekeeping missions were part of this effort. In addition, the United States used all available multilateral institutions such as ASEAN, ARF, and APEC to encourage greater interaction among regional countries.
3. Engaging China. The United States would not attempt to isolate the PRC but would seek to "encourage China to play a positive role in the region and remain a responsible member of the international community."
4. Alliances. This was the most important component of U.S. security strategy in the region, the cornerstone of which was the U.S.-Japan security alliance. In Northeast Asia, the U.S.-ROK alliance was a vital complement to the alliance with Japan in security matters.

The central role played by China in U.S. strategy and policy toward Asia continued to be acknowledged by the administration during its second term in office. Engagement was seen as essential to draw China into a positive role in helping to maintain peace and stability in East Asia and the Western Pacific, despite the tensions which arose between the United States and China over Taiwan in 1995 and 1996. The Clinton administration consistently adhered to its strategic goal of integrating China into the evolving Pacific community, the building of which comprised U.S. grand strategy toward the region.

The close connection between the strategy of engagement, the new Pacific community, and the integration of China could be seen in statements from the administration during 1997 and 1998. One example was the 1997 White House national security strategy statement, which described U.S. policy toward Asia as pursuit of the vision of a new Pacific community.[31] In particular, the United States pursued the goal of cementing "America's role as a stabilizing force in a more integrated Asia Pacific region."

The national security statement said: "An overarching U.S. interest is China's emergence as a stable, open, secure and peaceful state. The prospects for peace and prosperity in Asia depend heavily on China's role as a responsible member of the international community. China's integration into the international system of rules and norms will influence its own political and economic development, as well as its relations with the rest of the world."

According to the White House document, key U.S. national security objectives with China included sustaining a strategic dialogue with high-level exchanges; promoting the resumption of the cross-Strait dialogue between Beijing and Taipei, and a smooth transition in Hong Kong; gaining PRC adherence to international nonproliferation norms, establishing a comprehensive export control system, and implementing agreements on the peaceful use of nuclear energy; and encouraging the PRC's constructive role in international security affairs through active cooperation in APEC, ARF, and the Northeast Asia Security Dialogue.

These by now common themes were reiterated by Assistant Secretary of State for East Asian and Pacific Affairs Stanley Roth in May 1998 to the House Foreign Relations Committee.[32] Roth noted that peace and stability in East Asia and the Pacific was a "fundamental prerequisite for U.S. security." He emphasized the key importance of security alliances and relationships in the region and pointed to four specific challenges facing the United States: Korea, maritime territorial disputes, the security implications of the Asian financial crisis, and China.

Korea continued to be "one of the most dangerous places on earth," with the United States working closely with the ROK on confidence-building measures to reduce tensions on the peninsula, on responding to the North Korean food crisis, and on nuclear and missile proliferation issues.

Roth said that while the United States takes "no position on the legal merits of individual claims to sovereignty over the various islands and waters" contested in the East and South China Seas, Washington did have "a clear and abiding interest" in disputes over the Paracel Islands and the Spratly Islands. "Freedom of navigation and open sea lines of communication in these waters are ... vital interests for the United States."

The financial crisis which erupted in Asia in 1997 and continued through 1998 "had broad implications for U.S. security policy." Among U.S. concerns were that North Korea might seek to take advantage of the South's economic difficulties by initiating a conflict on the Korean peninsula; that ASEAN might suffer a severe setback due to the economic hardships suffered by Thailand, Indonesia, Malaysia, and the Philippines; and that Indonesia might fall victim to domestic political violence, which would affect many regional organizations such as ASEAN, APEC, and ARF, as well as security issues with which Indonesia was involved.

In terms of China, Roth said demographics, economic achievements, diplomatic prominence, and growing military strength meant that "China in the 21st century will profoundly shape the very nature of our world." He explained that "the Clinton Administration's strategy of comprehensive engagement toward China is based on the premise that it is in our interest to work toward the emergence of China as a major power that is stable, open, and non-aggressive; that embraces political pluralism and international rules of conduct; and that works with us to build a secure international order as well as peace and stability in the Asia-Pacific region." On Taiwan, Roth emphasized U.S. support for dialogue across the Taiwan Strait as the best way to find a peaceful resolution of the Taiwan issue. He said:

> No analysis of security issues involving China would be complete without a discussion of Taiwan. As we saw in March 1996, cross-Strait tensions can rapidly and dangerously escalate. U.S. policy on PRC-Taiwan relations remain unchanged: the United States continues to support peaceful resolution of the Taiwan question, and believes that cross-Strait dialogue provides the most promising mechanism through which to defuse tensions. In that regard, we are encouraged by signs of a renewed willingness on both sides of the Taiwan Strait to resume their dialogue. Last month, representatives from the PRC's ARATS and Taiwan's SEF, the two "unofficial" organizations which carry out direct contacts between Beijing and Taipei, met in Beijing for two days of talks, marking the first real step toward the resumption of formal cross-Strait dialogue since Beijing suspended the talks in June 1995.

Roth said the United States welcomed the renewed dialogue, believing "that improvement in cross-Strait relations will promote peace and stability in the entire region. Any deteriorating in Beijing-Taipei relations along the lines of what took place in 1995–1996 would be costly and counterproductive for both sides, and dangerous to the stability of the entire region."

Thus, in the wake of the Taiwan crisis, the administration placed renewed emphasis on the importance of both sides reaching a peaceful resolution of their differences through dialogue. The administration believed the best way to achieve this goal was to encourage cross-Strait talks and greater compromise on both sides. As will become apparent in the chapters which follow, however, the administration may have vastly underestimated the difficulty of building a bridge between the two Chinese sides.

Conclusion

Bill Clinton, like George Bush, chose a strategy of integration to replace containment as his administration's post-Cold War approach to the new era in international relations.[33] Both presidents concluded that if integration were to work, China would have to be brought into the new world order as a cooperative partner of the United States. And both presidents were willing to go to great lengths to ensure that engagement with the PRC would survive the inevitable twists and turns in Sino-American relations. But this renewed emphasis on the strategic importance of China had at least two unexpected results: first, it brought into sharper focus the many divergent interests between the PRC and the United States, making cooperation and partnership an elusive goal, at least through the time of writing in mid-1999; and second, it created the ironic impression that Taiwan, already a member of the community of market democracies, was an obstacle to the realization of the community of market democracies in Asia because of China's obdurateness over the Taiwan issue.

This chapter focused on Clinton administration strategy on global and regional levels, and China's role in those strategies. The next several chapters will examine in greater detail U.S. policy toward China and Taiwan through 1998. Chapter 5 provides an overview of the Taiwan issue from 1949 through 1992. Chapters 6 through 8 review Clinton administration policy toward China and Taiwan during the crucial period of 1993–1996, while Chapter 9 considers major events in Sino-American relations in 1997 and 1998.

Notes

1. *Washington Post*, January 14, 1993, p. A12.
2. *Washington Post*, March 23, 1993, p. A1.
3. Quoted in *Washington Post*, May 26, 1993, p. A1.
4. *Washington Post*, May 28, 1993, p. A34.
5. *Washington Post*, June 13, 1993, p. A33.
6. The strategy of assertive multilateralism was put into effect through Presidential Decision Directive 13 (PDD-13), signed by President Clinton in August 1993. The directive committed the United States to support U.N. peacemaking and peacekeeping operations, as well as to help the United Nations expand its headquarters staff to better handle international emergencies. The directive rejected U.S. support for a U.N. rapid deployment force, but it did earmark U.S. assets to assist U.N. operations on a case-by-case basis. American commanders serving under U.N. command in these operations were instructed to disobey U.N. orders if they were illegal or "militarily imprudent." For a discussion of PDD-13, see *Washington Post*, August 5, 1993, p. A1. For background to the document, see *Washington Post*, June 18, 1993, p. A1.
7. Anthony Lake, "From Containment to Enlargement," speech delivered to the Johns Hopkins University School of Advanced International Studies, Washington, D.C., September 21, 1993, ms.
8. See *A National Security Strategy of Engagement and Enlargement* (Washington, DC: The White House, July 1994); ibid., February 1995.
9. *A National Security Strategy for a New Century* (Washington, DC: The White House, May 1997), p. 5.
10. Les Aspin, *Report on the Bottom-Up Review* (Washington, DC: Department of Defense, October 1993). In most areas of strategy and policy, the review was similar to the 1992 JMNA report of the Bush administration.
11. William S. Cohen, *Report of the Quadrennial Defense Review* (Washington, DC: Department of Defense, May 1997).
12. The revolution in military affairs (RMA) and in business affairs referred to exploiting new technologies to give U.S. forces battlefield superiority and reengineering defense infrastructure and support activities to increase efficiency. The RMA was especially critical and involved the Joint Chiefs of Staff's blueprint for future military operations found in *Joint Vision 2010*. One of the key elements of *Joint Vision 2010* was to "create and exploit

information superiority to achieve full spectrum dominance through the synergy of four new operational concepts: dominant maneuver, precision engagement, focused logistics, and full-dimensional protection." China was also very concerned with modernizing the PLA along lines required by the revolution in military affairs. See Michael Pillsbury, ed., *Chinese Views of Future Warfare* (Washington, DC: National Defense University Press, 1997).

13. Winston Lord, "A New Pacific Community: Ten Goals for American Policy," opening statement at confirmation hearings for Assistant Secretary of State, Bureau of East Asian and Pacific Affairs, Senate Foreign Relations Committee, March 31, 1993, ms.

14. "Remarks by the President to Students and Faculty of Waseda University" (Tokyo: The White House, Office of the Press Secretary, July 7, 1993).

15. "Remarks by the President in Address to the National Assembly of the Republic of Korea" (Seoul: The White House, Office of the Press Secretary, July 10, 1993).

16. See "Statement of Secretary of State Warren Christopher at the ASEAN Post Ministerial Conference, Six-plus-Seven Open Session" (Singapore: U.S. Department of State, Office of the Spokesman, July 26, 1993).

17. For details of the economic interdependency in 1992, see Raphael Cung, "The United States and The Asia-Pacific Economic Cooperation Forum (APEC)," *Business America* 114, 7 (April 5, 1993), pp. 2-4.

18. "Asia-Pacific Economic Cooperation (APEC): Fact Sheet" (Washington, DC: Bureau of East Asian and Pacific Affairs, U.S. Department of State, October 26, 1998).

19. "Remarks by the President to Seattle APEC Host Committee" (Seattle: The White House, Office of the Press Secretary, November 19, 1993).

20. "Remarks by the President in Statement Regarding APEC Leader Meeting, Blake Island, Washington" (Seattle: The White House, Office of the Press Secretary, November 20, 1993).

21. "APEC Economic Leaders' Declaration of Common Resolve," Bogor, Indonesia, November 15, 1994.

22. From "Joint Statement of the Asia-Pacific Economic Cooperation Ministerial Meeting, November 17-19, 1993, Seattle, Washington."

23. Admiral Charles R. Larson, "United States Pacific Command: Posture Statement, 1994" (Honolulu: United States Pacific Command, March 1994).

24. *United States Security Strategy for the East Asia-Pacific Region* (Washington, DC: Department of Defense, Office of International Security Affairs, February 1995).

25. According to the document, six core U.S. security commitments in the Asian Pacific would remain "inviolable" in the 1990s: the U.S.-Japan security treaty of September 8, 1951; U.S.-South Korean security treaty of October 1, 1953; U.S.-Australia security treaty of September 1, 1951; U.S.-Philippine security treaty of August 30, 1951; U.S.-Thailand security treaty of September 8, 1954; and Compact of Free Association with the Republic of the Marshall Islands, the Federated States of Micronesia, and the Republic of Palau of November 4, 1986.

26. In October 1994, after sixteen months of intensive negotiations, Washington and Pyongyang reached an important, if controversial, agreement on the Korean nuclear program. Under the agreement, North Korea halted the operation of its existing graphite reactor and stopped construction on two larger gas graphite reactors. In their place Pyongyang would receive from the United States and its South Korean and Japanese allies nuclear components for light water reactors whose plutonium would be less useful in fabricating nuclear weapons. To compensate North Korea for the loss of energy production

in halting operation of its existing and projected nuclear reactors, the three allies would provide Pyongyang with 500,000 tons of heavy fuel oil annually. See "U.S.-Democratic People's Republic of Korea Agreed Framework," *Fact Sheet*, U.S. Arms Control and Disarmament Agency, Geneva, Switzerland, October 21, 1994.

27. The ASEAN Regional Forum (ARF) was the region's first broadly based, consultative body concerned with security issues. It first meeting was held in July 1994 with the United States, Canada, Japan, South Korea, Australia, New Zealand, China, Russia, Vietnam, Laos, the European Union, Papua New Guinea, Malaysia, Indonesia, Singapore, Brunei, Thailand, and the Philippines participating.

28. Winston Lord, "Building a Pacific Community: Statement before the Commonwealth Club, San Francisco, California, January 12, 1995" U.S. Department of State *Dispatch* 6, 3 (January 16, 1995), pp. 34-40; Winston Lord, "U.S. Policy Toward East Asia and the Pacific," prepared statement given to the Asia and Pacific Affairs Subcommittee, House International Relations Committee, February 9, 1995, ms.

29. Joseph S. Nye Jr., "Strategy for East Asia and the U.S.-Japan Security Alliance," speech to Pacific Forum Center for Strategic and International Studies/Japanese Institute of International Affairs Conference, San Francisco, March 29, 1995, *Defense Issues* 10, 35 (n.d.).

30. William J. Perry, "Ever Vigilant in the Asia-Pacific Region," remarks by the Secretary of Defense to the Japan Society, New York City, September 12, 1995, *Defense Issues* 10, 87 (n.d.); and "Alliance Forged in War, Tempered by Regional Challenges," prepared remarks to the Council on Korean Security Studies, Washington, D.C., October 26, 1995, *Defense Issues* 10, 100 (n.d.).

31. *A National Security Strategy for a New Century*, pp. 23-25.

32. "Stanley O. Roth, Assistant Secretary of State for East Asian and Pacific Affairs, Testimony before the Subcommittee on East Asian and Pacific Affairs of the House Foreign Relations Committee, May 7, 1998," ms.

33. For an early argument in favor of integration as U.S. grand strategy in the Pacific, see the author's "Beyond Containment in Asia: An American Strategy for the 1990s," *Korean Journal of Defense Analysis* 3, 2 (Winter 1991), pp. 83-104.

5

U.S. Policy Toward China and Taiwan, 1949–1992

The Taiwan conundrum in U.S. China policy is not a recent phenomena. It has roots in the Second World War, when the United States was allied with the Nationalist government of Chiang Kai-shek but sought the assistance of the Chinese Communists under Mao Zedong to prosecute the war against the Japanese. The emotions of that period ran high, with accusations of betrayal of U.S. interests from those who supported Chiang and those who urged greater support for Mao's rural reformers. The Chinese civil war continued after the cessation of hostilities with Japan, and U.S. involvement in that struggle became mired in differing perceptions of the Nationalist and the Communists. U.S. policy was condemned from those who believed not enough was being done to support the Nationalists in their life-and-death struggle with the Communists and from those who saw U.S. aid to the Nationalists being wasted in a sink hole of corruption and mismanagement on the part of Chiang and his government. In 1949 after their defeat by the Communists, remnants of Chiang's government and military retreated to the island of Taiwan, administered by the Nationalists after the surrender of Japan.

Historical Overview

For centuries Taiwan had a loose attachment to China, with a Chinese expeditionary force sent to the island in 239 A.D. and Chinese emigration occurring from at least the Tang dynasty (618–907), but the island never was considered a vital part of the Middle Kingdom. During the sixteenth century the Portuguese gave the island the name Formosa, and during the seventeenth century the Spanish and Dutch occupied parts of Taiwan, with the Dutch establishing control after 1642.

The Dutch were forced to withdraw in 1663 by the Ming rebel and pirate Koxinga (Cheng Ch'eng-kung). Twenty years later, the Manchu of the Ch'ing (Qing) dynasty forced the heirs of Koxinga to surrender, and Taiwan formally became part of Fukien (Fujian) province. The Taiwan ports of Keelung and Tamsui became ports of call for Western ships in the mid-1850s, and Commodore Oliver Perry and Townsend Harris suggested that the United States establish a presence on Taiwan or purchase it outright from the Chinese government.

After its victory over China in the 1894-1895 Sino-Japanese War, Japan was given Taiwan "in perpetuity" in the 1895 Treaty of Shimonoseki. Virtually all ties between Taiwan and the mainland of China were cut off by Japan during the fifty years of its administration, and Japan transformed the island into a prosperous colony. Tokyo used Taiwan as a key base of military operations during World War II, particularly toward Southeast Asia. The United States bombed Taiwan during the war, and there was consideration of invading the island as a stepping stone to Japan. But the cost of the operation—an estimated 300,000 American troops to defeat 32,000 Japanese soldiers on the island—was deemed too high, and Okinawa became the target of U.S. amphibious operations.[1]

In the Cairo Conference of 1943 and the Potsdam Declaration of 1945, the United States agreed to return Taiwan to China. Even today, there is some disagreement over the legitimacy of Nationalist rule over Taiwan, but the reality is that Chiang's troops did occupy Taiwan and assumed political control of the island in October 1945. Since then, Taiwan has been ruled by the government of the Republic of China with the Kuomintang as the ruling party. Unfortunately, that rule was not always benign or enlightened. The infamous February 28, 1947, incident occurred when riots broke out throughout the island after Nationalist security personnel killed a Taiwanese street vendor. Thousands of Taiwanese were killed, as well as numerous mainlanders, in the riots and crackdowns that followed. Despite the fact that the official responsible for the disaster was ousted and later executed by Chiang Kai-shek, the damage to Taiwanese-mainlander relations had been done. The resentment many Taiwanese families feel toward the mainlanders is palatable still today, although the years of intermingling, intermarriage, the lifting of martial law, official apologies, and the fact that Taiwanese now largely control the destiny of the island have blunted somewhat the bitter memories of the past. The desire of the Taiwanese to be independent of mainlander Chinese control—Communist or Nationalist—in large measure stems from the heavy-handed KMT rule from 1945 until the 1980s.

Many Americans, including a large percentage of Congress, blamed the Harry Truman administration, especially the State Department, for the "loss" of China to the Communists in 1949.[2] In response to this criticism, the State Department issued a "white paper" on U.S. relations with China in August 1949 saying responsibility for the collapse of the Republic of China was due mostly to inefficiency on the part of the Nationalist government.[3]

In December 1949 the National Security Council in document NSC 48/2 recommended to President Truman that the United States use diplomatic and economic means to deny Formosa (Taiwan) and the Pescadores to the Chinese Communists.[4] But the report also recognized that these means might fail. The NSC noted that the Joint Chiefs of Staff considered Formosa to be of strategic importance to the United States, but that "the strategic importance of Formosa does not justify overt military action . . . so long as the present disparity between our military strength and our global obligations exists."

In January 1950 President Truman announced that the United States would not give military assistance or advice or military people to the forces on Taiwan.[5] Also in January, Secretary of State Dean Acheson declared that the United States was establishing a "defensive perimeter" running from Aleutian Islands to Japan, the Ryukyu Islands, and the Philippines. Both Korea and Taiwan were excluded.[6]

In the 1948-1949 period the Truman administration sent several signals to Mao Zedong's communist movement and to the new PRC regime established in October 1949 that Washington was willing to formalize contact. These initiatives were rejected, however, apparently because Mao had already decided to align with Moscow.[7] In February 1950 China signed a thirty-year treaty of friendship, alliance, and mutual assistance with the Soviet Union.

Many in the Congress were exasperated with the administration's China policy. In March 1950 Senator Joseph R. McCarthy began to attack alleged communist members and sympathizers in the State Department and in the American academic community whom he felt were responsible for losing China to the communists. These charges fell on some guilty and many innocent people, and left a lasting legacy of political sensitivity when dealing with the Taiwan and China issues in American politics—with Congress and the State Department often not seeing eye-to-eye.

Domestic disagreement over China policy was overshadowed in June 1950, when North Korea launched a surprise attack against South Korea. On June 25, while the Soviet Union was boycotting Security Council meetings in an attempt to have the PRC replace the ROC in the United Nations, the council adopted a resolution calling for a cease fire and withdrawal of North Korean troops. Two days later, President Truman sent the Seventh Fleet into the Taiwan Strait, proclaiming:

> The attack upon Korea makes it plain beyond all doubt that communism has passed beyond the use of subversion to conquer independent nations and will use armed invasion and war. It has defied the orders of the Security Council of the United Nations issued to preserve international peace and security. In these circumstances, the occupation of Formosa by communist forces would be a direct threat to the security of the Pacific area and to the United States forces performing their lawful and necessary functions in that area.
>
> Accordingly, I have ordered the Seventh Fleet to prevent any attack on Formosa. As a corollary of this action, I am calling upon the Chinese Government on Formosa

to cease all air and sea operations against the mainland. The Seventh Fleet will see that this is done. The determination of the future status of Formosa must await the restoration of security in the Pacific, a peace settlement with Japan, or consideration by the United Nations.[8]

The decision to send the Seventh Fleet into the Taiwan Strait was a major reversal in U.S. policy toward China and Taiwan. Thereafter, Washington determined that preventing the collapse of the Nationalist government on Taiwan was in U.S. interests; and the United States took military, political, and economic steps to ensure ROC survival. At least through the early 1970s, Taiwan also became a critical component of the U.S. strategy of containment in the Western Pacific. With the outbreak of the Korean conflict, U.S. policy toward the PRC became hardened, with Beijing viewed as a Cold War enemy and the source of much of the revolutionary turmoil in Southeast Asia. An embargo on U.S. trade with China was put into effect in December 1950, remaining in place until 1971 when it was lifted by President Richard Nixon.

U.S. economic and military assistance to the ROC played a major role in that government's ability to survive and eventually prosper on Taiwan. Total U.S. aid from 1949 exceeded $5.9 billion, with $1.7 billion in economic assistance and $4.2 billion in military assistance. U.S. economic assistance was phased out in 1965 and military assistance ended in the mid-1970s.[9]

Although the United States recognized the ROC as the legitimate government of China from 1951, the Truman administration was careful not to expand the Korean War to the Chinese mainland. Truman turned down the Nationalist offer to open an offensive against the communists on the mainland, a proposal strongly supported by General Douglas MacArthur, who felt the president was not allowing him to achieve a military victory on the peninsula. MacArthur also considered Taiwan an "unsinkable aircraft carrier" and advised turning the island into an American stronghold on the coast of Asia. These sentiments found support among many Americans, and thousands participated in various pro-ROC organizations to lobby for U.S. assistance to Taiwan. Truman's policy toward China became even more unpopular after the PRC invasion of Tibet in 1950-1951 and Beijing's statements that it intended to liberate Taiwan and to aid the communists in Indochina and the Philippines. As a result, China policy became a heated political issue in the presidential campaign of 1952, as it did during the elections of 1956, 1960, 1964, 1968, 1980, 1992, and perhaps in 2000.

The Republican victory under Dwight D. Eisenhower brought a change in U.S. policy toward China and Taiwan. President Eisenhower announced in his first State of the Union message that the Seventh Fleet would no longer prevent the Nationalists from attacking the mainland. That statement, plus his comments in July 1953 that he might use nuclear weapons against China, were thought to pressure Beijing into signing the July 1953 armistice ending the Korean War.

As the Korean War ended, however, a new crisis arose in French Indochina. The United States decided not to aid the French in retaining control of their colony, but Washington did see the Viet Minh victory as a threat to U.S. security interests in Southeast Asia. In September 1954 Secretary of State John Foster Dulles helped to create the Southeast Asian Treaty Organization as part of an alliance system designed to contain China.

Taiwan was brought formally into that alliance structure in December 1954, when Washington and Taipei signed the U.S.-ROC Mutual Defense Treaty. The treaty with Taiwan followed similar arrangements with the Philippines, South Korea, and Japan. The U.S.-ROC treaty came largely in response to the September 1954 PRC attack against Quemoy and other offshore islands. The treaty gave the United States the right to dispose forces around Taiwan and the Pescadores to aid in their defense. However, the treaty did not include the offshore islands of Quemoy (Kinmen) and Matsu (Mazu), both of which were near the coast of Fujian Province; nor were the offshore islands included in the Taiwan Relations Act some twenty-five years later. The United States attempted unsuccessfully to convince Chiang Kai-shek to abandon these offshore islands, but the ROC leader refused, seeing them—as did Mao Zedong—as evidence of the ROC claim of there being only one China and Taiwan as being part of China. In January 1955 Congress passed the Formosa Resolution, giving the president the authority to defend Quemoy and Matsu if he felt it necessary for the security of Taiwan and the Pescadores. This was done during the Quemoy crises of 1958.

The Vietnam War had an important impact on U.S. relations with both China and Taiwan. Even though the United States viewed the PRC as a threat, there was a perception long held in Washington that it would be in U.S. strategic interests to drive a wedge between Beijing and Moscow. Accordingly, the United States kept open a line of communication with Beijing first in Vienna in 1954 and thereafter in Warsaw. The ambassadorial discussions did not achieve a great deal, but they were valuable in keeping the two sides informed as to each other's intentions and policies. Even during these talks, there was fundamental disagreement over Taiwan: the U.S. side wanting Beijing to renounce the use of force in resolving the issue, and the PRC refusing to give such a promise because the Taiwan issue was, in Beijing's view, an internal affair of China.

One of the main justifications for U.S. involvement in the Vietnam War was to prevent the expansion of Chinese influence among the communist movements in Southeast Asia. During the height of the war, China repeatedly warned the United States not to invade North Vietnam. The United States did not do so, partially influenced by its experience in the Korean War when Beijing warned Washington not to come too close to the Yalu River.

As the Vietnam War dragged on and became politically divisive at home, debate began anew over U.S. policy toward China. In 1966 the Senate Foreign Relations Committee held hearings on U.S. China policy, and strong recommendations were heard that U.S. policy on containing the PRC be lifted. One of the popular ideas in circulation at the time was that the United States should adopt a "two-Chinas" policy, in which Washington would retain its official relationship with the ROC but also have official relations with Beijing, permitting both the ROC and PRC to have seats in the United Nations. Indeed, Richard Nixon said he preferred the "two-Chinas" solution, but found it untenable due to opposition from President Chiang Kai-shek, who insisted that there was only one China (the Republic of China) and that Taiwan was part of China.[10]

In 1969 there was a series of military clashes along the Sino-Soviet border, which brought the Sino-Soviet split into the open. According to Henry Kissinger, Soviet Ambassador to the United States Anatoly Dobrynin floated the idea that now was the time for both the United States and the Soviet Union to intervene directly in Chinese affairs to eliminate the growing PRC threat.[11] Seeing an opportunity to signal China of its peaceful intentions, the Nixon administration rejected the Soviet offer and instead indicated through various channels that it would view a Soviet attack on China as being against U.S. interests. Other friendly gestures by the administration included the easing of trade and travel restrictions between the United States and China, as well as public statements by Nixon that he wished a more normal and constructive relationship with the PRC. The shifts in policy and more favorable comments about China from the Nixon administration paid off in July 1971, when Kissinger was able to travel secretly to Beijing for meetings with Zhou Enlai. The long process of normalization of Sino-American relations had begun, with the elements of the current Taiwan conundrum already well established.

Principles Governing the Taiwan Issue

From 1971 until the present, Sino-American relations have endured many ups and downs, often due to disagreement over the Taiwan issue. Gradually, certain principles governing the Taiwan issue evolved. The three U.S.-PRC joint communiqués on which Sino-American relations were built—the Shanghai Communiqué of February 28, 1972, the communiqué on the establishment of U.S.-PRC diplomatic relations on January 1, 1979, and the communiqué of August 17, 1982—were agreed to only after intense negotiations over the status of Taiwan. The basic principles contained in these documents continue to be cited by both Washington and Beijing as pillars in their relationship. Perhaps more important from the U.S. side—since it is the law of the land and the communiqués are but statements of administration policy—are the policy guidelines found in the 1979 Taiwan Relations Act (TRA).

These basic principles and guidelines governing the Taiwan issue in Sino-American relations bear repeating here. Usually they are cited verbatim below, but sometimes they are summarized for readability. As will be seen, the principles provide ample justification for continued American support to Taiwan as well as closer relations with Beijing, adding yet another layer to the conundrum of Taiwan in U.S. China policy.

Shanghai Communiqué

In the case of the 1972 Shanghai Communiqué, the two sides agreed to state separately their respective views of the Taiwan question. Most of these statements remain the bedrock of both government's position on the Taiwan issue today. China made the following points:

- The Taiwan question is the crucial question obstructing the normalization of relations between China and the United States.
- The Government of the People's Republic of China is the sole legal government of China.
- Taiwan is a province of China which has long been returned to the motherland.
- The liberation of Taiwan is China's internal affair in which no other country has the right to interfere.
- All U.S. forces and military installations must be withdrawn from Taiwan.
- The Chinese Government firmly opposes any activities which aim at the creation of "one China, one Taiwan," "one China, two governments," "two Chinas," an "independent Taiwan" or that advocate that "the status of Taiwan remains to be determined."

For its part, the U.S. side declared:

- The United States acknowledges that all Chinese on either side of the Taiwan Strait maintain there is but one China and that Taiwan is part of China.
- The United States Government does not challenge that Chinese position.
- The United States reaffirms its interest in a peaceful settlement of the Taiwan question by the Chinese themselves.
- With this prospect in mind, the United States affirms the ultimate objective of the withdrawal of all U.S. forces and military installations from Taiwan.
- In the meantime, the United States will progressively reduce its forces and military installations on Taiwan as tensions in the area diminish.

Omitting those points regarding U.S. military personnel and installations, which were removed as part of the 1978-1979 Sino-American normalization agreement, the non-negotiable principles of the two sides can be summarized as follows: The PRC claimed to be the sole legal government of China, considered Taiwan to be Chinese territory, and said it would not tolerate U.S. interference in the eventual reunification of China. The United States acknowledged and did not challenge the view of both the PRC and ROC governments that there was but one China and that Taiwan was Chinese territory. The sole U.S. interest was that the Taiwan issue be settled peacefully by the Chinese themselves. These principles reflected fundamental PRC and U.S. interests over which little compromise is possible even today.

It is important to note that the United States only acknowledged the Chinese position that Taiwan was part of China; the United States did not accept the Chinese position as being correct. As in subsequent statements of U.S. policy, the "Chinese" position referred to was the view held by both the PRC and the ROC governments that Taiwan was part of China. Of course, "China" to Beijing was the People's Republic of China, while "China" to Taipei was the Republic of China. Moreover, the "Chinese" on both sides of the Taiwan Strait did not take into account the views of the majority Taiwanese population of Taiwan. Thus, the so-called "one-China" principle is itself ambiguous, open to differing interpretations, ignores the views of the Taiwanese, and remains a source of much controversy in U.S.-PRC-ROC relations today. That being said, however, the "one-China" principle adhered to by Washington, Beijing, and Taipei enabled Sino-American normalization to proceed and, after 1979, provided cover for the United States to follow a dual-track policy of maintaining close but unofficial relations with Taiwan even while diplomatically recognizing the PRC.

The semantics of "one China" did not really pose a problem until after the mid-1980s, when democratic reform on Taiwan allowed the majority Taiwanese population to claim that their views were not being adequately considered. The term "Chinese" on both sides of the Taiwan Strait, it was argued by some, actually referred to mainlanders living on the two sides; it did not include the Taiwanese, many of whom did not consider themselves Chinese and who doubted Taiwan was really part of China. In the 1990s, as the Taiwanese rapidly gained control over the island's political parties, government, and institutions, disagreement on Taiwan over the validity of the "one-China" principle added elements of uncertainty and danger to the Taiwan conundrum.

The period between 1972 and 1977 were turbulent ones in the domestic politics of both the United States and China. The two sides established liaison offices in each other's capitals in 1973 and extended diplomatic immunities and privileges, but the Watergate affair and its aftermath in the United States and the leadership transition in China from Mao Zedong to the Gang of Four, Hua Guofeng, and finally Deng Xiaoping did not allow much progress to be made toward normalization of Sino-American relations.

Normalization Agreement

President Gerald Ford retained Henry Kissinger as his Secretary of State and sent him to Beijing in November 1974 and October 1975 to explore the prospects of normalization. Ford himself visited China in December 1975. On all occasions the Americans found Chinese leaders inflexible, repeating demands made since early 1973 that three conditions had to be met for the normalization of relations: termination of official U.S. relations with the ROC, termination of the 1954 U.S.-ROC Mutual Defense Treaty, and withdrawal of American troops and military installations from Taiwan. These demands were unacceptable to Nixon and Ford, who were politically handicapped in any case by Watergate and by the 1975 fall of Laos, Cambodia, and South Vietnam.

Normalization of Sino-American relations could only proceed under a new president, and Jimmy Carter came to office in 1977 with the intention of establishing diplomatic relations with Beijing.[12] Fortunately for Carter, his election closely coincided with the 1976 arrest of the Gang of Four by Hua Guofeng and the subsequent rehabilitation of Deng Xiaoping the following year. At first, President Carter suggested through Secretary of State Cyrus Vance that an American embassy be established in Beijing while a liaison office, similar to that then existing in Washington and Beijing, be established in Taipei. The PRC rejected this proposal, one of the last formal efforts by the United States to attempt a "two-Chinas" or "one China, one Taiwan" solution to the Taiwan question.

The incentive for Washington and Beijing to move more rapidly toward normalization gained momentum through the activities of the Soviet Union, which supported Vietnam's invasion of Cambodia in January 1978 and deployed SS-20 mobile intermediate-range ballistic missiles along the Sino-Soviet border. In the United States, National Security Adviser Zbigniew Brzezinski forcefully argued that U.S. strategic cooperation with the PRC was necessary to counter the Soviet Union.

According to Carter's account of events, the United States informed China during the Huang Hua-Leonard Woodcock talks—the discussions working out the details of normalization—that Washington would not press Beijing for a pledge of the nonuse of force in the Taiwan Strait but that it would continue to sell defensive arms to Taiwan. The Carter administration insisted that Beijing not contradict U.S. statements that the Taiwan issue should be settled peacefully and with patience. In late November 1978 the Chinese leadership accepted these conditions for normalization, as well as reached decisions resulting in the final consolidation of Deng Xiaoping's power and the use of Chinese military force against Vietnam to punish it for its invasion of Cambodia.[13]

On December 15, 1978, the United States and the People's Republic of China announced they would exchange diplomatic recognition on January 1, 1979. As noted momentarily, the PRC also softened its policy toward Taipei, calling for "peaceful reunification" rather than the "liberation" of Taiwan. During his highly successful trip to the United States in January 1979, Deng Xiaoping said that the only two circumstances under which the PRC would use force against Taiwan would be "if there was an extended period of no negotiation or if the Soviet Union entered Taiwan."[14]

In the joint communiqué on the establishment of U.S.-PRC diplomatic relations on January 1, 1979, and the accompanying official statements by both governments, the United States and China furthered defined their views on the Taiwan issue. The principles noted in the joint communiqué included the following:

- The United States recognized the Government of the People's Republic of China as the sole legal Government of China.
- Within this context, the people of the United States will maintain cultural, commercial, and other unofficial relations with the people of Taiwan.
- The United States and the PRC reaffirmed the principles agreed on by the two sides in the Shanghai Communiqué.
- The United States acknowledged the Chinese position that there is but one China and Taiwan is part of China.

Other principles intended by the Carter administration to govern U.S. relations with Beijing and Taipei were found in the official American statement accompanying the communiqué. These principles included the termination by the United States of the 1954 Mutual Defense Treaty in accordance to the provisions of the treaty, which allowed either party to end the treaty with one year's notification; the withdrawal of remaining American military personnel from Taiwan within four months; adjustments to U.S. laws and regulations to permit the maintenance of non-governmental relationships with the people of Taiwan; and statements to the effect that the United States had confidence that the people of Taiwan faced a peaceful and prosperous future, and that the United States had a continued interest in the peaceful resolution of the Taiwan issue, expecting that the issue will be settled peacefully by the Chinese themselves.

In its official statement, Beijing reiterated the following in regards to Taiwan: the Government of the People's Republic of China is the sole legal government of China; Taiwan is part of China; the question of Taiwan was the crucial issue obstructing the normalization of relations between China and the United States; the issue has now been resolved in the spirit of the Shanghai Communiqué and through joint efforts, thus enabling the normalization of relations desired by the people of the two countries; as for the way of bringing Taiwan back to the embrace of the motherland and reunifying the country, it is entirely China's internal affair.

In these documents, the fundamental policies of the two countries in regards to Taiwan were formalized as follows: The People's Republic of China, having been recognized as the sole legal government of China, insisted that Taiwan was part of China and that the means of achieving unification was strictly a Chinese internal affair. The United States accepted the government of the PRC as the sole legal government of China, continued to acknowledge that Taiwan was regarded by the Chinese on both sides of the Taiwan Strait as being part of China, affirmed its intention to maintain non-governmental relations with the people of Taiwan, and reaffirmed U.S. interest in a peaceful settlement of the Taiwan issue between the Chinese themselves.

Taiwan Relations Act

For its part, the U.S. Congress expressed dismay over the manner in which the Carter administration normalized relations with the PRC and severed diplomatic ties with Taipei. The Senate in July 1978 had requested by unanimous consent that the administration consult with that body before any action was taken to abrogate the U.S.-ROC Mutual Defense Treaty. This request was written into an amendment in the 1979 security aid authorization bill and signed into law by President Carter in September 1978. The administration chose to ignore the request and secretly moved forward on normalization while Congress was in recess and least able to react.

When Congress returned from its recess, congressional concerns quickly focused on the inadequacies of the legislation proposed by Carter to handle ties with Taiwan in the post-normalization period.[15] The most glaring of these were neglect of Taiwan's security and the close relationship between Taiwan and U.S. security interests in the Western Pacific. After holding extensive hearings, the Taiwan Relations Act (TRA) was enacted overwhelmingly by both Houses of Congress and signed into law by President Carter in April 1979.[16] Thereafter the TRA became one of the most important statements of U.S. interests, intentions, and policy toward Taiwan, containing many guidelines which continue to govern the Taiwan issue in Sino-American relations. Congress declared that it was the policy of the United States:

1. to preserve and promote extensive, close, and friendly commercial, cultural, and other relations between the people of the United States and the people on Taiwan, as well as the people on the China mainland and all other peoples of the Western Pacific area;
2. to declare that peace and stability in the area are in the political, security, and economic interests of the United States, and are matters of international concern;
3. to make clear that the U.S. decision to establish diplomatic relations with the People's Republic of China rests upon the expectation that the future of Taiwan will be determined by peaceful means;
4. to consider any effort to determine the future of Taiwan by other than peaceful means, including by boycotts or embargoes, a threat to the peace and security of the Western Pacific area and of grave concern to the United States;
5. to provide Taiwan with arms of a defensive character; and

6. to maintain the capacity of the United States to resist any resort to force or other forms of coercion that would jeopardize the security, or the social or economic system, of the people on Taiwan.

Congress specified that the enactment of the TRA was necessary to help maintain peace, security, and stability in the Western Pacific. Policy guidelines in the area of Taiwan's security were especially important to Congress. These specified that the United States will make available to Taiwan such defense articles and defense services in such quantity as may be necessary to enable Taiwan to maintain a sufficient self-defense capability. Henceforth, the president and the Congress would determine the nature and quantity of such defense articles and services based solely upon their judgment of the needs of Taiwan, in accordance with procedures established by law. Such determination of Taiwan's defense needs would include review by U.S. military authorities in connection with recommendations to the president and the Congress. The president was directed to inform the Congress promptly of any threat to the security or the social or economic system of the people on Taiwan and any danger to the interests of the United States arising therefrom. The president and the Congress would determine, in accordance with constitutional processes, appropriate action by the United States in response to any such danger.

The Congress, making clear that the U.S. relationship with Taiwan was a special case, gave itself an unprecedented role in U.S. foreign policy. More specific in many ways than the abrogated U.S.-ROC Mutual Defense Treaty, the TRA placed into U.S. law fairly specific guidelines for the administration to follow in handling Taiwan's security. Although the definition of what constituted "a sufficient self-defense capability" was left open to interpretation—a definition that eludes consensus yet today—the Congress made clear its perception that Taiwan's security (defined very broadly) was directly related to U.S. security interests.

Peaceful Reunification

The TRA specifically linked the normalization of U.S. relations with the PRC to continued efforts by Beijing to resolve the Taiwan question by peaceful means. In fact, prior to 1978, PRC policy toward Taiwan was mostly expressed in terms of "liberation," often by military means. As late as March 1978, Hua Guofeng told the Fifth National Party Congress: "The Chinese People's Liberation Army must make all the preparations necessary for the liberation of Taiwan."[17] In September of that year, a slight shift in PRC tactics could be seen, with Vice Premier Li Xiannian saying to Japanese visitors, "Whether by peaceable means or by force, we must consider the liberation of Taiwan from an overall strategic standpoint."[18]

In December 1978 a significant change in strategy toward Taiwan was approved at the Third Plenary Session of the Eleventh Party Central Committee. It was decided to reject "armed liberation" and "peaceful liberation" and to adopt instead a strategy of "peaceful reunification."[19] Numerous developments had converged to make a new approach to Taiwan both possible and necessary. These developments included the consolidation of Deng Xiaoping's power and the adoption of his "four modernizations" as the pragmatic basis for China's economic development; the normalization of relations with the United States and greater opening to the outside world; the necessity of teaching a military "lesson" to Vietnam for its invasion of Cambodia; and Chinese concerns about aggressive Soviet behavior in Afghanistan and elsewhere around China's periphery.

One of the earliest signs of China's new Taiwan policy was the New Year's Day Letter to Taiwan Compatriots released January 1, 1979, by the National People's Congress Standing Committee. The letter called for Taiwan and the mainland to arrange for mutual visits and tours, establish postal and transportation services, set up various academic and cultural exchanges, and open up trade.[20] Although progress has been incremental, in the years since 1979 most of these links and exchanges have been established in one way or another.

From the outset, however, the PRC placed conditions on its approach to peaceful reunification. Deng Xiaoping told Senator Sam Nunn in January 1979 that Beijing would still consider the use of force against Taiwan if its authorities refused over a long period of time to enter into negotiations or if there were an attempt by an outside power to interfere in Taiwan affairs.[21] Later that month, Deng told Hedley Donovan of *Time* magazine, "ten years is too long a time" to wait for reunification.[22] Liao Chengzhi, head of the PRC Office of Overseas Chinese, added in May 1979: "If some countries arm Taiwan in their own interests, and make the Taiwan authorities become self-conceited and disregard the common wish of the entire Chinese people, then we cannot assure definitely not to use means other than peaceful ones."[23]

Despite warnings to Taiwan not to wait too long for unification and to the United States to avoid interfering in the Taiwan issue, the 1979 period ushered in a new era of PRC strategy and policy toward both Washington and Taipei. There was direct connection between Beijing's decision to normalize relations with the United States and its decision to pursue peaceful reunification with Taiwan. These fundamental policies, in turn, were closely linked to the emergence of Deng Xiaoping as China's paramount leader, the adoption of his pragmatic economic reforms, the growing security threat from the Soviet Union, and the pending war with Vietnam.

Arms Sales

The PRC's reaction to the enactment of the Taiwan Relations Act was muted at first, partly because of the complex linkages discussed above and partly because President Carter promised to implement the TRA in ways not contravening the normalization communiqué with the PRC. Moreover, Carter placed a one-year moratorium on arms sales to Taiwan. During the 1980 presidential campaign, however, arms sales to Taiwan became a hot issue when Republican candidate Ronald Reagan indicated that he would provide advanced defensive weapons to Taiwan. More importantly, as he said in a Los Angeles speech in August 1980, "I would not pretend, as Carter does, that the relationship we now have with Taiwan, enacted by our Congress, is not official."[24]

Beijing was furious at Reagan's remarks, interpreting them to mean a retrogression in Sino-American relations. As a result, Chinese relations with the United States for much of the first two years of the Reagan presidency were bitter—even though Beijing approved of Reagan's tough policy toward the Soviet Union—with most controversy focused on arms sales to Taiwan. Washington and Beijing were not able to get their relationship back on track until the summer of 1982 with the signing of the August 17 communiqué.

Arms sales to Taiwan became a critical test in Sino-American relations for several reasons. First, with President Carter's one-year moratorium, there was genuine concern over Taiwan's security, especially in the post-normalization period when feelings of uncertainty and insecurity ran high on Taiwan. Second, there was recognition that a war in the Taiwan Strait would have serious impact on U.S. interests, for reasons discussed earlier, and that therefore the United States had to ensure Taiwan's adequate self-defense. Third, there was residual anger over Carter's derecognition of Taiwan and a sense, in the Reagan camp at least, that some gesture of continued American support for Taiwan was due.

From the PRC perspective, the incoming Reagan administration needed to be taught a lesson that it could not have its way over Taiwan after establishing diplomatic relations with Beijing. In terms of its relations with Taiwan, the PRC was concerned that renewed U.S. arms sales would strengthen Taipei's resolve to resist the more moderate reunification proposals being offered by the mainland. The PRC framed the issue to Washington in a stark choice: the Reagan administration had to choose between strategic cooperation with China against the common Soviet threat or improved U.S. relations with Taiwan. Such a diehard position by the Chinese ensured that the Republican White House and its supporters would face an excruciating dilemma.

The various considerations coalesced around the so-called FX issue in 1981 and 1982. The FX was intended to be a uniquely defensive fighter designed to replace Taiwan's aging fleet of F-5Es and F-104s. The ability to maintain air superiority over the Taiwan Strait and Taiwan itself was key to Taiwan's defense. The Carter administration approved the presentation of FX designs to Taipei by both Northrop and General Dynamics in June 1980, but the following month Premier Zhao Ziyang protested strongly to a visiting congressional delegation that such arms sales to Taiwan were incompatible with the normalization agreement.[25] When the Dutch government sold Taiwan two *Zwaardvis* submarines in November 1980, the PRC downgraded relations with The Hague to the level of chargé d'affaires. The Chinese government made plain that its action was intended to be an object lesson for the United States, particularly for the incoming Reagan administration which had indicated its intention to approve the FX sale to Taiwan.[26]

Although many Reagan supporters were inclined to sell the FX to Taiwan, the Republican administration was even more concerned about the growing threat from the Soviet Union. This pragmatic, anti-Soviet faction of the Republican party advised Reagan that a strategic partnership with China was necessary to protect American national security interests. Witnessing the strong PRC reaction to the Dutch submarine sale, the administration decided in January 1982, after a year of intense international and domestic debate over arms sales to Taiwan, that the FX sale would not go forward. In announcing the decision, the State Department said, "no military need for such aircraft exists."[27] The intense diplomatic confrontation led the United States and China into extended, acrimonious negotiations over a third communiqué, one dealing specifically with arms sales to Taiwan. The debates over the FX issue and the August 17 communiqué are excellent case studies of one of the major aspects of the Taiwan conundrum in Sino-American relations: how to ensure Taiwan's security while serving U.S. interests in strategic cooperation with Beijing?[28]

August 17 Communiqué

In the August 17, 1982, communiqué, the United States and China sought to resolve the issue of U.S. arms sales to Taiwan by placing parameters around future sales. Both sides reaffirmed their principles governing the Taiwan issue and added certain others. The principles found in the August 17 communiqué include the following:

- The United States recognizes the Government of the People's Republic of China as the sole legal government of China, and it acknowledges the Chinese position that there is but one China and Taiwan is part of China.
- The United States will continue to maintain cultural, commercial, and other unofficial relations with the people of Taiwan.
- Respect for each other's sovereignty and territorial integrity and non-interference in each other's internal affairs constitute the fundamental principles guiding United States-China relations.
- The Chinese government reiterated that the question of Taiwan is China's internal affair.
- Since January 1, 1979, the Chinese government had pursued a fundamental policy of striving for peaceful reunification of the motherland, thus striving for a peaceful solution to the Taiwan question.

- The United States has no intention of infringing on Chinese sovereignty and territorial integrity, or interfering in China's internal affairs, or pursuing a policy of "two Chinas" or "one China, one Taiwan."
- The United States understood and appreciated the Chinese policy of striving for a peaceful resolution of the Taiwan question.
- China's policy of peaceful reunification provided favorable conditions for the settlement of U.S.-China differences over the question of U.S. arms sales to Taiwan.
- Having in mind China's striving for peaceful reunification and the favorable conditions making possible the settlement of the arms sales issue, the United States Government stated that it does not seek to carry out a long-term policy of arms sales to Taiwan, that its arms sales to Taiwan will not exceed, either in qualitative or in quantitative terms, the level of those supplied in recent years since January 1, 1979, and that it intends to reduce gradually its sales of arms to Taiwan, leading over a period of time to a final resolution.

In the presidential statement accompanying the August 17 communiqué, Ronald Reagan stated that it was in the U.S. national interest that the U.S.-PRC strategic relationship be advanced. The communiqué would make that possible, consistent with U.S. obligations to the people of Taiwan. He said he was committed to maintaining the full range of contacts between the people of the United States and the people of Taiwan—cultural, commercial and people-to-people contacts—which were compatible with unofficial relations. Such contacts would continue to grow and prosper, and would be conducted with the dignity and honor befitting old friends. Reagan said U.S. policy in regards to arms sales to Taiwan, as set forth in the communiqué, was fully consistent with the Taiwan Relations Act. U.S. arms sales would continue in accordance with the TRA and with the full expectation that the approach of the Chinese government to the resolution of the Taiwan issue would continue to be peaceful. The president said the United States attached great significance to the Chinese statement in the communiqué regarding China's fundamental policy of striving for a peaceful resolution of the Taiwan issue. Future U.S. actions would be conducted with this peaceful policy in mind. He affirmed that the Taiwan question was a matter for the Chinese people, on both sides of the Taiwan Strait, to resolve. The United States would not interfere in this matter or prejudice the free choice of, or put pressure on, the people of Taiwan. At the same time, he emphasized, the United States had an abiding interest and concern that any resolution be peaceful.

Further indication of the Reagan administration's guiding principles on the Taiwan issue were contained in six assurances given Taipei on the eve of the communiqué. According to the ROC statement on the August 17 communiqué, these included assurances that the United States:

- has not agreed to set a date for ending arms sales to the Republic of China
- has not agreed to hold prior consultations with the Chinese communists on arms sales to the Republic of China
- will not play any mediation role between Taipei and Peiping [Beijing]
- has not agreed to revise the Taiwan Relations Act
- has not altered its position regarding sovereignty over Taiwan
- will not exert pressure on the Republic of China to enter into negotiations with the Chinese communists.[29]

In its official statement on the August 17 communiqué, the PRC government insisted that the U.S. sale of arms to Taiwan was an issue which affected Chinese sovereignty. The communiqué reaffirmed the principles of respect for each other's sovereignty and territorial integrity and non-interference in each other's internal affairs. The question of U.S. arms sales to Taiwan must be settled on these principles. According to Beijing, the final resolution referred to in the communiqué implied that U.S. arms sales to Taiwan must be completely terminated over a period of time. The Chinese side referred in the joint communiqué to its fundamental policy of striving for peaceful reunification of the motherland, demonstrating its sincere desire to strive for a peaceful solution to the Taiwan question. But this issue was purely China's internal affair; no misinterpretation or foreign interference was permissible. The joint communiqué was based on the principles embodied in the joint communiqué on the establishment of diplomatic relations between China and the United States and the basic norms guiding international relations and had nothing to do with the Taiwan Relations Act formulated unilaterally by the United States. According to the PRC, the TRA seriously contravened the principles embodied in the joint communiqué on the establishment of diplomatic relations, and the Chinese Government had been consistently opposed to it. Thus, all interpretations designed to link the August 17 communiqué to the TRA were in violation of the spirit and substance of the Communiqué and were unacceptable. The Chinese side noted that the agreement reached between the governments of China and the United States on the question of U.S. arms sales to Taiwan only marked the beginning of the settlement of the issue.

In terms of basic principles guiding the Taiwan issue, the August 17 communiqué made the following major points: the Chinese side emphasized that U.S. arms sales to Taiwan were a violation of China's sovereignty and an interference in its internal affairs; the United States, on the other hand, noted that its arms sales to Taiwan were consistent with earlier principles governing Sino-American relations, that U.S. interests in a peaceful settlement of the Taiwan issue continued, and that the requirements of the Taiwan Relations Act would be met. Both sides accepted the communiqué as a first step toward the resolution of the arms sales issue. China accepted the communiqué because the United States promised to limit future arms sales to Taiwan, while the United States expected China to continue its policy of peaceful reunification as a condition of reduced U.S. arms sales. As the administration made clear in testimony before Congress, the United States reserved the right to increase arms sales to Taiwan should the PRC threat to Taiwan's security increase.[30] Moreover, the administration told Congress that the TRA, being the law of the land, took legal precedence over the joint communiqué, which was a statement of intended policy by the administration.[31]

The Reagan administration's decision to proceed with the August 17 communiqué, and the justification for the agreement once it had been signed, were based on the need to preserve a strategic partnership with the PRC to counter the growing Soviet threat. Further, the administration wanted to assist Deng Xiaoping in his contest with hardliners in the PRC government over the direction and pace of economic reform. This argument was very much supported by Secretary of State Alexander Haig, who—much in the manner of Kissinger and Brzezinski—preferred to keep sensitive negotiations with the Chinese secret. When news of a draft agreement on arms sales became public, Haig and other State Department officials denied its existence. As Senator Barry Goldwater commented at the time, "It was clear to me and to the White House that President Reagan, Vice President Bush, and national security adviser William Clark had been lied to by the State Department about what they were planning." After key Members of Congress expressed outrage over this apparent duplicity when they were briefed on June 23, 1982, the president informed Haig the next day that he would accept his resignation.[32]

PRC Independent Foreign Policy

Ironically, in September 1982, one month after the signing of the August 17 communiqué, General Secretary Hu Yaobang formally announced at the Twelfth CCP Congress that China had decided to improve relations with the Soviet Union as part of its "independent" foreign policy.[33] The strategic partnership which justified the communiqué and which Haig and others had pursued so diligently never materialized. The Chinese used the Reagan administration's concern over the Soviet Union, and the U.S hope that strategic cooperation with Beijing was possible, to persuade Washington to sign an agreement that not only seemingly contradicted the Taiwan Relations Act but that over time could also seriously undermine Taiwan's security by limiting future arms sales. Possibly related to the adoption of an independent foreign policy was Deng's effort to placate hardliners who severely criticized the PRC Foreign Ministry for agreeing to continued arms sales in the August 17 communiqué.

Beijing used Moscow's concerns over a potential Sino-American strategic alliance to gain Soviet concessions on removing the "three obstacles" (large Soviet deployments along the Chinese border, Soviet assistance to Vietnam's occupation of Cambodia, and Soviet occupation of Afghanistan) as conditions to improve Sino-Soviet relations. With skillful bargaining, China was able to win concessions from both Washington and Moscow and to pursue an independent foreign policy of nonalignment with either superpower. A year later, Huan Xiang, director of China's Institute for International Affairs, explained why China decided to pursue an independent foreign policy rather than "coordinated measures" with the United States against Moscow:

> What has changed is the international situation. In the early seventies the Soviet Union had very strongly expanded toward the outside militarily and had become a threat to everybody. For this reason China offered cooperation to each state that felt threatened by the Soviet Union.
> Near the end of the Carter administration's term and at the beginning of the term of the Reagan administration, the Americans determinedly and energetically put up a front against the Soviet Union politically and militarily in the struggle for superiority in nuclear armament, in the matter of the European intermediate range weapons, in the Caribbean region, in the Middle East and, finally, also in Asia.
> This stopped the Soviet Union, and the rivalry of the two superpowers considerably intensified throughout the world. It seems the Russians still do not feel strong enough to react to the U.S. offensive. In our view, a certain balance between the two has emerged, especially in the military field.[34]

Since 1982 the PRC repeatedly has tried to convince the United States to negotiate another joint communiqué—recent attempts being made, for example, during the Clinton-Jiang summits in 1997 and 1998. To date, however, the United States has refused to enter into formal talks over a fourth communiqué. Thus, the basic principles governing the Taiwan issue in Sino-American relations have been in place for nearly two decades. Nonetheless, some important policy adjustments have been made by the Reagan and subsequent administrations.

Precedents in U.S. Taiwan Policy Under Reagan

Having learned the lesson of Chinese hardball in international politics, the Reagan administration assumed a more pragmatic policy toward the PRC and the Taiwan issue. The most evident example of this was the use of creative ambiguity in interpreting the communiqué's arms sales provisions. Senator S. I. Hayakawa's words apparently were taken to heart by the administration: the "communiqué means either what you want it to mean or what you fear it means. There is enough ambiguity in the document, it seems, that no one need take offense. . . . What we have in the communiqué is a situation not uncommon in human affairs: total ambiguity."[35]

In March 1983 the State Department announced that it would set ceilings on arms sales to Taiwan at $800 million for fiscal year 1983 and $760 million for fiscal year 1984. These figures were much higher than actual sales in 1979, 1980, and 1981—the base years referred to in the communiqué—with sales being $598 million, $601 million, and $295 million, respectively. To reconcile these numbers, the State Department explained that an "inflationary index" had been applied: the $598 million in 1979 had been equivalent to $830 million in current, inflated dollars.[36] The administration added a qualitative index to this quantitative index as well, selling Taiwan additional fighter aircraft, missiles, tanks, and other equipment shortly after the communiqué's signing and—perhaps most important—replacing obsolete equipment in Taiwan's inventory with newer equipment if suitable replacements could not be found. Moreover, the United States began to supply Taiwan with defense technology to build its own sophisticated weapons such as an indigenous fighter, the so-called IDF.

Thus, the Reagan administration, as well as the Bush and Clinton administrations following, chose to interpret the August 17 arms sales provisions in ways both beneficial and harmful to Taiwan. On the one hand, continued high levels of weapons sales occurred—as evidenced in President Bush's sale of 150 F-16s to Taiwan in 1992 (which some interpreted as actually nullifying the August 17 communiqué). On the other hand, the United States began to reduce the dollar amount of U.S. arms sales by about $20 million a year, a reduction in the "Taiwan bucket" that compelled Senator Murkowski to seek to amend the TRA as discussed in Chapter 2.

Another important precedent of the Reagan administration was the rejection of Beijing's appeal for the United States "to do something" to help China's reunification. As mentioned earlier, the PRC in January 1979 shifted its strategy toward Taiwan from one of liberation to peaceful unification. This was formalized in the January 1, 1979, New Year's day message to Taiwan from China's National People's Congress. The next major PRC initiative on the Taiwan issue came in the form of Ye Jianying's "nine-point" proposal on September 30, 1981.

Unification Proposals

Ye's nine points contain the essence of the PRC approach to resolving the Taiwan issue yet today and thus should be noted in some detail. The first point called for talks between the KMT and the CCP "on a reciprocal basis" so that national reunification could be achieved. Second, the PRC proposed that "the two sides make arrangements to facilitate the exchange of mails, trade, air and shipping services, and visits by relatives and tourists as well as academic, cultural and sports exchanges." Third, Beijing promised that after reunification, "Taiwan can enjoy a high degree of autonomy as a special administrative region and it can retain its armed forces." Further, "the [PRC] Central Government will not interfere with local affairs on Taiwan." Fourth, after reunification, "Taiwan's current socio-economic system will remain unchanged, so will its way of life and its economic and cultural relations with foreign countries." The PRC promised that "there will be no encroachment on the proprietary rights and lawful right of inheritance over private property, houses, land and enterprises, or on foreign investments." Fifth, various leaders in Taiwan can "take up posts of leadership in national political bodies and participate in running the state." Sixth, the PRC would assist Taiwan economically, "when Taiwan's local finance is in difficulty." Seventh, people on Taiwan can have "freedom of entry and exit" on the mainland, will not be discriminated against, and may live on the mainland if they choose. Eighth, Taiwan's industrialists and businessmen "are welcome to invest and engage in various economic undertakings on the mainland, and their legal rights, interests and profits are guaranteed." Ninth, Ye called upon all residents of Taiwan to stick to the "one-China" principle, oppose the creation of "two Chinas," and work with the Chinese on the mainland to achieve "the reunification of the motherland."[37]

The ROC rejection of the nine points also reflects a perception that has not greatly changed over the past two decades.[38] First, "the problem is not talks but two different ways of life." Taipei argued that China should be united but under a system that is free, democratic, and in the interests of the people. Unification under a communist system is not acceptable. Second, the free exchange of mail, trade, visits, and services are not offered the people on the mainland, so how can Beijing offer them to the people of Taiwan, who already enjoy those freedoms in any case? Third, since the ROC already enjoys freedom and its own armed forces, there is no reason why it should accept Beijing's offer to become a special administrative region. Fourth, it is naive to think that the communists will allow the capitalist system on Taiwan to remain indefinitely in place. Fifth, the participation by democratically elected Taiwan leaders in the communist government of the mainland makes little sense. Sixth, Taiwan does not need the economic assistance of the PRC; indeed, the mainland needs investments and technology from Taiwan. Seventh, the people of Taiwan already have freedom of movement, and it is unrealistic to expect that the mainland will allow such freedom to Taiwan residents while denying that freedom to its own residents. Eighth, Taiwan businessmen operating on the mainland have not found their enterprises to be especially profitable. Ninth, it is hard to imagine that the communist authorities will take policy suggestions from Taiwan seriously, since criticism of CCP policy on the mainland is punishable.

Essentially, the ROC argued that Ye's proposals offered nothing to Taiwan that it did not already have and that, hence, the offer probably was nothing more than a public relations gimmick for international audiences in the United States and elsewhere. More fundamentally, the ROC on Taiwan adamantly refused to accept unification under a central government controlled by the CCP.

Despite the ROC rejection of Ye's proposal, Beijing amended its constitution in December 1982, with Article 31 providing for "special administrative regions" within China. Peng Zhen, who explained the amendment to the National People's Congress, said the article was specifically designed for Taiwan, Hong Kong, and Macau. He said that China was unequivocal on the principle of sovereignty, unity, and territorial integrity; but that it was highly flexible in terms of specific policies and measures to bring about reunification.[39] Over the next year, Chinese authorities fleshed out the specifics of their unification proposals for Taiwan, often in interviews with Chinese scholars with good political connections in Taiwan.[40]

During the negotiations with Great Britain over returning Hong Kong to Chinese sovereignty in 1997, PRC peaceful reunification policies were formalized into the "one country, two systems" formula. As Deng Xiaoping explained to a group of Hong Kong businessmen in May 1984, China had "discussed the policy of two systems in one country for several years. It is now approved by the NPC." In regards to Taiwan, Deng said:

> What is the solution to this problem? Is it for socialism to swallow up Taiwan, or for the "Three Principles of the People" preached by Taiwan to swallow up the mainland? The answer is that neither can swallow up the other. If the problem cannot be solved peacefully then it must be solved by force. This would do neither side any good. Reunification of the country is the aspiration of the whole nation. If it cannot be reunified in one hundred years, then it will be reunified in one thousand years. In my opinion, the only solution to this problem is to practice two systems in one country.[41]

China promised that Taiwan could enjoy even more autonomy than Hong Kong under the "one country, two systems" formula. It is useful, therefore, to summarize the main points laid out in the December 1984 Sino-British agreement on the return of Hong Kong to Chinese sovereignty in July 1997.[42]

- The principles of one country, two systems shall be enshrined in a Basic Law of the Hong Kong Special Administrative Region of the People's Republic of China.
- The Basic Law will stipulate that after 1997 the socialist system and socialist policies shall not be practiced in the Hong Kong Special Administrative Region and that Hong Kong's previous capitalist system and life-style shall remain unchanged for fifty years.
- A high degree of autonomy shall exist, except in foreign and defense affairs, which will be the responsibility of Beijing.
- An executive, legislative, and independent judicial power shall be established with the current laws remaining basically unchanged.
- An executive shall be appointed by Beijing on the basis of local elections or consultations, and held accountable to the legislature.
- A legislature shall be constituted by elections, which may on its own authority enact laws in accordance with the provisions of the Basic Law and legal procedures, and report them to the Standing Committee of the National People's Congress for the record.
- The laws of the Hong Kong Special Administrative Region (SAR) shall be from three sources: the Basic Law, the laws previously in force in Hong Kong, and laws enacted by the Hong Kong SAR legislature.

- Judicial power in Hong Kong shall be vested in its own courts. The courts shall exercise judicial power independently and free from any interference. The power of final judgement shall be vested in the court of final appeals in the Hong Kong SAR.
- The Hong Kong Special Administrative Region shall maintain the capitalist economic and trade systems previously practiced in Hong Kong. Hong Kong shall retain the status of a free port and continue a free trade policy, including the free movement of goods and capital. Hong Kong may on its own maintain and develop economic and trade relations with all states and regions.
- The current social and economic systems in Hong Kong will remain unchanged, and so will the life-style. Rights and freedoms, including those of the person, of speech, of the press, of assembly, of association, of travel, of movement, of correspondence, of strike, of choice of occupation, of academic research and of religious belief will be ensured by law. Private property, ownership of enterprises, legitimate right of inheritance and foreign investment will be protected by law.
- Hong Kong will remain a separate customs territory. It will remain an international financial center, and its markets for foreign exchange, gold, securities and futures will continue. There will be free flow of capital.
- The Hong Kong dollar will continue to circulate and remain freely convertible. Hong Kong will have independent finances and Beijing will not levy taxes on Hong Kong.
- Mutually beneficial economic relations may be established with the United Kingdom and other countries, whose economic interests in Hong Kong will be given due regard.
- Under the name "Hong Kong, China," the Special Administrative Region may on its own maintain and develop economic and cultural relations and conclude relevant agreements with states, regions and relevant international organizations.
- Hong Kong may issue its own travel documents and maintain its own public security forces.
- Apart from displaying the national flag and national emblem of the People's Republic of China, Hong Kong may use a regional flag and emblem of its own.
- The Hong Kong Special Administrative Region shall maintain the educational system previously practiced in Hong Kong.

The ROC steadfastly has refused any comparison between Hong Kong and Taiwan. As summarized in September 1997 by Mainland Affairs Council Vice Chairman Lin Chong-pin: "We wish to reiterate that the 'one country, two systems' formula is by no means applicable to cross-Strait relations. The ROC has been a sovereign state since 1912. Hong Kong was and Macao [Macau] still is a colony.

We have had an independent foreign policy and a self-defense capability, which Hong Kong and Macao never had. The timing of sovereignty transfer of Hong Kong and Macao were stipulated under international treaties; we do not have such time limit. The Sino-British agreement reached in 1984 on Hong Kong's sovereignty transfer was made without consulting the Hong Kong people, a practice categorically impossible for us, now a full-fledged democracy."[43]

A formal counterproposal for unification came from Taipei in 1991 in the "Guidelines for National Unification."[44] This document, prepared by the National Unification Council under the Office of President Lee Teng-hui, contained the basic principles and timetables governing Taipei's policy of reunification with the mainland. The fundamental principles of the unification plan, which remains ROC policy today, included the following:

1. Both the mainland and Taiwan areas are parts of Chinese territory. Helping to bring about national unification should be the common responsibility of all Chinese people.
2. The unification of China should be for the welfare of all of its people and not be subject to partisan conflict.
3. China's unification should aim at promoting Chinese culture, safeguarding human dignity, guaranteeing fundamental human rights, and practicing democracy and the rule of law.
4. The timing and manner of China's unification should first respect the rights and interests of the people in the Taiwan area, and protect their security and welfare. It should be achieved in gradual phases under the principles of reason, peace, equity, and reciprocity.

In terms of the timetable of unification, no specific dates were specified in the guidelines but a three-stage process was outlined. The immediate first phase was one of building "exchanges and reciprocity." During this period, exchanges across the Taiwan Strait would increase, while at the same time "not endangering each other's safety and stability . . . and not denying the other's existence as a political entity." In this stage, the PRC would begin to implement democratic reform, and Taiwan would accelerate its constitutional reform. This stage was intended to address Taiwan's immediate needs, specifically to end the PRC threat to use force against Taiwan and to allow the ROC to play a normal role in international affairs without interference from Beijing. At the same time, during this phase the mainland was intended to phase out communism. All exchanges between the two sides would be through intermediary organizations such as the Straits Exchange Foundation and its PRC counterpart, the Association for Relations Across the Taiwan Straits. The two private organizations had been set up in 1991 to handle day-to-day interaction between the two Chinese sides. According to ROC officials, as of March 1999, "we are still in the short-term stage" during which "the two sides should work on reducing hostility."[45]

The mid-term phase of Taiwan's unification plan focused on building "mutual trust and cooperation." During this stage, "Direct postal, transport and commerce links should be allowed." Also, Taipei and Beijing would cooperate economically to develop the coastal areas to narrow the gap between the two sides' standards of living. "Official communication channels on equal footing" would be established, both sides would assist each other "in international organizations and activities," and "high-ranking officials on both sides" would exchange visits.

The final stage would be one of "consultation and unification." During this phase, a consultative organization for unification would be established to "jointly discuss the grand task of unification and map out a constitutional system to establish a democratic, free, and equitably prosperous China."

In contrast to the PRC proposal of one country, two systems—which set forth fairly generous conditions under which Taiwan could become part of the People's Republic of China as an autonomous region with a high degree of autonomy—the ROC proposal called for the PRC to give up communism and for Taiwan and the mainland to unify under a democratic system. The PRC proposal had a much shorter time frame than did the ROC proposal. In essence, the one country, two systems approach called for the KMT and ROC to give up all claims of representing China and to accept local government status, while the ROC national guidelines called for the CCP and PRC to give up their ideology and claims to represent China. Nice sounding phrases and generosity aside, both the PRC and ROC proposals had in mind the surrender of the other and the establishment of control over China under its own auspices. Yet another aspect of the Taiwan conundrum becomes clear: peaceful unification is a distant dream, not a foreseeable reality, under present circumstances.

Despite the reluctance of Taiwan to accept the one country, two systems formula and Beijing's refusal to take seriously Taipei's guidelines, the level of pragmatic exchanges between the two sides increased dramatically in the late 1980s and early 1990s. For example, between 1987 and 1992, Taiwan residents made more than four million trips to the PRC, and about 40,000 mainland residents visited Taiwan. In 1992 alone, more than 18 million pieces of mail were exchanged and nearly 27 million phone calls were placed.[46]

U.S. Policy Toward Unification

U.S. policy toward China's reunification was described in December 1986 by Gaston Sigur, assistant secretary of state for East Asian and Pacific affairs, who explained that the United States "viewed this issue as an internal matter for the PRC and Taiwan to resolve themselves. We will not serve as an intermediary or pressure Taiwan on the matter. We leave it up to both sides to settle their differences: our predominant interest is that the settlement be a peaceful one."[47] In March 1987 Secretary of State George Shultz further explained U.S. policy toward China's unification: while the "principles of one China and a peaceful resolution of the Taiwan question remain at the core of our China policy . . . the situation [in the Taiwan Strait] itself has not and cannot remain static." U.S. policy was to "support a continuing evolutionary process toward a peaceful resolution of the Taiwan issue." The pace of that process, however, "will be determined by the Chinese on either side of the Taiwan Strait, free of outside pressure. . . . Our steadfast policy seeks to foster an environment within which such developments [as indirect trade and increasing human interchange] can continue to take place."[48] Thus, toward the end of the Reagan administration, the United States had added to its fundamental policies of one China and the peaceful resolution of the Taiwan issue the added caveat that the United States would help foster an environment making increased cross-Straits exchanges possible.

The statements of Shultz and Sigur reflected an important element of U.S. policy: the United States would not take a position of supporting a *particular outcome* of the Taiwan issue but rather would support the *peaceful process* of resolving the Taiwan issue by the two Chinese sides themselves. In other words, the key U.S. interest was that the issue be resolved peacefully; U.S. interests were not tied to a particular formula for the resolution of the issue. The understanding that the United States would not oppose an agreement reached peacefully by Taipei and Beijing remains U.S. policy today. Much of the confusion surrounding U.S. Taiwan policy exists because of differences in interpretation as to what Washington means when it says it supports a "one-China" policy and does not support Taiwan independence. What is actually meant by that statement is that the United States is not seeking to divide China and that it will support any peaceful resolution of the Taiwan issue agreed to by the two sides of the Taiwan Strait.

Under the Reagan, Bush, and Clinton administrations there were several periods of debate over whether American policy should advocate or promote a certain outcome in the dialogue between Beijing and Taipei. Although fuzziness was introduced during the Clinton administration with some officials alluding to the United States seeking peaceful reunification of China, all three administrations concluded that active U.S. involvement in the outcome of cross-Strait talks would probably be counterproductive. There were several reasons for this caution, reasons which remain valid today.

First, there was no indication that the people of Taiwan wanted unification with the PRC anytime in the foreseeable future. For one thing, the people of Taiwan had not reached a consensus on what kind of political relationship Taiwan should have with mainland China. The majority of people favored a continuation of the status quo in the Taiwan Strait, if only because of great uncertainty as to the future policies of the PRC. For another, the "one country, two systems" formula for Hong Kong was not deemed appropriate for Taiwan because it had not been put to the test of time and because there were substantial differences between Hong Kong and Taiwan. Moreover, although China seemed to be set firmly on the path of economic modernization and some signs of political liberalization had appeared, the PRC remained a communist dictatorship. Few people on Taiwan, experiencing democracy and government accountability, wanted to fall under the jurisdiction of a communist government which was subject to the whims of individual leaders or the dictates of a single political party with no effective system of checks and balances. And, since peaceful unification assumed the non-coerced agreement of Taiwan and China over terms of unification, and since such agreement seemed a distant reality, U.S. support for reunification would be premature at best.

Second, early unification was not necessarily in the U.S. interest, especially if the people of Taiwan did not desire it. The status quo in the Taiwan Strait had served U.S. interests quite well since the 1950s. The U.S. "one-China" policy, which was based on the acknowledgment that both sides of the Taiwan Strait considered Taiwan to be part of China—albeit a different view of what comprised "China"—enabled the United States to pursue mutually beneficial relationships with both Taiwan and the PRC. Given the delicate nature of the Taiwan issue, any substantive change in U.S. Taiwan policy would have to be approached very cautiously and—in view of Taiwan's political support in the United States—only with adequate cause. Also, because of the important role the United States played in the Taiwan issue, any U.S. backing of a certain outcome for the resolution of the Taiwan issue likely would result in a significant weakening of Taipei's bargaining position and thus place the future of the Taiwan people at risk to the whims of the PRC government. Moreover, although the communist ideological threat to U.S. interests in the Asian Pacific had disappeared, the possibility that China would one day become a more traditional rival, perhaps even a threat, could not be ruled out. To most observers, there was very little incentive for the United States to enhance Chinese power by "giving" it Taiwan, when the future direction of China was unknown and Beijing might one day use its enhanced power against the United States.

Finally, the Taiwan issue—while central to China's territorial integrity and the completion of the Chinese civil war—was not the most fundamental issue in Sino-American relations from Washington's point of view. The nature of the U.S.-China relationship was governed by higher level issues such as whether the United States and China could coexist as superpowers in East Asia and whether China would participate in or oppose an American-led security, political, and economic system in East Asia. From this larger perspective, the resolution of the Taiwan issue would not change substantially future relations between Washington and Beijing. As long as the United States conceived of itself as a superpower with vital interests in the Western Pacific and China considered itself the rightful leader of the region, U.S. compromise over Taiwan made very little sense. This final point was central in determining U.S. policy.

For these and other reasons the Reagan, Bush, and Clinton administrations all decided not to become too involved in the dialogue between the PRC and Taiwan, other than to encourage the dialogue and to applaud the reduction of tensions in the

Taiwan Strait. From the point of view of U.S. interests, the heart of the matter was to ensure that the settlement of the Taiwan issue would be peaceful.

Bush Policy Toward China and Taiwan

The basic principles governing the Taiwan issue established during Reagan's term in office remained in place throughout the George Bush presidency. However, two developments during the Bush administration had a profound impact on the Taiwan issue. The first of these was the June 1989 Tiananmen incident, which severely weakened Sino-American relations and resulted in several sanctions being imposed on the PRC. The second major development was President Bush's decision in September 1992 to sell 150 F-16s to Taiwan—a decision based on many factors, including the U.S. desire to see a continued balance of power in the Taiwan Strait. Overall, the Bush administration adhered to a dual-track approach of seeking cooperative engagement with China—a strategy which enjoyed some success, particularly in Chinese cooperation on nonproliferation issues—and continued friendly but unofficial relations with Taiwan.

As noted earlier, President Bush was faced with the challenge of devising a post-containment strategy for the United States both globally and regionally. Relations with China were also under review, since the collapse of the Soviet Union removed much of the strategic foundation on which cooperative Sino-American relations had been built. Having served in the PRC as America's liaison officer prior to recognition, President Bush had a keen sense of the importance of China. He strongly favored engagement with the PRC as the best way to serve U.S. interests while helping to moderate Chinese domestic and foreign policies. Despite his determination to expand cooperative relations with China, Bush's efforts were thwarted almost from the outset of his administration by the June 1989 Tiananmen Square episode. In this unfortunate event, the People's Liberation Army (PLA) killed several hundred pro-democracy demonstrators and large numbers of innocent onlookers. Seen live on television by millions of Americans, the brutal crackdown profoundly influenced American attitudes toward Beijing. Instead of seeing a communist system gradually evolving into a market democracy through the reforms introduced by Deng Xiaoping, the Chinese communist regime came to be viewed as oppressive, antiquated, and untrustworthy.

Tiananmen destroyed the consensus on U.S. China policy that had been painstakingly built over two decades. That consensus had rested in large part on two foundations: the need for the United States and China to cooperate against the common Soviet threat, and the belief that engagement with China would result in that country's economic and then political liberalization. The first foundation eroded with the weakening and then collapse of the Soviet empire. The second foundation was severely weakened by Tiananmen. Since 1989, the administrations of George Bush and Bill Clinton have tried to define new rationales for engaging

China and have fought an uphill battle in trying to convince the American people and the Congress to support a new consensus on China policy. To date, the need for engagement has been largely accepted, but consensus on China policy remains elusive—in part because of Beijing's policies, in part because of domestic politics in both countries, in part because of conflicting Sino-American interests, and in part because of the Chinese and American policy conundrum over Taiwan.

In response to Tiananmen, the Bush administration ordered several sanctions against Beijing. These included the suspension of U.S. military sales to the PRC, the postponement of high-level military exchanges, the postponement of all official exchanges above the level of assistant secretary, and U.S. recommendations to international financial institutions to postpone further lending to Beijing. The United States also encouraged its European and Japanese allies to impose similar sanctions.

For its part, the PRC did little to improve its negative image. For a time, the Chinese communist leadership seemed ideological, xenophobic, and arrogant—attitudes that heightened the sense of alienation between Beijing and the American people. Human rights abuses increased, many of them directed against students, workers, and intellectuals involved in the May-June 1989 demonstrations in Beijing. Statements by Chinese Communist Party leaders stressed that the preservation of the party's hold on power was necessary to ensure social stability. There was a return to ideological work among the masses, wide repression of political opposition, and a slowdown of both political and economic reform.

In the view of perhaps most Americans, if the CCP had to maintain authoritarian control to ensure social stability, then society must not approve of CCP rule. Moreover, PRC persecution of political and economic reformers contrasted sharply with the liberalizing trends taking place in Eastern Europe, the Soviet Union, and most other socialist countries. The impression, reinforced by statements from PRC leaders themselves, was that China had become the last major bastion of communism, standing in the way of the democratic tide of history. Adding to this negative perception of the PRC were Chinese policies at sharp variance with U.S. interests. These included not only gross violations of human rights, but also a rapidly growing U.S.-PRC trade imbalance in China's favor and the Chinese sale of advanced missiles and nuclear technology to countries in the Middle East and South Asia. As a result of Tiananmen and these policies, there was a growing perception in the United States that China was becoming the greatest post-Cold War threat to traditional U.S. interests in security, trade, and democratic values in Asia. Among a large number of PRC power elite, a mirror image was being held of the U.S. threat to China.

One explanation for the widening gulf between American and Chinese interests and policies could be found in their contrasting visions of how the post-Cold War world should be ordered. President Bush advanced the idea of the creation of a new world order characterized by an expanding community of market democracies. The PRC ridiculed this idea, having no intention of accepting a world order dominated by the United States and its ideals. In place of a new world order based on democratic values and the free market system, China proposed a new international order based on former Premier Zhou Enlai's five principles of peaceful coexistence: mutual respect for sovereignty and territorial integrity, mutual non-aggression, non-interference in each other's internal affairs, equality and mutual benefit, and peaceful coexistence. Under Beijing's plan, each country would determine its own political, economic, and social standards free from outside interference.

PRC analysts pointed to several weaknesses in Bush's vision of a new world order.[49] For one thing, Chinese scholars felt the United States did not have the strength to fulfill its ambition of leading the new world order. According to this view, the American people did not support such an activist role for the United States in the post-Cold War era. Moreover, even allies of the United States held different visions of how the new world should be ordered. Some, such as France, objected to the United States assuming a dominant role. Another problem in the U.S. vision was that U.S.-Russian relations were unpredictable, yet that relationship was a crucial basis on which the new world order was to be built. The main problem with the U.S. vision of a new world order, however, was that it stressed U.S. values too much and did not allow individual countries to have their own national values. The rest of the world simply would not accept American domestic values as universal standards. Definitions of such concepts as democracy, freedom, and human rights were issues to be decided domestically by each country, not universal standards to be imposed by the United States. Because of these weaknesses, the PRC concluded that the new world order proposed by President Bush was doomed to failure.

In contrast to the U.S. version of a new world order, China proposed a plan for a new international order based on the fundamental right of all nations to choose their own social system, ideology, political and economic model, and path of development in view of their unique national characteristics. PRC scholars argued that differences in these areas were inevitable given the world's diversity, but that these national differences should not impede normal relations and cooperation between states. International relations should be based solely on mutual interests. All countries—big and small, rich and poor—should have equal rights in discussing and handling world affairs. Disputes between sovereign states should be solved through peaceful negotiations. No country should impose its will upon others or use or threaten the use of force in a unilateral way. The new international order should include not only a new political order but also a new economic order. Principles of the new economic order should include the right of every country to choose its own economic system, to control its own resources, and to participate in international economic affairs on an equal basis. No political strings should be attached to economic assistance from the developed world to the developing world.

The differences between the U.S. and PRC visions of the post-Cold War world order led to several contradictions in policy. For example, the United States was attempting to build and to lead a new Pacific partnership based on an "enduring sense of community" centered around common security, political, and economic interests and common values of prosperity, democracy, and freedom. By contrast, the PRC wanted a multipolar world and did not support U.S. leadership in Asia or support a Pacific community dominated by market democracies. China strongly opposed what it saw as an increased tendency for ideological intervention by the United States in the affairs of other countries, especially the PRC.

Further, as reflected in its East Asia strategic initiative documents, the United States believed its forward deployed military forces played an essential role as the "balance wheel of Asia." China, on the other hand, thought Washington greatly overestimated its importance in this regard and argued that Asian countries were capable of defining and managing a new power balance in the region. The PRC wanted the U.S. military presence in Asia to be reduced significantly and chiefly oriented toward containing Japan. Many senior Chinese leaders and military officers believed U.S. forces in Asia after the Cold War were intended primarily to contain Chinese power.[50]

Also, the United States believed that communism was collapsing worldwide, and that democracy had won the ideological battle for the hearts and minds of the world's peoples. The United States believed it had a moral mission to use its commercial strength and technology, especially mass communications, to promote the cause of freedom and human rights in China. The CCP, on the other hand, insisted that it would not tolerate a multiparty political system but would continue to adhere to multiparty cooperation under the leadership of the Chinese Communist Party. Some PRC leaders saw "bourgeois liberalization" and "peaceful evolution" as evidence of a continued class struggle in which the CCP battled for survival against anti-socialist forces on the mainland supported by outside powers such as the United States. Many in Beijing considered the long-term U.S. strategy to be a "soft attack" to undermine socialism—a correct assessment if presidential statements justifying China policy were true.

In yet another policy area, the United States believed human rights were universal, that minimal standards of decent conduct by governments toward their citizens were not culturally based but held in common by all mankind. The United States felt it had a special responsibility to point to higher standards and to protect human rights around the world, in a pragmatic fashion. China felt that human rights were not universal but rather defined by each individual nation in view of its particular historical and social conditions. The PRC argued that the United States, in pressing for other countries to adhere to its standards of human rights, was interfering in the internal affairs of sovereign states.

Although China was not directly involved in the Persian Gulf War, which started when Iraq invaded Kuwait in August 1990 and ended with the U.S.-led coalition victory over Baghdad in January 1991, the war influenced Sino-American relations in several ways. First, China's cooperation in not vetoing U.N. resolutions against Iraq convinced many Western governments that the Tiananmen sanctions had outlived their usefulness. Most Western countries after the Persian Gulf War were in favor of lifting the sanctions and returning to normal their relations with Beijing. The United States persisted in maintaining its sanctions, but Beijing's actions in the U.N. reinforced American government perceptions of China's importance as a powerful country with which the United States had to deal carefully and pragmatically if American interests were to be served.

Second, the quick U.S. victory in the war convinced many Americans that the time was ripe for the United States to pursue more aggressively its promotion of freedom and democracy. Since Beijing's communist leadership was widely despised after Tiananmen, the PRC became a primary target for renewed American ideological criticism. From the point of view of many in China, growing American hostility on ideological grounds—coupled with its willingness to use its unrivaled military power and the collapse of the Soviet counterbalance—meant that the United States posed the greatest single foreign threat to China in the post-Cold War period.

Third, the effectiveness of U.S. high-tech weapons in the Gulf War called into question PLA military strategy and demonstrated that Chinese weapons were no match for those of the West. The vulnerability of the PLA to modern U.S. weapons resulted in a decision to quicken the pace of China's military modernization. A sharp increase in the PRC defense budget was authorized, and Beijing began purchasing advanced military equipment and defense technology from Russia and other countries. Partly to finance these purchases, the PLA sold advanced weapons of its own to Third World nations, sales seen as threats to U.S. counterproliferation efforts.

At the same time, however, some Chinese analysts believed the Persian Gulf War to be the zenith for U.S. forces built to counter the Soviet Union. From this perspective, the United States actually was entering a period of decline, increasingly unable to fulfill its ambitions to create a new world order. According to PRC scholar Wang Jisi, for example: "Generally speaking, the United States has started a strategic withdrawal as the Soviet threat has faded. While ensuring its capacity for quick responses to major regional conflicts, the United States will substantially reduce its military spending, eliminate outmoded nuclear weapons, and trim its overseas military presence. The role of future U.S. overseas military strength will be to cope with abrupt occurrences like the [Persian] Gulf crisis, and to guarantee continuing political influence."[51]

U.S. policy toward the PRC under President Bush reflected his personal views on how best to deal with Beijing. The president explained his China policy in a commencement address to Yale University in May 1991.[52] According to the president, the United States needed to remain engaged with China in order to try to change Chinese behavior in ways closer to U.S. ideals. These ideals included freedom, democracy, human rights, and freer trade. It was in U.S. interests to find opportunities to cooperate with the PRC because of China's size, enormous population, and ability to affect the stability of East Asia. The Chinese also played central roles in Cambodia, Korea, and in many multinational organizations such as the U.N. Its cooperation in the United Nations, for example, was essential to pass U.N. resolutions against Iraq's invasion of Kuwait.

Nonetheless, the president explained, the United States would not hesitate to take appropriate action against the Chinese government when problems arose in its behavior. The United States was the first nation to condemn the use of violence against the peaceful demonstrators in Tiananmen, and it was the first to guarantee the rights of Chinese students to remain in the United States after Beijing cracked down on dissidents. The United States was also the first nation to impose sanctions against the PRC, and it was one of the last Western democracies to keep the sanctions in place. The president noted that his administration also cited China under the trade rules of a Special 301 for pirating U.S. copyrights and patents. He took strong issue with the Chinese government on its exports of missiles and nuclear technology.

In a key statement explaining why the United States should pursue constructive engagement with China, the president argued: "If we pursue a policy that cultivates contacts with the Chinese people, promotes commerce to our benefit, we can help create a climate for democratic change. No nation on Earth has discovered a way to import the world's goods and services—while stopping foreign ideas at the border. Just as the democratic idea has transformed nations on every continent—so, too, change will inevitably come to China."

Trade and proliferation were prominent issues in Sino-American relations under President Bush. In 1990 the PRC enjoyed a $10.4 billion trade surplus with the United States, and in 1991 it grew to $12.7 billion, second in the world behind that of Japan. By 1992 the PRC surplus had grown to about $18 billion. The rate of growth of China's trade surplus with the United States was of concern to Washington not only because of its size but also because it was at least partially achieved through what Americans perceived to be unfair trading practices. These practices included failure to honor U.S. intellectual property rights, refusal to remove protectionist barriers against imports from the United States, illegal PRC textile shipments through third countries, and Chinese exports made by political prisoners.

Both Houses of Congress were under the control of the Democratic Party, and the Congress as a whole strongly disagreed with President Bush's efforts to maintain cooperative relations with Beijing after Tiananmen. Democratic members frequently condemned his policy as one of "coddling" the PRC and its elderly leaders, a theme effectively taken up by Bill Clinton in the presidential campaign of 1992.

Beginning in 1990, the focus of White House-congressional disagreement over China centered on the annual debate over whether to grant unconditional most-favored-nation (MFN) trading status to China. The debate had its legal basis in the Jackson-Vanik amendment to the Trade Act of 1974, which stipulated that the president must certify annually that nonmarket economies receiving MFN provide freedom of emigration to their citizens. In the case of China, Congress sought to impose by law various other conditions on MFN, such as improvement in human rights behavior, removal of unfair trading practices, and ending proliferation. President Bush successfully vetoed all such bills on the grounds that MFN was the ordinary basis of world trade and that ending MFN would hurt those in China whom the United States wanted most to encourage: individuals and provinces seeking to expand the free market, trade, and contact with the West.

Another area of great concern to the United States was proliferation, particularly Chinese missile and nuclear technology transfers to the Third World. As noted earlier, the United States placed proliferation issues near the top of perceived threats to U.S. security after the Cold War. In 1987 China shipped around a dozen CSS2 intermediate-range missiles to Saudi Arabia. In 1991 it was reported that U.S. intelligence had warned that Beijing was ready to sell M-9 short-range ballistic missiles to Syria and M-11 short-range ballistic missiles to Pakistan. The M-9 had a range of about 370 miles, giving Syria the ability to hit military targets in Israel with great accuracy and reliability. The M-11 could carry an 1,100 pound bomb 185 miles to targets in India.[53] According to U.S. intelligence officials interviewed in 1998, China and Pakistan also agreed in 1988 that the PRC would help Pakistan build a factory complex in the Punjab town of Fatehjung to manufacture its own M-11s. Moreover, some 30-34 M-11s were shipped to Pakistan in late 1992, where they probably remained in crates in 1998 at Sagodha Air Base west of Lahore.[54] Because of political instability in the Middle East and South Asia, Washington saw the missile sales as a potential threat to regional peace and thus against U.S. interests in nonproliferation. In mid-1991 the United States began pressuring China to adhere to the Missile Technology Control Regime (MTCR) participated in by sixteen nations to halt the spread of ballistic missiles.

The United States was also deeply concerned by Chinese shipments of nuclear materials and technology to Pakistan and perhaps other countries. China had a long history of this practice. According to one report, in 1983 the PRC gave Pakistan the design of a tested nuclear weapon with a yield of about 25 kilotons; Beijing also provide Pakistan with enough weapons-grade uranium for at least two nuclear weapons.[55] Chinese scientists worked in Pakistan's Kahuta complex, where nuclear weapons research took place. Between 1982 and 1987, Beijing reportedly sold India about 150 tons of heavy water, which is used to make plutonium. In addition, China sold uranium to South Africa, uranium and heavy water to Argentina, enriched uranium to Brazil, and a heavy water reactor to Algeria. In view of these practices, the United States exerted pressure on Beijing to join the Nuclear Non-Proliferation Treaty (NPT), which China agreed to do in late 1991.

In November 1991, President Bush sent Secretary of State James Baker to China, the highest-level visit by an American official since Tiananmen. A number of important issues were discussed, including developments in Asia in general, the rise of Japan as a regional power, and the future security architecture in Asia. In addition, the Bush administration wanted to address specific areas of mutual concern with the Chinese. These included several nonproliferation issues, such as China's agreement in principle to sign the NPT; Chinese cooperation on Middle East arms control, particularly missile sales to countries like Syria; Beijing's stated commitment to join the Missile Technology Control Regime; the need to secure ironclad Chinese assurances not to sell nuclear technology to countries like Iran, Syria, or Pakistan; and the need for Chinese assurances not to sell ballistic missiles to these same countries. Trade issues were also on the agenda, including barriers to U.S. imports, a rapidly growing Chinese trade surplus with the United States, and Beijing's agreement to discuss not exporting goods to the United States made with prison labor. In addition, various human rights issues needed to be aired, especially the release of political prisoners arrested in the aftermath of Tiananmen.

In some of these negotiations the Bush administration found the Chinese to be unyielding, but in other talks progress was made, particularly toward the end of the Bush presidency. To the president and his advisers, the very scope of these negotiations proved the importance of continued engagement with China.

In terms of the Taiwan issue, the most important policy decision made by President Bush was his sale of 150 F-16s to Taipei in 1992.[56] As mentioned briefly in the context of the FX sale, one of the keys to Taiwan's defense is ROC air supremacy over the Taiwan Strait. If the ROC can control the skies, then a PRC amphibious invasion of Taiwan is impossible and an effective blockade of the island is prohibitively costly. For more than fifteen years Taiwan sought to replace the backbone of its air defense system, the F-5E Tiger II, with a newer and more advanced U.S. fighter such as the F-16 Fighting Falcon, F-4C Phantom, or F-5G Tiger Shark (later designated the F-20, one of the FX models). However, in January 1982 the Reagan administration decided not to sell a new fighter to Taiwan to avoid a possible rupture in Sino-American relations. The signing of the August 17 communiqué made it even more difficult for Taiwan to acquire an advanced fighter from the United States. Taiwan was also unsuccessful in purchasing the Kfir fighter from Israel, in this case because of Saudi Arabia's objection (the Saudis were one of the ROC's most important diplomatic friends at the time and had promised to supply Taiwan's oil needs).

Unable to purchase an advanced fighter from abroad, Taiwan concentrated on building its own indigenous fighter, the IDF program. The IDF was given design and equipment assistance from U.S. companies such as General Dynamics, Lear Siegler, and Garrett Engine. The first IDF prototype, dubbed the *Ching-kuo* fighter after President Chiang Ching-kuo, appeared in 1988. Problems persisted with the aircraft, principally due to its need for a more powerful engine. The IDF was mocked by Taiwanese critics as "It Doesn't Fly," but after improvements, the ROC military decided to produce 130 of the fighters.

In the post-Cold War environment of the 1990s, Taipei renewed its efforts to acquire foreign fighters, concentrating on the F-16 and the French-built Mirage 2000-5. Taiwan was able to purchase sixty Mirage 2000-5 fighters from France in 1992 at a price of about $6 billion, a deal that reportedly included over 1,500 Mica air-to-air missiles. The French were said to have offered Taiwan an additional sixty Mirages, but Taipei declined when the United States agreed to sell Taiwan the F-16.

In reaction to the French sale of the Mirage, Beijing ordered France to close its consulate in Guangzhou and banned French companies from participating in a $1 billion subway project. Pressured by French industrialists who felt they were being denied business opportunities in the PRC, Paris agreed in January 1994 to a communiqué stating, "the French Government pledges not to authorize French enterprises to participate in arming Taiwan in the future." However, France also said that arms sales already approved for Taiwan would go forward, including the sale of six *LaFayette*-class frigates and the Mirage fighters.[57] The communiqué was a blow to Taiwan's defense establishment, which had looked to France as an alternative source of weapons and technology.

President Bush announced his decision to allow the F-16 sale to Taiwan in September 1992 in Fort Worth, Texas, home of General Dynamics. His decision was influenced by many factors: concern over maintaining Taiwan's capabilities to deter the Su-27s and other weapons being purchased by the PRC from Russia; the need to maintain a balance of power in East Asia and a military balance in the Taiwan Strait; the difficulty in supplying spare parts for the outdated aircraft in Taiwan's inventory; the desire to ensure that American companies got the ROC's arms business, not French enterprises or those of other countries; mounting congressional pressure to sell Taiwan the F-16; to give a boost to American defense industries; to preserve U.S. influence over Taiwan's military; and to help Bush's presidential campaign in Texas, a critical state in the presidential primary.[58]

Taipei and Washington signed a letter of offer and acceptance for 150 F-16s in November 1992. On-island delivery of the first planes began in April 1997 and should be completed by the end of 1999. The F-16s initially offered Taiwan were older model A (single-seat) and B (two-seat) versions, in use by the U.S. Air Force for over a decade and generally considered inferior to the Su-27. Taiwan wanted the more advanced F-16C/D models, but the United States refused because of the plane's offensive capabilities. A compromise was worked out whereby Taiwan would receive new F-16 MLU (Mid-Life Upgrade) aircraft similar to models scheduled to be flown by American and European air defense pilots. The F-16 MLU is a more advanced model of the F-16A/B, with some functions identical to the F-16C/D. The cost of the 150 MLU versions of the F-16A/B sold to Taiwan was about $6 billion.

The Chinese were upset by the F-16 sale, calling it a major retrogression in relations; however, their purchase of the Russian Su-27 and other advanced weapons systems diluted the effectiveness of their protests. On the other hand, the sale was well received by most Americans, including Democratic presidential candidate Bill Clinton.

During the last two years of his administration, President Bush became increasingly tough with China. At the same time, the PRC began to display a greater willingness to accommodate some American demands. In this favorable negotiating environment, the Bush administration persuaded China to sign several important agreements with the United States. These included three trade agreements (protecting intellectual property rights, prohibiting the shipment to the United States of goods made by prison labor, and eliminating 70 percent of the PRC's non-tariff barriers to imports over a period of five years); and three international agreements designed to limit arms proliferation (the Nuclear Non-Proliferation Treaty signed by China, the Missile Technology Control Regime to which China said it would adhere, and the Biological and Chemical Weapons Conventions to which China agreed).

In response to these positive signals from China, the Bush administration at the end of 1992 began to loosen U.S. sanctions on the PRC. The December 1992 visit to China by Commerce Secretary Barbara Franklin was seen by both sides as a turning point in the relationship, in part meant to restore Sino-American commercial relations (U.S. investment in China totaled about $6 billion at the end of 1992), as well as to placate the Chinese after Bush's decision to sell F-16 fighters to Taiwan and to send U.S. Trade Representative Carla A. Hills to Taipei in December 1992.

Also in December 1992 the Bush administration announced that it was lifting its ban on sales of certain kinds of military technology to China. The decision allowed the conclusion of four arms sales to China stalled when the ban was imposed after the Tiananmen incident. The completed weapons transfers included avionics for China's F-8-II fighter, two counter-artillery radars, four antisubmarine torpedoes, and the production of munitions. The equipment was shipped with no follow-up support, spare parts, training, maintenance, or guarantees by the United States on equipment capability or working condition.[59]

Conclusion

The Taiwan conundrum in U.S. policy can be traced to many historical developments. Several were highlighted in this brief overview of U.S. policy toward China and Taiwan through 1992: e.g., the strategic imperative for cooperative Sino-American relations; Beijing's uncompromising demands that Washington limit its relations with Taipei as a price for strategic partnership with China; the unwillingness of Taiwan to be drawn into unification talks with the PRC; the difficulty in defining an appropriate arms sales level to Taiwan, especially as the PLA modernizes; fundamental differences between Washington and Beijing on a host of issues not related to Taiwan; the domestic controversy in the United States over U.S. policy toward China and Taiwan; the difficulty in defining a new balance of power between the United States and China in the post-Cold War era; American and Chinese differences over the new world order; the unique role of Congress in

U.S. China-Taiwan policy; and the ambiguities inherent in the principles governing the Taiwan issue.

Generally speaking, China has been viewed as being more important to U.S. interests than Taiwan, primarily because of the mainland's size and status as a great power. Taiwan, however, has enjoyed enormous support in the American body politic, making the abandonment of Taiwan impossible to contemplate seriously and the weakening of U.S. support for Taiwan a political risk. Because of the sensitivity of the Taiwan issue to both Washington and Beijing, a set of principles have evolved to manage the issue while pursuing other aspects of Sino-American relations. These principles, which remain valid today, were mostly in place by 1982. They include:

- Washington recognizes Beijing as the sole legal government of China.
- The United States acknowledges that Chinese on both sides of the Strait consider Taiwan to be part of China.
- The United States will continue to have close, friendly, but unofficial relations with the people of Taiwan.
- The PRC will attempt to settle the Taiwan issue peacefully.
- Washington will sell only limited defensive weapons to Taiwan.
- The United States will not seek to mediate differences between Beijing and Taipei.
- The United States does not promote a particular outcome of the Taiwan issue, but it does insist that the issue be settled peacefully.
- The United States will not seek to divide China by supporting "two Chinas," "one China, one Taiwan," or "Taiwan independence."

As long as all three sides—Washington, Beijing, and Taipei—adhered to a one-China policy, these principles were flexible enough to permit the United States to pursue a "dual-track" China policy that served American interests in both the PRC and the ROC, including advanced arms sales to Taiwan. The U.S. hope for a strategic partnership with Beijing never fully materialized, however, and after the August 17 communiqué the PRC went on to adopt an independent foreign policy.

President Bush wanted to deal pragmatically with the PRC to serve U.S. security, trade, and cultural interests. However, the collapse of the Soviet Union and the slaughter at Tiananmen changed forever the foundations of Sino-American relations. With great effort, Bush managed to engage the Chinese but he could not overcome the growing list of divergent interests between the United States and the PRC: conflicting visions of the new world order; proliferation issues involving ballistic missiles, advanced conventional weapons, and nuclear weapons technology; trade issues such as China's large surplus with the United States and the extension of MFN trading status to the PRC; and Beijing's flagrant violations of human rights and opposition to democratic reform within China. Taiwan once again became an issue because of Bush's decision to sell F-16s to Taipei, but

Beijing's reaction was muted because of its own acquisition of advanced weapons from Russia. The F-16 sale demonstrated, however, that the qualitative and quantitative restrictions of the August 17 communiqué would not deter the United States from correcting serious weaknesses in Taiwan's security.

President Bush justified cooperative engagement with the PRC on the grounds that it would help to change China in a positive direction. This explanation was taken as proof by some in Beijing that the United States was seeking to undermine the CCP. Witnessing systemic change in Eastern Europe and the Soviet Union, Chinese leaders could see that once the foundations of socialism and communist party control were eroded, the communist state would quickly crumble. The CCP was determined not to repeat the mistakes of Mikhail Gorbachev and therefore refused to allow political reform to keep pace with economic reform.

In spite of many points of contention between the United States and China, the two countries were able to agree to certain trade and proliferation regimes and to cooperate in international crisis such as the Persian Gulf War. Bush's policies toward China were condemned by congressional Democrats and by the Clinton presidential campaign as coddling Chinese dictators. Once in office, however, President Bill Clinton adopted with little change the strategy of engagement followed by his predecessor. The Taiwan conundrum continued, not because of faulty policy but because ambiguity was necessary to serve U.S. interests in both China and Taiwan. This ambiguity did not harm Taiwan too much; although on those occasions when policy had to be clarified, Taiwan usually, but not always, found its position eroded somewhat.

Notes

1. "Legislative History, P.L. 96-8 (Taiwan Relations Act)," *U.S. Code Congressional and Administrative News*, 4 (June 1979), 96th Cong., 1st sess., p. 661.

2. An excellent collection of essays regarding the early postwar period of U.S.-China relations can be found in Harry Harding and Yuan Ming, eds., *Sino-American Relations, 1945-1955: A Joint Reassessment of a Critical Decade* (Wilmington, DE: Scholarly Resources, 1989).

3. A useful summary of American involvement in postwar China through 1980 can be found in *China: U.S. Policy Since 1945* (Washington, DC: Congressional Quarterly, 1980).

4. "A Report to the President by the National Security Council: The Position of the United States with Respect to Asia," NSC/48 (December 30, 1949), in Stephen P. Gibert and William M. Carpenter, eds., *America and Island China: A Documentary History* (Lanham, MD: University Press of America, 1989), pp. 80-85. The Gibert and Carpenter collection contains a wealth of documents related to U.S. policy toward China and Taiwan through 1988.

5. "U.S. Secretary of State Acheson's Statement on U.S. Military Involvement in Formosa," in ibid., pp. 88-90.

6. "U.S. Secretary of State Acheson's Statement on U.S. Defense Perimeter in Pacific Area," ibid., pp. 91-92.

7. See William N. Stokes' contributions in Marshall Green, John H. Holdridge, and William N. Stokes, *War and Peace with China: First-hand Experiences in the Foreign Service of the United States* (Bethesda, MD: Dacor Press, 1994).

8. *American Foreign Policy, 1950–1955: Basic Documents, II* (Washington, DC: GPO, 1957), p. 2467.

9. *U.S. Overseas Loans and Grants and Assistance from International Organizations* (Washington, DC: Agency for International Development, 1984), p. 83.

10. Richard M. Nixon, *RN: The Memoirs of Richard Nixon* (New York: Grosset and Dunlap, 1978), p. 556.

11. Henry A. Kissinger, *White House Years* (Boston: Little, Brown and Co., 1979), p. 173.

12. For his views on China, see Jimmy Carter, *Keeping Faith: Memoirs of a President* (New York: Bantam Books, 1982), pp. 186-211.

13. Carter, p. 197.

14. Carter, pp. 209-210.

15. Carter's draft legislation, along with the reaction of many Members of Congress, can be found in Robert L. Downen, *The Taiwan Pawn in the China Game: Congress to the Rescue* (Washington, DC: Center for Strategic and International Studies, Georgetown University, 1979).

16. One of the most important sources of information about U.S. policy toward Taiwan through 1978 can be found in the record of Senate hearings on Taiwan: U.S. Congress, Senate, Committee on Foreign Affairs, *Taiwan* (Washington, DC: GPO, 1979). One of the best discussions of the formulation of the TRA within the Congress can be found in Lester L. Wolff and David L. Simon, *Legislative History of the Taiwan Relations Act* (New York: American Association for Chinese Studies, 1982).

17. *Xinhua*, March 6, 1978, in *FBIS-China*, March 7, 1978, p. D31.

18. *Kyodo*, September 19, 1979, in *FBIS-China*, September 19, 1978, p. A1.

19. Li Jiaquan, "Formula for China's Reunification," *Beijing Review*, February 3, 1986, p. 19.

20. See *Xinhua*, December 31, 1978, in *FBIS-China*, January 2, 1979, p. E1.

21. AFP, January 9, 1979, in *FBIS-China*, January 9, 1979, p. A4.

22. *Washington Star*, January 29, 1979, p. 1.

23. *Xinhua*, May 21, 1979, in *FBIS-China*, May 24, 1979, p. D8. Liao told a meeting of the National Association of Overseas Chinese in February 1979: "After China has achieved peaceful unification the long-term road for Taiwan will be the socialist road. Under the leadership of a single, proletarian political party, there is no reason why one segment should have a socialist system while the other follows the capitalist road." Translated in *Inside China Mainland* (Taipei), May 1982.

24. "Ronald Reagan on U.S. Policy Toward Asia and the Pacific," Reagan for President Press Release, Los Angeles, CA, August 25, 1980, ms.

25. *Xinhua*, July 8, 1980, in *FBIS-China*, July 9, 1980, p. B2.

26. *Xinhua*, January 17, 1981, in *FBIS-China*, January 19, 1981, p. G2.

27. "No Sale of Advanced Aircraft to Taiwan," *Department of State Bulletin* 82, 2059 (February 1982), p. 39.

28. For linkage between U.S. arms sales to Taiwan and Sino-American strategic cooperation, see the author's *The Taiwan Issue in Sino-American Strategic Relations* (Boulder, CO: Westview Press, 1984) and *Policy in Evolution: The U.S. Role in China's Reunification* (Boulder, CO: Westview Press, 1989).

29. "ROC Statement on August 17 Communiqué, August 17, 1982," issued by the Coordination Council of North American Affairs, Washington, D.C. The Coordination Council of North American Affairs (CCNAA) was the private corporation created by the ROC government to handle its affairs in Washington after January 1, 1979. The corresponding U.S. corporation was the American Institute in Taiwan (AIT), authorized by the Taiwan Relations Act. CCNAA changed its name in 1994 to Taipei Economic and Cultural Representative Office in the United States (TECRO).

30. See the testimony of Assistant Secretary of State John Holdridge in U.S. Congress, House of Representatives, Committee on Foreign Affairs, *China-Taiwan: United States Policy* (Washington, DC: GPO, 1982), pp. 2-29.

31. See the prepared statement of State Department Legal Adviser Davis Robinson before the Senate Committee on the Judiciary, Subcommittee on Separation of Powers, on September 27, 1982.

32. *Washington Post*, July 2, 1982, p. A26; *Washington Times*, July 2, 1982, p. 1.

33. Hu Yaobang, "Create a New Situation in All Fields of Socialist Modernization," *The Twelfth National Congress of the CPC* (Beijing: Foreign Languages Press, 1982), pp. 58-59.

34. Interview in *Der Spiegel*, December 26, 1983, in *FBIS-China*, December 29, 1983, pp. A7-A8.

35. S. I. Hayakawa, "Ambiguity: The China Syndrome," *New York Times*, August 30, 1982, p. A17.

36. *Washington Post*, March 22, 1983, p. A12.

37. Ye's nine-point proposal was given in an interview with *Xinhua* on September 30, 1981. See *FBIS-China*, September 30, 1981, p. U1.

38. Summarized from "China's Reunification: Is the 'Nine-Point Proposal' a Yesable Solution" (Taipei: China Mainland Research Center, May 1982).

39. See *Xhongguo Xinwen She*, November 28, 1982, in *FBIS-China*, November 30, 1982, p. K19.

40. Two of the most informative were Hu Yaobang's interview with Parris Chang in May 1983 and Deng Xiaoping's interview with Winston Yang in June of that year. See *Hsia Pao*, June 28, 1983, in *FBIS-China*, June 28, 1983, p. W1; *Xinhua*, July 29, 1983, in *FBIS-China*, August 1, 1983, pp. U1-U2; and *Chishih Nientai*, August 1, 1983, in *FBIS-China*, August 4, 1983, pp. W1-W6.

41. *Xinhua*, June 30, 1984, in *FBIS-China*, July 2, 1984, pp. E1-E2.

42. See *A Draft Agreement between the Government of the United Kingdom of Great Britain and Northern Ireland and the Government of the People's Republic of China on the Future of Hong Kong* (London: Her Majesty's Government, September 26, 1984).

43. Lin made his comments in a press conference held in Taipei on September 12, 1997. See *MAC News Briefing* 41 (September 16, 1997).

44. "Guidelines for National Unification" (Taipei: National Unification Council, 1991).

45. "MAC Vice Chairman, Spokesman Sheu Ke-sheng, at the March 26, 1999, News Conference," *MAC News Briefing* 118 (March 29, 1999), p. 2.

46. For details of cross-Strait interaction through 1991, see Ralph N. Clough, *Reaching Across the Taiwan Strait: People-to-People Diplomacy* (Boulder, CO: Westview, 1993).

47. Gaston J. Sigur, Jr., "China Policy Today: Consensus, Consistence, Stability," U.S. Department of State, *Current Policy* 901 (December 1986), p. 4.

48. "Remarks by the Honorable George P. Shultz, Secretary of State, Shanghai Banquet, Shanghai, China, March 5, 1987," Department of State, *Press Release* 59 (March 10, 1987).

49. Chinese scholars wrote extensively on Beijing's view of the new international order. See, for example, Han Xu, "New World Order: A Chinese Perspective," *Beijing Review*, September 9-15, 1991, pp. 31-34; Qian Qichen, "Establishing a Just and Equitable New International Order," ibid., October 7-13, 1991, pp. 11-16; and Pan Tongwen, "New World Order—According to Mr. Bush," ibid., October 28-November 3, 1991, pp. 12-14.

50. See, for example, Hu Yang, "Summary of Symposium with the U.S. National Defense University," *Beijing Review*, December 14-20, 1992, pp. 31-32.

51. Wang Jisi, "United States: Formulating New Global Strategy," *Beijing Review*, March 9-15, 1992, pp. 33-35.

52. "Remarks by the President in Commencement Address to Yale University," (Kennebunkport, ME: The White House, Office of the Press Secretary, May 27, 1991).

53. *Washington Post*, June 11, 1991, p. A14; ibid., June 13, 1991, p. A36. For a more up-to-date report, see *Wall Street Journal*, December 15, 1998, p. A14.

54. *Wall Street Journal*, December 15, 1998, p. A14.

55. See Gary Milhollin and Gerald White, "A New China Syndrome: Beijing's Atomic Bazaar," *Washington Post*, May 12, 1991, p. C1.

56. For a discussion of the F-16 sale and other security-related matters, see the author's *The Changing of the Guard: President Clinton and the Security of Taiwan* (Boulder, CO: Westview, 1995).

57. *New York Times*, January 13, 1994, p. A11; *Far Eastern Economic Review*, January 27, 1994, pp. 12-14.

58. For details, see Dennis Van Vranken Hickey, *United States-Taiwan Security Ties: From Cold War to Beyond Containment* (Westport, CT: Praeger, 1994), pp. 77-93.

59. *China Post*, December 24, 1992, p. 2; *China News*, December 25, 1992, p. 1.

6

Clinton's Policy Toward China and Taiwan: The Formative Years, 1993-1994

The period 1993-1994 brought home the fact that U.S. policy toward China was itself a conundrum, the dilemma being how best to manage pragmatic relations with the PRC while pursuing larger U.S. objectives of integrating China into the community of market democracies and, in Asia particularly, the new Pacific community. The Taiwan conundrum in Sino-American relations during the Clinton administration became most apparent during 1995-1996, when Lee Teng-hui's visit to the United States ushered in several months of intense, but nonviolent, hostility between Beijing and both Washington and Taipei.

This chapter provides an overview of U.S. policy toward China and Taiwan during the formative years of the Clinton administration, 1993 through 1994. The next two chapters examine his policies in 1995 and 1996. The final chapter of the book considers President Clinton's policies toward China and Taiwan during 1997 and 1998, highlighting the renewed efforts of Washington and Beijing to establish a "constructive strategic partnership" and the implications this might have for Taiwan.

Clinton Defines His China Policy

As noted in the previous chapter, U.S. policy toward China once again became highly politicized after the 1989 Tiananmen Square incident, with President Bush defending his policy of engagement with China and the Democratic-controlled Congress criticizing the administration for "coddling" the communist rulers of Beijing. The 1992 Democratic Party Platform cited "the hero who stood in front of a tank in Beijing" as an example of "the tide of democracy" that arose in China but which was "only reluctantly" supported by President Bush. The platform said the Democratic Party approved the "conditioning of favorable trade terms for China on respect for human rights in China and Tibet, greater market access for U.S. goods, and responsible conduct on weapons proliferation." Overall, the platform called for the reordering of American interests in the post-Cold War era, giving a much higher priority to economic affairs and the promotion of human rights and American values in policies toward China.[1]

Because of the intensity of Democratic criticism of Bush's China policy, there was every expectation that Bill Clinton would be confrontational toward China, especially in the area of human rights. During the early stages of the presidential campaign, candidate Clinton said: "The administration continues to coddle China, despite its continuing crackdown on democratic reforms, its brutal subjugation of Tibet, its irresponsible exports of nuclear and missile technology, its support for the homicidal Khmer Rouge in Cambodia, and its abusive trade practices."[2] Clinton promised that, unlike Bush, he would link MFN trading status for China to its improvements in human rights observations, good trade behavior, and restraint in the export of weapons and defense technology.[3] At the same time, Clinton said he supported President Bush's decision to sell Taiwan F-16 jet fighters and promised to implement the sale if elected. He also voiced firm support for the U.S. commitment to help Taiwan defend itself under the TRA.[4]

During the televised presidential campaign debate in St. Louis on October 12, 1992, Clinton was asked how he would use U.S. power to influence China. First, he said, the U.S. relationship with China was important and China should not be isolated. Second, it was wrong for President Bush to send National Security Adviser Brent Scowcroft to China immediately after Tiananmen to toast their leaders. Third, it should be recognized that China agreed to stop exporting goods made by prison labor to the United States and to do something about their $15 billion trade surplus with the United States, not because the Bush administration "coddled them," but because of pressure by Congress. Fourth, he "would be firm" with China, saying: "If you want to continue most-favored-nation status for your government-owned industries as well as your private ones, observe human rights in the future, open your society." Fifth, Clinton said the United States should stand up for its economic and democratic interests in China, because by doing so the Chinese people will be more reliable partners in the long run.[5]

However, as it became apparent he would likely win the election, Clinton began to moderate his position on China. During a transition meeting with President Bush in mid-November 1992, Clinton said: "We have a big stake in not isolating China. . . . But we also have to insist, I believe, on progress in human rights and human decency. And I think there are indications in the last few months that a firm hand by our government can help to achieve that."[6] By December, Clinton was saying it would not be necessary to revoke China's MFN status if the PRC continued its course of economic reform and improved human rights. He told participants in the national economic conference in Little Rock, Arkansas: "I don't think we'll have to revoke the MFN status . . . if we can achieve continued progress along [present] lines." Clinton noted that China recently had agreed to stop exporting products made by prison labor to the United States and to open some markets to U.S. goods, after "the Bush administration finally agreed to put a little heat on the Chinese." Clinton said, "I don't want to isolate China for political and economic reasons. I don't want to dislocate any industries here. . . . But I do think in the aftermath of Tiananmen Square . . . that we have an obligation to at least continue to be consistent about the things in which we believe."[7]

During the period of the presidential transition, China signaled its desire to improve relations with the United States. In mid-November 1992, Deputy Trade Minister Tong Zhiguang said China would further liberalize its economy in order to qualify for GATT. Tong said China's purchase of two million tons of U.S. wheat that month was a signal that it wanted to advance trade ties with the United States.[8] In early December, Jiang Zemin told visiting U.S. Senators that the PRC was willing to set aside for the moment the issue of F-16 sales to Taiwan in order to try to work closely with President Clinton to put Sino-American relations back on a sound footing. At about the same time, China announced that it would cut tariffs on more than 3,000 imports to bring its trading regulations into alignment with GATT requirements.[9]

President Yang Shangkun, Vice President Wang Zhen, and Premier Li Peng sent separate messages of congratulations to the new president. The PRC Foreign Ministry said, "The Chinese government always attaches importance to Sino-U.S. relations and is ready to work with the new U.S. administration for improvement and development of bilateral relations."[10] In late January 1993, the PRC released two prominent political prisoners, Wang Xizhe, arrested twelve years before after taking part in the 1978–1979 Democracy Wall Movement, and Gao Shan, an economist jailed in connection with the 1989 Tiananmen Square protests. A few weeks later, China released Wang Dan, a prominent student leader imprisoned after the Tiananmen incident. And in mid-1993, China released Xu Wenli, a political activist imprisoned for twelve years in solitary confinement for advocating political reform within the communist system during the Democracy Wall Movement.[11] China also sent special buying missions to the United States during the first few months of 1993 to purchase more than $1 billion of U.S. planes, cars, and oil equipment.

Clinton responded favorably to these Chinese overtures. In February 1993 he sent a trade delegation to China to discuss Beijing's entry into GATT and U.S. access to the Chinese market. During the same month, he told an American University audience that the United States wanted to continue its "partnership" with China, "but I also think we have a right to expect progress in human rights and democracy"[12]

Clinton's early China policy was explained by designated Assistant Secretary of State for East Asian and Pacific Affairs Winston Lord in his March 1993 confirmation hearing before the Senate Foreign Relations Committee.[13] Lord said one of the principal U.S. goals in Asia was "restoring firm foundations for cooperation with a China where political openness catches up with economic reform." To accomplish this, the administration would follow a nuanced policy toward China, balancing U.S. interests in maintaining cooperative relations with the PRC because of its importance, while seeking improvement in China's record of human rights and the termination of policies harmful to U.S. interests. Lord said Chinese "leaders cling to an outdated authoritarian system" in which serious human rights and other abuses persisted. "Chinese leaders are gambling that open economics and closed politics will preserve their system of control," but it will prove to be "a gamble that sooner or later will be lost."

Lord pinpointed the U.S. policy conundrum with respect to Beijing: "Our policy challenge therefore is to reconcile our need to deal with this important nation with our imperatives to promote international values. We will seek cooperation with China on a range of issues. But Americans cannot forget Tiananmen Square." This required the United States to "conduct a nuanced policy toward Beijing until a more humane system emerges." He cautioned: "Shunning China is not an alternative. We need both to condemn repression and preserve links with progressive forces which are the foundations for our longer term ties." Lord defined the fundamental elements of President Clinton's China and Taiwan policies in terms similar to those of Presidents Carter, Reagan, and Bush:

1. The United States "will continue to be guided by the three Sino-American communiqués that have provided a flexible framework for our relations."
2. "It is up to China and Taiwan to work out their future relationship; we insist only that the process be peaceful."
3. "Consistent with our undertakings not to challenge the principle of 'one China,' we will continue to build upon our unofficial relations with Taiwan based on the Taiwan Relations Act."

Lord pointed to several issues in Sino-American relations that would be addressed by the new administration: widespread human rights violations on the mainland and in Tibet; Chinese exports of dangerous weapons and technology to volatile areas of the world; the fastest growing trade deficit of the United States, second only to that of Japan; continuous need for collaboration at the United Nations and on regional conflicts; and emerging challenges like the environment and illegal drugs. These and other issues required the United States and China to "work together where our interests converge and bargain hard over differences." Lord said, "Our approach will reflect that China is a great nation. In response to positive movement by the Chinese, we are prepared to address their concerns and strengthen our ties." He promised the new administration would support the democratic aspirations of the Chinese people, but "without arrogance—recognizing that the Chinese people will determine their own destiny, but confident that we are aligning ourselves with the future."

Clinton's Policy: The Formative Years

Thus, from at the outset of the Clinton administration, U.S. policy toward China was concerned with issues carried over from previous administrations: trade, human rights, security, proliferation, and Taiwan. The continuity of these issues, as well as the continuity of U.S. interests in China, ensured that Clinton's policies would be very similar to those of his predecessors. This can be seen in a brief review of some of the major policy issues faced by the new administration. Initially, the most visible of these issues was the linkage between MFN and human rights.

Trade and Human Rights

During the first two years of the Clinton administration, trade and human rights were closely intertwined in U.S. China policy. This linkage reflected the strong pro-human rights faction in the Democratic Party that supported Clinton in his campaign for the presidency. But as China's economy grew in importance to U.S. business, this linkage proved increasingly difficult to sustain, finally being broken by the administration in 1994.

When Bill Clinton assumed office in January 1993, the U.S.-PRC trade relationship had become one of the most important in the world. Trade between the United States and China topped $33 billion in 1992, with Chinese exports to the United States totaling $25.8 billion and U.S. exports to China totaling $7.5 billion. China was the fastest growing export market for U.S. goods in Asia, with American exports increasing by 19 percent. The United States absorbed 30 percent of Chinese exports in 1992, and between June 1989 and June 1993 China accumulated a $40 billion trade surplus with the United States.

China signed a market access agreement with the United States in 1992, promising to phase out 70 to 80 percent of China's non-tariff trade barriers over the next four years. In addition, an Intellectual Property Rights agreement was signed, along with a Memorandum of Understanding under which U.S. officials could inspect facilities suspected of producing goods for export made with prison labor. Earlier, in October 1991, China had promised to ban the export of such products altogether.

Despite campaign promises to link MFN and human rights, the Clinton administration indicated after the election that it might continue China's MFN status without conditions. In March 1993 Secretary of State Warren Christopher told the House Appropriations Subcommittee on Commerce, State, Judiciary and related agencies that the administration wanted to renew MFN for China in 1993 without conditions, but that it would tie renewal in 1994 to progress in human rights and certain other areas.[14] The following month, identical legislation was introduced in the House and Senate extending MFN to China into 1994 without conditions, but requiring that the president certify "significant progress" in areas such as human rights and proliferation before MFN would be extended after 1994. The bill called on China to release political prisoners and to permit individuals claiming political persecution to emigrate freely. The bill also asked China to end its sale of missiles to other countries and to allow greater U.S. product access to the Chinese market.

In May Clinton formally announced his 1993 MFN decision on China, accompanied by comment on China policy in general.[15] Stating that the United States must "recognize both the value of China and the values of America," the president said China occupied "an important place in our nation's foreign policy." He noted, however, "the American people continue to harbor profound concerns about a range of practices by China's communist leaders." These included the continued imprisonment of Chinese political activists and pro-democracy leaders; the lack of international access to Chinese prisons; continued reports of Chinese abuses against the people and culture of Tibet; the proliferation of dangerous weapons, such as M-11 missile transfers to Pakistan; China's $18 billion trade surplus with the United States; and Chinese practices to block American goods and services from being imported into the PRC. There were many signs of progress in China, Clinton said, but "the question we face today is how best to cultivate these hopeful seeds of change in China while expressing our clear disapproval of its repressive policies"— an excellent statement of the China conundrum. According to Clinton, the core of his China policy was "a resolute insistence upon significant progress on human rights in China." He would extend MFN status for China for the next twelve months through an executive order. "Whether I extend MFN next year, however, will depend upon whether China makes significant progress in implementing its human rights record."

On the same day Clinton announced his MFN decision, the administration sent a report to Congress which explained U.S. China policy in detail.[16] The report said that, while the United States would unconditionally renew MFN for 1993, renewal in 1994 would be conditioned on "significant progress" in a number of areas, including:

1. Respecting the fundamental human rights recognized in the Universal Declaration of Human Rights.
2. Complying with China's commitment to allow its citizens, regardless of their political views, freedom to emigrate and travel abroad (excepting those who were imprisoned, had criminal proceedings pending against them, or had received court notices concerning civil cases).
3. Providing an acceptable accounting for and release of Chinese citizens imprisoned or detained for the peaceful expression of their political views, including Democracy Wall and Tiananmen activists.
4. Taking effective steps to ensure that forced abortion and sterilization were not used to implement China's family planning policies.
5. Ceasing religious persecution, particularly by releasing leaders and members of religious groups detained or imprisoned for expression of their religious beliefs.

6. Taking effective actions to ensure that prisoners were not being mistreated and were receiving necessary medical treatment; granting access to Chinese prisons by international humanitarian organizations.
7. Seeking to resume dialogue with the Dalai Lama or his representatives, and taking measures to protect Tibet's distinctive religious and cultural heritage.
8. Continuing cooperation concerning U.S. military personnel who were listed as prisoners of war or missing in action.
9. Ceasing the jamming of Voice of America broadcasts.

The 1993 MFN decision thus linked 1994 MFN with human rights; however, the May 1993 policy also removed the linkage between MFN and other issues in Sino-American relations such as arms control and trade. On nonproliferation issues, the White House said it would approach China through existing legislation and international agreements. Trade issues also would be handled separately from MFN considerations, including the implementation of bilateral agreements with China on market access, intellectual property rights, and prison labor. If necessary, the administration promised to use Section 301 of the 1974 Trade Act "to ensure our interests are protected and advanced in the areas of market access and intellectual property rights."

The 1993 extension of MFN to China left several trade issues unresolved. First, in the area of market access, the PRC had agreed in October 1992 to eliminate most non-tariff and other informal trade barriers to U.S. goods and services over a five-year period, but progress had been slow. Secret and arbitrary import regulations permeated the system, and they were used frequently to keep American products out of China or to solicit bribes from U.S. businessmen and Chinese importers. Second, China continued to impose many irrational standards on American products, especially foods and medicines, as a way to protect its own agricultural and medicinal industries. Third, even though China promised to eliminate the practice, reports persisted that the PRC exported about $1 billion worth of prison-made goods to the United States each year through various forms of subterfuge. Fourth, U.S. customs officials estimated that China annually exported at least $2 billion of illegally labeled textiles, despite its promise to abide by international rules prohibiting mislabeling practices. Washington warned Beijing that the United States would unilaterally reduce textile quotas for the PRC unless it agreed to U.S. terms by the end of 1993, when the five-year Sino-American textile agreement would expire. And fifth, despite having laws on the books protecting intellectual property rights, Chinese violations persisted with little enforcement, resulting in billions of dollars in losses to U.S. audio and video tape producers.

Clinton's 1993 MFN policy was explained on June 8 by Assistant Secretary of State Winston Lord in a hearing before the House Ways and Means Committee.[17] Expressing the U.S. policy conundrum toward China, Lord said that trying to balance U.S. international goals in maintaining cooperative relations with Beijing with U.S. interests in promoting human rights and democracy in China was no easy task. Many different approaches had been considered to find "the best means to remain engaged with China while pressing Beijing for responsible behavior in core areas of concern." The administration believed "economic reform produces—and requires—political reform. In today's world, nations cannot prosper for long without opening up their societies. Technology and information, the forces of modernization, and global democratic trends have been eroding communism and totalitarianism across the globe." Lord assured the members of the committee that "change continues in China," including the "erosion of Marxist-Leninist orthodoxy."

Lord said the guiding principle of Clinton's policy toward China was this: "The Chinese Government cannot expect to enjoy the full fruits of membership in the international community . . . unless it abides by universally recognized standards regarding treatment of its citizens, global commerce, and the transfer of weapons of mass destruction and sensitive technology." The U.S. policy challenge with China was "to reconcile our need to deal with this important nation with our imperative to promote international values." Above all, "the U.S. has a basic national interest in a more open, prosperous, and humane China, which will also be a more peaceful and cooperative member of the world community."

The Clinton administration was drawn into the same dilemma which had confronted previous administrations: how to engage China without sacrificing U.S. values? The U.S. strategy was based on the simple assumption that engagement would change China, so that, eventually, U.S. values—as well as U.S. interests— would be served. The problem was that China refused to follow U.S.-defined international rules and standards, and it rejected the notion that economic reform would lead to the demise of the communist state. China pursued engagement with the United States to further Chinese interests; the United States pursued engagement with China not only to serve American interests but also to change China.

Not surprisingly, the Chinese response to Clinton's 1993 MFN policy was acidic, with the PRC Foreign Ministry lodging a protest with the United States for its adding conditions to the extension of MFN in 1994. Beijing said these conditions "constitute an open violation of the principles set forth in the three Sino-U.S. joint communiqués and the agreement on trade relations between the two countries, and is a serious interference in China's internal affairs. . . . [It is] unacceptable to China that the United States has politicized the trade issue. . . . If the United States should insist on this, it will seriously impair Sino-U.S. relations and economic and trade cooperation, eventually hurting the vital interest of the United States."[18]

Differences between the Clinton administration and China surfaced repeatedly in the area of human rights. In large measure, this reflected China's profound disagreement with the U.S. definition of universal human rights. Vice-Foreign Minister Liu Huaqiu, head of the Chinese Delegation to the World Conference on Human Rights held in Vienna, spelled out Chinese views on this issue in June

Clinton's Policy: The Formative Years 163

1993, listing four "principled proposals" on which China's policy on human rights were based:[19]

1. The international community should give its primary attention to the massive gross violations of human rights resulting from foreign aggression and occupation and continue to support those people still under foreign invasion, colonial rule or apartheid system in their just struggle for national self-determination.
2. World peace and stability should be enhanced and a favorable international environment created for the attainment of the goals in human rights protection. To this end, countries should establish a new type of international relationship of mutual respect, equality, amicable coexistence and mutual beneficial cooperation in accordance with the U.N. Charter and the norms of international law. All international disputes should be solved peacefully in a fair and reasonable manner and in the spirit of mutual accommodation and mutual understanding, and consultation on equal footing, instead of resorting to force or threat of force. No country should pursue hegemonism and power politics or engage in aggression, expansion and interference.
3. The right of developing countries to development should be respected and guaranteed. To create a good international economic environment for the initial economic development of developing countries, the international community should commit itself to the establishment of a fair and rational new international economic order.
4. The right of each country to formulate its own policies on human rights protection in light of its own conditions should also be respected and guaranteed. Nobody should be allowed to use the human rights issue to exert political and economic pressures on other countries. The human rights issue can be discussed among countries. However, the discussions should be conducted in the spirit of mutual respect and on an equal footing.

China demonstrated repeatedly that it would not allow interference from the United States on PRC treatment of its own citizens. This attitude deeply offended many Americans. Reflecting this sense of outrage, Congress voiced strong opposition to the idea of Beijing hosting the Summer Olympic Games in the year 2000. In July 1993 the U.S. House of Representatives adopted a resolution urging the International Olympic Committee (IOC) to reject Beijing's bid to host the games because of China's poor human rights record. In August nearly two-thirds of the Senate signed a letter to all ninety members of the IOC with the same message of opposition.

Faced with this opposition, China sought to improve its human rights image and win the honor of hosting the 2000 Olympics. In mid-September 1993, just a few days before the IOC was to make its final decision, the PRC released Wei Jingsheng, China's most famous political prisoner.[20] Immediately after losing its

Olympic bid to Sydney, Australia, Beijing again cracked down on dissidents by arresting several throughout China. The government also passed regulations restricting the personal use of satellite dishes, pagers, and cordless telephones. PRC leaders reportedly were extremely angry over U.S. opposition to China's hosting the Olympic Games, with senior political and military officials demanding that Jiang Zemin adopt a tougher stance in Sino-American relations. Perhaps reflecting this opinion, Jiang reportedly said in late August 1993 that the West was pursuing a two-tracked strategy toward China: trying to Westernize it by promoting democracy, human rights, and other bourgeois ideals and culture, and trying to weaken China by splitting it through separatism and by promoting the independence of Hong Kong, Taiwan, Xinjiang, and Tibet. Jiang said the West wanted capitalism to succeed in China but that it did not want China to become a major Pacific power.[21]

Alarmed at deteriorating relations with China, the Clinton administration concluded that it needed to do something. In mid-September 1993, President Clinton adopted a strategy of "reengagement" to help resolve the growing list of problems that had emerged with the PRC since 1989. According to press reports, Clinton sent a personal letter to Jiang Zemin along with a document clarifying U.S. intentions in Sino-American relations. The documents were said to mentioned a U.S. "commitment to a 'unified' China."[22] If true, such a commitment would be a significant change in U.S. policy, which previously had supported the process of peacefully resolving the Taiwan issue without backing a specific outcome of that process.

As part of his strategy of reengagement, Clinton sent several top officials to Beijing for discussions on a wide range of issues. These included Treasury Secretary Lloyd Bentsen and Agricultural Secretary Mike Espy to discuss trade, State Department Assistant Secretary John Shattuck to discuss human rights, and Assistant Secretary of Defense Charles Freeman to discuss resuming U.S.-PRC military ties. Secretary of State Warren Christopher met Foreign Minister Qian Qichen in New York in September, and Clinton himself met Jiang Zemin during the Asian Pacific Economic Cooperation (APEC) meeting in Seattle in November 1993.

In his meeting with Jiang, President Clinton said he reaffirmed U.S. support for the three joint communiqués "as the bedrock of our one-China policy."[23] According to the president, "I emphasized to President Jiang the need for early concrete progress on aspects of China policy and practice that are of deep concern to the American people—human rights, including Tibet, trade practices, and nonproliferation." The five human rights areas raised by Clinton in his meeting with Jiang were Red Cross visits to Chinese prisons, the release of political prisoners, beginning a dialogue with the Dalai Lama, prohibiting prison labor to produce goods for exports, and permitting relatives of Chinese dissidents exiled in the United States to emigrate to the United States.

The Clinton administration also was concerned over the U.S.-PRC textile trade. In 1993 China was the largest textile exporter to the United States, accounting for more than 13 percent of total U.S. textile and clothing imports and as much as 25 percent of total textiles sold in the United States. Legal Chinese textile exports to the United States were about $4.7 billion. In addition, some $2.2 billion in Chinese silks were exported to the United States. On top of these legal sales, the administration claimed China was illegally exporting about $2 billion worth of textiles and apparel by mislabeling products as being made in other countries. The previous five-year U.S.-PRC textile agreement was due to expire at the end of 1993, and the United States threatened to impose unilateral reductions of China's textile quotas if the illegal exports were not stopped.

By mid-January 1994, however, the two sides approved a new textile agreement. Under the previous agreement, China had been allowed to increase its textile exports to the United States at a rate of 4.4 percent annually. The new agreement limited PRC textile exports to the United States to annual increases of 1 percent in 1995 and 1996. To compensate for previous illegal shipments, China's quota for 1994 was frozen at the 1993 level. The agreement provided for unannounced inspections by joint U.S.-Chinese teams to ensure that Chinese factories were not mislabeling the country-of-origin tags on their products. In a separate pact the two sides agreed to limit the growth in Chinese silk exports to the United States to 1 percent a year.[24]

In March 1994 intellectual property rights (IPR) once again became an issue. U.S. Trade Representative Mickey Kantor told the House Foreign Affairs Committee that the administration had placed China on a priority watch list for flagrant IPR violation. In addition to IPR issues, Kantor's office was concerned over restrictions on U.S. access to Chinese agricultural markets.[25]

In early 1994, as the question of the renewal of China's MFN status moved to the fore, there was sharp debate within the administration over whether U.S. interests in human rights were more important than U.S. commercial interests in interacting with the fastest growing economy in the world. The State Department's annual report on the status of human rights around the world, released in early February 1994, described China's "overall human rights record in 1993 [as falling] short of internationally accepted norms as it continued to repress domestic critics and failed to control abuses by its own security forces." As a result, the State Department concluded that China's human rights record was not sufficient to justify renewal of MFN in 1994.[26]

A few days after the State Department's report, Beijing released three political prisoners held in connection with the Tiananmen demonstrations, but it still detained high-level political prisoners such as Wang Juntao and Bao Tong. Then, in early March, the PRC arrested several political dissidents, including Wei Jingsheng. Wei was soon released, however, when it became known that Secretary of State Christopher might cancel his first trip to Beijing, scheduled for later that month. In Australia at the time, Christopher commented: "It is hard to overstate the strong distaste we all feel for the recent detentions and hostile measures taken by the Chinese. Certainly these actions will have a negative effect on my trip."[27]

Christopher's comments proved prophetic. When he visited the PRC in March, the secretary informed the Chinese government that President Clinton intended to link China's MFN status in 1994 to its human rights conduct which, to date, was not satisfactory. He received an exceptionally cold reception, although progress in some areas of human rights was made. According to the secretary, he was able to secure from the Chinese a joint declaration to end exports to the United States of goods produced by prison labor; assurances on inspections of all Chinese facilities suspected of producing such goods; promises to resolve a few of the outstanding emigration cases; an agreement to review interference with Voice of America radio signals; a promise to talk with Red Cross officials regarding visits to prisoners of conscience; information regarding some 235 prisoners specified by the United States; and promises to provide information on 106 Tibetans imprisoned in China.[28]

Upon his return from China, the Secretary of State was severely criticized for his handling of China policy in general. Some thought he should have canceled his trip to Beijing because of China's harassment of leading dissidents; others regarded the linkage of trade with human rights as counterproductive. Business groups with an interest in trading with the PRC found strong allies with those in the administration who were responsible for trade and economic policy. The president himself seemed ambivalent on the issue, and different departments and agencies within the U.S. government contradicted each other in statements as to whether China's MFN would be extended in 1994.[29]

The PRC continued its tough posture. Foreign Minister Qian Qichen observed that the importance of China's trade with the United States was overrated, insisting that his government would not be pressured by attempts to link trade and human rights. According to Qian, the U.S. president had "enmeshed himself in a web of his own spinning" in which "he will only have his own hands and feet bound."[30]

Concerned that the rift in its China policy was growing, the White House held a series of top level meetings shortly after Christopher's return from Beijing. One outcome of these meetings was an increased role by the departments of Treasury and Commerce in the formulation of China policy, ostensibly to ensure greater balance between U.S. security, human rights, and commercial interests. A few years later this decision returned to haunt the administration when the Commerce Department did not adequately consult the Defense and State departments on the transfer to China of information related to sensitive missile and satellite technology.[31] After March 1994, the president continued to speak of the need to improve human rights in China, but his administration placed much greater emphasis on maintaining a positive relationship with China.[32] This was reflected in the administration's final MFN decision for 1994.

As required by executive order, the Department of State issued a report in May on China's human rights performance as part of the MFN determination for 1994.[33] The report noted China's compliance with two mandatory conditions: the

Clinton's Policy: The Formative Years

resolution of all pending emigration cases and the ending of exports of prison labor to the United States. On the other hand, China "has not achieved the 'overall, significant progress' in the five additional areas identified in the 1993 executive order," thus falling short of the required standard. Nonetheless, "Our judgment is that revocation of China's MFN status would serve neither the interests of promoting human rights progress in China nor the interests this nation has in maintaining mutually advantageous ties with China. . . . We believe that our human rights objectives may now be best pursued with China without conditioning MFN eligibility." In a sharp about-face, the State Department was recommending that the link between MFN and human rights be ended.

On May 26 President Clinton announced that he had accepted the State Department's recommendations: "I have decided that the United States should renew Most Favored Nation trading status toward China. This decision, I believe, offers us the best opportunity to lay the basis for long-term sustainable progress in human rights, and for the advancement of our other interests with China. Extending MFN will avoid isolating China and instead will permit us to engage the Chinese with not only economic contacts but with cultural, educational and other contacts, and with a continuing aggressive effort in human rights—an approach that I believe will make it more likely that China will play a responsible role, both at home and abroad."[34]

Accordingly, the president said he would "delink human rights from the annual extension of Most Favored Nation trading status for China. That linkage has been constructive during the past year. But I believe, based on our aggressive contacts with the Chinese in the past several months, that we have reached the end of the usefulness of that policy, and it is time to take a new path toward achievement of our constant objectives. We need to place our relationship into a larger and more productive framework." In language remarkably similar to that of President Bush, Clinton said in the May 26 announcement:

> I believe the question, therefore, is not whether we continue to support human rights in China, but how we can best support human rights in China and advance our other very significant issues and interests. I believe we can do it by engaging the Chinese. I believe the course I have chosen gives us the best chance of success on all fronts. We will have more contacts. We will have more trade. We will have more international cooperation. We will have more intense and constant dialogue on human rights issues. We will have that in an atmosphere which gives us the chance to see China evolve as a responsible power, ever-growing not only economically, but growing in political maturity so that human rights can be observed.

Clinton's revised human rights policy toward the PRC included the following major elements: (1) renewing China's MFN status; (2) delinking MFN renewal from human rights issues, other than the statutory requirements of the Jackson-Vanik amendment regarding freedom of emigration; (3) banning the import of Chinese munitions (mostly small arms and ammunition), valued at $200 million in

1994; (4) maintaining the existing Tiananmen sanctions, including the denial of participation in the U.S. Trade and Development Assistance Program, Overseas Private Investment Corporation, and the U.S.-Asia Environment Partnership Program; continued U.S. opposition to non-basic human needs loans to China by the World Bank and other multilateral development banks; suspension of weapons deliveries; and denial of licenses for dual-use civilian technology and U.S. munitions list items; and (5) implementing a new human rights strategy for China. The components of that new human rights strategy were: (a) intensifying high-level dialogue with the Chinese on human rights; (b) increasing the number of exchanges between Chinese and American legal specialists, jurists, prison administrators, and human rights organizations; (c) working with the American business community to develop a voluntary set of principles to advance human rights in China; (d) increasing radio and television broadcasts to the Chinese people from the Voice of America; (e) inaugurating Radio Free Asia; (f) increasing multilateral pressure on China to improve its human rights practices through the United Nations and other international forums; (g) working more closely with Chinese and American non-governmental organizations to improve human rights conditions; and (h) working through international organizations to address Tibet's human rights problems and promoting discussions between the Dalai Lama and the Chinese government.[35]

Anthony Lake, the president's national security adviser, called the new policy "a tactical shift" designed to serve the "very important strategic objective" of building "a relationship with China within which we can seriously pursue human rights as well as our other security and economic interests."[36] For their part, the Chinese responded favorably to the new pragmatism in U.S. policy. In contrast to the frigid reception given Warren Christopher during his trip to Beijing in March, PRC leaders went out of their way to welcome Secretary of Commerce Ronald Brown during his visit in late August and early September 1994. Brown was accompanied by twenty-four chief executives of American corporations seeking to do business in China. Emphasizing U.S. commercial interests in dealing with the PRC and downplaying human rights issues in all public statements, Brown and his entourage were able to obtain $5-6 billion in contracts,[37] although less than a tenth of the promised business had materialized after a year.[38]

Proliferation Issues

By the time Clinton assumed office in January 1993, China had become a party to all major agreements on nonproliferation, acceding to the Nuclear Non-Proliferation Treaty (NPT) in March 1992,[39] adhering to the Missile Technology Control Regime (MTCR) guidelines and parameters,[40] and becoming an original signatory to the Chemical Weapons Convention in January 1993.[41]

Seeking full Chinese compliance with these multilateral obligations and its support for international nonproliferation goals was a top administration priority.

From the outset, the administration said it was prepared to employ the resources under U.S. law and executive determination—including the imposition of sanctions —if the PRC engaged in transfers that violated its commitments. In practice, the Clinton administration was often reluctant to impose these penalties, often choosing to ignore American intelligence detailing Chinese proliferation activities.[42]

The U.S. intelligence community released an unclassified report in January 1993 stating, "it is highly probable that China has not eliminated its BW [biological warfare] program" as it agreed to do in 1984.[43] In May 1993, U.S. intelligence officials said that new evidence had surfaced of China's violation of the Missile Technology Control Regime. The violation occurred with the shipment of M-11 ballistic missile components to Pakistan in November 1992. Mobile launch vehicles for the M-11 had been sighted inside of Pakistan in early 1991. The MTCR banned the sale of missiles and associated technology with a range of more than 186 miles and payload capabilities over 1,100 pounds. Although the M-11 had a range of slightly less than 186 miles, the United States concluded that China's sale of M-11 technology and components violated the MTCR because these could be used by Pakistan to produce longer-ranged missiles capable of carrying nuclear, chemical, or biological warheads.

President Clinton's security strategy toward China was to integrate the PRC more fully into regional affairs as a means of moderating Beijing's behavior and, hopefully, to avoid the consequences of having China become an enemy of the United States in the twenty-first century. In his July 10, 1993, speech before the Korean National Assembly, Clinton specifically mentioned China, along with North Korea, as threats to the security interests of the new Pacific community.[44] Still, he indicated that U.S. strategy toward China was one of integration, welcoming Beijing's participation in new regional security dialogues: "The goal of all these efforts is to integrate, not isolate, the region's powers. China is a key example. We believe China cannot be a full partner in the world community until it respects human rights and international agreements on trade and weapon sales. But we also are prepared to involve China in building this region's new security and economic architectures. We need an involved and engaged China, not an isolated China." Secretary of State Warren Christopher reiterated the president's remarks in Singapore during the ASEAN Post-Ministerial Conference in late July 1993.[45] At the same time, he warned China about shipments of M-11 missile components and technology to Pakistan, saying such shipments might result in U.S. sanctions.[46]

Although China denied violating its pledge to abstain from shipping such missiles, the administration formally concluded in August 1993 that the PRC, while refraining from the sale of certain items since joining the international agreements, in fact had in November 1992 transferred to Pakistan MTCR-class M-11 missiles and related equipment in violation of China's MTCR commitment.[47] Specifically, the U.S. government determined that Chinese and Pakistani organizations had engaged in transfers of Category II MTCR annex items related to the M-11 missile.

Such transfers required the imposition of sanctions under U.S. law. Accordingly, on August 25, 1993, the administration announced a ban on the export of certain high-technology goods to China for two years. The U.S. sanctions were mandated by an amendment to the 1990 Arms Export Control Act requiring that if a nonmarket economy violated MTCR guidelines, all U.S. activities affecting the development or production of electronics, space systems or equipment, and military aircraft would be subject to sanctions. In a decision affecting about $1 billion in U.S. sales, the administration prevented American companies from obtaining export licenses to sell China rocket systems and rocket subsystems, avionics equipment, launch-support equipment, software, satellites, and advanced computers.

China reacted strongly to the U.S. sanctions, claiming the American decision "was a wrong judgment based on inaccurate intelligence." Vice-Foreign Minister Liu Huaqiu said that China had done nothing to violate its February 1992 commitment to the MTCR. Liu pointed out that the PRC agreement to act in compliance with the MTCR guidelines and parameters "was predicated on U.S. withdrawal of all its sanctions on China." With the resumption of the sanctions, "the Chinese government has no alternative but to reconsider its commitments to MTCR," with the United States being "held fully responsible for all the consequences."[48]

Another proliferation issue in 1993 involved the Chinese cargo ship *Yinhe* destined for Iran. The United States strongly suspected the ship carried thiodiglycol for mustard gas and thionyl chloride for nerve gas in violation of the recently negotiated Chemical Weapons Convention scheduled to take effect in 1995. After weeks of heated exchanges in which the United States demanded that it be allowed to search the ship, *Yinhe* was inspected in the Saudi port of Damman in early September. No banned chemicals were found. American officials believed the chemical containers had been dumped at sea or that U.S. agencies had been fed disinformation by Chinese intelligence services for the purposes of embarrassment.

The Chinese Foreign Ministry said on September 4 that the U.S. action in the *Yinhe* incident was "a show of hegemony and power politics, pure and simple." China demanded the United States make a public apology and compensate China for all financial loses. The Foreign Ministry said, "China has committed itself publicly not to produce or possess chemical weapons, nor does it export chemical products that may be used for the purpose of making chemical weapons."[49] Other Chinese commentators said, "the United States has once again tried to play the role of 'world cop,' revealing itself to be a hegemonic bully."[50]

On September 29 Foreign Minister Qian Qichen denounced the United States before the United Nations for "hegemonic conduct of a self-styled 'world cop' who tramples upon international law and norms of international relations." Referring to the U.S. sale of F-16s to Taiwan in 1992 and sanctions against China in 1993 for the alleged sale of M-11 components to Pakistan, Qian said China was opposed to the use of sanctions "under the pretext of controlling arms transfers while engaging in massive arms sales of one's own which jeopardize the sovereignty and security of the country concerned." The Foreign Minister called for more tolerance of "differences and diversities" among the countries of the world, adding that China strongly opposed "any attempt to impose a particular model" of government on other nations.[51]

Adding fuel to the nonproliferation issue was China's detonation of an underground nuclear weapon in October 1993. China had become a nuclear power in 1964. As of October 1993, it had conducted thirty-eight tests, the previous one in September 1992. By way of comparison, the United States had conducted 942 tests, while the combined tests of Russia, France, and Great Britain totaled 969.[52] China's October 1993 test was carried out despite repeated requests from President Clinton and twenty other nations that Beijing join the world's other nuclear powers in foregoing nuclear testing. Saying it deeply regretted the PRC test, the White House called on Beijing to refrain from further nuclear tests and to join the other nuclear powers in a global moratorium.[53]

Despite these highly visible episodes, the Clinton administration tried to handle proliferation problems with the PRC in private diplomatic exchanges, believing that greater compliance could be gained in this manner. Also, private exchanges would make the management of China policy easier by removing from public eye one of the most contentious issues in Sino-American relations. But once again, this approach proved embarrassing to the administration a few years later with the 1999 release of the Cox report, detailing years of Chinese espionage activities to acquire American missile and weapon technologies.[54]

One aspect of the September 1993 reengagement strategy was the gradual reestablishment of U.S. military links with the People's Liberation Army (PLA), banned by President Bush in 1989 as a result of Tiananmen. This decision enjoyed fairly wide consensus among American China specialists, who felt more dialogue with the PLA would be wise in view of several considerations: the PRC was expanding its power projection capabilities and aspired to be a world power; there was greater tendency on the part of China to challenge the United States in Asia; the PLA's strength was steadily increasing; many senior Chinese military leaders were convinced that the United States had become China's principal enemy; the PLA was directly involved in many areas of controversy in Sino-American relations such as proliferation of nuclear weapons technology and ballistic missiles; the PLA exerted strong influence within the conservative wing of the PRC leadership; the military would play a vital role in the future political direction of China; and greater contact with the PLA would enable the United States to learn more about Chinese military thinking and perhaps to influence the PLA in ways beneficial to U.S. interests.

To reopen military-to-military talks with the PRC, Assistant Secretary of Defense Charles Freeman visited Beijing in early November 1993. His trip produced no significant agreements, although a wide range of issues were discussed, including regional security, Chinese participation in U.N. peacekeeping operations, the problem of converting defense industries to civilian production, and U.S. concerns about proliferation of weapons of mass destruction. Sharp differences were reported over Chinese missile sales to Pakistan and U.S. weapons sales to Taiwan. Freeman said it was not likely U.S.-PRC military cooperation would return to the level maintained during the Cold War and that there was no talk of weapons sales to China. Other U.S. officials said Washington would continue to ban the sell of weapons to Beijing and would not approve manufacturing licenses for military-related goods.[55]

A few weeks after the Freeman visit, the administration approved the sale to China of a Cray supercomputer slated for use in weather prediction but which could also be used to develop nuclear weapons and ballistic missile systems. The computer sale was accompanied by a decision to allow China to launch three of eight communications satellites earlier banned because of the M-11 missile sanctions. In return for the lifting of high-tech sanctions, Washington asked Beijing to make more specific its promise to abide by the requirements of the Missile Control Technology Regime. China agreed to do so, and in October 1994, a joint statement was signed on missile proliferation and fissile materials for nuclear weapons.[56] In the agreement the United States promised to lift the sanctions imposed in August 1993, at which time the PRC "will not export ground-to-ground missiles featuring the primary parameters of the Missile Technology Control Regime (MTCR)—that is, inherently capable of reaching a range of at least 300 km with a payload of at least 500 kg." The Chinese accepted the U.S. definition of inherent capability: "Under this concept, the missile would be included in the ban if it could generate sufficient energy to deliver a 500 kg payload at least 300 km, regardless of its demonstrated or advertised combination of range and payload." The two sides agreed to work toward China's eventual membership in the MTCR. At the same time, "the two countries agreed to work together to promote the earliest possible achievement of a multilateral, non-discriminatory, internationally and effectively verifiable convention banning the production of fissile materials for nuclear weapons or other nuclear explosive devices."

China's cooperation on nonproliferation issues gradually improved after the October 1994 agreement, although there were periods of curtailment of cooperation following Lee Teng-hui's visit to the United States in 1995 and the accidental missile attack on the Chinese embassy in Belgrade in 1999 during the Kosovo conflict. In 1995 China supported the indefinite and unconditional extension of the Nuclear Non-Proliferation Treaty; in 1996 it signed the Comprehensive Test Ban Treaty and agreed to seek an international ban on the production of fissile nuclear weapons material. Also in 1996 China committed not to provide assistance to unsafeguarded nuclear facilities. In 1997 it became a member of the NPT Exporters Committee and issued detailed nuclear export control regulations. In the same year China ratified the Chemical Weapons Convention. By 1998 China was implementing regulations which established controls over nuclear-related dual-use items, and it also pledged not to engage in new nuclear cooperation with Iran. As a result of these efforts, Clinton in 1998 brought back into force the 1985 U.S.-China Agreement on Peaceful Nuclear Cooperation.[57]

Despite this progress, proliferation problems with China continued to plague Sino-American relations through 1998. In that year, for example, the principal issue was the illegal transfer of missile technology to the PRC from American companies using China's satellite launching vehicles. Following Secretary of State Christopher's controversial trip to China in March 1994, it was decided that the Department of Commerce would have a larger say in the sale of high-tech, dual-use equipment and technology to China. This removed several layers of control over the export of sensitive technology, a problem formally addressed by Congress through two committees charged with investigating the transfer of sensitive space technology to China. The committees found several instances—specifically involving a Hughes satellite blown up in a Chinese rocket in 1995 and a Loral Space & Communications satellite similarly destroyed in 1996—in which American companies inadvertently provided China with information that might be used to improve the reliability and accuracy of China's ICBMs.[58] A Pentagon report given Congress in late 1998 faulted the Commerce Department for approving contacts between these companies and China without alerting other U.S. agencies responsible for preventing militarily sensitive information from going to foreign governments.[59]

Policies Toward Taiwan

Taipei did not expect great improvement in relations with the United States under President Clinton, but it signaled early that it hoped for at least two changes in U.S. policy: (a) the lifting of the administrative directive established by the Carter administration forbidding U.S. government officials above the assistant secretary level to visit Taiwan and prohibiting other forms of official contact, such as denying the right of Taiwan diplomats to visit the State Department; and (b) the renaming of Taiwan's representative office in the United States, the Coordination Council for North American Affairs, "so that newcomers will not be confused."[60] Both of these changes were implemented in 1994 as part of the administration's Taiwan policy review.

Moreover, Clinton indicated on several occasions his recognition of the importance of Taiwan to U.S. interests. During the campaign, Clinton said he approved of President Bush's decision to sell F-16s to Taiwan and promised to proceed with the sale if elected. Clinton also voiced support for the U.S. commitment to help Taiwan defend itself under the Taiwan Relations Act. Clinton's campaign promises to take strong action against the PRC for its human rights abuses and missile proliferation contributed to a perception in Taiwan that ties with the United States might actually improve slightly under the new president.

It soon became clear, however, that Clinton's policies toward Taiwan would be the same as those of his predecessor. Ambassador Winston Lord in his confirmation hearing in March 1993 said the Clinton administration would "continue to be guided by the three Sino-American communiqués that have provided a flexible framework for our relations." Reiterating past policy, he said, "It is up to China and Taiwan to work out their future relationship; we insist only that the process be peaceful. . . . Consistent with our undertakings not to challenge the principle of 'one China,' we will continue to build upon our unofficial relations with Taiwan based on the Taiwan Relations Act."[61]

President Clinton spoke favorably of Taiwan on several occasions during the first year of his administration. In his Waseda University speech in Tokyo in July 1993, for example, Clinton referred to Taiwan as an example of the forces of market democracy at work in Asia. During the same speech Clinton said that Taipei, along with Seoul, Bangkok, and Shanghai, were "providing consumer goods and services to people who could not have even dreamed of them just a generation ago." He spoke favorably of Taiwan's trade practices, which he contrasted with those of Japan, noting that Taiwan "moved closer to trade balance with the U.S. as [it became] more prosperous."[62]

These positive themes were reiterated by Natale Bellocchi, chairman of the American Institute in Taiwan (AIT), in several of his speeches under the new administration. In Boston in June 1993, Bellocchi suggested the Clinton administration might broaden U.S. support for Taiwan's participation in international organizations, saying:

> it is in everyone's interest that Taiwan should not only follow but also where appropriate, participate in establishing trade and other standards. Taiwan is a member of APEC and the GATT accession process has begun, both of which are positive developments. It is still barred from most international economic and scientific organizations and agreements. International organizations in finance, in trade, in environment, in transnational issues such as narcotics, police, terrorism, etc., in humanitarian efforts, and in regulatory bodies, all could benefit from Taiwan's involvement. [However], in dealing with international organizations the form of [Taiwan's] involvement becomes a multilateral matter, not a bilateral one and thus it becomes much more complex.[63]

In 1993 Taiwan was the sixth largest trading partner of the United States with U.S. imports from Taiwan totaling $23.5 billion and exports to the ROC valued at $16.7 billion. The potential for expansion of U.S. trade and investment with Taiwan was large. In 1992, for example, one-third of the increase in global exports to the Pacific Rim were to Taiwan. It represented the largest market in the world for infrastructure work and equipment. The American Institute in Taiwan said in its March 1994 report on Taiwan's economy that one of the most important future U.S. interests in Asia was commercial ties with Taiwan.[64]

Clinton's Policy: The Formative Years

Clinton's intention to maintain friendly relations with Taiwan was demonstrated also by the level of arms sold to Taipei during his administration. In addition to promising to implement President Bush's decision to sell F-16s, the Clinton administration completed many arms transfers and authorized several new sales. During 1993 and 1994, these transactions included the following:

- In March 1993 it was announced that Taiwan and Raytheon Company, manufacturer of the Patriot missile system, were negotiating the coproduction of the hardware and software for a Patriot derivative known as the Modified Air Defense Systems (MADS). MADS would replace Taiwan's existing air defense system, based on the Nike, considered incapable of protecting the island against air attacks from China.[65]
- In September 1993 the United States agreed to sell Taiwan forty-one Harpoon antiship missiles for $68 million. The Harpoon had been sought by Taiwan for almost as long as the F-16.[66]
- In October 1993 it was reported that the United States would sell Taiwan the Stinger ground-to-air missile installed on military vehicles.[67]
- In October 1993 the ROC Navy placed into service three *Knox*-class frigates leased from the United States, with six more to be acquired in 1994 and 1995.[68]
- In March 1994 it was reported that Taiwan would take delivery in September 1995 of four Hawkeye early warning command and control aircraft valued at $760 million. The deal included logistics, personnel training, and a software development lab on Taiwan.[69]
- In April 1994 the ROC Army announced that it would purchase 200 Patriot missiles at a cost of about $377 million.[70]
- In August 1994 the ROC army announced it had purchased 160 M-60A3 tanks from the United States at a cost of $91 million. The tanks were equipped with thermal sights.[71]
- In August 1994 the United States announced it would sell Taiwan 80 electronic-countermeasures (ECM) pods for the F-16s sold to Taipei at a cost of $150 million.[72]

Despite these signs that Clinton would maintain friendly U.S. relations with Taiwan and pursue the "dual-track" China-Taiwan policy in place since 1979, there were several problem areas in the U.S.-Taiwan relationship. The most serious trade issue was Taiwan's violation of U.S. copyrights. AIT Chairman Bellocchi said in March 1993 that the Clinton administration would include Taiwan on a list subject to Section 301 U.S. Omnibus Trade Act sanctions if Taipei did not take concrete action in resolving its copyright violations. Bellocchi also said the United States would continue to support Taiwan's entrance into GATT, but that Washington would focus on four areas of needed improvement in regards to that membership:

intellectual property rights (IPR), agricultural subsidies, transparency of government procurement, and regulation of telecommunications.[73]

In May 1993 the Clinton administration placed Taiwan, along with Hungary, on a "priority watch list" for IPR violations. U.S. Trade Representative Mickey Kantor said, "We have given Taiwan and Hungary very special action plans, and expect them to meet the plans by the end of July. . . . Taiwan needs to enact legislation to legitimize cable TV systems, control copyright piracy by cable TV stations in Taiwan and eliminate piracy of videogames." At the same time, Kantor praised Taiwan for clamping down on IPR violators, approving a strict bilateral copyright agreement, and banning unauthorized parallel imports of copyrighted works. By August 1993 the United States declared its satisfaction with Taipei's efforts to end industrial piracy.[74]

In December 1993 the administration presented the ROC with a list of 2,800 import items on which Washington wanted Taipei to reduce tariffs or make duty-free in order to advance Taiwan's GATT application process in Geneva. During the same period, the ROC legislature approved amendments to Taiwan's Trademark Law strengthening IPR protection for U.S. products as a means of avoiding possible future trade sanctions under Section 301 and to move Taiwan's regulations closer into alignment with GATT requirements. Another area of contention in 1993–1994 was U.S. sanctions placed on Taiwan for trade in endangered species such as tigers and rhinoceroses, parts of which were used in traditional Chinese medicines.[75] (As of mid-1999, Taiwan still had not been admitted to the WTO, primarily because of China's insistence that it be admitted first.)

It was also during this 1993–1994 period that a longer-term problem began to emerge in the U.S.-Taiwan relationship. A larger number of American foreign policy specialists started to express concern that Taiwan's democratization might eventually pose a problem for the United States in its relations with China. Since the late 1980s, the political fate of Taiwan rested ever more firmly in the hands of the Taiwanese people. Since virtually no one on Taiwan wanted to unify with the mainland as long as it was controlled by the communists and a considerable portion of Taiwanese apparently wanted national independence instead of any form of unification with China, a fundamental contradiction began to arise in U.S. China policy. For decades the United States had supported democracy on Taiwan, while acknowledging since the early 1970s the Chinese position on both sides of the Taiwan Strait that there was only one China with Taiwan being considered part of China.

But democratization on Taiwan had brought into political power the majority Taiwanese, many of whom did not consider Taiwan to be part of China. Therefore, as democratization took hold on the island, there existed an increased possibility of a democratically elected government on Taiwan abandoning the ROC's traditional "one-China" policy and pursuing either "two Chinas" or Taiwan independence. Such a decision on the part of Taipei would place the United States in the awkward position of having either to change its one-China policy or to ignore the democratic choice of the Taiwanese people. This would require hard policy choices which no administration wanted to face, particularly the Clinton administration with its dual emphasis on supporting market democracies in Asia while seeking cooperative relations with Beijing.

For the first two years of his administration, Clinton was careful not to allow unofficial U.S. ties with Taiwan to undermine Sino-American relations. For example, it was decided not to allow President Lee Teng-hui to attend the first APEC meeting of Asian-Pacific heads of state in Seattle in 1993, despite Clinton's invitation to all leaders of APEC. Taiwan had been a full and equal member to APEC since 1991 under the designation "Chinese Taipei." The PRC insisted that Taiwan's president or prime minister could not be invited because they represented only a local government, not a country. After intensive negotiations between Washington, Beijing, and Taipei, it was agreed that President Lee Teng-hui would decline President Clinton's invitation to attend the summit and instead send Vincent Siew as his personal representative. At the time, Siew was head of the ROC Council for Economic Planning and Development.[76]

As already noted, in keeping with the low profile given Taiwan, the State Department in May 1994 refused to allow President Lee Teng-hui to stay overnight in Honolulu or Los Angeles en route to Latin America. Congressional reaction to this and other slights prompted numerous resolutions in support of Taiwan and several invitations to Lee to visit individual states. An irritated Congress began in earnest to pressure the administration to adjust its Taiwan policy, with several pieces of legislation earlier discussed. Congress also passed binding legislation incorporating such amendments as that introduced by Senator Murkowski on arms sales—all in an attempt to ensure that some degree of balance was maintained in U.S. relations with China and Taiwan.

Congress did not oppose U.S. relations with China, nor did it call for a reversal of diplomatic ties with Taipei. But it did insist that the administration show more respect to an old friend and ally. As noted earlier, partly as a result of growing pressure from Congress, the administration finalized a year-long interagency review of U.S. policy toward Taiwan. Announced in September 1994, U.S. policy toward Taiwan was refined in a few areas. These included the establishment, under AIT auspices, of a sub-cabinet economic dialogue with Taiwan; exchange visits between high-level U.S. and Taiwan government officials from economic and technical agencies; permission for high-level Taiwan political officials to transit but not visit the United States, a restriction that also applied to U.S. political leaders; permission for undersecretary-level U.S. officials in the State and Defense Departments to meet with Taiwan counterparts in unofficial settings, while high-level economic and trade officials from Taiwan would be able to meet with U.S. counterparts in official settings; acknowledgment that Taiwan had a legitimate role to play in international organizations such as APEC, GATT, and some additional international organizations, but not the United Nations; allowing Taiwan to change the name of its representative office in the United States to the "Taipei Economic and Cultural Representative Office in the United States"; and a promise that the United States would continue to provide material and training for Taiwan's self-defense as mandated by the TRA, while at the same time adhering to the August 17 communiqué.

For the most part, Congress was not satisfied with the adjustment in Clinton policy toward Taiwan, the general feeling being that it was more cosmetic than substantive in nature. Nonetheless, as the administration had predicted, Beijing's reaction to the Taiwan policy review was bitter. Deputy Foreign Minister Liu Huaqiu handed an official protest to U.S. Ambassador to China J. Stapleton Roy, warning that Washington should "correct its erroneous action on the question of Taiwan to spare our relationship from severe damage." Liu told the U.S. ambassador: "If not handled properly, the question of Taiwan will become an explosive issue for China and the United States. . . . In that case, the growth of our bilateral relations will not only be stalled, but also retrogress. . . . We demand that the U.S. government approach the question of Taiwan with every seriousness and caution."[77]

One reason the PRC reacted so strongly to the slight improvement in U.S.-Taiwan relations was the frustration Beijing felt in its unsuccessful efforts to convince Taipei to enter into negotiations over eventual unification. Many in the PRC were convinced that the longer the ROC delayed political talks, the greater the possibility that Taiwan could move in the direction of independence. In truth, however, there were both encouraging and discouraging signs of increased interaction across the Taiwan Strait.

Cross-Strait Relations

To manage the growing interaction across the Taiwan Strait, Taipei and Beijing established institutions with quasi-official status to represent their interests. In February 1991 the ROC created the Foundation for Exchanges Across the Taiwan Strait (or Straits Exchange Foundation, SEF) with the major responsibilities of accepting, ratifying, and forwarding on entry and exit documents from the two Chinese sides; verifying and delivering documents issued on the mainland; deporting fugitives on both sides of the Taiwan Strait; arbitrating trade disputes; promoting cultural and academic exchanges; providing consultation on general affairs; and helping to protect the legal rights of ROC citizens during their visits to the mainland. For its part, Beijing created in December 1991 the Association for Relations Across the Taiwan Straits (ARATS), an organization closely tied to the Taiwan Affairs Office of the PRC State Council. The ROC and PRC representative offices act in strict accordance with their governments' instructions and they serve as convenient middlemen between the two governments to avoid the appearance of official contact (the ROC concern) or state-to-state relations (the PRC concern).

In an historic meeting between the two sides, the chairmen of Beijing's Association for Relations Across the Taiwan Straits and Taipei's Straits Exchange

Foundation (Wang Daohan and Koo Chen-fu, respectively) met in Singapore in April 1993 to discuss a variety of non-political bilateral issues. The meeting produced four documents. Three dealt with the delivery of registered letters, document verification, and the schedule of future contacts between the two organizations. The other accord set forth the areas in which both sides wanted greater cooperation: fishing disputes, repatriation from Taiwan of illegal immigrants from the mainland, joint efforts to fight crime, protection of intellectual property rights, and efforts to reconcile differences in the two sides' legal systems. The joint exploitation of natural resources was also discussed, along with cooperation in science, culture, and education. The two sides were unable to agree on the protection of Taiwan investments on the mainland, partly because Taipei wanted Beijing to sign a bilateral investment accord giving Taiwan a claim to be an equal political entity in relations with the mainland. The PRC side refused to do this, proposing instead that it provide investment guarantees directly with individual investors.[78]

Subsequent meetings over the next few months between the Straits Exchange Foundation and the Association for Relations Across the Taiwan Straits were not productive. Differences over definitions of sovereignty effectively blocked agreements on trade and cultural links throughout the remainder of 1993. Practical problems such as airline hijacking (ten PRC airlines were hijacked to Taiwan in 1993 alone), fishing disputes, immigration, and extradition could not be resolved due to their political implications. Essentially, the PRC refused to give Taipei any semblance of political equality, while the ROC refused to compromise on key issues as long as Beijing placed obstacles in the way of Taipei's participation in international affairs and did not rule out the use of force in resolving the Taiwan issue.

In early 1994 the two sides continued their discussions with a less formal agenda. In August the two organizations were able to reach agreement in principle on three issues: each side would handle its own citizens who hijacked planes, procedures for handling illegal entrants, and procedures for settling fishing disputes. Little progress was made on the protection of Taiwan business interests on the mainland, travel safety, press freedom, or the return of previous hijackers.

In large measure, the slow progress of the talks reflected ROC caution over political contact with the PRC. Beijing, on the other hand, sought to expand official contact with Taiwan as soon as possible. This coincided with the apparent interests of the two Chinese governments: the ROC wanted to postpone reunification until such time as the Chinese Communist Party could no longer dominate the mainland's political system; the PRC wanted to expedite reunification while its position was stronger than that of Taipei.

The formal positions of the two sides continued to be refined, although with little substantive change. In August 1993, the PRC published a major policy statement on "The Taiwan Question and the Reunification of China."[79] This rather hardline document is worth examining in detail because it shows the extent to which the PRC wants to restrict Taiwan's participation in the international community.

As its fundamental premise, the white paper, as it was called, noted that the Taiwan issue was a remnant of China's dismemberment in the past, a period of history that could not be brought to a close until Taiwan and the mainland were reunited. Most of the blame for the continued division of China was placed on the United States, citing U.S. support for the KMT during World War II, the passage of the Taiwan Relations Act, and continued arms sales to Taiwan. The PRC document stated that "the U.S. Government is responsible for holding up the settlement of the Taiwan question."

The white paper said the PRC's "basic position" on Taiwan issue was "peaceful reunification; one country, two systems." The main contents of this policy were as follows:

1. *Only one China*. There is only one China in the world, Taiwan is an inalienable part of China and the seat of China's central government is in Beijing. This is the premise for a peaceful settlement of the Taiwan question. The Chinese Government is firmly against any words or deeds designed to split China's sovereignty and territorial integrity. It opposes "two Chinas," "one China, one Taiwan," "one country, two governments," or any attempt or act that could lead to the "independence of Taiwan." The Chinese people on both sides of the Straits all believe that there is only one China and espouse national reunification. Taiwan's status as an inalienable part of China has been determined and cannot be changed. "Self-determination" for Taiwan is out of the question.

2. *Coexistence of two systems*. On the premise of one China, socialism on the mainland and capitalism on Taiwan can coexist and develop side by side for a long time without one swallowing up the other. This concept takes account of the actual situation in Taiwan and the practical interests of compatriots there. It will be a unique feature and important innovation in the state system of a reunified China. After reunification, Taiwan's current socio-economic system, its way of life as well as economic and cultural ties with foreign countries can remain unchanged. Private property, including houses and land, as well as business ownership, legal inheritance and overseas Chinese and foreign investments on the island will all be protected by law.

3. *A high degree of autonomy*. After reunification, Taiwan will become a special administrative region. It will be distinguished from the other provinces or regions of China by its high degree of autonomy. It will have its own administrative and legislative powers, an independent judiciary and the right of adjudication on the island. It will run its own party, political, military, economic, and financial affairs. It may conclude commercial and cultural agreements with foreign countries and enjoy certain rights in foreign affairs. It may keep its military forces and the mainland will not dispatch

troops or administrative personnel to the island. On the other hand, representatives of the government of the special administrative region and those from different circles of Taiwan may be appointed to senior posts in the central government and participate in the running of national affairs.

4. *Peace negotiations.* It is the common aspiration of the entire Chinese people to achieve reunification of the country by peaceful means through contacts and negotiations. People on both sides of the Straits are all Chinese. It would be a great tragedy for all if China's territorial integrity and sovereignty were to be split and its people were to be drawn into a fratricide. Peaceful reunification will greatly enhance the cohesion of the Chinese nation. It will facilitate Taiwan's socio-economic stability and development and promote the resurgence and prosperity of China as a whole. In order to put an end to hostility and achieve peaceful reunification, the two sides should enter into contacts and negotiations at the earliest possible date. On the premise of one China, both sides can discuss any subject, including the modality of negotiations, the question of what parties, groups and personalities may participate as well as any other matters of concern to the Taiwan side. So long as the two sides sit down and talk, they will always be able to find a mutually acceptable solution. Taking into account the prevailing situation on both sides of the Straits, the Chinese Government has proposed that pending reunification the two sides should, according to the principle of mutual respect, complementarity and mutual benefit, actively promote economic cooperation and other exchanges. Direct trade, postal, air and shipping services and two-way visits should be started in order to pave the way for the peaceful reunification of the country.

The white paper warned, however, that the use of force cannot be ruled out to achieve unification: "Peaceful reunification is a set policy of the Chinese Government. However, any sovereign state is entitled to use any means it deems necessary, including military ones, to uphold its sovereignty and territorial integrity. The Chinese Government is under no obligation to undertake any commitment to any foreign power or people intending to split China as to what means it might use to handle its own domestic affairs."

Despite signs of progress in cross-Strait relations in recent years, several obstacles to reunification were of grave concern to the PRC: "It should be pointed out that notwithstanding a certain measure of easing up by the Taiwan authorities, their current policy vis-a-vis the mainland still seriously impedes the development of relations across the Straits as well as the reunification of the country. They talk about the necessity of a reunified China, but their deeds are always a far cry from the principle of one China. They try to prolong Taiwan's separation from the mainland and refuse to hold talks on peaceful reunification. They have even set up barriers to curb the further development of the interchanges across the Straits." Even more disturbing to the PRC were calls for Taiwan independence:

In recent years the clamors for "Taiwan independence" on the island have become shriller, casting a shadow over the course of relations across the Straits and the prospect of peaceful reunification of the country. The "Taiwan independence" fallacy has a complex socio-historical root and international background. But the Taiwan authorities have, in effect, abetted this fallacy by its own policy of rejecting peace negotiations, restricting interchanges across the Straits and lobbying for "dual recognition" or "two Chinas" in the international arena. It should be reaffirmed that the desire of Taiwan compatriots to run the affairs of the island as masters of their own house is reasonable and justified. This should by no means be construed as advocating "Taiwan independence." They are radically distinct from those handful of "Taiwan independence" protagonists who trumpet "independence" but vilely rely on foreign patronage in a vain attempt to detach Taiwan from China, which runs against the fundamental interests of the entire Chinese people including Taiwan compatriots. The Chinese Government is closely following the course of events and will never condone any maneuver for "Taiwan independence."

The white paper went on to condemn "certain foreign forces who do not want to see a reunified China" that "have gone out of their way to meddle in China's internal affairs. They support the anti-Communist stance of the Taiwan authorities of rejecting peace talks and abet the secessionists on the island, thereby erecting barriers to China's peaceful reunification and seriously wounding the national feelings of the Chinese people."

The white paper was especially strong in defining the PRC's position on Taiwan's role in international affairs: "As part of China, Taiwan has no right to represent China in the international community, nor can it establish diplomatic ties or enter into relations of an official nature with foreign countries." However, "the Chinese Government has not objected to non-governmental economic or cultural exchanges between Taiwan and foreign countries." In addressing Taipei's pragmatic diplomacy, the report said: "In recent years the Taiwan authorities have vigorously launched a campaign of 'pragmatic diplomacy' to cultivate official ties with countries having diplomatic relations with China in an attempt to push 'dual recognition' and achieve the objective of creating a situation of 'two Chinas' or 'one China, one Taiwan.' The Chinese Government is firmly against this scheme." In terms of Taiwan's participation in international organizations:

The Government of the People's Republic of China, as the sole legal government of China, has the right and obligation to exercise state sovereignty and represent the whole of China in international organizations. The Taiwan authorities' lobbying for a formula of 'one country, two seats' in international organizations whose membership is confined to sovereign states is a maneuver to create 'two Chinas.' The Chinese Government is firmly opposed to such an attempt. . . . Only on the premise of adhering to the principle of one China and in the light of the nature and statutes of the international organizations concerned as well as the specific circumstances, can the Chinese Government consider the question of Taiwan's participation in the activities of such organizations and in a manner agreeable and acceptable to the Chinese Government.

Special mention was made of the United Nations, where Taipei had been attempting to gain reentry in some capacity: "All the specialized agencies and organizations of the United Nations system are inter-governmental organizations composed of sovereign states. After the restoration of the lawful rights of the People's Republic of China in the United Nations . . . the issue of China's representation in the U.N. system has been resolved once and for all and Taiwan's re-entry is out of the question." Taiwan's efforts to return to the United Nations were actually "an attempt to split state sovereignty, which is devoid of any legal or practical basis."

Nonetheless, Taiwan could participate in certain kinds of international organizations with the concurrence of Beijing:

> As to regional economic organizations such as the Asian Development Bank (ADB) and the Asia-Pacific Economic Cooperation (APEC), Taiwan's participation is subject to the terms of agreement or understanding reached between the Chinese Government and the parties concerned which explicitly prescribe that the People's Republic of China is a full member as a sovereign state whereas Taiwan may participate in the activities of those organizations only as a region of China under the designation of Taipei, China (in ADB) or Chinese Taipei (in APEC). This is only an ad hoc arrangement and cannot constitute a "model" applicable to other inter-governmental organizations or international gatherings.

In the future, Taiwan's participation in non-governmental international organizations would have to be approved by "relevant bodies of the People's Republic of China." An understanding would have to be reached whereby "China's national organizations would use the designation of China, while Taiwan's organizations may participate under the designation of Taipei, China or Taiwan, China." The document also defined a highly restricted policy in regards to international airline service to Taiwan: "The opening of aviation services with Taiwan by any airlines, including privately-operated ones, of countries having diplomatic relations with China is a political issue affecting China's sovereignty and cannot be regarded as a non-political transaction. State-run airlines of countries having diplomatic relations with China certainly must not operate air services to Taiwan. Privately-operated airlines must seek China's consent through consultations between their government and the Chinese Government before they can start reciprocal air services with privately-operated airlines of Taiwan."

Not surprisingly, the document paid special attention to foreign arms sales to Taiwan, thought by the PRC to firm up Taipei's will to resist unification under Beijing's terms:

The Chinese Government has always firmly opposed any country selling any type of arms or transferring production technology of the same to Taiwan. All countries maintaining diplomatic relations with China should abide by the principles of mutual respect for sovereignty and territorial integrity and non-interference in each other's internal affairs, and refrain from providing arms to Taiwan in any form or under any pretext. Failure to do so would be a breach of the norms of international relations and an interference in China's internal affairs.

All countries, and especially big powers shouldering major responsibilities for world peace, are obligated to strictly abide by the guidelines laid down by the five permanent members of the U.N. Security Council to restrict the proliferation of conventional weapons so as to contribute to maintaining and promoting regional peace and stability. However, at a time when relations across the Taiwan Straits are easing up, certain powers have seen fit to renege on their undertakings under international agreements and to flout the Chinese Government's repeated strong representations by making arms sales to Taiwan, thereby whipping up tension between the two sides of the Straits. This not only constitutes a serious threat to China's security and an obstacle to China's peaceful reunification, but also undermines peace and stability in Asia and the world at large. It stands to reason that the Chinese people should voice strong resentment against this conduct.

It is clear from this and other documents that Beijing has no intention to view Taipei as an equal or even competing government of China. The PRC argues that the issue has been decided on the battlefield in China in 1949 and in most capitals of the world since 1971. At most, the PRC is willing to allow the people of Taiwan to continue their lifestyle for an undisclosed period of time and to permit the government of Taiwan to function as a local government with limited participation in international non-governmental organizations as a part of China. Basically, the 1993 PRC white paper demanded that the ROC surrender its claim as a rival government of China, abandon the KMT's goal of a united, democratic China, and accept the inevitability of communism and socialism one day replacing democracy and capitalism on the island. As might be expected, Taipei continued to rejected Beijing's terms of peaceful reunification.

In September 1993 the ROC Mainland Affairs Council responded to the PRC white paper on Taiwan in a document titled "There Is No 'Taiwan Question'; There Is Only a 'China Question.'"[80] Some of the major points in the ROC document were as follows:

First, "there is no Taiwan question, only a question of the future of China and how to make the country democratic and free." In so arguing, Taipei attempted to change the impression that Taiwan was a problem in international politics, particularly in Sino-American relations. Instead, China was a problem because of its threatening attitude. Specifically, the major issue in regional and global politics was the future of China: would the mainland be communist or would it be democratic?

Second, the PRC cannot be equated with China. "The term 'China' connotes multifaceted geographical, political, historical and cultural meanings. We have always asserted that both the mainland and Taiwan are Chinese territories. [But it is also] an undeniable fact that the two have been divided and ruled separately since 1949. Although the Chinese Communists have enjoyed jurisdiction over the mainland area, they cannot be equated with China. They can in no way represent China as a whole, much less serve as the 'sole legal government of all Chinese people.'"

Third, the ROC already is and will remain a member of the international community; the PRC never has nor can it represent the people of Taiwan. "The Chinese Communists have never extended their governing power to the Taiwan area, so they are not entitled to represent Taiwan in the international community, nor have they advocated the rights or fulfilled the obligations of the people in the Taiwan area in any international organizations."

Fourth, the "main obstacle to China's reunification" is the PRC's one country, two systems proposal. "It is clear that the 'one country, two systems' premise is nothing but a demand for the Taiwan area to surrender to the Chinese Communists. Thus, objectively, 'one country, two systems' is infeasible, and, subjectively, it is unacceptable to the people in the ROC."

Fifth, "the ROC government pursues China's unification not only to unify the territories of China through peaceful and reasonable means," according to the MAC report. "The loftier goal is to allow the 1.2 billion people on the Chinese mainland to enjoy the same democratic, free and equitably prosperous lifestyle and the basic human rights and freedom that the people in the Taiwan area do."

Sixth, whereas "the two sides of the Taiwan Straits should resolve the unification question peacefully," Taiwan believes "that so long as the Chinese Communists do not implement democracy and the rule of law, and do not renounce the use of force to resolve problems, the threat they pose to the stability and prosperity of Asia, and even the world, will continue."

In conclusion, the ROC document stated:

> We believe that the value of national unification lies not in a single jurisdiction over China's territories but in enabling the people on the Chinese mainland to enjoy the same democratic, free and equitably prosperous lifestyle as is enjoyed by the people in the Taiwan area....
> We sincerely call upon the Chinese Communist authorities to quickly relinquish the anachronistic communist system; commit themselves to political, economic and social reforms on the Chinese mainland; and place the fundamental rights and welfare of the 1.2 billion Chinese people above the narrow interests of the Chinese Communist Party....
> We would also like to once again urge the Chinese Communist authorities to recognize the reality that the two sides of the Taiwan Straits are divided and ruled separately, and to renounce the use of force in the Taiwan Straits.

As is fairly obvious from the PRC and ROC documents, the positions of the two Chinese governments allow very little room for compromise on the key issues of sovereignty, political legitimacy, and territorial integrity. The PRC is unlikely to give up the communist system—a requirement under the ROC plan of unification, and the ROC is unlikely to place Taiwan under PRC jurisdiction, a requirement under Beijing's plan. Although most observers would consider the PRC to be in the stronger negotiating position, it should be noted that the ROC draws strength from four incontestable realities: (1) Taiwan never has been under the control of the PRC; (2) the people of Taiwan enjoy a much higher standard of living and quality of life than do their compatriots on the mainland; (3) Taiwan is not easily conquered militarily; and (4) Taiwan enjoys the support of the United States and other members of the international democratic community. As a result, at least through mid-1999, Taiwan could safely reject the "one country, two systems" formula and insist that unification can only take place when the CCP allows the mainland to enjoy the fruits of freedom and democracy—quixotic perhaps, but not that different from the China-transforming goals of engagement.

Conclusion

For the first two years of the Clinton administration, U.S. policies toward Taiwan and China were very similar to those of President Bush. Both administrations accepted China as an emerging major power and acknowledged its expanding role in regional and global affairs. Clinton continued the Bush strategy of engagement with China, believing Beijing would eventually improve its behavior with respect to proliferation, trade, and human rights.

To maintain public support for their engagement policies, both Bush and Clinton told the American people that constructive engagement with the PRC would help bring about positive change in China. Having experienced this Western strategy since the sixteenth century,[81] it was not surprising that Chinese leaders believed these statements and that many of them came to view the United States and its "soft" strategy of peaceful evolution as the greatest threat to their positions of power.

Increasingly, the Clinton administration found that China, not Taiwan, represented the larger conundrum in U.S. policy. At first, Clinton tried to link what China wanted—MFN trading status with the United States—to what many of his supporters wanted—progress in China's human rights behavior. This never worked, leading the president eventually to delink MFN and human rights, as well as to delink MFN from China's policies on proliferation and specific trade issues such as IPR enforcement.

The Chinese leadership under Jiang Zemin believed that China needed cooperative relations with the United States, but Beijing refused to accept the rules of international behavior defined by Washington. Some in China saw the United States as a declining power in Asia, but one that continued to interfere in Chinese internal affairs by seeking to change China into a democracy and to weaken China by helping Taiwan resist unification. For China, it was vital to become stronger to resist this new form of imperialism. The challenge for Beijing was to maintain good relations with the United States to further the goal of modernization, yet to protect Chinese independence, sovereignty, and territorial integrity, particularly in the case of Taiwan. If a choice had to be made, however, Beijing made clear it would choose the protection of its sovereignty and territorial integrity over good relations with the United States.

At the same time, the United States and China recognized each other as powerful nations whose pragmatic interests dictated that they avoid confrontation and cooperate in areas of mutual benefit. These areas of cooperation included maintaining peace on the Korean peninsula; counterbalancing the potential rise of Japan or Russia as a threatening power in the Western Pacific; maintaining an increasingly interdependent trade relationship; modernizing China's economy and ensuring its smooth integration into regional and global economic systems; and accommodating a strong, modern China in the post-Cold War international political system in a way that stabilized, not destabilized, the new international order.

President Clinton tried to serve both American values and American interests in dealing with China, but this proved difficult because Beijing often refused to cooperate when its interests were at risk or when it felt undue pressure from Washington. Clinton's efforts to "reengage" China after September 1993 and his May 1994 decision to renew China's MFN trade status in spite of dissatisfaction over PRC human rights practices reflected a triumph of American strategic and (particularly) economic interests over its moral values. Thereafter, President Clinton sounded very much like President Bush in arguing that sanctions on the PRC hurt the United States and harmed progressive elements within China. The best U.S. strategy, according to both presidents, would be to integrate China into the global community rather than attempt to isolate her. Clinton's more pragmatic approach pleased the Chinese, but it did little to resolve the substantive problems in Sino-American relations.

Most changes on Taiwan since the mid-1980s had been in directions favorable to U.S. goals and interests in East Asia. Accordingly, the Clinton administration worked to improve unofficial ties with Taiwan, albeit within tight parameters. This was demonstrated by positive presidential comments about Taiwan, public commitments to honor the Taiwan Relations Act, cordial trade relations, expanding cultural and educational ties, support for Taiwan's own engagement with mainland China, slighter more support for Taipei's participation in some international organizations, continued advanced arms sales, and a minor upgrading of relations as a result of the 1994 Taiwan policy review. But the Clinton administration would not improve relations with Taiwan beyond those permitted by three Sino-American communiqués. There was no change in the U.S. "one-China" policy, despite democratization on Taiwan and increased demands on the part of Taiwanese for a greater voice in their future relationship with the mainland. On the fundamental question of China's unification, there was no progress as both the PRC and ROC remained inflexible on issues of sovereignty.

The next two chapters will examine President Clinton's policies toward China and Taiwan during 1995 and 1996, a period of intense activity over the Taiwan issue and one in which the Taiwan conundrum was brought forcefully to the forefront of Sino-American relations.

Notes

1. "The Democratic Party Platform, 1992," p. 14.
2. *China News*, November 24, 1992, p. 7.
3. *Far Eastern Economic Review*, November 12, 1992, pp. 10-11.
4. *China News*, August 15, 1992, p. 1.
5. *China News*, October 13, 1992, p. 7.
6. *China News*, November 24, 1992, p. 7.
7. *China News*, December 16, 1992, p. 1.
8. *China News*, November 23, 1992, p. 1. On the eve of Clinton's victory in November 1992, China purchased over 1.6 million tons of subsidized American wheat, the largest one-day purchase by any country since the U.S. Export Enhancement program began in 1985. Earlier, Chinese officials had threatened to boycott American wheat after Bush announced the sale of F-16s to Taiwan.
9. *China News*, December 5, 1992, p. 4.
10. *China News*, December 6, 1992, p. 1.
11. Other leading dissidents released by China included Han Dongfang, Wang Youcai, Luo Haixing, Xiong Yan, Yang Wei, Wang Zhixin, Zhang Weiguo, Bao Zunxin, and a number of Catholic clergy and lesser known political activists.
12. *Washington Post*, February 27, 1993, p. C1.
13. Winston Lord, "A New Pacific Community: Ten Goals for American Policy," opening statement at confirmation hearings for Assistant Secretary of State, Bureau of East Asian and Pacific Affairs, Senate Foreign Relations Committee, March 31, 1993, ms.
14. *Washington Post*, March 11, 1993, p. A25.
15. "Statement by the President on Most Favored Nation Status for China" (Washington, DC: The White House, Office of the Press Secretary, May 28, 1993).
16. "Report to Congress Concerning Extension of Waiver Authority for the People's Republic of China" (Washington, DC: The White House, Office of the Press Secretary, May 28, 1993).
17. "Assistant Secretary of State Winston Lord, Opening Statement, House Ways and Means Committee, International Trade Subcommittee, June 8, 1993," ms.
18. *Beijing Review*, June 6-13, 1993, p. 4.
19. Liu Huaqiu, "Proposals for Human Rights Protection and Promotion," *Beijing Review*, June 28-July 4, 1993, pp. 8-11.
20. Wei Jingsheng had been in jail for more fourteen years for urging democracy as the "fifth modernization" to go along with Deng Xiaoping's "four modernizations" in Chinese agriculture, industry, science and technology, and defense.
21. *Far Eastern Economic Review*, October 7, 1993, pp. 12-13.

22. Don Oberdorfer, "Replaying the China Card: How Washington and Beijing Avoided Diplomatic Disaster," *Washington Post*, November 7, 1993, p. C3. Also, Julian Baum, "On the Sidelines: Taipei Anxious about US-China Warming," *Far Eastern Economic Review*, November 25, 1993, p. 20.

23. "Remarks by the President After Meeting with President Jiang of China" (Seattle, WA: The White House, Office of the Press Secretary, November 19, 1993).

24. *Washington Post*, January 18, 1994, p. C1; *Wall Street Journal*, January 18, 1994, p. A3; *New York Times*, January 18, 1994, p. D1.

25. Mickey Kantor's testimony before the U.S. House of Representatives, Committee on Foreign Affairs, March 2, 1994, was televised by C-Span that day.

26. *New York Times*, February 2, 1994, p. A8.

27. *Washington Post*, March 9, 1994, p. A13; March 10, 1994, p. A34.

28. Warren Christopher, "My Trip to Beijing Was Necessary," *Washington Post*, March 22, 1994, p. A17.

29. Evidence of disputes within the administration over China policy can be found in *Washington Post*, March 20, 1994, p. A20 and H1; and *Wall Street Journal*, March 22, 1994, p. A1.

30. Quoted in the *New York Times*, March 21, 1994, p. A1.

31. See Stephen Fidler and Tony Walker, "Cox Report: U.S. Inquiry Cites Security Lapses," *Financial Times* (Internet version), February 12, 1999.

32. See *New York Times*, March 24, 1994, p. A5; March 25, 1994, p. A12.

33. For the official abridged version, see "China's MFN Status: Summary of the Report and Recommendations of Secretary of State Warren Christopher" (Washington, DC: The White House, Office of the Press Secretary, May 26, 1994).

34. "Press Conference of the President" (Washington, DC: The White House, Office of the Press Secretary, May 26, 1994). For background on the 1994 MFN decision, see articles in the *New York Times*, May 27, 1994, pp. A1, D1.

35. See "Fact Sheet: China MFN Decision" and "Fact Sheet: New Initiatives in U.S. Human Rights Policy for China" (Washington, DC: The White House, Office of the Press Secretary, May 26, 1994).

36. "Press Briefing by National Security Adviser Tony Lake, Assistant Secretary of State for Human Rights John Shattuck, Assistant Secretary of State for Asian and Pacific Affairs Winston Lord, and Assistant to the President for Economic Policy Bob Rubin" (Washington, DC: The White House, Office of the Press Secretary, May 26, 1994).

37. For reports of Brown's trip to China, see *Washington Post*, September 1, 1994, p. B10; *New York Times*, September 2, 1994, p. D1; *Wall Street Journal*, September 9, 1994, p. A1.

38. *Wall Street Journal*, August 15, 1995, p. A13. See also *Washington Post*, October 13, 1995, p. A27.

39. The NPT was open for signature on July 1, 1968, at which time the United States and Soviet Union signed. Signatories to the NPT which possess nuclear weapons agree not to transfer nuclear weapons to non-nuclear weapon states or assist non-nuclear weapon states to acquire nuclear weapons. Signatories to the treaty which are non-nuclear states agree not to receive, manufacture, or otherwise acquire nuclear weapons. All NPT parties have the right to develop nuclear energy for peaceful purposes. Non-nuclear weapon states party to the treaty agree to accept safeguards as negotiated with the International Atomic Energy Agency (IAEA) and agree to IAEA safeguards to ensure compliance.

40. The MTCR was a multilateral political agreement announced on April 16, 1987, between the United States and its G-7 partners (Canada, France, Germany, Italy, United Kingdom, and Japan) to control the export of missile-related technologies. Two categories of restricted items were established. Category I items are ballistic missiles and other unmanned delivery systems, their complete subsystems, and their production facilities. Category II items are components for Category I items.

41. The Chemical Weapons Convention (CWC) was signed on January 13, 1993, in Paris by 130 countries, including the United States and China. When in force, the CWC will ban the development, production, acquisition, stockpiling, retention, and direct or indirect transfer of chemical weapons. It also prohibits the use or preparation for use of chemical weapons and the assistance, encouragement, or inducement of anyone else to engage in activities prohibited by the CWC.

42. Perhaps out of frustration on the part of analysts, many of these damaging intelligence reports found their way into American newspapers, particularly in articles written by Bill Gertz of the *Washington Times*. For a collection of the highly classified documents, see Bill Gertz, *Betrayal: How the Clinton Administration Undermined American Security* (Washington, DC: Regnery, 1999).

43. See *Washington Post*, February 24, 1993, p. A4.

44. "Remarks by the President in Address to the National Assembly of the Republic of Korea" (Seoul: The White House, Office of the Press Secretary, July 10, 1993).

45. "Statement of Secretary of State Warren Christopher at the ASEAN Post Ministerial Conference, Six-plus-Seven Open Session, July 26, 1993" (Singapore: U.S. Department of State, Office of the Spokesman). An ASEAN official said that the challenge was "how to ensure that China is enmeshed in a web of relationships" to integrate it with the region but keep it from projecting military power into the area.

46. *Washington Post*, July 26 1993, p. A10; June 27, 1993, p. A1.

47. See *Washington Post*, May 18, 1993, p. A9.

48. *Beijing Review*, September 6-12, 1993, pp. 6-7.

49. "Foreign Ministry on 'Yinhe' Incident," *Beijing Review*, September 13-19, 1993, p. 4.

50. Tiao Yue, "US Breaches International Law on the 'Yinhe' Incident," *Beijing Review*, September, 20-26, 1993, pp. 12-13.

51. *Washington Post*, September 30, 1993, p. A15.

52. *Wall Street Journal*, October 6, 1993, p. A12; *Washington Post*, October 6, 1993, p. A1.

53. See "Statement by the Press Secretary" (Washington, DC: The White House, Office of the Press Secretary, October 5, 1993).

54. *House Report 105-851: Report of the Select Committee on U.S. National Security and Military/Commercial Concerns with the People's Republic of China* (Washington, DC: GPO, 1999). Representative Christopher Cox was chairman of the committee.

55. *Washington Post*, November 1, 1993, p. A1 and November 3, 1993, p. A12; *New York Times*, November 3, 1993, p. A13.

56. "Joint United States-People's Republic of China Statement on Missile Proliferation" and "Joint United States-People's Republic of China Statement on Stopping Production of Fissile Materials for Nuclear Weapons," U.S. Arms Control and Disarmament Agency *Fact Sheet*, October 4, 1994.

57. These nonproliferation efforts are summarized in "Background Notes: China" (Washington, DC: Bureau of East Asian and Pacific Affairs, U.S. Department of State, October 1998).

58. See the Cox report previously cited in note 53.

59. For the unclassified version of the report, see "Department of Defense Initial Assessment of Certain Documents Concerning an Investigation by Hughes Space and Communications Company into the Failure of the Launch of the APSTAR II on China's Long March 2E Launch Vehicle, December 7, 1998," *Aviation Week & Space Technology, Headline News* (Internet edition), n.d. As an example of the many newspaper articles discussing the issue, see *Washington Post*, December 9, 1998, p. A22; *Wall Street Journal*, December 10, 1998, p. B2.

60. *China News*, December 19, 1992, p. 3.

61. Winston Lord, "A New Pacific Community: Ten Goals for American Policy."

62. "Remarks by the President to Students and Faculty of Waseda University" (Tokyo: The White House, Office of the Press Secretary, July 7, 1993).

63. Natale H. Bellocchi, "Speech to New England-Taiwan Business Council," Boston, MA, June 22, 1993, ms. See also his "Speech to the Dallas Chinese Community," Dallas, TX, April 10, 1993, ms.

64. "Foreign Economic Trends and Their Implications for the United States: Taiwan" (Taipei: American Institute in Taiwan, March 1994).

65. *Free China Journal*, March 12, 1993, p. 1.

66. *Far Eastern Economic Review*, September 16, 1993, p. 11; *Free China Journal*, September 10, 1993, p. 1.

67. *Far Eastern Economic Review*, November 4, 1993, p. 15.

68. *Free China Journal*, October 8, 1993, p. 1.

69. *Free China Journal*, March 25, 1994, p. 1

70. *Free China Journal*, April 22, 1994, p. 1.

71. *Free China Journal*, September 2, 1994, p. 1.

72. *Far Eastern Economic Review*, August 11, 1994, p. 13.

73. *China Post*, March 25, 1993, p. 1.

74. *Wall Street Journal*, May 3, 1993, p. A13; August 4, 1993, p. A5.

75. *Free China Journal*, December 3, 1993, p. 3.

76. *Far Eastern Economic Review*, October 7, 1993, p. 20.

77. *Washington Post*, September 11, 1994, p. A26; Reuters report from Beijing, September 10, 1994.

78. Hungdah Chiu, *Koo-Wang Talks and the Prospect of Building Constructive and Stable Relations Across the Taiwan Straits* (Baltimore: University of Maryland School of Law, 1993).

79. "The Taiwan Question and the Reunification of China" (Beijing: Taiwan Affairs Office and Information Office, State Council, August 1993). An English version of the document can be found in *Beijing Review*, September 6-12, 1993, pp. I-VIII.

80. For a summary of the document, see *Free China Journal*, September 24, 1993, p. 7.

81. For a record of these attempts, see Jonathan Spence, *To Change China: Western Advisers in China, 1620-1960* (New York: Penguin Books, 1980).

7

Clinton's Policy Toward China and Taiwan: The Lee Teng-hui Visit and Repercussions

This chapter focuses on the 1995 period in U.S.-PRC-ROC relations, a year characterized by extreme fluctuations in cooperation and tension between China and both the United States and Taiwan. Because of the complexity of the relationships—made even more dynamic due to internal developments in China and Taiwan—the Clinton administration had great difficulty in defining its China policy. "Engagement" and "one China" were convenient terms, and dearly loved by Washington spin doctors, but they did little to clarify—not to mention resolve—the many problems that were arising in U.S. policies toward both Taiwan and China.

The administration found it necessary to explain U.S. policy repeatedly during 1995, as rapid change in both the PRC and Taiwan challenged various aspects of the Clinton approach to both Chinese nations. Clearly, the United States valued its relationships with both Beijing and Taipei, and preferred stability and the status quo in the Taiwan Strait, but the two Chinese sides were moving in directions that made the status quo increasingly untenable. For its part, China was trying to come to grips with a post-Deng leadership (Deng having retired from most decision making and Jiang Zemin not yet firmly in control), and the future of the reform movement was not clear even to the Chinese themselves. At the same time, China was becoming more powerful internationally and better able to assert and protect its interests in areas of competition with the United States. On Taiwan, the processes of democratization and Taiwanization had taken firm root, resulting in policies that in substance if not in name raised questions of whether the ROC would continue the traditional Nationalist policy of eventual reunification with the mainland.

Taiwan's creative use of "pragmatic diplomacy" (whereby the ROC sought to expand its international presence through all available means), "vacation diplomacy" (unofficial trips abroad by high-ranking officials), and "dollar diplomacy" (whereby Taipei attempted to secure and maintain diplomatic and other relations through generous financial assistance), was strongly opposed by the PRC and viewed by some in Washington as "pushing the envelope" beyond what was acceptable behavior.

The key issue really was the PRC's reaction. In and of itself, Taiwan's efforts to expand its international presence were neither exceptional nor illegitimate. The difficulty arose because Beijing claimed these efforts were directed toward the independence of Taiwan—or, almost as bad, "two Chinas" or "one China, one Taiwan." Concerned that opportunity for unification under Beijing's terms might be slipping away, China reacted with varying degrees of hostility to Taiwan's efforts to gain "international living space." Since Beijing blamed Washington for much of Taipei's arrogance and transgression, the PRC's unease over the Taiwan issue tended to affect other areas of Sino-American relations. At times, the PRC made direct linkage between issues such as U.S. sales of arms to Taiwan and Chinese cooperation on nonproliferation issues; at other times, China's suspicion of U.S. motives poisoned the general atmosphere of Sino-American relations, as in the case of Beijing's sense of betrayal over the visa given to Lee Teng-hui despite assurances to the contrary by the U.S. Secretary of State.

Regardless of the Taiwan factor in increased tensions in Sino-American relations during this period, a fundamental geopolitical reality was that China was emerging as a great power in East Asia, determined to adjust regional spheres of influence to reflect a greater Chinese role in international affairs. The United States, on the other hand, remained the predominant power in the Western Pacific, determined as always to maintain a favorable balance of power to protect its security, political, economic, and ideological interests. The maintenance of a favorable balance of power required the United States to counterbalance any potential hegemon, which, in the post-Cold War era, meant China. But rather than confront China or to seek somehow to contain its power, Washington chose to engage China in the expectation that Beijing would then moderate its policies and in fact join the United States as a cooperative partner in creating a mutually beneficial new world order. The Clinton administration was convinced that its dual policies—balance of power and engagement—served the long-term interests of most Asia-Pacific states as well, by providing the security necessary to enable the region to continue its rapid economic growth and progress toward democratization. The problem (and an additional element in the Taiwan conundrum) was how to engage China while supporting Taiwan, when the foundations of the "one-China" principle seemed to be eroding on Taiwan and Beijing seemed to be losing its patience.

Since the root of much of the difficulty in Sino-American relations during 1995 was attributable to differences between Beijing and Taipei, the state of cross-Strait relations before Lee's visit to the United States in June needs to be understood.

Eight-Point and Six-Point Proposals

As noted earlier, the PRC wanted progress on unification as early as possible, while the ROC wanted to preserve indefinitely the status quo in the Taiwan Strait for purposes of survival and flexibility. Each side had its reasons. Beijing, for instance, felt its position vis-à-vis Taiwan to be exceptionally strong during this period; Chinese leader Jiang Zemin, not yet confident of the permanency of his position, wanted progress toward unification to be a hallmark of his administration; nationalism on China was increasing, and recovery of the lost territory of Taiwan assumed great symbolic importance; developments on Taiwan suggested that unification might become more difficult in the future, as native-born Taiwanese assumed greater control over the direction of the island's policies; and China's ambition to be a truly great power in Asia could never be realized until the Taiwan issue had been settled satisfactorily. Taipei, on the other hand, felt its bargaining position with the mainland to be relatively weak and thus saw no incentive to enter into negotiations over unification; the political dynamics on the island made it impossible for the KMT or the ROC government to negotiate without popular support with either the CCP or the PRC; the vast majority of the people on Taiwan favored the status quo in the Taiwan Strait and did not support early political talks with the mainland; nearly everyone on Taiwan viewed early unification with the PRC as surrender to the communists; and there was confidence that, despite mounting pressure from Beijing, Taiwan could hold out almost indefinitely, feeding hope that Taiwan's position might improve in the future.

In view of these interests, the two sides remained far apart politically even as their economic, cultural, and communications ties strengthened considerably due to the mostly private initiatives of residents on both sides of the Strait, but especially from Taiwan. At the same time, both Beijing and Taipei knew the world was looking over their shoulders, with the United States encouraging at every opportunity increased dialogue and reduced tension.

In this environment, China and Taiwan tried to appear reasonable on the unification issue but without giving ground on their respective positions. As noted, the fundamental PRC goal was to have Taiwan join the mainland under conditions ensuring the leadership of the CCP of a united China. Beijing cared little what kind of system was on Taiwan, as long as it was a *local* government and economic system. The ROC rejected this and proposed an alternative model for unification, one in which the CCP would first allow democratization to come to the mainland. This the PRC refused to consider. Nonetheless, with an eye toward the United States, Beijing and Taipei continued to make suggestions for China's unification. Two of the most important during 1995 were Jiang Zemin's "Eight-Point" proposal and Lee Teng-hui's "Six-Point Proposal." Since both sides point to these proposals today, their content should be noted.

President Jiang's "Eight Points" were offered in a speech on January 30, 1995.[1] In his speech, Jiang emphasized the usual formulation of China's position: "We will never allow there to be 'two Chinas' or 'one China, one Taiwan.' We firmly oppose the 'independence of Taiwan.' There are only two ways to settle the Taiwan question: One is by peaceful means and the other is by non-peaceful means. The way the Taiwan question is to be settled is China's internal affairs, and brooks no foreign interference. We consistently stand for achieving reunification by peaceful means and through negotiations. But we shall not undertake not to use force." He went on to reaffirm the main points in China's existing reunification plan:

> After Taiwan is reunified with the mainland, China will pursue the policy of "one country, two systems." The main part of the country will stick to the socialist system, while Taiwan will retain its current system. . . . After Taiwan's reunification with the mainland, its social and economic systems will not change, nor will its way of life and its non-governmental relations with foreign countries, which means that foreign investments in Taiwan and the non-governmental exchanges between Taiwan and other countries will not be affected. As a special administrative region, Taiwan will exercise a high degree of autonomy and enjoy legislative and independent judicial power, including that of final adjudication. It may also retain its armed forces and administer its party, governmental and military system by itself. The Central Government will not station troops or send administrative personnel there. What is more, a number of posts in the Central Government will be made available to Taiwan.

Jiang commented favorably on the growing exchanges that had taken place between the two sides over the past decade. He then set forth eight points as "views and propositions on a number of important questions that have a bearing on the development of relations between the two sides and the promotion of the peaceful reunification of the motherland."

First, "adherence to the principle of one China is the basis and premise for peaceful reunification. China's sovereignty and territory must never be allowed to suffer split. We must firmly oppose any words or actions aimed at creating an 'independent Taiwan' and the propositions 'split the country and rule under separate regimes,' two Chinas over a certain period of time,' etc., which are in contravention of the principle of one China."

Second, "we do not challenge the development of non-governmental economic and cultural ties by Taiwan with other countries. . . . However, we oppose Taiwan's activities in 'expanding its living space internationally' which are aimed at creating 'two Chinas' or 'one China, one Taiwan.'"

Third, "it has been our consistent stand to hold negotiations with the Taiwan authorities on the peaceful reunification of the motherland. Representatives from the various political parties and mass organizations on both sides of the Taiwan Straits can be invited to participate in such talks." Jiang went on, "I suggest that, as the first step, negotiations should be held and an agreement reached on officially ending the state of hostility between the two sides in accordance with the principle that there is only one China. . . . As regards the name, place and form of these political talks, a solution acceptable to both sides can certainly be found so long as consultations on a equal footing can be held at an early date."

Fourth, "we should strive for the peaceful reunification of the motherland since Chinese should not fight fellow Chinese." Explaining China's refusal to rule out the use of force, Jiang said: "Our not undertaking to give up the use of force is not directed against our compatriots in Taiwan but against the schemes of foreign forces to interfere with China's reunification and to bring about the 'independence of Taiwan.'"

Fifth, "in face of the development of the world economy in the twenty-first century, great efforts should be made to expand the economic exchanges and cooperation between the two sides of the Taiwan Straits so as to achieve prosperity on both sides to the benefit of the entire Chinese nation. We hold that political differences should not affect or interfere with the economic cooperation between the two sides." Continuing, "since the direct links for postal, air and shipping services and trade between the two sides are the objective requirements for their economic development and contacts in various fields, and since they are in the interests of the people on both sides, it is absolutely necessary to adopt practical measures to speed up the establishment of such direct links. Efforts should be made to promote negotiations on certain specific issues between the two sides. We are in favor of conducting this kind of negotiations on the basis of reciprocity and mutual benefit."

Sixth, five thousand years of Chinese culture is "the tie keeping the entire Chinese people close at heart and constitutes an important basis for the peaceful reunification of the motherland. People on both sides of the Taiwan Straits should inherit and carry forward the fine traditions of the Chinese culture."

Seventh, "the 21 million compatriots in Taiwan, whether born there or in other provinces, are all Chinese and our own flesh and blood. We should fully respect their life style and their wish to be the masters of our country and protect all their legitimate rights and interest." Jiang said, "all parties and personages of all circles in Taiwan are welcome to exchange views with us on relations between the two sides and on peaceful reunification."

Eighth, "leaders of the Taiwan authorities are welcome to pay visits in appropriate capacities. We are also ready to accept invitations from the Taiwan side to visit Taiwan."

Many observers on Taiwan believed Jiang's proposals indicated greater flexibility in holding substantive, practical talks in an atmosphere of more equality. A formal response to Jiang's eight points soon came from President Lee Teng-hui in the form of a six-point counterproposal which was, in the main, a restatement of the 1991 guidelines for national unification.

In a speech to the ROC National Unification Council on April 8, 1995, Lee set forth six principles that should govern unification.[2] The first principle, Lee said, is to "seek China's unification on the reality of separate rules across the Strait." According to Lee, this principle was based on the fact that the two sides of the

Taiwan Strait have been governed since 1949 by the PRC and ROC respectively, with neither political entity subordinated to the other. "To solve the unification problem, we must be pragmatic and respect history, and we should seek a feasible way for national unification based on the fact that the two shores are separately governed."

A second principle is to "step up cross-Strait exchange on the basis of the Chinese culture." Exchanges based on traditional Chinese culture could help "elevate the national sentiment of common existence and common prosperity" and "further increase exchange and cooperation in the information, academic, science and technology, sports, and other fields."

A third principle is to "increase cross-Strait economic and trade exchanges and develop mutually beneficiary and supplementary relations." Lee suggested that "Taiwan should make Mainland China its hinterland in developing its economy, whereas Mainland China should draw lessons from Taiwan in developing its economy." Taiwan was willing to help the mainland improve its agriculture through technology and to help develop the mainland's economy through investment and trade. The ROC president noted that cross-Strait business and shipping exchanges were complicated and required communications between the two sides "to thoroughly understand the problems and exchange views."

A fourth principle is that the two sides should "join international organizations on equal footing and leaders of the two sides will naturally meet each other on such occasions." Lee said the most natural setting for leaders from the two sides to meet would be in international organizations to which their respective governments belonged. Such meetings "will be conducive to developing bilateral relations and to promoting the process of peaceful reunification." The status of the two sides in such organizations, however, should be equal.

As a fifth principle, the two sides "should persist in using peaceful means to resolve disputes." Lee noted that in 1991 the ROC announced that it would no longer use force against the mainland. He said, "the mainland authorities should show their goodwill by renouncing the use of force against Taiwan, Penghu, and Kinmen and Matsu." Should this occur, "a preliminary consultation on how to end the state of hostile confrontation between the two sides will be held at a most appropriate time and opportunity."

Sixth, "the two sides should jointly maintain the prosperity of and promote democracy in Hong Kong and Macao."

The Lee proposal, like that of Jiang, was not noteworthy in terms of new ideas; but it was an important indicator that Taipei, like Beijing, was favorably inclined to increase the level of cross-Strait dialogue if the sensitive issue of terms of unification could be set aside and immediate focus given instead to pragmatic areas of possible cooperation. Neither side was willing to compromise its basic principles: Beijing insisted that Taiwan was a province of the PRC and the ROC government was a local government; Taipei insisted that unification could be achieved only when the PRC stopped threatening Taiwan with force, accepted the reality of a divided China ruled by two equal governments, and agreed to unite China under a democratic form of government. Despite these differences, the two sides were talking; and many American observers were optimistic that light had been sighted at the end of tunnel.

As a sign of meaningful progress in reducing tension in the Taiwan Strait, in May 1995 the SEF and the ARATS held and successfully concluded preliminary consultations for a second round of Koo-Wang talks scheduled for July in Beijing. According to the ROC, the basis of those talks was that "the meaning of one China is subject to the interpretations of the two sides."[3] However, a few days later, Beijing found out that Lee Teng-hui would be invited to the United States. ARATS notified the SEF by letter than the Koo-Wang talks would have to be postponed and that Taipei would be contacted at an appropriate time in the future. High-level discussions between ARATS and SEF were abruptly terminated by the PRC and did not resume until 1998.

Persistent Problems in Sino-American Relations

Throughout 1995, Sino-American disagreements continued over trade, security, human rights, proliferation, democratic values, and Taiwan, although some agreements were reached. In the area of trade, for example, in late December 1994 the Clinton administration threatened to impose steep tariffs against $2.8 billion in Chinese-made goods if the PRC did not satisfactorily address U.S. concerns over the theft of intellectual property in China. Washington demanded China close down twenty-nine factories in southern China annually producing some 75 million counterfeit discs, laser discs, and CD-ROMs. For its part, Beijing warned that if these sanctions were imposed, it would retaliate by cutting off investment opportunities for American firms. In early January 1995, the PRC amended its copyright law enacted three years previously and urged its citizens to boycott pirated goods.[4] Nonetheless, in early February the administration announced that it would impose 100 percent tariffs on over $1 billion worth of Chinese products to protest the lack of adequate Chinese response to Washington's IPR complaints. China retaliated with a 100 percent tariff on several categories of U.S. goods. Both tariffs were to go into effect February 26, thus setting a deadline for the two sides to reach an agreement before a trade war erupted. At stake was a considerable amount of trade. In 1994, for example, bilateral trade between China and the United States totaled about $45 billion, with China enjoying a $30 billion surplus.

While U.S. Trade Representative Mickey Kantor threatened to impose economic sanctions, Energy Secretary Hazel R. O'Leary worked to convince the Chinese to purchase $8 billion in American electric-power systems. The administration also announced that it would expand its program of subsidized wheat sales to China, saving the PRC some $20 million. Kantor brushed aside suggestions of inconsistency in these policies: "You have to pick your punitive actions with surgical precision. In this business, you have to walk and chew gum at the same time. You can't be a slave to a false notion of consistency that is not in our interest."[5] Echoing the administration's policy of not allowing problems in one area of Sino-American relations to damage other areas, Kantor said, "It's harmful to U.S. interests to let one trade dispute color our ability to work with China in other areas."[6]

But this policy led to some interesting episodes. In late February 1995, for example, there were two different American delegations on separate floors of the China World Hotel in Beijing. On one floor was a delegation headed by Deputy Trade Representative Charlene Barshefsky battling the Chinese over IPR violations. On another floor was a delegation headed by O'Leary and comprising American corporate executives seeking expanded business opportunities in China.[7] On this occasion, both delegations were successful. At the last minute before the February 26 deadline, the USTR was able to secure an agreement from China that it would take immediate steps to curtail infringements on American intellectual property rights, improve enforcement to prevent future abuse, and increased market access for U.S. companies seeking to conduct business in China. At the same time, Secretary O'Leary signed an agreement giving China access to U.S. civilian nuclear technology, although its implementation could not go forward until Clinton certified to Congress that China's nuclear trade with Iran and Pakistan was appropriate under NPT guidelines.

The IPR agreement was signed in Beijing on March 11 by Mickey Kantor and his Chinese counterpart, Madame Wu Yi. However, the two sides immediately began to argue over whether the United States was preventing China from joining the World Trade Organization (WTO), the successor to GATT. For several years China had tried unsuccessfully to join GATT. The United States and other developed countries wanted China to be member of GATT and the WTO, but they insisted that membership must be the result of China's adherence to the commercial obligations and responsibilities accepted by other members. China argued that it was a developing country and therefore should be admitted under much less stringent rules.

In March the United States and China agreed on a series of measures to help the PRC gain entrance into the WTO, not as a developing country (which China had demanded) and not as a developed country (as the United States had sought) but as a hybrid member with a status falling somewhere in between. In the eight-point trade agreement, China agreed to lift suspension of the 1992 market access agreement with the United States; both sides agreed to pursue talks on U.S. telecommunications services and on market access for U.S. insurance services; both sides agreed to implement a letter of intent on agriculture and to pursue talks on wheat and citrus fruit; the United States agreed to support China's accession into the WTO as a founding member; and both sides agreed to pursue talks on China's WTO entry on a pragmatic, flexible basis. In the agricultural accord the two sides agreed to expand their imports of the others' agricultural products.[8] As of mid-1999, however, China still had not been admitted to the WTO, in part because of continuing disagreement with the United States over market access in the PRC and in part because of domestic opposition to Sino-American relations in both countries.[9]

In the area of human rights, a similar pattern of only incremental improvement in U.S.-PRC relations could be found. It will be recalled that President Clinton removed the linkage of improved human rights behavior from the renewal of China's MFN trading status in May 1994 in the expectation that expanded contact between the United States and the PRC would result in gradual improvement in human rights. In mid-January 1995, however, U.S. Assistant Secretary of State for human rights John Shattuck met with Chinese officials, but with no results. In fact, by the time of Shattuck's visit, the State Department had concluded that China's human rights record had worsened since Clinton's MFN decision, with renewed crackdowns on dissidents, the media, and in Tibet.[10]

Human rights issues were raised in virtually every meeting between Chinese and American officials, but the overall human rights situation in the PRC continued to deteriorate. In May 1995, a month before Clinton had to determine once again China's MFN status, the Senate Foreign Relations Committee held hearings in which a number of witnesses testified that China carried out an illicit international trade in kidneys, corneas, and other organs extracted from executed prisoners. Others charged that China engaged in the sale of aborted human fetuses in the form of health tonic. The charges gained wide attention in the media, and the State Department promised to look into the matter.[11]

As promised in 1994, the administration completed a new "code of conduct" for American businessmen to be applied voluntarily in countries such as China where human rights abuses were widespread. The "Model Business Principles" included suggestions such as: provide a safe and healthy workplace; institute fair employment practices, including avoidance of child labor and avoidance of discrimination and respect for the right to organize and bargain collectively; practice responsible environmental protection; comply with U.S. and local laws promoting good business practices, including laws prohibiting illicit payments and ensuring fair competition; and maintain a corporate culture that respects free expression and does not condone political coercion in the workplace. Amnesty International and other organizations concerned with human rights in China called the administration's business principles "essentially milquetoast."[12]

Despite concerns over human rights abuses in China, President Clinton extended unconditional MFN to the PRC in June 1995. Beijing did not respond graciously to the MFN extension, but instead criticized the annual U.S. renewal process as being "outdated" and one that "should be consigned to history."[13]

In the area of security, in mid-January 1995, Defense Secretary William Perry commented that, while "China has quite clearly a substantial military capability," the United States did not consider it "a significant threat, either on a global scale or on a regional scale. Nor do I believe the Chinese government has aggressive or offensive intentions."[14] A month later, the PRC seized and occupied Mischief Reef in the Spratly Islands about 130 miles off the coast of the Philippines. China raised its flag and erected a structure on the tiny shoal. Beijing then said it was willing to settle disputes over the Spratly Islands on the basis of international law, including the 1982 Law of the Sea Treaty which the PRC had not yet ratified. The seizure led to a number of minor confrontations between the Philippines and China, and it raised ASEAN's concerns that China was intent on seizing its claims to virtually the entire South China Sea. The U.S. response to rising tensions in the South China Sea was to urge a peaceful settlement of the disputes, insisting that international waters be respected since the right of free passage through the waters was deemed vital by the U.S. military. The State Department said: "We do not exert a legal opinion on the status of the Spratlys, but we are continually in touch with the claimants to exert our view that any conflicts over the Spratlys ought to be discussed peacefully, free from the threat of force or the use of force."[15] (By mid-1999, China was "reinforcing" its presence in the South China Sea, the Philippines were poised to sign a new military pact with the United States, and most of the rest of ASEAN was silent on the South China Sea issue.)[16]

The *USS Bunker Hill*, a guided missile cruiser and one of the most sophisticated antiair platforms for the U.S. Navy, visited Qingdao, China, for a four-day courtesy call on March 22–25, 1995. It was the first U.S. warship to visit China since 1989 and the third such port call since 1949. During the same period, it was announced that Lt. Gen. Xiong Guankai, assistant to the chief of the PLA's general staff, would visit the United States in late March to discuss China's defense strategy, structure, and budget. Xiong's presentations were in exchange for those of Assistant Secretary of Defense for strategy and requirements Ted Warner, who briefed Chinese officers on U.S. defense strategy and budgets in December 1994. Thus, by early 1995 the U.S. and PRC militaries were again exchanging high-level visits, a politically sensitive issue for both sides since Tiananmen, but one deemed highly important to learn more of the other side's capabilities and intentions, to establish personal relationships between military leaders, and to defuse potential military confrontations in the future.

While military-to-military contacts increased in 1995, there were persistent problems in the nonproliferation aspects of U.S.-China security relations. In mid-April, for example, there was widespread concern expressed in the United States over China's impending deal to transfer technology capable of furthering Iran's nuclear weapons program. Strictly speaking, the deal was not in violation of Nuclear Non-Proliferation Treaty (NPT) guidelines, but the dual-use technology could assist Iran in ways opposed by Washington. Secretary of State Christopher raised U.S. concerns to Foreign Minister Qian Qichen during a meeting in New York on April 17. Qian rebuffed Christopher and said, "There is no international law or international regulation or international agreement that prohibits such cooperation in the peaceful use of nuclear energy."[17]

Clinton's strategy of comprehensive engagement was intended to allow Sino-American relations to go forward in some areas even if it retrogressed in others.

The justification was that the overall relationship was too important to be dragged down by specific issues. The strategy was in part a result of the failure of Clinton's initial approach to China, which attempted to pressure Beijing by linking trade, human rights, proliferation, and other issues. When Beijing resisted American pressure through these linkages, the Clinton administration adopted a strategy of cooperating where possible and confronting when necessary, but not allowing confrontation in some areas to undermine cooperation in others. In theory, the strategy of engagement made sense in view of China's growing power and importance, but in practice the strategy had at least two major weaknesses: first, it left the administration vulnerable to manipulation by Beijing, for if Sino-American relations were too important to be undermined by specific issues, then China could threaten the overall relationship to gain concessions on specific issues; and second, the strategy and resulting policy were confusing to both Americans and Chinese.[18]

Policy Explanations

As a result of continued difficulties in Sino-American relations and apparent inconsistencies in policy, the Clinton administration spent considerable time before Congress and the American public trying to explain U.S. engagement with China. Interestingly, the Department of Defense often was more articulate than other bureaucracies; and, in fact, the Pentagon played a highly influential role in China policy during this period.

The U.S. military explanation of engagement was offered in the 1995 Posture Statement of the Commander in Chief, United States Pacific Command.[19] Admiral Richard C. Macke told the Senate Armed Services Committee in February 1995 that the U.S. Pacific Command pursued a strategy of cooperative engagement with China (the USPACOM's version of comprehensive engagement) for important reasons of national security. Sino-American engagement helped to stabilize the Asia-Pacific region, increase mutual understanding between the PLA and American armed forces, moderate PLA policies, and avoid a military confrontation with China as it increased its role in Asian-Pacific affairs. Adm. Macke explained: "Although the Chinese say their military is not their central priority, the People's Liberation Army is clearly central to all their goals: internal stability, economic progress, and external respect. That is why our growing program of reassuring military contacts with the Chinese military is so important. As China's future unfolds, the PLA will play a pivotal role."

Admiral Macke noted that China continued to increase the pace and scope of its military modernization, and the USPACOM recognized the concerns of many regional nations over China's growing power projection capability. But, he said, "I do not see China's military as a near-term threat to the U.S. or to our interests in Asia." On the other hand, he warned that U.S. policy could make China an enemy in the future: "My assessment [of the Chinese threat] will change, however, if we choose to isolate, rather than engage and reassure China. I believe the best approach to be a coordinated engagement in the political, economic, and military arenas."

In May 1995 a fairly complete explanation of U.S. China policy was presented by Kent Wiedemann, Deputy Assistant Secretary of State for East Asian and Pacific Affairs.[20] His testimony before the House Ways and Means Subcommittee on May 23 was given in the context of the pending June decision to renew China's MFN trading status. Wiedemann said the administration believed U.S. national interests were served by developing and maintaining friendly relations with a China that was "strong, stable, prosperous, and open." As a guiding principle of policy, the administration believed engagement between the United States and China offered "the best way, over the long term, to promote the full range of U.S. interests with China, including our human rights, strategic, economic and commercial interests. . . . High-level engagement provides valuable opportunities to remind China of the need to adopt and fulfill international norms."

Wiedemann explained that the strategy of comprehensive engagement adopted by President Clinton in September 1993 had three purposes: (1) to pursue all U.S. interests at the levels and intensity required to achieve results; (2) to seek to build mutual confidence and agreement in areas where American and Chinese interests converged; and (3) through dialogue, to reduce the areas in which the United States and China had differences. While the engagement strategy had succeeded in helping to advance U.S. interests with China and encouraging China's continued integration into the international community, U.S. foreign policy toward China continued "to focus on three baskets of core concerns: human rights, nonproliferation and economic issues."

In the area of human rights, Wiedemann admitted, "we have not seen the kind of progress we would like on human rights in China over the past year." However, some progress had been made in terms of continued bilateral and multilateral dialogue on human rights, a voluntary set of principles for American companies doing business in China, increased Voice of America programming in China, ending forced labor practices at some Chinese factories, and expanded counternarcotics cooperation.

In terms of economics and trade, Wiedemann noted that the administration had deep concern over the nearly $30 billion trade deficit with China in 1994. The U.S. trade strategy was to urge Beijing to abide by international rules and discipline as the price for accession into the World Trade Organization. Wiedemann argued, "Through trade, U.S. concepts filter into the consciousness of all Chinese. Opening markets for America's idea industries—movies, CDs, interactive software, television—and for products that make communicating easier—such as fax machines and copiers—spread U.S. values and ideals."

In terms of nonproliferation concerns, Wiedemann said: "Since China is a major player in the international arms world, Chinese observance of the multilateral proliferation regimes is necessary to halt the spread of weapons of mass destruction and missiles. Proliferation is a high-level concern in our dealings with Beijing, and comprehensive engagement has helped us to move ahead on several fronts with the Chinese in this very important area of U.S. national interest." Wiedemann reported that results were mixed. On the negative side, the United States was concerned over China's nuclear cooperation with Iran and the PRC's own nuclear testing. On the positive side, the United States and China issued a Joint Statement on Missile Non-Proliferation in October 1994 in which China agreed to observe MTCR guidelines and parameters. China also sided with the United States on the indefinite and unconditional extension of the NPT.

Visit of Lee Teng-hui

As previously noted, one of the most controversial episodes in Sino-American relations during the Clinton administration was the visit of Taiwan President Lee Teng-hui to the United States in mid-June 1995. For almost a year afterward, China threatened and intimidated Taiwan with displays of military force, including missile tests over the island, and in March 1996 the United States confronted the PLA navy in waters near Taiwan to demonstrate American resolve that the use of force by Beijing would not be tolerated.[21]

The background to Lee's visit—including congressional pressure, State Department assurances to Chinese leaders that the trip would not take place, and President Clinton's eventual decision—were discussed earlier. The trip was important to Taiwan for at least three reasons: to increase Taiwan's international breathing space, to enhance Lee's political popularity at home, and to explain firsthand to a wide American audience Taipei's view on its relations with China. In his remarks at Cornell University, Lee emphasized, "We believe that mutual respect will gradually lead to the peaceful reunification of China under a system of democracy, freedom and equitable distribution of wealth."[22] Lee was quoted as saying in a private breakfast with Taiwanese-Americans at Cornell: "The Republic of China (Taiwan) is definitely not a part of the People's Republic of China, and neither is it a province of that country."[23]

In essence, Lee told his American audience that the ROC favored reunification with the mainland, but only under conditions of democracy. Taiwan would never unify under a communist government in Beijing. As greater economic and political reform took place on the mainland, Taipei was willing to improve relations with Beijing and gradually increase linkages between the two sides. However, this process of gradual interaction should take place under conditions of mutual respect—i.e., Beijing had to recognize Taipei as an equal government and to acknowledge that the two parts of China were governed by two separate, sovereign political entities. Further, mutual respect meant that Beijing had to renounce the use of force against Taiwan, not interfere in Taiwan's efforts to play a role in international affairs commensurate with the island's economic, political, and social development, and to protect the citizens of Taiwan as they invest, trade, tour, and otherwise interact with the mainland. To expedite these exchanges and to manage the day-to-day problems that would inevitably arise in the interchange, Taiwan was willing to deal pragmatically and on an equal basis with counterparts on the mainland.

In truth, contact between the peoples on both sides of the Taiwan Strait had increased remarkably since the mid-1980s. By 1995, millions of Taiwan residents had visited mainland China, and China had become Taiwan's most important source of export growth. In that year, out of Taiwan's total exports of $111.7 billion, ROC exports to Hong Kong, the main entrepôt of indirect trade with mainland China, totaled $26.1 billion, with Taiwan recording a $24.3 billion surplus.[24] On the other hand, Taiwan's increased exposure to mainland China had not resulted in Taiwanese wanting to embrace the motherland. Indeed, most Taiwan visitors to the mainland were shocked at how backward China was in many respects, how repressive its governing authorities were, how corrupt the system was in general, and how rampant its crime. Having just evolved into a democracy after four decades of authoritarian rule under the KMT, most Taiwan visitors returned to the island with greater determination to avoid unification with the communist-controlled mainland if at all possible.

Even while President Lee Teng-hui indicated a willingness to improve relations with mainland China, he also moved forward to expand Taiwan's international political representation. This was reflected in concerted efforts to rejoin the United Nations and to increase the scope of quasi-official trips abroad by high-ranking Taiwan authorities. Lee himself, for example, had made high profile visits to Indonesia, Thailand, the Philippines, three Central American countries, South Africa, and Singapore in 1994. In addition to his trip to the United States in 1995, Lee visited Jordan and the United Arab Emirates; and in 1996 he visited several Latin American countries.

These efforts at "vacation diplomacy" were widely supported on Taiwan, where several factors contributed to the more assertive ROC effort in foreign affairs. These factors included pressure from the DPP to break out of the diplomatic isolation imposed by the PRC; perceptions that Sino-American relations were not improving, despite Clinton's 1994 decision to delink human rights from China's most-favored-nation trading status; and evidence that the U.S. Congress and American media favored closer ties between the United States and Taiwan. In May 1995, for example, the U.S. Senate voted 97-1 in favor of H. Con. Res. 53 expressing the sense of Congress that President Lee should be permitted to make a private visit to his alma mater at Cornell University. No doubt, Lee's effort to secure a visa was motivated in part by his desire to be overwhelmingly chosen as Taiwan's first democratically elected president in March 1996. But mostly, Lee's trip to the United States, and the lobbying efforts the ROC orchestrated to facilitate such a trip, reflected Taiwan's determination to expand its international presence.

Any optimism Beijing may have felt in early 1995 about in its relations with Washington and Taipei faded on May 22, when the U.S. government announced that it would give permission to Lee Teng-hui to pay a private, unofficial visit to the United States. The PRC knew that President Clinton personally had made this decision and it hit Beijing unexpectedly and hard. According to PRC sources, Clinton himself had told Jiang Zemin in the 1994 Asia-Pacific summit in Indonesia that Lee Teng-hui would not be allowed to visit the United States, assurances repeated by Secretary Christopher and Assistant Secretary Lord.[25]

From Beijing's point of view, Taiwan's efforts to break out of international isolation threatened PRC interests in at least three important ways. First, it undermined the PRC strategy for peaceful reunification under the terms of the "one country, two systems" formula devised by Deng Xiaoping for Hong Kong, Macau, and Taiwan. This formula suited PRC interests because it perpetuated Beijing as the central government of China, while allowing the people of Taiwan to enjoy their way of life and capitalist system for some decades. Second, it preserved Taiwan's option to pursue a path of national independence in the future, thus leaving open the possibility of splitting the Chinese motherland and of encouraging separatist movements in Tibet and Xinjiang. And third, the U.S. invitation to Lee could encourage other nations to extend similar invitations.

Chinese leaders felt they had to take firm measures to counter Taiwan's efforts to expand its role in international affairs, especially when involving the United States. Beijing believed that if Taipei succeeded in its pragmatic diplomacy, the ROC government might draw out indefinitely political talks over eventual reunification. A successful pragmatic diplomacy might also lead to growing international recognition of "two Chinas" or increase international support for "one China, one Taiwan." There also was strong suspicion that Taiwan's efforts to expand its international presence were being supported by the United States in some secret strategy to contain China before it became a superpower in the twenty-first century. All of these developments would seriously harm PRC interests and therefore could not be tolerated by Beijing.

There is strong evidence that the Lee visit precipitated a major dispute within the Chinese leadership over control of policy toward Taiwan and the United States. According to May and June reports in the Hong Kong *Lien Ho Pao*, hardliners within the Chinese Communist Party seized upon Lee's invitation as an opportunity to criticize those departments responsible for relations with Taiwan and the United States as being too weak. In the wake of Lee's visit, the influence of the hardliners rose in policymaking circles, while the influence of the moderates declined. The hardliners insisted that cooperation with the United States in all areas be curtailed and that the Chinese ambassador to the United States be recalled in protest. The hardliners further insisted that Lee Teng-hui and his government were pursuing an independent Taiwan, a movement the mainland should no longer tolerate. This group lobbied hard against any further concessions to Taiwan and insisted that Taiwan's international activities be vigorously opposed.[26]

As noted previously, the PRC reaction to the U.S. invitation to Lee was exceptionally strident. The Foreign Affairs Committee of the National People's Congress Standing Committee issued a statement on May 24, 1995, calling the U.S. decision "an extremely serious move," and one that "will inevitably impair Sino-U.S. relations." The statement predicted: "Given Li's [Lee Teng-hui] position, his visit to the United States, under whatever name or in whatever way, will inevitably bring about the serious consequence of creating 'two Chinas' or 'one China, one Taiwan.'"[27] Also on May 24 the Foreign Affairs Committee of the Chinese People's Political Consultative Conference National Committee issued a statement which read in part: "The Taiwan issue is of vital importance to China's sovereignty, territorial integrity and the great cause of reunification. Allowing Li Teng-hui to visit the United States in whatever capacity by the U.S. administration will result in the severe consequence of creating 'two Chinas' or 'one China, one Taiwan,' in complete violation of the fundamental principles in the three Sino-U.S. joint communiqués."[28]

The next day, China's Foreign Ministry spokesman announced that several upcoming visits by important Chinese officials to the United States would be canceled to protest Washington's decision to invite Lee to the United States. The spokesman warned that the United States would "pay the price" for the invitation, hinting at linkage with other issues. The spokesman said: "The three Sino-U.S. joint communiqués are the very underpinning of the development of Sino-U.S. relations. If this underpinning is harmed then Sino-U.S. relations in other fields will unavoidably be affected.... For us nothing is more important than safeguarding China's sovereignty and reunification."[29] Beijing thereupon cut short the U.S. visit of the PLA Air Force Chief of Staff, canceled the visit of State Counselor Li Guixian, and postponed the trip of Defense Minister Chi Haotian. Chinese-American consultations on nuclear cooperation and controlling the spread of missile technology were postponed as well, as China openly linked U.S. policy toward Taiwan with Chinese cooperation with the United States in security matters.

According to the analysis of Chinese Academy of Social Sciences fellow Zhang Yebai, the United States had made three "major retrogressions" on the Taiwan issue in recent years. These included President George Bush's decision to sell F-16 fighters to Taiwan, the September 1994 readjustment of U.S. Taiwan policy by President Clinton, and Clinton's decision to extend a visa to Lee Teng-hui. Because of these challenges to Chinese sovereignty, "China has lost its trust in the United States" and is considering "whether or not it will take a cooperative attitude toward the United States on certain specific issues" such as security in the Asia-Pacific region and economic issues.[30]

One of the strongest reactions was in a commentary in Beijing's *Renmin Ribao* on May 26, which argued that the United States was using Lee's visit as part of a grand strategy to weaken China by keeping the nation divided:

Although the United States claims to recognize only one China, deep down it does not want China to be unified, and is always looking for an excuse to engineer "two Chinas" or "one China, one Taiwan" in an attempt to keep Taiwan as an "unsinkable aircraft carrier" for the United States. There have been new developments in cross-Strait relations in recent years. In particular, following President Jiang Zemin's eight-point proposal on the peaceful reunification of the motherland, cross-Strait relations have warmed up further, with good momentum appearing in economic exchanges, trade ties, and other areas. However, this is a development the United States does not want to see. The United States was seeking to disrupt and undermine the growth of cross-Strait relations and to obstruct China's peaceful reunification when it gave Li Denghui [Lee Teng-hui] permission to visit the country. . . . The Taiwan issue has a bearing on China's sovereignty, territorial integrity, and national reunification. On this key principle, which concerns China's fundamental interests, China's position is firm and unyielding. China has consistently valued its relations with the United States, but it absolutely will not tolerate the United States' wantonly undermining its sovereignty. The Chinese people will resolutely defend their national interests and dignity.[31]

Echoing the theme that the U.S. invitation to Lee was part of an American strategy to contain China, Beijing Central People's Radio editorialized on June 12, 1995: "The United States considers China the greatest obstacle standing in its way to achieving hegemony. . . . Guided by its hegemonic mentality, the United States does not want to see a unified China and, by hindering China through Taiwan, tries to maintain the status quo of a divided China and obstruct China from being an affluent and strong country."[32] A *Xinhua* commentary of June 17 said: "In the final analysis, the United States has never discarded the policy of regarding Taiwan as its 'unsinkable aircraft carrier'; and its attempts to play the 'Taiwan card,' and to curb China's development, growth, and reunification of China."[33]

Dire warnings were heard from the PRC that the United States was "playing with fire." On June 10, *Renmin Ribao* editorialized:

> The Taiwan issue is a powder keg. It is extremely dangerous to keep warming it up, no matter whether this is done by the United States or by Li Denghui. If their activities lead to its explosion, the consequences will be unimaginable.
>
> People who play with fire always think they know what they are doing and think it is fun. But elements such as fire and water are cruel and indifferent and have their own principles, after crossing a certain threshold, running independent of human will and ultimately burning the players, much to their surprise.
>
> We advise the U.S. Government, people like Li Denghui, and those who seek the "independence of Taiwan" in service of their immediate interests by warming up the powder keg: Be cautious, be cautious![34]

In addition to condemning the United States for its invitation to Lee Teng-hui, the PRC heaped special scorn on Lee himself for "embracing foreigners to earn himself dignity and for being willing to become a person condemned by history."[35]

Reflecting the view of many in China that Lee was leading Taiwan down a path of "two Chinas" or Taiwan independence, *Liaowang* in early June detailed the steps the Taiwan president had taken to redefine the island's status since coming to power in January 1988. The article said that Lee's government had made a concerted effort to drop the one-China commitment of its predecessors and to adopt a de facto two-Chinas position through such schemes as "one China, two reciprocal governments," "one country, two governments," "one country, two regions," "two reciprocal political entities," "mutual governmental recognition," "divided country under separate rule," "two Chinas as a phase in a long process leading toward one China," "the ROC in Taiwan," "Taiwan and the mainland are governed by two political entities," "the two sides of the Strait are divided under separate rule," and so on. According to the article, this evolution in Taipei's view was made possible because of three developments: democratization on the island which consolidated Lee Teng-hui's position; the rapid growth of the DPP threatened KMT rule, necessitating compromise between the two parties; and some Western countries [i.e., the United States] had pursued "a double-track policy toward China in a bid to 'use Chinese to control Chinese'" by maintaining diplomatic relations with the PRC but "substantive relations" with Taiwan.[36]

PRC Policy Adjustments

Influenced by these perceptions and by hardliners within the CCP who demanded a tougher policy line, the government of Jiang Zemin modified PRC relations with both Taiwan and the United States. In the case of Taiwan, the PRC banned some business and cultural exchanges and postponed indefinitely the next meeting between Wang Daohan of China's Association for Relations Across the Taiwan Straits and Koo Chen-fu of the ROC's Straits Exchange Foundation. It will be recalled that the first meeting between Wang and Koo was held in Singapore in 1993 and led to significantly expanded contact between the two sides. The second Wang-Koo talks were scheduled to be held in July 1995 and had been expected to open contact still further. The talks had helped to reduce tension in the Taiwan Strait and were pointed to by Washington as evidence of the success of its policies toward China and Taiwan. In addition to postponing the Wang-Koo talks, Beijing canceled routine discussion between lower-ranking officials in the two representative organizations, normally held every three months. The second round of talks between Wang and Koo did not occur until October 1998, by which time relations across the Taiwan Strait had returned to a degree of normalcy. The PRC ban on high-level contacts between the two quasi-official organizations responsible for managing day-to-day affairs across the Taiwan Strait continued through 1997, despite many efforts by Taipei to resume the dialogue. The PRC Foreign Ministry explained that Lee had "poisoned" the climate of cross-Strait relations.[37]

On June 16, 1995, the same day Beijing postponed the second round of Koo-Wang talks, China recalled its Ambassador to the United States, Li Daoyu. The recall of Ambassador Li for consultations coincided with the scheduled departure of U.S. Ambassador to China J. Stapleton Roy before his successor, former Senator James Sasser, had been accepted by Beijing or confirmed by the U.S. Senate. With no ambassadorial representation in either capital, Sino-American relations reached their lowest ebb since 1979. Ambassador Sasser did not arrive in Beijing until several months later. Earlier, it will be recalled, China had cut short the U.S. visit of the PLA Air Force Chief of Staff and postponed the visit of the PRC Defense Minister. Further, by postponing indefinitely U.S.-PRC consultations on nuclear cooperation and proliferation, China sought to punish the Clinton administration for its policy toward Taiwan.

While China felt confident it could exert considerable pressure on Taiwan, policy changes toward the United States were more problematic. On the one hand, Beijing recognized that Washington wanted to maintain cooperative relations with China, as demonstrated by continuous U.S. assurances that it was following its traditional "one-China" policy. On the other hand, the United States had shown greater support for Taiwan in recent years, as evidenced by the F-16 sale, the Taiwan policy review, and the invitation to Lee Teng-hui. Moreover, a growing number of Americans seemed to be concluding that, while the United States hoped to improve its relations with China, the two countries were likely to remain somewhat hostile to each other because of differences over arms sales, human rights, Taiwan, and Tibet.

Faced with these contradictory elements in U.S. policy, some CCP leaders apparently concluded that the United States was following a dual policy of cooperation and confrontation toward China, with the overall strategic objective to westernize and possibly split China. According to some commentaries, this Chinese perception of U.S. strategy led the PRC to adopt the following line: "strategically, the CPC will not make any concession on problems concerning its sovereignty and territorial integrity, while tactically, it will strike only after it has been struck." On the Taiwan issue, the PRC leadership believed that greater importance should be attached to the unification of the country than to Sino-U.S. relations. As a result, no further concessions on the Taiwan issue should be made by Beijing. Moreover, it was decided that if the United States did not return to the principles of the three joint communiqués, then friendly relations between the two countries would be difficult to maintain. It was in this context that China asked the United States to make some concrete gestures to eliminate the difficulties created by the Lee visit.[38]

Other analysis, reportedly from within the CCP itself, concluded that the United States was playing a "Taiwan card" to cause political instability on the mainland during the post-Deng leadership transition.[39] Lee Teng-hui was a willing participant in this maneuver, causing the PRC to conclude that Lee had "broken the rules of the game, plunging cross-Strait relations into a dangerous state." According to this analysis, CCP hardliners gained greater influence over policy during this period because the United States had not responded positively to the moderate sixteen-character Sino-American policy of Jiang Zemin ("enhancing confidence, reducing trouble, avoiding confrontation, and expanding cooperation") and because Lee Teng-hui had not responded positively to Jiang's eight-point proposal. The hardliners advocated a tougher diplomatic stand against the United States, in particular demanding that Washington make clear that it did not support Taiwan's pragmatic diplomacy. To bring Sino-U.S. relations back to a state of normalcy, the two sides needed, first, to "reciprocally dispatch special envoys to carry out political dialogue and to relax the strained relations, then visits by high-ranking officials should be made on a reciprocal basis so as to clear relations between the two sides, and finally both parties should accept each other's ambassadors, whose vacancies have not been filled yet, so as to normalize relations." Of the two relationships, however, it was deemed that relations with the United States were the most important and that relations with Taiwan were secondary. Until relations with the United States became more stabilized, PRC relations with Taiwan had to be put on hold, including postponing talks between Wang and Koo. China's handling of the Taiwan issue in relations with the United States was critical, according to these PRC sources, because international attention was focused on the issue. U.S. actions toward Taiwan would affect other countries' policies toward Taiwan.

Apparently, it was during these heated policy debates within the CCP that the PLA began to exert a more influential voice on policy toward Taiwan and the United States. The PLA was deeply concerned about Lee's visit to the United States, viewing this as evidence that Washington and Taipei were intent to pursue policies harmful to China's sovereignty and territorial integrity. According to one report, the CCP leadership reached two basic conclusions. First, the basic PRC policy toward Taiwan would remain unchanged, that is, "the mainland will continue to attach primary importance to economic construction, and secondary importance to reunification of the country, while resolutely preventing Taiwan independence." Second, preparation for possible military action against Taiwan had to be taken, since greater priority had to be given to sovereignty than to economic development.[40]

Other reports from Beijing indicated that Jiang Zemin, eager to increase his stature among the military in the post-Deng leadership transition, told PLA leaders: "The Taiwan independence movement is getting out of hand and we cannot let this go on. . . . We must heighten our guard and strengthen our resources and combat-readiness to curb" this movement. Jiang did not specify what action the military should take, but it was known that within the PLA there was considerable pressure from hawks to teach Taiwan a lesson. There was some concern among observers that Jiang might use the military's worries over Taiwan to enhance his leadership credentials, just as Deng Xiaoping had used the invasion of Vietnam to establish his credentials as a worthy successor to Mao Zedong.[41]

In early July 1995 *Xinhua* said the Chinese people "must use fresh blood and lives" to defend the nation against Taiwan independence.[42] A few days later, on

July 18, Beijing announced that it would conduct an eight-day missile launching drill from July 21 through July 28, with a target area only some 150 kilometers off Keelung in northern Taiwan. Later, a second round of guided missile exercises was held during August 15-25; and a third set of missile firings was held between March 8-15, 1996.

According to PRC officials, the missile tests were designed to show Beijing's dual tactics to resolve the Taiwan issue: by peaceful reunification or by armed liberation. The missile drills were intended to demonstrate China's military strength and to pressure Taipei to hold early peace talks with the mainland. If Taiwan refused to hold such talks, then the mainland could resort to the use of arms. According to these officials, Lee Teng-hui had become too arrogant because of backing by the United States. Therefore, to solve the Taiwan issue, China must first end the interference of the United States. Because of the dual nature of U.S. policy toward China, the PRC had decided to adopt a dual policy of its own toward the United States, namely, a desire for cooperation as the best policy but a willingness to confront the United States if necessary.[43]

Developments in the United States

As has often been the case, the United States after Lee's visit found itself under pressure from both China and Taiwan, with the two Chinese sides trying to convince the Clinton administration to adjust its policies. In early July 1995, for example, Jiang Zemin warned, "The U.S. side should take practical and effective measures immediately to thoroughly eliminate the adverse influences and consequences" of the Lee Teng-hui visit, which has "seriously shaken the foundation of Sino-U.S. relations."[44] At about the same time, Taiwan's Premier Lien Chan described U.S. policy as "absolutely outdated," saying, "If the United States continues its China policy based on the structure that Chinese communists represent China and Taiwan is a part of China, it has seriously lost political contact. . . . The two sides of the Strait have remained apart for nearly fifty years."[45]

Meanwhile, the American press obtained parts of a secret CIA report detailing M-11 missile part transfers from China to Pakistan. Some American analysts saw the transfers as Chinese efforts to circumvent prior nonproliferation agreements, while others viewed the transfers as PRC protests over Washington's policies toward Taiwan. As evidence of the latter interpretation, it was noted that in 1992 China sold M-11 surface-to-surface missiles to Pakistan in apparent retaliation to President Bush's decision to sell Taiwan 150 F-16s. Sanctions on China because of the 1992 missile sale were imposed by the United States in August 1993, but the sanctions were lifted in October 1994 after Beijing agreed to abide by MTCR guidelines. In addition to missile components being transferred to Pakistan, other leaked CIA reports said China was transferring technology and components to Iran, enabling its engineers to improve a new generation of Scud missiles received from

North Korea. These missiles were capable of carrying nuclear warheads. Earlier, China had refused to terminate the sale to Iran of two nuclear reactors believed capable of helping Tehran develop nuclear weapons. Washington also suspected China of selling chemical weapons technology to Iran. The fact that China had stopped proliferation talks with the United States on these and other matters in reaction to the Lee visit greatly concerned the administration. For its part, China said the missile, nuclear, and chemical weapons proliferation charges were "groundless," and it refused to accept a U.S. offer for high-level discussions until Washington took "concrete moves" to repair the damage caused by Lee's visit.[46] Aware of U.S. proliferation concerns, China demanded that the United States change its policy toward Taiwan before Beijing would join the MTCR and undertake further cooperation on proliferation and regional security issues.[47]

In part, China's tough stance reflected a growing perception in Beijing that U.S. strategy was to oppose China's larger role in regional and global affairs. On virtually every hand—whether in trade, in hosting the Olympic Games, in arms sales, in expansion of influence in the South China Sea, in resolving the reunification issue with Taiwan, in human rights, in Tibet, even in Hong Kong to some extent—the United States was the principal opposition to Chinese policies and the expansion of PRC influence. Rather than engaging China, as the Clinton administration claimed, the real U.S. strategy (according to this analysis) was to limit China's power and influence of China—in effect to contain China through a new cold war.[48] Even those Chinese who did not believe the United States was trying to contain China found this argument appealing; it could be used to push a sensitive button in Washington—i.e., causing Americans who supported engagement to rush forward with statements denying containment and urging cooperative relations with Beijing.

Sino-American relations became more strained in mid-June 1995, when Harry Wu, a Chinese-born American citizen, was arrested in Xinjiang Province. Wu had spent nearly twenty years in Chinese labor camps as a rightist before moving to the United States and becoming an American citizen. He wrote two books describing the Chinese Gulag and testified before Congress about the use of prison labor to produce goods for export to the United States. The administration strongly protested Wu's arrest, and both Houses of Congress passed resolutions demanding his immediate release. Beijing dismissed the U.S. protests and charged Wu with stealing state secrets and sneaking into China under an assumed name. Wu's arrest coincided with an overall crackdown on political dissent in China, including the re-arrest and imprisonment of veteran dissident Chen Ziming, whose medical parole in May 1994 had helped convince Clinton to delink human rights and MFN.[49]

In an effort to put Sino-American relations back on track, President Clinton on June 2 announced his intention to extend MFN trading status to China for another year. The White House said: "Last year, the President delinked China's MFN trade status from overall human rights considerations. He did so because he concluded that broad engagement with China, including on human rights issues, offers the best prospect for progress in all areas of concern to us." Although the United States would renew MFN, "we find China's record on human rights unacceptable. China continues to deny its citizens freedom of speech, association, and religion and fails to guarantee humane treatment of prisoners. Extrajudicial arrest and detention remain common practice." Nonetheless, the White House said, "We remain convinced that the broadest possible engagement with China offers the best opportunity over the long term to ensure that China abides by internationally-accepted norms. MFN status for China will enable us to continue to engage China in the comprehensive and constructive manner necessary to move forward on the full range of bilateral, regional and global issues."[50]

On June 27 Assistant Secretary of State Winston Lord and Assistant Secretary of Defense Joseph Nye testified before the House International Relations Committee on U.S. security policy toward East Asia, with special emphasis on China.[51] In his remarks, Lord said that since Lee's private visit earlier in June, "our relationship with China has entered a very difficult period." Beijing had retaliated for Lee's unofficial visit by postponing all scheduled visits and talks on nonproliferation and security matters. In addition, Chinese rhetoric had been severe, and the Chinese Ambassador had been recalled. In spite of the PRC reaction, Lord reaffirmed the continuation of long-standing U.S. strategy and policy toward China and Taiwan:

> There is a growing perception in some quarters of the PRC that the U.S.—and by this I mean the Administration as well as the Congress—is trying to foster an independent Taiwan as part of an effort to "contain" China and to prevent it from fully assuming its role as a great power. That is emphatically not United States policy. We seek to engage China, not contain it. Our relations with Taiwan will continue to be friendly but unofficial. For its part, Taiwan is seeking to gain the recognition and respect its people believe they deserve from the international community—and from the government in Beijing—for their impressive economic and political achievements.
>
> We have consistently declined to play a role in shaping the future between China and Taiwan. We leave this to the parties themselves, insisting only that the process be peaceful. Indeed, one of the great achievements of U.S.-PRC normalization was to take the U.S. out of the middle of the dispute between China and Taiwan, giving the U.S. the credibility to encourage both sides to improve cross-Strait ties—which has in fact occurred. The effect has been to facilitate a dramatic reduction of tension across the Taiwan Strait and to allow the burgeoning economic, tourist and other ties that have developed between Taiwan and the mainland. This, in turn, has been of importance to the economic growth of both sides and to the impressive political liberalization in Taiwan.

In his presentation to the House International Relations Committee, Joseph Nye said that, despite the current crisis in Sino-American relations, there were certain security facts which had to be faced: China was a nuclear weapons state; it was a leading regional military power; it was a global economic and political power with a permanent seat on the U.N. Security Council; it was essential for peace, stability, and economic growth in the Asia-Pacific region that China was stable and continued to develop friendly relations with its neighbors. It was therefore essential that the United States maintain a dialogue with China, working together when the two countries could agree and finding ways to influence the PRC when disagreements occurred.

Nye pointed to six reasons why the United States had to engage China on a broad range of security issues:

1. Security dialogues and military exchanges are important during periods of international transition and they are especially important to shape thinking, ease concerns, and enhance trust between major powers. Since the power of China is increasing, the United States "must engage its political/military leadership in a dialogue about their future role in the Pacific and work to integrate it into the larger international community. China's Pacific power and presence is still in a formative stage and outcomes can be influenced—that is why we choose to engage China, not contain it."

2. U.S. friends and allies in the Asian Pacific supported a policy of engagement. Nye said that allies such as Japan, South Korea, and Thailand have "pressed the U.S. to engage China on a broad array of issues, including security concerns. If we mistakenly decided to practice a broad policy of containment—rather than engagement—towards China, we would be going it alone in Asia, without the support of our key allies."

3. In terms of larger U.S. objectives in the Asian Pacific, the United States was "trying to promote transparency and mutual understanding" as a way to increase trust between nations and reduce the likelihood of misinterpretation of intentions and capabilities. Nye recalled, "in the 1980s, the U.S. made military technology and arms sales available to China as a counterweight to the Soviet Union. In this post-Cold War environment we want to promote transparency and build confidence in the Pacific—not arsenals."

4. One of the most important reasons to engage the PRC is that "China holds the key to progress in a variety of regional trouble spots and, increasingly, in global security issues." The assistant secretary noted China's role "behind the scenes in the negotiation of the North Korean nuclear framework agreement"; in discussions over Cambodia; in providing "avenues of discreet diplomacy on security and political matters to states such as Burma, Pakistan, and Iran"; in managing and eventual resolving "competing claims in the South China Sea"; and in establishing "effective international arms control and nonproliferation regimes." Nye stressed: "As a nuclear power and an arms exporter and importer, China's importance on these issues must not be underestimated and cannot be overemphasized. Even if there were no other reasons to do so, our proliferation concerns would require that we continue to engage China."

5. "The military and security elite in China will play a critical role during a period of political transition." The Pentagon believed that dialogue and engagement with these leaders would allow the United States "to gain valuable insights into the political changes sweeping the country" and to "have a measure of influence over their attitudes and behavior."
6. Sixth, since "the Chinese military is increasingly operating further from their shores, in international waters where US forces regularly deploy," it is likely in the future that China and the United States will operate in the same areas. "By beginning operational dialogues with our Chinese military counterparts we can work to improve mutual understanding between our maritime and air forces, so that they will understand each others' signals and operating procedures as they inevitably have increasing contact in the course of their routine operations."

Nye said five pillars comprised the U.S. military's policy of engagement with China: "high-level visits; functional exchanges; routine military activities and confidence-building measures; participation in multinational security fora; and the Joint Defense Conversion Commission."[52] Nye also carefully noted areas in which U.S. cooperation with China did not exist: "the ban on arms transfers and dual-use technologies continues and discussion of US military capabilities and intentions is limited to publicly available information."

An assessment of the current state of Sino-American relations was offered by Deputy Assistant Secretary of State Kent Wiedemann in testimony before the Senate Foreign Relations Committee on July 25.[53] Wiedemann said China was important to U.S. interests for many reasons: China was one of the five declared nuclear powers and a growing military power; its economy was expected to continue to grow between 8 and 10 percent annually through the year 2000; China purchased about $9.3 billion in U.S. goods and services in 1994 and its market for the United States was expected to grow; the PRC was a permanent member of the U.N. Security Council, possessing veto power over key global issues such as resolutions dealing with proliferation, peacekeeping, and sanctions against rogue states; China played a key role in regional security issues such as the North Korean nuclear issue, Cambodia, and the Spratlys; and Beijing's cooperation was critical on a number of bilateral, regional, and global issues such as interdiction of drug trafficking, illegal Chinese immigration, and protection of the environment.

He pointed to several achievements of President Clinton's policy of engagement with China:

- China reaffirmed its commitment to the Missile Technology Control Regime in October 1994.
- Beijing agreed to help establish an international convention to end the production of fissile materials for nuclear weapons use.

- The PRC agreed to further talks on nonproliferation issues such as missiles, MTCR guidelines, nuclear cooperation, and export controls—although China temporarily suspended these talks after Lee Teng-hui's visit to the United States in June 1995.
- China agreed to unconditional extension of the nuclear nonproliferation treaty and pledged to join the comprehensive test ban treaty in 1996—although the PRC had begun testing after its pledge.
- China continued to be a "quiet, but cooperative partner" in the North Korean nuclear issue and to help in the transition to a democratically elected government in Cambodia.
- China accepted an intellectual property rights agreement in March 1995.
- China approved billions of dollars in business deals during the visits of Secretaries Brown and O'Leary.
- China began military transparency talks with the United States.
- Beijing cooperated with the United States to stop alien smuggling activities.
- China continued its economic reform program, with some progress in legal reform and rule of law.

Because of these accomplishments, and despite the halt in some initiatives in the aftermath of President Lee's visit, the Clinton administration intended to continue its long-term strategy of engagement with China. There were, however, several problems area in Sino-American relations, including "very serious concerns about human rights abuses in China" and "myriad visible and invisible barriers to [U.S.] efforts to do more business in China."

Wiedemann then discussed the Taiwan issue in some detail.

> In recent months, Taiwan has again emerged as a principle bilateral issue between the United States and China. Since 1979, we have consistently declined to play an active role in shaping the future between Beijing and Taipei. We insist only that any resolution to the situation be achieved through peaceful means. Our actions regarding Taiwan have all been designed to serve that end. The result has been a burgeoning of economic, cultural and social ties between Taiwan and the mainland, with benefits accruing to both sides. In our view, this process is the best hope for a peaceful resolution of the differences between the two sides, and we must carefully avoid any action on our part that damages or disrupts it.
>
> Taiwan is of course changing. The people on Taiwan, with the energy characteristic of the citizens of a new democracy, are seeking greater recognition and respect from the international community—and the government in Beijing—for their economic and political achievements, and are increasingly unwilling to accept the status quo. This Administration believes that Taiwan's achievements should be acknowledged. That was one of the goals of our policy adjustments last September. We realize that many people both here and on Taiwan were dissatisfied with the results of that exercise, but our aim was to facilitate and to rationalize a number of the elements of our unofficial relationship with Taiwan while preserving the peace and stability which has proven so beneficial to all parties concerned.

It was not and is not, however, the objective of this Administration to preclude the eventual political reunification of Taiwan with the mainland—we do not seek, in the words of the Chinese, to create "two Chinas" or "one China, one Taiwan." We continue to adhere to the framework under which we normalized relations with the PRC: The United States of America recognizes the Government of the People's Republic of China as the sole legal government of China and acknowledges the Chinese position that there is but one China and Taiwan is part of China. Abandonment of this fundamental element of our policy would not only endanger our relationship with China but also threaten the security and stability of the whole East Asian region. The Administration's decision to admit Lee Teng-hui for an expressly private purpose does not change our basic policy.

Wiedemann's statement highlighted crucial differences in perceptions between the United States and China over the Taiwan issue. In being supportive of Taiwan, the United States did not intend to divide China. However, many PRC elite saw—or claimed to see—U.S. support for Taiwan as evidence of a possible plot to prevent the reunification of China. Because of this Chinese perception—which apparently gained influence in Beijing after Clinton approved Lee's visa—the PRC decided to "rattle the cage" of Sino-American relations to warn Washington not to proceed any further in improving ties with Taiwan. The Clinton administration saw this as "overreacting," but it was viewed by the Chinese as being necessary to establish a clear marker on the limits of their toleration.

The Clinton administration wanted to stabilize Sino-American relations as soon as possible after Lee's visit, but the pot kept simmering. Proliferation problems with the Chinese continued to be a major headache. It was reported in early July 1995 that U.S. intelligence sources believed storage crates at Pakistan's Sargodha Air Force Base contained more than thirty M-11 missiles. These same sources thought that the missiles had been in Pakistan since November 1992. China dismissed the allegations as "groundless," but the reports persisted. The administration hesitated to impose legally mandated sanctions since Sino-American relations already were severely strained. Rather than rely on circumstantial evidence, the administration asked for an incontrovertible "smoking gun," such as an admission by China or Pakistan that the crates actually contained missiles or a photograph of a missile inside a crate, before formally accusing China of violating its Missile Technology Control Regime pledge. In mid-July it was reported that the U.S. Arms Control and Disarmament Agency had determined that China had conducted illegal biological or toxin weapons work in the late 1980s and that it was highly probable the PRC was continuing its biological warfare program in violation of the 1972 Biological and Toxin Weapons Convention.[54]

In July the administration decided to normalize relations with Vietnam. U.S. officials insisted this was not designed to counterbalance China; however, some influential foreign policy specialists, including Senator John McCain of Arizona, explicitly argued that Vietnam was an important counterweight to the PRC in Southeast Asia.[55] Some Chinese strategists pointed to the U.S. decision to improve relations with China's traditional rival in Southeast Asia as yet another example of the American strategy of containing China. By mid-July, official PRC spokesmen began to promote this view more widely, adding Vietnam to such evidence as the United States selling Taiwan F-16 fighters in 1992; allowing Lee Teng-hui to visit the United States; undermining Beijing's bid to host the 2000 Summer Olympics; discouraging Chinese arms sales to Iran, Pakistan, and Burma; opposing China's entrance into the World Trade Organization; criticizing China's nuclear testing program; opening a U.S.-India security dialogue; warning China not to interfere with freedom of navigation in the South China Sea; expressing concern over Chinese policies toward Hong Kong; and pressuring China over human rights and trade issues.[56]

When House Speaker Newt Gingrich said in mid-July 1995 on the CBS program "Face the Nation" that the United States should recognize Taiwan as a free nation, he was immediately denounced by the Chinese for his remarks.[57] While perhaps undiplomatic, Gingrich's comments accurately reflected a growing sense of congressional dissatisfaction with Clinton's China policy, which successfully maintained a dialogue with the PRC but did little to moderate Chinese behavior. On July 20, the House of Representatives passed the China Policy Act by a vote of 416-10. Among other provisions, the act demanded that China end its human rights abuses, harassment of journalists, and discriminatory and unfair trading practices. It called for the immediate release of Harry Wu, urged China to abide by nuclear weapons and missile control treaties, and called on Beijing to moderate policies toward Tibet and to reduce tensions with Taiwan and over the Spratly Islands.[58] The PRC Foreign Ministry angrily demanded: "China wants the U.S. government to adopt concrete measures to prevent the act from being passed by the Congress so as to avoid further damages to the bilateral relations."[59]

As the above remark suggests, China was not very adept at working with Congress. One of the results of the Lee Teng-hui visit was an effort by the PRC leadership to acquire greater understanding of the role of Congress in U.S. foreign policy. Taiwan had long learned this lesson, with Madame Chiang Kai-shek an effective early advocate with the Congress for greater support to the Nationalist cause on the mainland. Over the years, the ROC developed one of the most proficient foreign government lobbying machines in Washington, second perhaps only to that of Israel. The PRC, on the other hand, learned to be very effective in dealing the executive branch.

While criticizing the United States for its Taiwan policy and U.S. efforts to "contain" China, Beijing also said it was willing to return Sino-American relations to normal if the Clinton administration would take "concrete actions" to repair the damage caused by the visit of Lee Teng-hui. These actions were said to include a personal commitment from President Clinton reaffirming that Beijing was China's sole legal government and that Taiwan was part of China, as well as a promise not to allow Lee Teng-hui back into the United States. In reply, the administration said its China policy had not and would not change; however, Secretary of State

Christopher went on to say: "I would not expect that there will be frequent visits of the kind President Lee made, but I can't rule out that there might be some similar situation, where it was a totally unofficial and private visit by some official of the Taiwanese government. But let me emphasize that it would be a rare occasion."[60]

Chinese Missile Exercises

In July 1995, China dramatically increased its pressure on Taiwan with a series of military maneuvers, including missile tests, near Taiwan. The exercises were intended to signal China's displeasure over Taiwan's efforts to expand its international role. Military exercises held early that month some 240 miles north of the Taiwan Strait caused the Taiwan stock market to drop about 2.5 percent. On July 18, the PLA announced it would test surface-to-surface missiles during a week-long exercise between July 21 and 28 in the East China Sea just north of Taiwan's port of Keelung. Taiwan's stock market immediately dived another 4.2 percent.

During the latter missile exercise, China fired four M-9 tactical missiles at targets near Taiwan, the closest landing some 87 miles north of the island. At the same time, Beijing's personal criticism of Lee Teng-hui mounted, with the *People's Daily* calling Lee's father a "100-percent traitor" and Lee himself "a schemer, pure politician and double dealer." Rather than undermining Lee's popularity on Taiwan, however, the missile exercises and personal attacks increased Lee's appeal among most Taiwanese.[61]

Deliberately adopting a low-key response at this point, the United States only mildly criticized the missile tests in public, saying, "we don't believe this test contributes to peace and stability in the area."[62] Jude Kearney, Deputy Assistant Secretary of Commerce for Service Industries and Finance, was in China during this period. She studiously avoided bringing up political issues such as Lee Teng-hui's visit and Harry Wu's arrest, explaining: "we have been very resolute in distinguishing between our diplomatic issues and our commercial ones as regards China."[63]

The Clinton administration was trying very hard to move beyond the Taiwan issue to other aspects of Sino-American relations.[64] These efforts were not always reciprocated by Beijing, however, for reasons that were interpreted by various American China specialists as a sign of weakness on the part of moderates in the PRC leadership, a reflection of a general hardening of PRC policies toward the United States, or simply good bargaining tactics proven in earlier confrontations with the United States over Taiwan.[65]

Regardless of the interpretation, it was also clear the Chinese did not want to sever ties completely with the United States or to damage irreparably Sino-American relations. On July 20, one day before missile splashdown near Taiwan, China announced it was sending a 250-member trade delegation to the United

States to encourage infrastructure and construction investment in the PRC. To break out of the diplomatic impasse, both sides attached great importance to the meeting scheduled on August 1 between Foreign Minister Qian Qichen and Secretary Christopher during the ASEAN Regional Forum in Brunei.

The Qian-Christopher meeting produced no major agreements, but it did mark the beginning of improved U.S.-PRC relations by reestablishing high-level dialogue between China and the United States. Christopher gave Qian a letter from President Clinton to President Jiang reaffirming the U.S. one-China policy, appealing for the release of Harry Wu, and expressing the belief that it was time to relax tensions and move forward in the bilateral relationship. The two statesman agreed to meet again in New York in September during the U.N. General Assembly session, and Christopher hinted that Clinton might meet with Jiang at the same time if Harry Wu was released by then. It was also agreed that other talks between the two countries postponed after Lee's visit could be resumed, including the visit to China of Undersecretary of State Peter Tarnoff. Reaffirming existing policy, but in a more direct statement, the administration promised China it would not support Taiwan's independence or entry into the United Nations—precedent for Clinton's 1998 Shanghai statement on the "three no's."[66]

While Christopher was meeting Qian in Brunei, it was reported that the White House was editing intelligence reports about China's shipments of M-11 missiles and components to Pakistan to avoid having to impose legally mandated sanctions against the PRC. The annual report of the Arms Control and Disarmament Agency (ACDA) was found to contain "before" and "after" editions which substantially changed intelligence assessments. According to the *Washington Post*, virtually the entire U.S. intelligence community had concurred that M-11 missiles were sitting in crates at a Pakistani air force base. If true, this could trigger substantial economic sanctions against China. The "before" version of the ACDA report stated, "we remain concerned about possible past transfer of M-11 missiles to Pakistan, and are urgently seeking clarification and resolution of this matter." The White House National Security Council edited the statement to read: "we remain concerned about possible past M-11-related transfers to Pakistan." The White House version said Washington was "continuing to monitor the situation closely." The editing was important, because under U.S. law there was a substantial difference between "missiles" and "missile-related" items. The transfer of ballistic missiles required automatic sanctions; the transfer of missile-related items gave the administration greater flexibility in its response.[67]

The continuous efforts by the Clinton administration to put a favorable "spin" on China-related developments greatly irritated Congress, which increasingly felt compelled to play a more assertive role in U.S. China policy. As part of its challenge to the administration, the House International Relations Committee met in August 1995 to consider a resolution promoting Taiwan's membership in the United Nations. These hearings were in addition to several others held to consider Chinese human rights violations.

At about the same time as the hearings, *Time* magazine editorialized that the United States should pursue a strategy of containing China and undermining the Chinese communist government. *People's Daily* ridiculed the editorial, but some in the Chinese government were said to believe that the magazine reflected the thinking of at least some top American policy makers.[68]

On August 16 the administration publicly criticized China for conducting missile tests some 84 miles north of Taiwan, the second such round of tests following Lee Teng-hui's visit to the United States. The two Dong Feng-21 intermediate range ballistic missiles were launched from a base in northern China. The DF-21, also known as the CSS-5, has a range of 1,800 kilometers and can carry a nuclear warhead yield of 250 kilotons. The following day, the PRC exploded an underground nuclear weapon at Lop Nor with a yield of between 20 and 80 kilotons. As in the previous test of May 15, the United States expressed deep regret and urged China to join the comprehensive test ban treaty.[69]

The PRC tried Harry Wu in late August, found him guilty of spying, sentenced him to fifteen years in prison, and then immediately expelled him from China. The relatively lenient treatment accorded Wu was seen as a gesture to remove obstacles to Clinton's possible meeting with Jiang at the 50th anniversary of the United Nations in late October and to provide the administration with political cover for the First Lady's possible participation in the United Nations Fourth World Conference on Women in Beijing in early September. The White House welcomed the news about Wu on August 24 and a few days later announced that Hillary Rodham Clinton would indeed attend the international women's conference. Undersecretary of State Peter Tarnoff, in Beijing at the time of Wu's release, said that chances were now good for a Clinton-Jiang meeting in October. He also said that while differences over Taiwan had not been resolved, both sides wanted to move forward in their overall relationship. Meanwhile, China announced that Ambassador Li Daoyu would be returning shortly to Washington. It was further announced that Gen. Li Xilin, commander of the Guangzhou military district, would attend ceremonies in Honolulu marking the 50th anniversary of the end of the Second World War. American officials confided to reporters that the relationship was "back on track," but that "we continue to have serious questions about [China's] nuclear testing, about some of their policies vis-à-vis transfer of missile technology, and some of their threatening behavior toward Taiwan."[70]

On September 5, Mrs. Clinton delivered a forceful speech in Beijing on the linkage between treatment of women and human rights.[71] Although she did not mention China by name, much of her statement was interpreted to be indirect reference to the PRC's poor record on human rights, including intrusive birth control practices such as forced abortions. The First Lady said:

> Our goals for this conference, to strengthen families and societies by empowering women to take greater control over their own destinies, cannot be fully achieved

unless all governments—here and around the world—accept their responsibility to protect and promote internationally recognized human rights.

The international community has long acknowledged—and recently affirmed at Vienna—that both women and men are entitled to a range of protection and personal freedoms, from the right of personal property to the right to determine freely the number and spacing of the children they bear.

No one should be forced to remain silent for fear of religious or political persecution, arrest, abuse or torture.... It is a violation of human rights when women are denied the right to plan their own families, and that includes being forced to have abortions or being sterilized against their will....

Let me be clear. Freedom means the right of people to assemble, organize, and debate openly. It means respecting the views of those who may disagree with the views of their governments. It means not taking citizens away from their loved ones and jailing them, mistreating them, or denying them their freedom or dignity because of the peaceful expression of their ideas and opinions.

On September 11 Vice President Al Gore met with the Dalai Lama in the White House. The president dropped by for a brief "chat," as he had done previously in 1993 and 1994. Although the United States considered Tibet an autonomous region within China, Congress had passed several resolutions recognizing the Dalai Lama as Tibet's leader. Beijing protested the Dalai Lama's meeting with the president as "gross interference in China's internal affairs." Rejecting the protest, the State Department said the meeting "was the courteous thing to do and it's been done in past years."[72]

Taking advantage of trends toward improved relations, China began to press the Clinton administration for a fourth Sino-American joint communiqué. Beijing wanted the new statement to be issued in the forthcoming Clinton-Jiang meeting in October. As a new agreement to join previous communiqués to form the basis of U.S.-PRC relations, Beijing envisioned a fourth communiqué in which the United States would reaffirm formally that Taiwan was part of China and perhaps pledge never again to invite Lee or other senior ROC officials to the United States. Beijing hinted such "concrete action" would help resolve tensions in Sino-American relations. The State Department opposed a new communiqué, however, unless the joint declaration also noted specific progress to be made in areas such as China's missile sales to Pakistan, nuclear sales to Iran, and human rights issues.[73]

Disagreement over the details of the proposed Clinton-Jiang meeting arose during the Christopher-Qian talks in New York in late September. The two sides could not agree on whether the meeting between the heads of state would occur in New York in a low-key visit (which the United States preferred) or in Washington with a high-profile state visit (which China wanted). After their meeting, Christopher announced that Qian had stated China would not proceed with its nuclear reactor sale to Iran. Qian corrected him and said the sale was suspended, not canceled.[74]

In early October the administration announced that Jiang Zemin would not be invited to Washington for a state visit on this occasion, because "a state visit is reserved for allies, for countries with which we have excellent relations. . . . [It] would have been inconsistent with relations [with China] that have been in the deep freeze." Instead, the two presidents would meet in New York on October 24 during the 50th anniversary of the U.N. General Assembly. The Chinese were clearly angered by the decision, Foreign Minister Qian Qichen retorting: "President Jiang has made overseas trips to over ten countries, big and small, including Germany, France, Russia, Japan, and some others. Every visit of his was a state visit."[75]

A few days later, Secretary Christopher confirmed that the remaining U.S. sanctions imposed on China in the aftermath of Tiananmen would remain in force. These included bans on weapons sales, denial for licenses to export dual-use civilian technology, and opposition to international lending to China except for humanitarian projects.[76] Clearly the relationship, although improving to the degree that talks were being held once again, was far from friendly: engagement without much cooperation.

On October 11, Assistant Secretary of State Winston Lord appeared before the Senate Foreign Relations Committee to discuss the status and rationale of U.S. policy toward China, particularly its security and military dimensions.[77] According to Lord, China's neighbors had several security concerns in regards to the PRC:

- China's military budget and strategic plans were largely opaque to the rest of the world, developed behind a cloak of secrecy.
- China, under the control of civilian leadership, had embarked on a modernization program in recent years aimed at developing a more professional army and at upgrading in particular its aerial and naval capabilities.
- China had sold technologies related to weapons of mass destruction, as well as missile delivery system technology, in sensitive regional hot spots.
- China had supported nuclear programs of concern in Pakistan and Iran.
- China's extensive claims in the South China Sea had been backed up by construction of a military installation on Mischief Reef, less than 150 miles from the main Philippine islands.
- Despite its general support for a Comprehensive Test Ban Treaty (CTBT), China continued nuclear testing and had been slow in negotiating a CTBT.
- China's two recent military exercises, including missile firings, in the vicinity of Taiwan had contributed to the region's sense of unease and instability.

While acknowledging that these and other activities were troubling, Lord argued that they did not in themselves mean that China was an enemy or a threat to the United States. Indeed, China's priorities remained, first and foremost, "economic development, its transformation from a poor developing into a wealthy country." China's foreign policy since the late 1970s had been "a function of this domestic priority." Lord said, "Put simply, China's development requires a peaceful international environment, and this has been China's goal in the last decade and a half." Toward this end, China ended its support of revolutionary movements in Asia; negotiated border agreements with Russia, Kazakhstan, and India; established diplomatic relations with South Korea; improved relations with Vietnam; supported a peace settlement in Cambodia; and established extensive trade and investment ties with Taiwan. In essence, China had opened up to the outside world, a process requiring that China abide by international regimes in trade, financial organizations, and multilateral security organizations.

According to Lord, recent improvements in China's international behavior included Beijing's support of the indefinite extension of the NPT; its restrictions on sale of missiles and agreement to the MTCR regime; its signing the Chemical Weapons Convention; its statements indicating a willingness to conclude a Comprehensive Test Ban Treaty in 1996; China's acceptance of the applicability of international law and the Law of the Sea Convention for disputes involving the Spratly Islands; and Beijing's help in defusing tensions over the North Korean nuclear program.

Since there were both troubling and encouraging aspects of China's security behavior, the Clinton administration would continue its policy of comprehensive engagement. Lord explained that engagement "assumes neither Chinese aggressiveness nor Chinese benevolence. It means neither acquiescence in what we see as inappropriate actions by China, nor attempts to isolate the PRC or frustrate its development. Containment would be a self-fulfilling prophecy of mutual enmity. And it would not be supported by our Asian partners. We seek to act in concert where we agree, foster greater consensus where the picture is mixed, and prevent or minimize conflict where we disagree."

From the long-term strategic point of view, Lord said, "the question is not whether China will be a major player in global as well as regional security affairs, but rather when and how. China's rapid economic development, its growing military capabilities, and its historic international role will make it a major power in the coming century." The challenge the United States faced was how to ensure, as China develops into a major global power, that "it does so constructively, as a country integrated into international institutions and committed to practices enshrined in international law."

On October 12 former Senator James Sasser testified before the Senate Foreign Relations Committee in his confirmation hearings as U.S. Ambassador to China. Sasser had a word of warning for Taiwan, noting that Taipei was "doing very well ... with the status quo" and that authorities in Taiwan would be "ill-advised" to press for international recognition as an independent political entity. Sasser's statement was one of several to be heard in subsequent months to the effect that the United States did not want Taiwan to press too hard for additional international political recognition. This was commonly referred to as "rocking the boat" in Washington salons, the idea being that Taiwan had done very well under the "one-

China" principle and that challenging that principle not only brought trouble to U.S.-PRC relations but also might have negative consequences for Taiwan as well. There was growing sentiment expressed in closed-door sessions in Washington that the United States might not support Taipei if it deliberately antagonized Beijing through policies aimed at independence. Interestingly, although the State Department quickly distanced itself from remarks made by Sasser to the effect that the PRC was within its rights to disband Hong Kong's Legislative Council after 1997, no such clarification was heard over his warnings to Taiwan.[78]

A few days prior to his October 24 meeting with President Clinton in New York, President Jiang Zemin told editors from *U.S. News and World Report* and *Newsweek* that the Taiwan issue was non-negotiable on two key points: "Having two Chinas, or one China and one Taiwan, is unacceptable. All other issues can be discussed." Jiang reiterated Deng Xiaoping's "one country, two systems" formula for Taiwan: Taiwan could maintain its own economy, government, military, legislature, judiciary, and social system and preserve its way of life without interference from the mainland. "But on one thing we are certain: If separatism emerges on Taiwan . . . then we might use nonpeaceful means to achieve reunification." He told the editors that Secretary Christopher had assured China that Lee Teng-hui's visit would not take place. "Secretary of State Christopher firmly replied that if Lee Teng-hui's visit took place, it would represent a violation of the three Sino-U.S. joint communiqués. However, after seven or eight days, all of a sudden, the White House announced the decision allowing Lee Teng-hui to make the visit, and [U.S. officials] said it was consistent with the principles enshrined in the three Sino-U.S. joint communiqués." Jiang said China would no longer be "bullied and humiliated by various powers. . . . We are resolutely opposed to the independence of Taiwan because this would undermine our sovereignty and territorial integrity and alter the grand course of the reunification of the motherland."[79]

Just prior to his meeting with Clinton, Jiang criticized the United States before the U.N. General Assembly, saying that "certain big powers" were meddling in the affairs of other nations "under the cover of 'freedom,' 'democracy' and 'human rights.'"[80] Jiang's sharp remarks were commonly interpreted by American China watchers as indicating that Clinton's sudden change of policy on Lee's visit had severely undermined Jiang's leadership and the position of Foreign Minister Qian at a time when internal politics in Beijing were heated and uncertain.[81]

On October 24, President Clinton met President Jiang in New York in an effort by both sides to improve U.S.-China relations. U.S. officials described the meeting as covering a wide range of bilateral, regional, and global issues. No specific agreements were reached, but Clinton promised Jiang that, while the United States could not rule out visits such as Lee Teng-hui's in the future, they would be considered on a case-by-case basis and would be "unofficial and private and rare." The president felt the meeting had been "very useful and very productive" in the sense that it "had structured a mechanism to deal with our differences, but placed that mechanism in the context of a much more comprehensive engagement across a much wider bilateral agenda in which the interests of both countries can be advanced."[82]

The meeting between Jiang and Clinton—and earlier meetings between Qian and Christopher—helped to move the two countries back into normal bilateral talks on strategic issues, proliferation, international crime, narcotics, the environment, sustainable development, energy, economic issues, opening China's markets, the World Trade Organization, intellectual property rights, human rights, and military exchanges. Washington and Beijing were unable to agree over Taiwan or to resolve any of the other outstanding issues in Sino-American relations. However, the two governments wanted to preserve their relationship because of its strategic importance. They were determined not to allow the visit of Lee Teng-hui or any other issue—including controversies within their own countries over U.S.-PRC ties—to undermine continued dialogue.

And, indeed, cooperation between the United States and China did improve during the last few months of 1995. In early November, Deputy U.S. Trade Representative Charlene Barshefsky visited Beijing to discuss China's entrance into the World Trade Organization. She gave her counterparts an eight-page "road map" detailing how China could gain WTO membership. Barshefsky said twenty-five to thirty obstacles remained, including the reopening of factories producing counterfeit CDs and CD-ROMs previously closed.[83] She also warned China that its trade with the United States was too imbalanced, with a trade surplus reaching $35 billion in 1995, a figure hotly denied by China and questioned by some scholars. Frank Ching of the *Far Eastern Economic Review*, for example, noted that about 70 percent of U.S. imports from China were routed through Hong Kong, but that the United States increased the value of those imports by 25 percent. On the other hand, U.S. exports to China routed through Hong Kong were considered exports to Hong Kong, not China. If one recalculated Chinese exports to the United States by subtracting the value-added in Hong Kong and recalculated American exports to China by including products routed through Hong Kong, then in 1994 the PRC trade surplus with the United States would be $19.7 billion, some $10 billion less than the official U.S. figure of $29.5 billion. A similar argument was made by Nicholas Lardy, who said that a more realistic deficit for the United States in its trade with China in 1995 was $23 billion, again, nearly $10 billion less than the official American figure.[84]

President Clinton was scheduled to meet again with President Jiang during the APEC summit meeting in Osaka, Japan, in late November 1995. At the last minute, however, the president canceled his participation due to budget disagreements with the Congress. In his place, Vice President Al Gore met with Jiang in an uneventful but cordial meeting. During the APEC conference, comments on U.S. China policy were heard from Secretary of State Christopher, who met with Chinese Foreign Minister Qian Qichen, and from Assistant Secretary of State Winston Lord, who briefed reporters about the Christopher-Qian meeting.

In their remarks to reporters, Christopher and Qian said their respective presidents had agreed in October in New York that Sino-American relations should be approached from a long-term strategic perspective on the basis of the three U.S.-PRC joint communiqués.[85] In his comments, Ambassador Lord said the Christopher-Qian talks were "resuming momentum in the relationship" that had been lost after the visit to the United States of Lee Teng-hui.[86] Both sides "acknowledged that there is a broad agenda between the two countries," and a series of meetings had been held or were scheduled to discuss protection of the environment; sustainable development; strategic issues; fighting international crime; United Nations activities; nonproliferation; a comprehensive ban on testing nuclear weapons; the peaceful uses of nuclear energy; military, economic, and human rights issues; and Chinese accession to the World Trade Organization.

Lord said the Taiwan issue was raised in the Christopher-Qian meeting, but "this is no longer a predominant issue in our discussions although it remains a very important and sensitive one," especially to the Chinese. Lord commented that Taiwan had been discussed in "almost every meeting with the Chinese" he had attended during his long career in government service. "In every administration, no meeting goes by without a mention of Taiwan. Obviously, the temperature goes up and down. So, I frankly would not be unhappy if we had a meeting without it being mentioned but I certainly would be surprised. The key thing is not whether it's mentioned, but the amount of time it takes and the tone of the discussion." In terms of U.S. policy on future visits from Lee and other top Taiwan officials, Lord said: "the four magic words [are] case by case, private, unofficial and rare."

At the APEC leader's meeting, President Jiang gained considerable attention by announcing China's plans to lower tariffs on 4,000 imported items from 35 percent to 25 percent. Beijing pointed to the trade concessions as evidence that now was the time for the developed nations to welcome China into the World Trade Organization. Washington did indeed welcome the announcement, but said it fell short of what would be required of China to gain entrance into the WTO.[87]

Thus, at the conclusion of 1995, Sino-American dialogue was back on track through considerable effort on the part of both governments. Major disagreements continued over Taiwan, however; and little progress was made in the areas of proliferation, trade, human rights, and other traditional problems in the relationship. But, with PLA forces exercising close to the shores of Taiwan, the situation had not returned to normal, as seen by the increasingly hard statements issued by the Pentagon.

U.S. Military Perspectives

The Department of Defense emerged as an articulate and influential voice in U.S. China policy during 1995. Secretary of Defense William Perry played an especially important role in China-Taiwan policy, arguing forcefully for comprehensive engagement with the PRC, even while gradually toughening his position against PLA exercises seeking to intimidate Taiwan. In late October 1995 Perry announced that a high-level U.S. delegation led by Assistant Secretary of Defense Joseph Nye would visit China in November to begin rebuilding defense contacts broken off by Beijing after Lee Teng-hui's visit in June. Secretary Perry explained the U.S. strategy of comprehensive engagement in a speech to the Washington State China Relations Council in Seattle on October 30.[88]

The secretary noted that a "new geopolitical order is being created in the Asia-Pacific region," and that China would play an "increasingly important role" in the security of the region "as one of the world's most ancient nations emerges as one of the world's most powerful nations." As China becomes a world power, "it is inescapable that China's interests will sometimes harmonize and sometimes conflict with those of the United States. The government of the United States recognizes this fundamental fact. Our response to it is a policy of comprehensive engagement with China. . . . We believe that engagement is the best strategy to ensure that as China increases its power, it does so as a responsible member of the international community. And we believe that is critical if peace, prosperity and stability are to endure in Asia and around the world." Thus, the Secretary of Defense directly linked U.S. engagement with China to America's overarching interests in peace and security in the new world order.

Perry said, "the overarching premise of this strategy is that whatever our differences with China we also have important common interests and that these interests make dialogue more rational than confrontation." Dialogue with China served U.S. interests by establishing cooperation where the two nations agreed and consultation where they disagreed. Moreover, "this dialogue will help us reinforce positive developments in China and encourage China to become a stabilizing influence in the region and in the world." Perry listed four key reasons why security engagement with China served U.S. interests:

1. Security engagement with China will help the United States "influence China's policies in ways that will help curb the spread of weapons of mass destruction."
2. Engagement gives the United States "an opportunity to influence China to play a positive role in regional instability where U.S. interests are very much at stake such as on the Korean Peninsula, the Asian subcontinent and Southeast Asia."
3. U.S. engagement "opens lines of communication with the People's Liberation Army." Since the PLA is a major player in Chinese politics, the Chinese military "wields significant influence on such issues as Taiwan, the South China Sea and proliferation. And if we are to achieve progress on these issues, we must engage PLA leaders directly."
4. By engaging the PLA directly, the United States "can help promote more openness in the Chinese national security apparatus, including its military

institutions." This increased "transparency about Chinese strategic intentions, procurement, budgeting and operating procedures will not only help promote confidence among China's neighbors, it will also lessen the chance of misunderstandings or incidents when our forces operate in the areas where Chinese military forces are also deployed."

Perry argued that if the United States attempted to contain rather than engage China, the PRC would likely be uncooperative with Washington in limiting the spread of weapons of mass destruction, including nuclear and missile technology. China probably would not implement the Nuclear Non-Proliferation Treaty, would not ratify the Comprehensive Test Ban Treaty, and would not support the U.S.-DPRK framework dismantling North Korea's nuclear weapons program. Instead, China would probably intensify its military modernization programs, thereby contributing to regional arms races and increasing the probability of conflict on the Korean Peninsula, in the Taiwan Strait, and over the South China Sea. U.S. allies in Asia would not support the containment of China; and if the United States pursued such a strategy, then its vital alliance structure in the region would be ruptured. Containment of China would probably result in the closing of Chinese markets to American businesses, resulting in billions of dollars of economic loss to the United States and perhaps start a trend of closing markets throughout the region. Also, if the United States should seek to contain China, the PRC would likely oppose U.S. initiatives in the United Nations and be much less cooperative with the United States in the U.N. and other multilateral institutions. Thus, containment should not be substituted for engagement as the U.S. strategy and policy toward China.

Engagement did not equal appeasement, however. Perry said the Clinton administration did not acquiesce to Chinese policies that were wrong or harmed U.S. interests. Rather, the U.S. strategy of engagement meant "that we will not try to isolate China because of them. Instead, engagement recognizes that the best way for changing China's policies that we don't like is firm diplomacy and dialogue. It recognizes that Chinese policies are unlikely to be changed by hostility, rhetoric and confrontation, and it recognizes that even when we strongly disagree with China, we cannot make our entire relationship hostage to a single issue—that we still have security reasons for maintaining lines of communication."

Perry argued that "history and time are on our side. In the long run, change is coming to China." Moreover, "the direction of these changes suggest it is more likely than not that long-term change in China will favor our interest. Seeking to contain and confront China can only slow down the pace of this change." Perry warned China, however: "Just as it takes two to tango, it takes two to engage." The United States "accepts China at its word when it says that it wants to become a responsible world power, but it also requires that China act like one. The United States government has tried very hard to send China the right messages. Now, it is time for China to start sending the right messages."

For example, we do not like it when China conducts nuclear tests, but we take China at its word that it will join the Comprehensive Test Ban Treaty. We look forward to China honoring that pledge.

We have also made it very clear to China that we are sticking to our one-China policy and the principles set forth in the U.S.-China communiqués of 1972, 1979 and 1982. And we have reaffirmed that we have no intention of advocating or supporting a policy of two Chinas or one China, one Taiwan.

Now China has to show that they too want a peaceful resolution to this issue. Conducting missile tests off Taiwan sends the opposite message. China sometimes claims that America is not sensitive to Chinese values, but China has to make a greater effort to be sensitive to widely accepted international values—values such as the freedom of travel and freedom of speech. When China shows gross insensitivity to these two values, it is not acting like a reasonable world power.

Perry said emphatically: "I am also willing to state quite plainly that engagement will not work if China is determined to ignore the security concerns of most members of the international community—and transfer to known terrorist states of the production technologies and the know-how of weapons of mass destruction does ignore those security concerns. . . . This administration is committed to engagement, but not engagement at any price. It is important for audiences on both sides of the Pacific to understand both parts of that sentence. We are committed to engagement, but not at any price."

In the question and answer session following his presentation, Perry said the Chinese navy, even with its modernization program, was not "a threat to the United States now or in the foreseeable future. The United States Navy is not only the most powerful navy in the world, it is more powerful than all the other navies in the world put together. . . . I do not see any nation or combination of nations being able to challenge the United States Navy's dominance of the seas any time in my lifetime." At the same time, the United States understood the modernization of China's military was of concern to its neighbors. If China developed its military "beyond where we're now projecting it," then the United States would be concerned as well. To help defuse this potential problem between China and its neighbors, the United States has "urged for much greater transparency on the part of Chinese in describing their budget, their programs, their deployments."

Following his trip to China in mid-November 1995, Assistant Secretary Joseph Nye briefed reporters on what had been accomplished. He said many differences existed between the two countries, but that he and Gen. Chi Haotian, vice chairman of China's Central Military Commission, had agreed that "engagement is better than containment, dialogue better than confrontation." Chi warned Nye that the Taiwan issue was "more important than anything else" and that the United States should not interfere with China's reunification. Nye said he was able to ease Chinese suspicions that the United States was seeking to contain China. He reported that Chi would visit the United States in 1996 and that General John Shalikashvili, chairman of the U.S. Joint Chiefs of Staff, would also visit China.[89]

A month later, Nye told reporters that during his trip to China, PLA officers had asked him how the United States would react to a military crisis over Taiwan. In a classic statement of ambiguity, but a statement that nonetheless was absolutely true, Nye said he responded: "Nobody knows." Citing the U.S. decision to go to war in Korea in 1950, he told the Chinese, "It shows that you cannot know the answer to these things." Nye warned, however, that the dangers of escalation in the Taiwan Strait "could be catastrophic."[90]

The U.S. military under President Clinton believed dialogue with the PLA and frequent high-level military-to-military exchanges were vital to prevent the United States and China from drifting into an adversarial relationship in the future. Such interaction, aimed at greater mutual understanding and transparency, was seen as urgent as both sides interacted with greater frequency in the Asian Pacific. At the same time, the Pentagon made it clear that U.S. interests in peace and stability in the Western Pacific remained unchanged. On December 19-20, 1995, the U.S. aircraft carrier *Nimitz* and its escort battle group sailed through the Taiwan Strait en route to a port call in Hong Kong, ostensibly because bad weather forced it to sail to the west as opposed to the east of Taiwan. Nearly everyone interpreted the transit as a military signal to Beijing to avoid using force against Taiwan,[91] which had just held a legislative election in which the KMT barely managed to sustain a majority.[92]

Conclusion

By 1995 the Clinton administration conceded that a new geopolitical order was being created due to the emergence of China as one of the world's most powerful nations. The United States was willing to accept that fact, as well as the inevitability that as China became a world power, there would be times when China's interests would parallel those of the United States and times when those interests would conflict. The administration determined that the best way to deal with an emerging China was to engage it in as broad a scope of contacts as possible. Containment was rejected as an alternative approach, but in fact few Americans wanted to contain or isolate China. The idea of engaging China was, of course, not new; it had been the policy of every administration since Richard Nixon. The U.S. objective also had been consistent: to ensure that as China increased its power, it would do so as a responsible member of the international community, cooperative with the United States, and not a spoiler of international security, political, and economic regimes.

During 1995 the Clinton strategy of comprehensive engagement with China was severely tested, as it would be in 1996. To preserve its strategy of engagement, the Clinton administration was very accommodating to the PRC on issues such as MFN and human rights, while generally protective of U.S. interests on issues such as Taiwan, trade, and nonproliferation. The Taiwan issue presented the most important challenge to the U.S. engagement strategy, particularly after President Lee Teng-hui's visit to the United States in June 1995. The private and very circumscribed trip of Lee was not seen by most Americans as threatening vital PRC interests or undermining the fundamental principles of Sino-American relations. Nor did the trip imply or lead to a change in U.S. policy toward Taiwan. And given the outrage expressed by Congress, the media, and general public over the inappropriateness of not inviting Lee, it was probably inevitable that the visit would be approved by President Clinton. In fact, as it had done in the past, Congress was intent on mandating changes in U.S. policy toward Taiwan through legislation unless the administration accommodated congressional on Lee's trip.

The administration recognized that Lee's visit would precipitate a temporary downturn in U.S. relations with China, but it was surprised by the fury of the PRC reaction. In trying to understand the Chinese reaction, American analysts concluded that it was due in large measure to the difficulties President Jiang Zemin was experiencing in assuming the leadership mantle from ailing senior leader Deng Xiaoping. President Jiang, Premier Li Peng, and other potential candidates for China's supreme leadership did not have unassailable positions of power like Deng, and thus they lacked the political authority to compromise too much with the United States on sensitive issues, particularly Taiwan. Heir apparent Jiang Zemin, for example, was known to actively seek political support from military and security forces, who often urged him to be more tough with Washington and Taipei. The Chinese sense of outrage at the visa being given to Lee, after China had been promised otherwise by American leaders, increased the influence of hardliners in Chinese policymaking for a while, at the expense of moderates and particularly in regards to relations with Taiwan and the United States.

Just as Jiang found his flexibility toward Taiwan and the United States limited by domestic political considerations, so President Clinton also was forced by domestic pressure in 1995 to assume a tougher line toward Beijing. This was because of at least two factors: first, the problems with China had not been resolved by comprehensive engagement and the policy of delinking human rights and MFN; second, members of the Republican-controlled Congress were looking for foreign policy issues on which to oppose Clinton, and China policy was highly vulnerable to criticism.

But there were more than domestic politics involved in U.S. and Chinese policies. An increasing number of analysts on both sides of the Pacific were troubled by the prospects of Sino-American cooperation at a time when confrontation between the two countries loomed ever more probable—not because of mutual hatred but because of seemingly immutable laws of international politics when the interests of two great powers collide, as that of China and the United States did in the Western Pacific. This presented a policy conundrum to both Washington and Beijing, and it led to the perhaps inevitable conclusion that while dialogue was better than confrontation, preparation for confrontation was necessary. Strategists on both sides could rationalize increased contact, but few could accept encroachment on important national interests by the other side, tending to view these as evidence of expanding Chinese hegemony, on the one hand, and a secret American strategy of containment, on the other. The conundrum on all sides was how to maintain engagement without compromising fundamental interests and values. As Perry said: engagement did not mean appeasement, nor would engagement be retained at any cost—a point of view no doubt echoed by his Chinese counterparts. The U.S. and PRC policy dilemma over Taiwan was that the issue straddled the line between what was tolerable and what was intolerable for both sides.

Nonetheless, as demonstrated in several policy areas in late 1995, the Clinton and Jiang governments would not allow a crisis over Taiwan to derail Sino-American relations. This determination to maintain dialogue and cooperation in some areas of mutual benefit played a key role in enabling the two sides to weather the pressures of the March 1996 crisis in the Taiwan Strait described in the next chapter. However, as indicated at the outset of the book and discussed more thoroughly in the concluding chapter, Clinton's determination to preserve Sino-American engagement tended to work to Taiwan's short-term disadvantage, since American policy specialists increasingly posed the question: should the United States make additional concessions over Taiwan to avoid a future U.S.-China conflict in the Taiwan Strait?

Notes

1. For the text of Jiang's speech, entitled "Continue to Promote the Reunification of the Motherland," see *Xinhua*, January 30, 1995, in *FBIS-China*, January 30, 1995.
2. The text of Lee's speech can be found in *Lien Ho Pao*, April 9, 1995, in *FBIS-China*, April 9, 1995.
3. See comments of MAC Chairman Chang King-yuh at January 26, 1998, news conference, in *MAC News Briefing*, February 2, 1998, p. 5.
4. *Washington Post*, January 5, 1995, p. A30; January 17, 1995, p. A16; January 20, 1995, p. B1; January 21, 1995, p. A10; *Wall Street Journal*, January 30, 1995, p. A14.
5. Quoted in *New York Times*, February 8, 1995, p. D1.
6. *Wall Street Journal*, February 9, 1995, p. A2.
7. *Washington Post*, February 24, 1995, p. A17.
8. See *Wall Street Journal*, March 13, 1995, pp. A3, D1; *Washington Post*, March 13, 1995, p. A9; Reuters report from Beijing, March 13, 1995.
9. Beyond the time frame of this book but proving the point is Premier Zhu Rongji's visit to the United States in April 1999. See "Joint Press Conference of the President and Premier Zhu Rongji of the People's Republic of China" (Washington, DC: The White House, Office of the Press Secretary, April 8, 1999).
10. *Wall Street Journal*, January 16, 1995, p. A10.
11. *Wall Street Journal*, May 5, 1995, p. A5A; *New York Times*, May 5, 1995, p. A10.
12. *Wall Street Journal*, May 20, 1995, p. A3; *Washington Post*, May 27, 1995, p. F1.
13. *Wall Street Journal*, June 5, 1995, p. A10; Reuters report from Beijing, June 4, 1995.
14. Reuters report from New Delhi, India, January 13, 1995.

15. UPI report from Washington, D.C., April 19, 1995.
16. See *Far Eastern Economic Review*, June 3, 1999, p. 27; ibid., June 10, 1999, pp. 28-30.
17. *Washington Post*, April 17, 1995, p. A1; April 18, 1995, p. A13; May 18, 1995, p. A22; Associated Press report from New York, April 18, 1995; Associated Press report from Washington, D.C., April 19, 1995.
18. See Daniel Williams, "China Finds 'Comprehensive Engagement' Hard to Grasp," *Washington Post*, February 13, 1995, p. A17.
19. See "Statement of Admiral Richard C. Macke, U.S. Navy, Commander in Chief, United States Pacific Command," before the Senate Armed Services Committee, February 16, 1995, ms.
20. "Testimony by Kent Wiedemann, Deputy Assistant Secretary of State for East Asian and Pacific Affairs before House Ways and Means Subcommittee on Trade, May 23, 1995," ms.
21. For a discussion of the crisis and its significance, see John W. Garver, *Face off: China, the United States, and Taiwan's Democratization* (Seattle: University of Washington Press, 1997).
22. Associated Press report from Ithaca, NY, June 9, 1995.
23. Quoted by Jason Hu, ROC government spokesman, in Reuters report from Ithaca, NY, June 9, 1995. For Lee's hope (à la 1999) for the future relationship between Taiwan and mainland China—his proposed abandonment of the idea of a central controlled "Great China" and the division of China into seven largely autonomous regions—see Lee Teng-hui, *Taiwan's Viewpoint* (Taipei: Liou Publishing Company, 1999). At the time of writing in mid-June 1999, the book was only available in Chinese. Needless to say, the proposal was quickly condemned by Beijing. See review of the Lee book by Antonio Chiang, "No Place Like Home?" *Far Eastern Economic Review*, June 17, 1999, p. 49.
24. Figures from ROC Ministry of Finance as reported in *Free China Journal*, January 12, 1996, p. 8.
25. See Jen Hui-wen, "Beijing Warns Li [Lee] Teng-hui Through Missile Training," *Hong Kong Hsin Pao*, July 19, 1995, in *FBIS-China*, July 21, 1995.
26. "Infuriated by Li Teng-hui's Visit, CPC Hardliners Call for Re-explanation of Jiang's Eight-Point Proposal to Curb Taiwan Independence Forces," *Lien Ho Pao*, May 26, 1995, in *FBIS-China*, May 26, 1995. A similar article appeared a few weeks later. See "Irritated by Le Teng-hui's Words and Deeds and Provoked by Taiwan's Military Exercises, Hardliners in China's Taiwan Affairs Departments Get the Upper Hand," *Lien Ho Pao*, June 11, 1995, in *FBIS-China*, June 11, 1995.
27. *Xinhua*, May 24, 1995, in *FBIS-China*, May 24, 1995.
28. Ibid.
29. From PRC Foreign Ministry weekly news conference of May 25, 1995, cited in Hong Kong AFP, in *FBIS-China*, May 25, 1995.
30. "China Is Correspondingly Readjusting Its Cooperation with the United States—Interviewing Zhang Yebai, Research Fellow of the CASS American Studies Institute," *Wen Wei Po*, June 1, 1995, in *FBIS-China*, June 1, 1995.
31. "Serious and Dangerous Retrogression," *Renmin Ribao*, May 26, 1995, in *FBIS-China*, May 26, 1995.
32. Huang Huiping commentary, "What Role Is Li Denghui Playing," Beijing Central People's Radio, June 8, 1995, in *FBIS-China*, June 12, 1995.

33. "Commentary: Where Does the United States Really Want to Lead Sino-U.S. Relations," *Xinhua*, June 17, 1995, in *FBIS-China*, June 17, 1995.
34. Bu Wen, "The United States Is Playing with Fire," *Renmin Ribao*, June 10, 1995, in *FBIS-China*, June 10, 1995.
35. Duanmu Laidi, "Commentary: It Is Unpopular to Embrace Foreigners to Earn Himself Dignity and to Split the Motherland," *Xinhua*, June 13, 1995, in *FBIS-China*, June 14, 1995.
36. Yan Jing, "Evidence of Violations of 'One-China' Principles by Taiwan Authorities," *Liaowang*, June 19, 1995, in *FBIS-China*, June 19, 1995.
37. *Zhongguo Xinwen She*, June 29, 1995, in *FBIS-China*, June 29, 1995.
38. For an extension of this argument, based on interviews with authoritative communist party leaders, see Jen Hui-wen, "Gradual Escalation of China's Strategy against United States, Taiwan," *Hong Kong Hsin Pao*, June 28, 1995, in *FBIS-China*, June 30, 1995.
39. See Wang Yu-yen, "Beijing Top Level Focuses Attention on Sino-U.S. Ties," *Lien Ho Pao*, July 2, 1995, in *FBIS-China*, July 2, 1995. See also Wang Mei-hui, "Koo-Wang Meeting Cannot Possibly Be Held This Year Unless China and the United States Resume Political Dialogue," *Lien Ho Pao*, July 10, 1995, in *FBIS-China*, July 10, 1995.
40. "Communist China to Comprehensively Review Policy toward Taiwan, Military Has No Plan for the Time Being to Conduct Large-Scale Military Exercises," *Lien Ho Pao*, July 4, 1995, in *FBIS-China*, July 4, 1995.
41. *South China Morning Post*, July 7, 1995, in *FBIS-China*, July 7, 1995.
42. Reuters report from Beijing, July 1, 1995.
43. Jen Hui-wen, "Beijing Warns Li Teng-hui Through Missile Training," *Hong Kong Hsin Pao*, July 19, 1995, in *FBIS-China*, July 21, 1995.
44. UPI report from Beijing, July 3, 1995; Reuters report from Beijing, July 3, 1995.
45. Quoted in Reuters report from Taipei, July 2, 1995.
46. UPI report from Beijing, June 20, 1995; Reuters report from New York, June 21, 1995; UPI report from Washington, D.C., June 22, 1995; Associated Press report from Beijing, June 22, 1995.
47. *Washington Post*, May 29, 1998, p. A36.
48. For expressions of concern over this growing sense of Chinese distrust, see *Washington Post*, June 21, 1995, p. A17; *Wall Street Journal*, June 23, 1995, p. A1; Associated Press report from Beijing, June 23, 1995.
49. See *Washington Post*, June 27, 1995, p. A14.
50. "Statement by the Press Secretary" (Washington, DC: The White House, Office of the Press Secretary, June 2, 1995).
51. "Statement of Ambassador Winston Lord, Assistant Secretary of State, Bureau of East Asian and Pacific Affairs, June 27, 1995, Before the House International Relations Committee, Asia and Pacific Affairs Subcommittee, U.S. Security Policy Toward East Asia and the Pacific," ms; "Statement by Dr. Joseph S. Nye, Jr., Assistant Secretary of Defense, International Security Affairs, Before the House International Relations Committee, Subcommittee on Asian and Pacific Affairs, June 27, 1995," ms.
52. The Joint Defense Conversion Commission was initiated in October 1994 during Secretary of Defense Perry's trip to China. The program was intended to establish channels of communications with elements of the PLA, increase transparency, monitor Chinese defense conversion activities, and seek commercial opportunities for American companies.

53. "Testimony by Kent Wiedemann, Deputy Assistant Secretary of State for East Asian and Pacific Affairs, before Senate Foreign Relations Committee, Subcommittee on East Asian and Pacific Affairs, July 25, 1995, Current State of U.S.-Sino Relations," ms.
54. *Washington Post*, July 15, 1995, p. A18.
55. Reuters report from Washington, D.C., July 9, 1995.
56. See, for example, *Washington Post*, July 9, 1995, p. A23.
57. Associated Press report from Washington, D.C., July 9, 1995; *Washington Post*, July 12, 1995, p. A16; Associated Press report from Washington, D.C., July 13, 1995.
58. UPI report from Washington, D.C., July 20, 1995; *Wall Street Journal*, July 21, 1995, p. A2.
59. Reuters report from Beijing, July 22, 1995.
60. UPI report from Washington, D.C., July 17, 1995.
61. UPI report from Beijing, July 24, 1995; Reuters report from Beijing, August 24, 1995; Reuters report from Taipei, August 27, 1995.
62. Reuters report from Washington, D.C., July 20, 1995.
63. Reuters report from Hong Kong, July 20, 1995.
64. See, for example, UPI report from Beijing, July 18, 1995; Reuters report from Beijing, July 18, 1995.
65. For a useful study of Chinese bargaining strategies and tactics, see Alfred D. Wilhelm, Jr., *The Chinese at the Negotiating Table* (Washington, DC: National Defense University, 1994).
66. *Wall Street Journal*, September 1, 1995, p. A4.
67. "An M-11 Missile Violation by Any Other Name," *Washington Post*, August 8, 1995, p. A29.
68. See UPI report from Washington, D.C., August 3, 1995; Reuters report from Beijing, August 4, 1995.
69. Reuters report from Jackson Hole, Wyoming, August 17, 1995.
70. *Wall Street Journal*, August 28, 1995, p. A10; *Washington Post*, August 28, 1995, p. A20; August 29, 1995, p. A1.
71. "First Lady Hillary Rodham Clinton, Remarks to the United Nations Fourth World Conference on Women, Beijing, China" (Washington, DC: The White House, Office of the Press Secretary, September 5, 1995).
72. *Washington Post*, September 12, 1995, p. A8; Associated Press report from Beijing, September 14, 1995; Associated Press report from Washington, D.C., September 14, 1995. See also Reuters report from Washington, D.C., August 8, 1995.
73. *Wall Street Journal*, September 14, 1995, p. A15; Reuters report from Washington, D.C., September 21, 1995.
74. *Wall Street Journal*, September 28, 1995, p. A22; Associated Press report from Washington, D.C., October 10, 1995.
75. *Washington Post*, October 1, 1995, p. A33.
76. Reuters report from Washington, D.C., October 3, 1995.
77. "Statement of Ambassador Winston Lord, Assistant Secretary of State, Bureau of East Asian and Pacific Affairs, October 11, 1995, before the Senate Foreign Relations Committee, Asia and Pacific Affairs Subcommittee, U.S. Policy Toward China: Security and Military Considerations," ms.
78. *Washington Post*, October 14, 1995, p. A24.

79. Associated Press report from Washington, D.C., October 14, 1995; *Washington Post*, October 15, 1995, p. A28. For additional background on the diplomatic confrontation between Washington, Beijing, and Taipei, see Don Oberdorfer, "Juggling the Two Chinas: Caught Between Beijing and Taiwan, Clinton Dropped the Ball," *Washington Post*, October 22, 1995, p. C4.

80. Reuters report from New York, October 24, 1995.

81. See, for example, *Washington Post*, August 26, 1995, p. A21; Reuters report from Washington, D.C., October 20, 1995.

82. See "Press Briefing by Assistant Secretary of State for East Asian and Pacific Affairs Winston Lord and [NSC] Director of Asian Affairs Robert Suettinger" (New York: U.S. Department of State, Office of the Spokesman, October 24, 1995).

83. In May 1998, the USTR office refused to acknowledge the existence of such a "roadmap" to the author, perhaps a reflection of the sensitivity of the forthcoming Clinton trip to China during which some progress might be made on China's entrance into the WTO.

84. See *Washington Post*, November 11, 1995, p. A23; *Wall Street Journal*, November 13, 1995, p. A1; Frank Ching, "Bashing China Is New U.S. Fad," *Far Eastern Economic Review*, February 22, 1996, p. 33; Nicholas Lardy, "China's No Renegade Mercantilist Trader," *Wall Street Journal*, February 7, 1996, p. A14.

85. "Press Availability with Secretary of State Warren Christopher and Chinese Foreign Minister Qian Qichen, New Otani Hotel, Osaka, Japan" (Osaka: U.S. Department of State, Office of the Spokesman, November 16, 1995).

86. "On the Record Briefing by Assistant Secretary for East Asian and Pacific Affairs Winston Lord, Royal Hotel, Osaka, Japan" (Osaka: U.S. Department of State, Office of the Spokesman, November 16, 1995).

87. *Washington Post*, November 24, 1995, p. F3.

88. William H. Perry, "U.S. Strategy: Engage China, Not Contain It," Remarks as delivered by the Secretary of Defense to the Washington State China Relations Council, Seattle, October 30, 1995, *Defense Issues* 10, 109 (n.d.).

89. Reuters reports from Beijing, November 17, 1995; Associated Press report from Beijing, November 17, 1995.

90. Reuters report from Washington, D.C., December 12, 1995.

91. Actually, American warships travel fairly routinely through the Taiwan Strait. The aircraft carrier *USS Independence* had passed through several times in recent years; the amphibious assault ship *USS Belleau Wood* traveled through the Strait in July 1995; and the guided missile frigate *USS McCluskey* and the destroyer *USS O'Brien* passed through on December 11-12. UPI report from Washington, D.C., January 26, 1996.

92. As a result of the election, the KMT held a paper-thin majority of 85 seats in the 164-seat Legislative Yuan, while the pro-independence DPP won 54 seats, the pro-unification New Party won 21 seats, and independents won 4 seats.

8

Clinton's Policy Toward China and Taiwan: The Military Crisis and Its Aftermath

The many elements of the Taiwan conundrum in U.S. China policy came to a head in 1996, as the United States faced a choice of either standing aside while the PRC threatened Taiwan with increasing bellicosity or intervening on Taiwan's behalf and thereby placing at risk the policy of engagement with China. As it turned out, the administration did intervene to demonstrate its resolve to protect American interests in a peaceful settlement of the Taiwan issue, and it managed to do so without derailing engagement. However, the possibility of war in the Taiwan Strait caused many—especially in the American academic community—to wonder anew whether the United States ought not to reduce its commitment to Taiwan to avoid such confrontations in the future.

In truth, there was very little threat of conflict between the United States and China in March 1996, but the face-off in waters near Taiwan did demonstrate three important facts about the Taiwan issue. First, Beijing was willing—and increasingly able—to use military force against Taiwan to prevent the island from moving in the direction of de jure, if not de facto, independence. Second, Washington continued to view a peaceful settlement of the Taiwan issue as being in the U.S. interest, an interest the United States was willing to use force to protect both to secure Taiwan's democracy and to demonstrate American credibility and resolve in Asia. And third, the government and people of Taiwan were increasingly willing to take risks to further their right of self-determination and to challenge a definition of "one China" that presupposed Taiwan to be part of the People's Republic of China. At the time of writing in mid-1999, none of these conditions had changed. A sign of future trouble or unforeseen compromise? Only time would tell.

The Taiwan Strait Crisis

In early January 1996 Taiwan's Vice President Li Yuan-zu applied for a U.S. transit visa so his aircraft could refuel en route to and from Guatemala on January 11 and 16. Such a visa was authorized in the 1994 Taiwan policy review, but the administration hesitated to approve the request because the PRC asked the United States not to grant the visa so as not to "harm the relations of the two countries, hurt the feelings of the Chinese people." After several days of internal debate, the administration decided to grant the visa. Beijing protested, "The Taiwan authorities are attempting to create 'two Chinas' or 'one China, one Taiwan' in the name of making a stopover in the United States and this is bound to meet the resolute opposition of all the Chinese people."[1] At about the same time, Jiang Zemin told visiting former President George Bush that Taiwan was the "most important and most sensitive" issue in Sino-American relations.[2]

In late January former defense official Charles Freeman said Chinese officers told him the PLA had prepared plans for a series of attacks on Taiwan, consisting of one missile strike a day for thirty days. A similar warning had been given earlier to professor John Lewis.[3] Partly because of these and similar reports, the ROC sought, on an emergency basis, Harpoon air-to-sea missiles from McDonnell Douglas, Avenger antiaircraft missiles, and French-made Mistral rockets. The White House held meetings on the growing tension in the Taiwan Strait, with the State Department saying that while "at the present time there is no imminent threat to Taiwan," it was "monitoring the situation very closely." The United States reminded China that Washington would "consider any effort to settle the status of Taiwan by force a threat to peace in the western Pacific area and of grave concern to the United States."[4]

From mid-January through March 1996, the atmosphere in Sino-American relations took a decidedly militant tone over Taiwan as sharp warnings were heard from Beijing, Taipei, and Washington about precipitating a dangerous accident in the Taiwan Strait. Whereas the PRC military threat to Taiwan had been dismissed by most American analysts for nearly a decade, the new Taiwan crisis resulted in several books and hundreds of newspaper articles and wire reports being written about the military balance in the Taiwan Strait, the PLA's capabilities to attack Taiwan, Taiwan's defense capabilities, and the probability of U.S. military intervention.[5] There also were several important U.S. policy statements made during this period. Perhaps most importantly, the crisis focused the attention of government officials, policy analysts, and the general public on the foundations of U.S.-Taiwan-China relations, with many wondering if the policies that had preserved an equilibrium in the Taiwan Strait for nearly twenty years had outlived their usefulness.

One of the major conclusions reached by most American and Taiwanese analysts examining the Taiwan Strait crisis in early 1996 was that the PLA did not have the military capability to invade Taiwan successfully. It was believed that if the PLA attempted such an invasion, it would likely be defeated. The determining factors were the lack of PRC amphibious capabilities and strong ROC ground defense forces, backed by significant air and naval assets. It was thought that Taiwan could do little, however, to stop PLA ballistic missile attacks or to prevent the capture of small offshore islands near the coast of China. More controversial were the PRC's ability to impose an effective naval blockade of Taiwan or to capture the major offshore islands of Kinmen (Quemoy) or Matsu, both of which were heavily fortified by Taiwan. If the United States were to aid in Taiwan's defense, then the PRC's ability to invade Taiwan, impose a blockade of the island, or seize Kinmen and Matsu would be negated completely. The United States could not, however, prevent the PRC from launching ballistic missile strikes against Taiwan, nor could it prevent Beijing's attacking smaller offshore islands other than Kinmen or Matsu, primarily because of the lack of ROC defenders and the islands' proximity to mainland coastal defenses.

Chinese Assessments of Taiwan's Strategic Value

One difficulty Western analysts faced in assessing the 1996 PRC threat to Taiwan was the inability to divine true Chinese perceptions of the likelihood of Taiwan moving in the direction of independence. Also, it was not clearly understood whether the PRC would actually fight the United States over Taiwan, even to preserve Chinese unity. These were perceptual problems, similar to those encountered in the Korean and Vietnam wars, when the United States had difficulty understanding and accepting the signals being sent by Beijing.

PRC analysts, on the other hand, attempted to be very clear that (1) China thought the government of Lee Teng-hui was moving in the direction of eventual independence for Taiwan and (2) China would attack to stop Taiwan independence even if it meant war with the United States. For example, Chu Shulong, director of the North American division of the China Institute of Contemporary International Relations, wrote in 1996 that there was considerable support in China for the PLA to fight the United States over Taiwan:[6]

> In the PRC, there is still a strong degree of support for the country's leadership to go to war with the United States over Taiwan. . . . Two major factors underpin this national feeling and national will. First, China is a nation with a history of roughly five thousand years. . . . Chinese tend to consider unification as normal and reasonable, while separation is temporary and wrong. . . . Second, and more importantly, for people in the PRC, Taiwan's separation from the mainland is a living example of China's humiliation in the last 150 years . . . . Taiwan is the last piece of land that other governments still want to take away from China . . . . The people in the PRC just cannot let this history of humiliation perpetuate itself, they have got to stop it.

Chu attempted to refute the view of some American analysts that China would show restraint or not fight the United States over Taiwan. He said the Chinese people used a different calculus to determine whether the costs of such a war would be the worth the effort:

> First, do not forget that the people of the PRC have fought with the United States [in the Korean War] directly by choice. Second, the people of the PRC may have a unique way of looking at the military balance between their country and the United States. These Chinese are realistic people. They know well that in fighting with the world's sole superpower, especially in a naval and air war in the Western Pacific, the PRC would be at a disadvantage. However, these Chinese also know that today's PRC does have the capability to kill US personnel and destroy US ships, and aircraft, including aircraft carriers in the Western Pacific.
> Third, different people have different standards in evaluating the result of a war; in other words, they have a different conception of victory. For the people of the PRC, to have the courage to fight with a superpower when that superpower tries to bully their country would itself be a victory. To destroy two capital ships of such stronger forces would be a victory, no matter whether eight or ten PRC ships were destroyed at the same time. . . . So it is correct for Dr. Joseph Nye, former assistant secretary of defense for international security affairs, to argue that the Chinese should not assume that the United States would not become involved. . . . However, it is equally important for Americans not to assume that, because the Chinese are afraid of US involvement, they would not do what they think they have to do.

Chu also provided partial insight into why the PRC had reacted so strongly to the visit of Lee Teng-hui to the United States the previous year: "For the PRC, what the United States does about Taiwan is the clearest indication of US intentions regarding the strategic goal of containing the PRC." The Chinese saw a series of events which, contrary to American explanations, were not isolated but rather part of a strategic plan to divide and weaken China. According to Chu, since the end of the Cold War these events included: starting from 1989, the United States had undertaken sanctions against the PRC and some were still in place; in 1992 the United States sold Taiwan 150 F-16s in clear violation of the August 17 communiqué; in the summer of 1993 the United States provoked the *Yinghe* incident in international waters; also in 1993 the United States worked hard to prevent China from hosting the year 2000 Olympic Games; in September 1994 the Clinton administration's Taiwan policy review legalized high-level official visits and contacts between the United States and Taiwan; in the spring of 1995 the U.S. government allowed Lee Teng-hui to visit and even treated him as a president in some ways; and in March 1996 the United States sent two aircraft carrier battle groups to the Taiwan area to provoke and intimidate the PRC and encourage and protect Lee Teng-hui.

Chu said it was "possible to identify some strategic policies that seem to lie behind those actions." These included:

- In the spring of 1992 the Bush administration adopted a grand strategy to prevent any country in the world from becoming another superpower to challenge the U.S. position. The current challenger is seen to be the PRC.
- In the autumn of 1993 the Clinton administration adopted a strategy of enlargement, calling the PRC a backlash state, and pursuing a strategic goal of changing the PRC from a non-democratic into a democratic state.
- In early 1995 the East Asia and Pacific strategic report of the Pentagon was issued, and subsequent actions in 1996 indicated that in the post-Cold War period the chief threats to regional security were seen as North Korea and the PRC.
- In April 1996 the United States and Japan issued a joint declaration on their security alliance which both identified the PRC as a new target and enlarged the area of the alliance coverage to include the Taiwan Strait and the South China Sea.

Accordingly, said Chu, "the 'Taiwan card' seems to be a strategic card that the United States can play against the PRC. Compared with other cards—such as human rights, trade sanctions, or nonproliferation—the Americans have found the Taiwan card is more effective in dealing with the PRC, simply because it can hurt the PRC most and serve all the purposes that the United States pursues."

> When you want to "democratize" the PRC, Taiwan can be a good Chinese example in adopting the American system; when you do not want to see the PRC becoming too strong, a united China is a nightmare; when you want to keep China weak by dividing the country, as happened in the USSR, Taiwan is the best starting place—Hong Kong, Macau, Tibet, and Xinjiang are more difficult to use. Playing the Taiwan card can also cause the PRC's neighbors to become concerned about the PRC, so they follow US interests more closely.

Chinese analysts believed that Taiwan had great strategic value to China, not simply "moral value" as Taiwan appeared to many Americans. In the Chinese view, Taiwan was not merely territory to be recovered but also an extremely important geostrategic possession which China needed to control in order to fulfill its destiny of once again becoming the most powerful nation in Asia. According to PLA researchers Jiang Minfang and Duan Zhaoxian: "China is semi-enclosed by the first island chain. If it wants to prosper, it has to advance into the Pacific in which lies China's future. Taiwan, facing the Pacific to the east, is the only unobstructed exit for China to move into the ocean. If this gateway is opened for China, then it becomes much easier for China to manouevre in the western Pacific." Jiang and Duan went on to note that the PLA also assesses the geostrategic value of Taiwan in terms of its being adjacent to critical sea lines of communication, enabling it "conveniently to control the Balin and Bashi Straits in the south, to block Gonggu and Naguo waterways in the north, and to protect the mainland in the east. As such, it may be used to adversely affect US forward deployment, Japan's economic lifeline, and Russia's freedom of manouevre. So if Taiwan returns to the PRC, it will not only help to resolve the South China Sea problem but also disrupt the United States' strategic chain in the Asia-Pacific region."[7]

A similar view was taken by Chinese scholar Lu Junyuan, who wrote in 1996 that "Taiwan's national security value derives mainly from its unique geographical location."[8] Noting that "Taiwan also plays a pivotal role in the mainland's security," Lu said that from the geostrategic perspective, Taiwan's strategic significance for China was at least threefold:

> First, Taiwan directly impacts the mainland's security status. The island of Taiwan stands guard off China's southeastern coast, the nation's only large island in that area. Taiwan is superb as a shield for southeastern China, a "screen for several provinces in the hinterland." Taiwan is one of the "two eyes," the other being Hainandao, in China's southeasterly coastal defense. If China controls Taiwan, mainland security is assured. Conversely, if Taiwan is under the control of hostile forces, the mainland's security environment would deteriorate. . . .
>
> Second, Taiwan influences the strategic links between the two major bodies of water off north and south China. Between the island of Taiwan and Fujian is a wide waterway known as the Strait of Taiwan. The northern entrance to the strait separates the mouth of the Min Jiang from Fuguijiao at the northern tip of Taiwan. The southern entrance separates Nanaodao, which is where the two provinces of Fujian and Guangdong meet, from E'luanbi at the southern end of Taiwan. . . . The Strait of Taiwan is a shortcut between the East China Sea and South China Sea and a vital shipping lane in the western Pacific. Just about all strategic links between China's eastern and northern coasts and the waters off its southern coast run through the Strait of Taiwan. If it falls under the control of hostile forces, China would have difficulty asserting total control over the strait. Not only will this threaten shipping lanes in China's coastal waters, but the strategic linkage between the two major bodies of water in the north and south would also be in danger of being severed, which would divide the theater of naval warfare off the Chinese coast and prevent joint action. In a certain sense, therefore, China has no coastal defense without Taiwan.
>
> Third, Taiwan is critical to the preservation and development of China's naval power. China is both a land power and a sea power with a very long coastline and extensive maritime interests and rights. However, only a small portion of China's coastline opens directly to the Pacific Ocean. Its oceanic shipping lanes are liberally dotted with geographical barriers. The Yellow Sea and East China Sea are blocked by Japan and the Ryukyu Islands while the South China Sea is all but encircled by the various Southeast Asian nations. Taiwan, on the other hand, hubs the Philippine Sea. The waters to the east of Taiwan are the only part of the Pacific over which China has sovereignty and where it enjoys economic interests, providing China with its lone direct strategic entrance to the Pacific Ocean. And what a passageway it is, safe, wide, affording freedom of movement. All of that is immensely helpful to China as it develops naval power in the Pacific Ocean. If Taiwan and the mainland cannot be reunified, China would lose its only direct passageway to the Pacific Ocean and its drive for naval power would be severely hampered.

According to Lu, it is precisely because Taiwan has outstanding geostrategic value that the United States has been interested in Taiwan. "Casting a covetous glance toward Taiwan's strategic position, they often interfere and meddle in Taiwan's affairs, which is a major external factor in the Taiwan issue." Not only is Taiwan "China's sacred territory," Lu argued, it has "extraordinary significance for China's national security. National reunification must be achieved to protect China's fundamental interests."

These and other articles from Chinese sources suggest that many PLA strategists view Taiwan as being strategically vital for several reasons:

- Taiwan controls vital shipping lanes in the Western Pacific.
- Taiwan is the gateway to the Pacific for China's future blue water navy.
- Taiwan is the key to an effective defense of eastern China.
- Taiwan is well positioned as a communications and financial hub for all of Asia.
- In hostile hands, Taiwan would be an ideal base from which to attack China.
- Taiwan must be denied to the United States and Japan to prevent these nations from dividing and weakening China.
- Taiwan is used by the United States in its strategy to contain the PRC.
- Taiwan is home to the last major political opposition to the Chinese Communist Party asserting control over all of China.
- Taiwan is the last major territory seized from China that must be returned in order to effect the nation's reunification.
- Taiwan is essential to China if Beijing is to be able to project military force into the Pacific at some time in the future.
- Taiwan is essential to protect China's interest in the South China Sea, as well as to defeat the hegemonic intentions of Japan and the United States.

The harsh PRC reaction to Lee Teng-hui's visit to the United States becomes more understandable in view of these PLA strategic perceptions. For China's strategic and security purposes—as well as the more frequently expressed sovereignty and territorial integrity reasons—Taiwan cannot be allowed to pursue independence. Convinced that Lee was attempting gradually to separate Taiwan from China and that this effort was being abetted—willfully or through ignorance—by the United States, Beijing had to act forcefully to stop Lee and to warn the United States. Although many in the PLA favored engagement with the United States as a means of reducing tensions with Washington, the PLA also felt it necessary to demonstrate China's resolve to protect its security at whatever cost. After Lee's visa was issued, the PLA gained considerable influence over China's policies toward Taiwan and the United States. Hence, the Taiwan crisis did not end in late 1995, as it appeared it might with improved Sino-American ties. The Taiwan crisis had to run its course before all sides concluded that their interests lie in managing the issue in a more cautious way.

The Taiwan Issue Heats Up

For the first few weeks in 1996, U.S.-PRC relations moved along fairly normally. The American and Chinese military establishments, despite their differences and considerable domestic pressure opposing closer collaboration, made efforts to expand their relationship during this period. On January 29, a Chinese military delegation headed by Maj. Gen. Wen Guangchun, assistant director of the PLA's general logistics department, arrived in the United States to discuss logistics modernization, joint logistics, and logistics training and education. Two days later, the *USS Fort McHenry* paid a port call at Shanghai, the first U.S. naval ship to visit the city since 1989. Troubling to the U.S. military, however, was Iran's testing of a new low-flying antiship cruise missile made by China. A significant number of Iranian patrol boats were being modified to carry the C-802, which had a range of about sixty miles. Because of the threat the missile might pose to U.S. warships in the Persian Gulf, the missile transfers raised, once again, concerns in the halls of Congress and within U.S. intelligence agencies over PRC proliferation practices.

In early February 1996, the PRC again made "strong representations" to Washington for issuing another travel visa to ROC Vice President Li Yuan-zu for brief stops on U.S. soil on February 3, 4, and 11 during trips to and from Haiti. Beijing warned the United States not to create "fresh troubles," but Washington said the granting of the visa was "nothing to be concerned about." The State Department carefully explained the limitations placed on Vice President Li during his brief stay in the United States: "He cannot hold public meetings. He cannot stand up in the middle of a park and give a speech. We certainly don't want to see any interviews on television. I think the Taiwan authorities are very clear about our wishes in granting this transit visa—no public activities."[9] The State Department was making every reasonable effort to ensure that Li's transit was short, private, and unofficial.

On February 5, Washington-area newspapers reported that U.S. intelligence agencies had evidence that the PRC planned to conduct large military exercises in the Taiwan Strait as part of an effort to intimidate Taiwan during its March 23 presidential elections, the first in the ROC's history. Some forty warships were said to be involved, along with 100 or so military aircraft. This would be the largest exercise in China's coastal waters for decades. As a result of this activity, the United States increased its intelligence gathering in the region and set up task forces throughout the government to study how the United States might respond. After decades, Taiwan was emerging once again as one of the most dangerous points of confrontation in the Asian Pacific. The Clinton administration conveyed its concerns to visiting Vice Foreign Minister Li Zhaoxing.[10]

Public pressure began to build on the administration to take a firm stance against the PLA buildup. The *Washington Post* editorialized on February 6, 1996: "the United States would have no choice but to help Taiwan—a flourishing free-market democracy—defend itself against attack by Communist China. No treaty or law compels this response, but decency and strategic interest demand it. An American government that allowed the issue of Taiwan's future to be settled by China's force would be in disgrace as well as in error."[11]

In a question and answer period following a speech at the Aspin Institute on February 6, Secretary of Defense William Perry was asked about China's military threat to Taiwan. He said, "I do not see the prospects for military confrontation between China and Taiwan in the foreseeable future. But, I am concerned. I'm concerned about the military maneuvering that the Chinese are doing to, in not so subtle ways, threaten Taiwan, trying to influence their election. I'm concerned about the military buildup that's going on in China today. I do not see that as a threat yet, but I am concerned about it. . . . [We] have to watch both of these very carefully, both what the Chinese are doing in developing their military capability and what they are saying and threatening relative to Taiwan or other neighbors." When asked what the U.S. response would be if China attacked Taiwan, Perry referred to Joseph Nye's answer to a similar question from Chinese military officers a few months earlier: "We don't know what we would do, and you don't—because it going to depend on the circumstances."[12]

Winston Lord addressed U.S. concerns over the security of Taiwan in testimony before the Senate Foreign Relations Committee on February 7, 1996.[13] His comments were among the best statements of U.S. policy toward Taiwan during the Clinton administration. Referring to rising tensions in the area, including surface-to-surface missiles being fired into the ocean a hundred miles north of Taiwan, the assistant secretary said:

> We are concerned by any rise in tension in the region, we have conveyed this to Beijing, and we are watching developments closely. However, having examined all of the available evidence, we cannot conclude that there is an imminent military threat to Taiwan. While it is abundantly clear that the PRC wishes its military activities to be noticed, to influence Taiwan's legislative and presidential elections, and to have a restraining effect on Taiwan's international activities, they do not in our judgment reflect an intention to take military action against Taiwan. Perhaps more importantly, the Taiwan authorities have reached the same judgment. Though the scale of some of these recent exercises is substantial, the pattern of such exercises in connection with elections in Taiwan is not new; such activities have been observed since 1988. PRC authorities have stated publicly, as well as to us in diplomatic exchanges, that there is no change in their intention to seek a peaceful resolution of the Taiwan question. We, as always, will continue to monitor closely the situation in the Taiwan Strait. But all evidence at our disposal at this time leads to the conclusion that the PRC has no intention to initiate military action.

Lord said the United States viewed China's demonstrations of military strength as efforts "to send a message to the Taiwan authorities to curb what the PRC regards as efforts to establish a separate, independent identity for Taiwan. . . . The Chinese position, of course, is that Taiwan is a part of China, and it thus views the issue as vital to its interests. Some PRC commentators have charged Lee Teng-hui with the intention of abandoning, or postponing indefinitely, the Taiwan authorities' long-standing goal of eventual reunification with the mainland."

Lord said that Taiwan's leadership desires "recognition of Taiwan as a sovereign entity for now," but has "repeatedly reaffirmed its interest in eventual reunification." What Taiwan wants now is "greater respect and recognition from the international community." Moreover, "it is also apparent that the majority [of people on Taiwan] wish to remain separate from the People's Republic of China, at least until political and economic conditions on both sides of the Strait make reunification more attractive."

Nonetheless, the assistant secretary warned of a danger of military confrontation in the Taiwan Strait due to "growing nationalism on the mainland and increased efforts by Taiwan's democratic polity to obtain greater recognition of its own identity and improve its international status":

> Although neither Taiwan nor the PRC wants a military confrontation, there is a danger that Chinese nationalism in the PRC may collide with Taiwan's search for international recognition and status. Democratic development in Taiwan has permitted the free expression by a portion of the Taiwan populace of a desire for a separate Taiwan identity, expression of which has been largely suppressed under the previous political leadership in Taiwan. Some in Beijing interpret this development as challenging the assumption underlying the political status quo and source of stability in the Taiwan Strait—the acceptance of a single Chinese state by both sides.

Lord carefully explained U.S. policy on the Taiwan question: "It is vital to keep in mind U.S. interests in the Taiwan issue. We insist that the PRC and Taiwan work out their differences peacefully, so as not to disturb the security of the region and the people there. At the same time, our approach is to strictly avoid interference in the process whereby the two sides pursue resolution of differences." The basis of U.S. policy toward the security of Taiwan is contained in the 1979 Taiwan Relations Act: "Its premise is that an adequate defense in Taiwan is conducive to maintaining peace and security while differences remain between Taiwan and the PRC." Lord then reaffirmed section 2 (b) of the TRA:

> It is the policy of the United States ... to consider any effort to determine the future of Taiwan by other than peaceful means, including by boycotts or embargoes, a threat to the peace and security of the Western Pacific area and of grave concern to the United States; to provide Taiwan with arms of a defensive character; and to maintain the capacity of the United States to resist any resort to force or other forms of coercion that would jeopardize the security, or the social or economic system, of the people on Taiwan.

He went on to cite section 3 of the TRA, which provides that the "United States will make available to Taiwan such defense articles and defense services in such quantity as may be necessary to enable Taiwan to maintain a sufficient self-defense capability." Further, Lord said, the TRA stipulates: "The President is directed to inform the Congress promptly of any threat to the security or the social or economic system of the people on Taiwan and any danger to the interests of the United States arising therefrom. The President and the Congress shall determine, in accordance with constitutional processes, appropriate action by the United States in response to any such danger."

Lord also highlighted key elements of United States' policy toward the Taiwan question that were contained in the three U.S.-PRC joint communiqués:

- The United States recognizes the Government of the PRC as "the sole legal Government of China."
- The United States acknowledges the Chinese position that "there is but one China and Taiwan is part of China."
- In 1982, the United States assured the PRC that it has no intention of pursuing a policy of "two Chinas" or "one China, one Taiwan."
- Within that context, the people of the United States will maintain cultural, commercial, and other unofficial relations with the people of Taiwan.
- The United States has consistently held that the resolution of the Taiwan issue is a matter to be worked out peacefully by the Chinese themselves: "Our sole and abiding concern is that any resolution be peaceful."

Lord said these statements from the TRA and joint communiqués "express precisely the governing principles of our policy. They serve U.S. interests today just as well as in past decades." He further explained why the August 17, 1982, joint communiqué was "extremely important to Taiwan's security":

In this document, the PRC stated that its "fundamental policy" is "to strive for a peaceful resolution to the Taiwan question." Based on that PRC assurance, the United States Government made reciprocal statements concerning our intentions with respect to arms sales to Taiwan—that we did not intend to increase the quantity or quality of arms supplied and, in fact, intended gradually to reduce these sales. At the time the Joint Communiqué was signed, we made it clear to all parties concerned that our intentions were premised on the PRC's continued adherence to a policy of striving for peaceful reunification with Taiwan. We continually review our assessment in light of events, particularly during periods of heightened tension. Our judgment is that the PRC has not changed this policy, and we have abided by our commitments.

Lord argued that "U.S. arms sales to Taiwan have been consistent with both the TRA and the 1982 Joint Communiqué." Taiwan now had a defensive capability "as strong as at any time since 1949," including systems purchased or leased from the United States in recent years such as various types of military aircraft, ships, and air-defense and antiship missiles. In addition, "the U.S. has provided significant technical support for Taiwan's own production of the Indigenous Defense Fighter and *Perry*-class frigates." These systems, Lord noted, had been complemented with purchases from other countries, such as Mirage fighters and *LaFayette*-class frigates from France.

Lord said, "Although there may be other defensive systems which Taiwan will seek to obtain for its self-defense, the basic inventory of equipment which Taiwan has or will have in its possession will, in our view, be sufficient to deter any major military action against Taiwan." The assistant secretary went on to explain why the administration would continue to be cautious in selling advanced military equipment to Taiwan:

> While our arms sales policy aims to enhance the self-defense capability of Taiwan, it also seeks to reinforce stability in the region. We will not provide Taiwan with capabilities that might provoke an arms race with the PRC or other countries in the region. Moreover, our policy must be applied with a long-term perspective. Any transfer of a complicated modern weapon system generally requires years of lead time before the capability is fully in place. Each new system, moreover, demands a U.S. commitment for continuing logistical and technical support in order to remain effective. Decisions on the release of arms made without proper consideration of the long-term impact both on the situation in the Taiwan Strait and on the region as a whole would be dangerous and irresponsible.

Lord emphasized that many U.S. interests would be harmed if armed conflict broke out between Taiwan and the mainland. Both Chinese societies would suffer, with political and economic gains in Taiwan put at risk and China's economic progress set back as well.

> Conflict would also be costly to the United States and to our friends and allies in the region. Taiwan is an important economic actor throughout East Asia. It is located along one of the main sea lanes in the western Pacific. Any confrontation between the PRC and Taiwan, however limited in scale or scope, would destabilize the military balance in East Asia and constrict the commerce and shipping which is the economic life-blood of the region. It would force other countries in the region to re-evaluate their own defense policies, possibly fueling an arms race with unforeseeable consequences. It would seriously affect the tens of thousands of Americans who live and work in Taiwan and the PRC. Relations between the U.S. and the PRC would suffer damage regardless of the specific reaction chosen by the President in consultation with Congress. For all these reasons, we are firmly determined to maintain the balanced policy which is best designed to avoid conflict in the area.

If hostilities were to break out, Lord said, "the Administration would immediately meet its obligations under the TRA to consult with the Congress on an appropriate response." He said the "circumstances leading to this situation would be important in determining our response—what caused the breakdown? Both sides have a responsibility to act in ways that promote stability and avoid needless provocation." Indirectly, he warned the PRC that the U.S. response might be strong:

Clinton's Policy: The Military Crisis

"I hardly need remind this committee that the people of the United States feel strongly about the ability of the people of Taiwan to determine their future peacefully. This sentiment must not be underestimated." As to the current crisis, Lord said:

> we will continue to make clear to the PRC through diplomatic and other channels that any attempt to resolve the Taiwan question through other than peaceful means would seriously affect the interests of the United States. This position comprises a fundamental premise that underlies our policy: that the PRC will pursue a peaceful settlement. Over the past months, and indeed recent days, we have made clear in our diplomatic dialogue with Beijing our deep concern over the exercises and the dangers of escalation. We also have used and will continue to use our military-to-military relationship with the PRC to communicate these concerns directly to PLA leaders.
>
> We must, though, avoid unwarranted actions that could further add to tensions. We should maintain our present prudent and effective policy on arms sales, within the framework of the TRA and in conformity to the 1982 Joint Communiqué. We have an enormous stake in preserving stability in Asia and maintaining a productive relationship with the PRC. We will continue to engage the Chinese Government on issues of mutual interest and encourage the PRC's positive participation in the international community. We seek engagement, not confrontation. We expect the Taiwan authorities as well to avoid any actions which could potentially put at risk the interests of all parties concerned.

Lord closed by saying the two Chinese sides ultimately must work out their own differences:

> Taiwan and the PRC must eventually find some sort of common ground, if they are to continue to enjoy the peace and prosperity that exists in the Strait area today. Both sides need to avoid provocative political or military actions that have the potential to destabilize the situation. They must together actively seek ways to address their differences peacefully. This is the only long-term guarantee of Taiwan's security. It is also the only long-term guarantee of peace and stability in East Asia. Only through the resumption of positive dialogue directly between Beijing and Taipei can the route to a peaceful and lasting settlement be found. We understand that the Taiwan authorities are prepared to resume cross-Strait talks. The PRC has also indicated their willingness to expand ties with Taiwan in a number of areas as long as the Taiwan authorities continue to embrace the principle of "one China." We hope the two sides will agree as soon as possible to take up again the dialogue that was suspended last June [following Lee Teng-hui's visit to the United States].

Lord's testimony, and statements from other administration officials, demonstrated that continuity rather than change continued to characterize U.S. policy toward Taiwan under the Clinton administration—despite U.S. efforts to broaden engagement with Beijing, despite China's growing national power, despite Taiwan's efforts to seek an expanded role in the international community, and despite the PLA's threats in the Taiwan Strait. U.S. policy toward Taiwan was certainly challenged by these developments, but the continuity of the policy, laboriously worked out over many years and retained because of its utility, persisted through the crisis of 1996.

Other Issues Resurface

Taiwan was not the only security issue straining Sino-American relations in 1996. In the midst of growing tensions in the Taiwan Strait, the CIA concluded that China had sold nuclear-related equipment and technology to Pakistan in 1995. The equipment involved specialized magnets shipped to the Abdul Qadeer Khan Research Laboratory in Kahuta. The ring magnets were to be installed in high-speed gas centrifuges to help in the enrichment of uranium for nuclear weapons. The leaked CIA report followed earlier intelligence pinpointing the location in Pakistan of crated, Chinese-made, medium-range M-11 ballistic missiles and the export of antiship cruise missiles to Iran. If interpreted literally, U.S. law would require the termination of billions of dollars in Sino-American trade because of these Chinese activities. Boeing and Westinghouse, among other large corporations, lobbied the administration to waiver the sanctions required under the 1994 Nuclear Proliferation Prevention Act to cut off loan guarantees by the U.S. Export-Import Bank and other assistance. The American media, however, was less sympathetic. The *Washington Post* editorialized: "It is already established that the Clinton administration is putting trade over human rights in its China policy, even though the mellowing that trade was expected to bring about is so far not in sight. Now it is being established that the administration is putting trade . . . over nonproliferation as well. The administration's China policy is at the edge of incoherence."[14]

According to the *Washington Post*, China's arms sales and technology transfers were in possible violation of at least four U.S. laws: the 1968 Treaty on the Non-Proliferation of Nuclear Weapons that barred any state from transferring "equipment or material especially designed or prepared" for making fissionable material not subject to international inspection; the 1976 Symington Amendment that barred U.S. economic and military assistance for countries that delivered or received nuclear enrichment equipment, materials or technology not subject to international safeguards; the 1992 Iraq-Iran Arms Non-Proliferation Act that required the United States to vote against international loans to any country that helped Iran or Iraq "acquire destabilizing numbers and types of advanced conventional weapons" and to suspend for a year all exports of military-related or sensitive commercial technology or products; and the 1994 Non-Proliferation Act that (a) barred the U.S. government from purchasing from foreign companies that "knowingly and materially" contributed to the development of nuclear arms by a non-nuclear state; (b) barred the sale or lease of military-related equipment to any country that violated the NPT; (c) required sanctions against those who financed improper nuclear-related cooperation; and (d) barred Export-Import Bank loan guarantees for business deals in countries that aided or abetted the development of nuclear arms by a non-nuclear state.[15]

The PRC attempted to link its arms proliferation policies to the U.S. sale of arms to Taiwan. Beijing also renewed its demand that Washington end arms sales to Taiwan as a condition for lowering tensions in the Taiwan Strait. China claimed that tensions with Taiwan "come mainly from some countries, including the United States, selling huge amounts of advanced weapons to [Taiwan].... These countries in reality are encouraging the Taiwan authorities to create 'two Chinas' or 'one China, one Taiwan,' harming the process of peaceful reunification."[16] At the same time that China made these demands, it was reported that Beijing had signed a new contract with Moscow to purchase an additional seventy-two Su-27 fighters. China further warned the United States not to invite senior Taiwan officials to attend the 1996 Olympic Summer Games in Atlanta, saying it will "react fiercely and sharply ... to interference in China's domestic affairs."[17]

Meanwhile, on the economic front, U.S. Trade Representative Mickey Kantor threatened to impose trade sanctions on $1 billion worth of Chinese imports unless Beijing immediately stopped—as it had promised in 1995—the piracy of U.S. compact disks, videos, and software. The deadline for the enforcement of the 1995 agreement was February 26. The U.S. sanctions were put into force, but then rescinded a few hours later when China agreed to greater protection of intellectual property rights (IPR). At the same time, however, the USTR began to consider sanctions of more than $2 billion if the promised improvement in IPR protection was not implemented by China. Kantor said the U.S. trade deficit with China in 1995 was a record $33.8 billion, up 15 percent from $29.5 billion in 1994, a trade deficit he claimed was due to China's unfair trading practices.[18]

China's belligerency and lack of cooperation on issues such as nonproliferation and trade created serious domestic political problems for the administration's engagement policies. Even Democrats in the Congress felt Clinton was coddling the PRC, and Republicans were quick to condemn the president for being too soft on China. Several high-level meetings on China policy were held by the administration, and by mid-February the United States began to adopt a tougher line toward Beijing, particularly in statements issued by the Department of Defense.

On February 13, Secretary of Defense Perry delivered a speech at the National Defense University in Washington, D.C., in which he discussed Asia-Pacific strategy and specifically called on China "to start sending the right message."[19] Perry said that with the end of the Cold War, the United States was reducing its nuclear arsenal and military forces and placing "strong emphasis on preventive defense." In the Asia-Pacific region, the preventive defense strategy was "based on four pillars: alliances, regional confidence building, constructive engagement with China, and the framework agreement with North Korea." Most of his comments were directed at U.S. engagement with China. Perry noted that the policy of engagement had been in place for more than twenty years and "will remain our policy because China is playing an increasingly important role in the security of the region." He cautioned: "China is a power of global significance, not of simply regional significance, [and] it is a fundamental fact that the United States and Chinese interests will sometimes be in harmony and sometimes be in conflict." Nonetheless, the basic assumption of constructive engagement was that "through a healthy, honest dialogue we can work together where our interests are in harmony for our mutual benefit, and we can work together to reduce tensions when our interests conflict."

Perry said containment of China would harm U.S. security interests: "A China that feels encircled by U.S. containment policy is quite unlikely to cooperate on U.S. vital security objectives. And containment could actually *create* security problems for the United States. It could push China to accelerate its defense modernization, contributing to regional arms races and increasing the likelihood of military conflict in regional spots like North Korea, the South China Sea, and the Taiwan Strait."

At the same time, Perry emphasized that if constructive engagement was to work, China must also keep its word to become a responsible world power. Echoing a theme he made in 1995, Perry said, "China sends quite the opposite message when it conducts missile tests and large military maneuvers off Taiwan, when it exports nuclear weapons technology, or abuses human rights. It is time for China to start sending the right messages."

The Secretary of Defense explained that the one-China policy of the United States rested on "three legs": (1) Washington-Beijing relations, built around constructive engagement and based on the Shanghai communiqués; (2) Washington-Taipei relations, which include Taiwan's ability to defend itself as called for in the Taiwan Relations Act; and (3) the promotion of healthy Beijing-Taipei relations, based on increased trade, investment, and other peaceful activities across the Taiwan Strait, which benefit the regional economy and stability. Perry said: "Inherent in each leg is dialogue which serves to diminish tension, missteps and misunderstanding over perceived slights or unwelcome actions. . . . Ultimately, it is the responsibility of both Beijing and Taipei to build healthy relations. But it is in the abiding interest of Beijing, Taipei and Washington that relations maintain a healthy, peaceful course without provocation or overreaction by any capital."

In late 1995 and early 1996 U.S. intelligence chiefs began to hedge somewhat on their predictions of Sino-American relations in the future. CIA Director John Deutch told the Senate Select Committee on Intelligence on February 22, 1996, that China, along with Russia, was "in the process of metamorphosis" with its final shape "still very much in question." Even though China "is emerging as a major economic, political, and military actor in East Asia and the world in the next decade . . . we still know very little about Beijing's future leadership and intentions." China's new military strength—including purchases of twenty-six Russian Su-27s, two *Kilo* attack submarines, and several battalions of Patriot-class SA-10 SAMS—"is changing the region's security environment." Also, "Chinese military exercises in the Taiwan Strait have increased tensions and raised serious questions about Beijing's intentions."[20]

Similar reference to potential problems in Sino-American relations were heard from Toby Gati, Assistant Secretary of State for Intelligence and Research (INR).[21] He placed emphasis on U.S. interests in a peaceful, cooperative China, while at the same time sounding a warning. Gati said: "The importance of a strong, stable, prosperous, and open China working in concert with its Asian neighbors and the US cannot be overemphasized. China is seeking a global stature commensurate with its size, population, and permanent membership in the U.N. Security Council, participating actively in multilateral organizations like APEC and the ASEAN Regional Forum (ARF)." The INR director warned, however:

> China is modernizing its armed forces, acquiring advanced military systems, including fighter aircraft and surface-to-air missiles, to complement indigenous weapons development programs which have achieved only limited success. The People's Liberation Army (PLA) is also allocating resources to support more sophisticated training and the transition from a cumbersome ground army primarily oriented to the Soviet threat to a more mobile, streamlined force capable of dealing with regional conflicts, defending territorial claims in the South China Sea, or enforcing claimed sovereignty over Taiwan. The new Chinese threat buzzwords—"local and limited conflicts"—are thinly veiled reference to the Spratly Islands and Taiwan.

As a result of these activities, Gati said, "China's emergence as a major regional power affects longtime American allies, who are unsure of China's capabilities and intentions during a period of leadership transition. Fueled by strong economic growth, China's neighbors are also modernizing their forces, primarily in response to new uncertainties about regional stability."

The U.S. intelligence community, which repeatedly made less benign assessments of China's intentions and capabilities than the Clinton White House, was concerned that the combination of China's new assertive nationalism, its claims to the South China Sea and Taiwan, and its enhanced power projection capabilities being acquired through purchases from Moscow could work to destabilize the region and undermine the confidence of other Asian countries in their long-term security.

Tensions Increase

The United States privately and publicly criticized the PRC military maneuvers in the Taiwan Strait, but Washington did not believe China was actually going to attack Taiwan, particularly in an invasion. General John Shalikashvili, Chairman of the Joint Chiefs of Staff, said on February 15: "We do not believe that [the Chinese] have the capability to conduct amphibious operations of the nature that would be necessary to invade Taiwan. . . . Secondly, we don't see them gathering the kind of forces and the kind of support that you would need to conduct that kind of operation. . . . The story is not whether that capability exists or not. The story is that we do not see a change that has occurred that would make us believe somehow that they decided to invade the island of Taiwan." The general used the analogy of the invasion of France over the twelve-mile English Channel in World War II, which was "an extraordinarily complex operation." With its current capabilities, China could not send thousands of troops across the 130-mile Taiwan Strait and keep them supplied. "All of you who have studied history can well image what it takes in terms of amphibious shipping to project a force just across the English Channel. Here, we are talking about distances that are considerably greater." He did say, however, that China had the capability of blockading Taiwan, although he did not believe China planned such action.[22]

Despite U.S. urging to avoid any further military assertiveness in the Taiwan Strait, China moved some 150,000 PLA troops opposite Taiwan. Reacting to the PLA buildup and military maneuvers, Senator Frank Murkowski announced while in Taipei: "If the security of Taiwan is at risk, the President has the obligation to report to the Congress, and I think Taiwan has many friends in the Congress. . . . We would be compelled to take appropriate action."[23] Murkowski's remarks accurately reflected the mood of Congress, which became increasingly active in calling for a stronger U.S. response to the escalating Taiwan Strait crisis.

With pressure from several fronts on his China policy, President Clinton adopted a two-track approach toward the PRC. On the one hand, he became more forceful on issues of concern to the United States; on the other hand, he expanded high-level talks with the Chinese to demonstrate U.S. acceptance of China as a major power. Clinton's new approach was the result of a month-long series of policy meetings and was based on the assumption that, over the longer term, China and the United States had much more in common than in conflict. A significant portion of Clinton's new approach to China was an improved public relations campaign in the United States to convince the American people of the need for closer relations with the PRC.[24]

As part of its new approach, the administration asked the Ex-Im Bank to stop financing business deals in China during March while the U.S. government decided what to do about the PRC's nuclear technology sales to Pakistan. The Clinton administration did not want to take action that would harm U.S. companies and give China's business to other countries. On the other hand, congressional pressure was mounting to take some action in conformity with U.S. law. Even leading Democrats, including House Democratic leader Richard Gephardt, threatened to oppose China's MFN status in June if nothing was done.[25]

The Taiwan issue also began to have an impact on U.S. presidential politics. Senator Robert Dole, who secured the delegates necessary for the GOP nomination for the presidential election in November, said in early March that if elected president, "I would support Taiwan having a seat in the U.N. Whether I could get that accomplished or not, I don't know." Dole also said he would tell China to be careful about its militant stance toward Taiwan, "because if they make a move we're committed to help Taiwan." Asked whether President Lee Teng-hui could repeat a private visit to the United States, the senator said, "it would be all right with me."[26] A week later, Dole said that while the United States wanted to "dialogue with China . . . they also have to understand that if they start messing with Taiwan, they're going to strain our relationship and set back China entering the modern world for years and years."[27] The Republican Study Committee in the U.S. House of Representatives described Clinton policy toward China and Taiwan as "supine," saying, "House Republicans strongly support a clear and unambiguous policy of friendship toward, and commitment to the defense of Taiwan, designed to unmistakably deter the People's Republic of China from invading, attacking, or blockading Taiwan."[28]

Meanwhile, China's *People's Daily* published an essay by Yan Xuetong, deputy director of the China Institute of Contemporary International Relations, suggesting that China would substantially reduce the size of its military if the United States stopped selling advanced weapons to Taiwan. Yan argued that the U.S. military equipment encouraged separatists on the island and undermined China's strategy for peaceful reunification, necessitating the rapid modernization of the PLA beyond what would be normal for the PRC's level of development.[29]

On March 5 Chinese Premier Li Peng opened the annual National People's Congress with a speech outlining government policy in various areas, including Taiwan and the United States. "The question of Taiwan is China's internal affair," he said, "and China will brook no interference by outside forces under whatever pretext and in whatever form." While China wanted peaceful reunification, "we shall not undertake to renounce the use of force." He reiterated that force would not be directed "against our compatriots in Taiwan, but against the schemes of foreign forces to interfere with China's reunification and to bring about the 'independence of Taiwan.'" China wanted "normal relations" with the United States, Premier Li said, but "the question of Taiwan has always been the most sensitive and important aspect of Sino-American relations."[30]

The Taiwan Crisis Escalates

As Li Peng spoke, Beijing announced it would conduct another series of missile tests in two areas close to Taiwan's main ports, Keelung and Kaohsiung. The weeklong tests effectively imposed a missile blockade of the island for the period March 8–15, 1996. The tests were in areas about thirty miles southwest of Kaohsiung and twenty miles northeast of Keelung. These were the third and fourth missile tests off Taiwan since Lee Teng-hui's visit to the United States in June 1995. In the tests, China test-fired unarmed M-9 guided missiles, similar to Russian-made Scuds used by Iraq during the Persian Gulf War.[31]

The United States condemned the new tests as risky and unnecessary. Secretary of Defense Perry commented, "I deplore that decision on their part and I will express my concern to them. . . . It's taking a risk which is unnecessary." The State Department said, "These missile exercises are designed to intimidate the people of Taiwan before Taiwan's elections. We're concerned about these missile tests [and] those concerns have been raised in Beijing and here in Washington."[32] House Speaker Newt Gingrich described the missile tests as "an act of terror."[33]

At about the same time as the PRC announced its new missile tests near Taiwan, the State Department released its annual report on human rights practices, once again highly critical of China. The report said in part: "During the year, the [PRC] government continued to commit widespread and well-documented human rights abuses, in violation of internationally accepted norms, stemming both from the authorities' intolerance of dissent and the inadequacy of legal safeguards and basic freedoms. Abuses included arbitrary and lengthy incommunicado detention, forced confessions, torture and mistreatment of prisoners. Prison conditions remained harsh. The government continued severe restrictions on freedom of speech, the press, assembly, association, religion, privacy, movement and worker rights."[34]

During this period of PLA missile tests, it was reported that U.S. intelligence agencies had concluded that Chinese companies were selling complete factories able to produce poison gas to Iran. If true, this again would have violated U.S. law, as well as Beijing's pledge to abide by the Chemical Weapons Convention (a treaty both China and Iran had signed), which barred any nation from developing or producing chemical weapons. However, the multinational treaty had not yet taken effect, since only forty-seven of the required sixty-five nations had ratified it.[35]

On March 7 a very specific warning to China about its provocative actions in the Taiwan Strait was given by Secretary of Defense Perry, Secretary of State Christopher, and National Security Adviser Anthony Lake to visiting Chinese Vice Foreign Minister Liu Huaqiu during a meeting in Washington. Perry said the next day,

> I told the Chinese delegation that I thought the action that they took with these missile firings was reckless. It was not just that they were having missile tests in the open ocean—which they've done before and we've done before—but that they were firing them so close to Taiwan, to the populated areas there, that it could only be viewed as an act of coercion. And it had the danger that—if the firings had any malfunctions at all—that some parts of the missile could have landed on populated areas. That's why I thought it was reckless. So, I made that point very clearly and very unequivocally. I deplore that action and we made our position on that very clear.[36]

In response to a comment about U.S. "strategic ambiguity" lacking a clear signal to the Chinese, thus perhaps influencing their belligerent behavior, Perry said, "I believe the message which the President has communicated—and the message which we communicated at dinner last night—was very clear and very straight forward." Perry then confirmed that the United States had stationed the aircraft carrier *Independence* within a few hundred miles of Taiwan, as well as a guided missile cruiser and guided missile destroyer. He noted that an American guided missile cruiser was close enough to observe the missile test and that the United States also had monitored the test through various reconnaissance systems.

Two days later, China announced that it would hold live-fire exercises in the Taiwan Strait between March 12 and 20 to complement its missile tests. It also announced that the PLA would hold army exercises after the March 23 presidential elections on Taiwan. Secretary of State Christopher called the PLA actions "risky" and said they "smack of intimidation and coercion." He warned, "There will be really grave consequences if they try to resolve that problem [Taiwan] by force." Because of the growing crisis, Christopher said the *Independence* would move closer to Taiwan. Meanwhile, the Pentagon announced that the nuclear-powered aircraft carrier *Nimitz* and five or six accompanying ships would be sent to the Taiwan area from the Persian Gulf, arriving around the time of the March 23 presidential election. The navy task force included between 110-130 carrier-based strike aircraft, over 200 Tomahawk cruise missiles, and at least three nuclear-powered attack submarines. The U.S. Pacific Fleet announced on March 13 that the following ships would be deployed around Taiwan: the nuclear attack submarines *Portsmouth*, *Columbus*, and *Bremerton*; the aircraft carriers *Independence* and *Nimitz*; the destroyers *O'Brien* and *Hewitt*; the guided missile frigate *McClusky*; the oiler *Pecos*; and the guided missile cruiser *Bunker Hill* with the *Independence*; and the cruiser *Port Royal*; the destroyers *Callaghan* and *Oldendorf*; the frigate *Ford*; and the replenishment ships *Willamette* and *Shasta* with the *Nimitz*.[37] The U.S. armada was one of the largest deployed to the region since the Vietnam War.

Secretary Perry said of the deployments, "We do not believe China plans to attack Taiwan. We do not expect military conflict there. Nevertheless, we are increasing our naval presence in that region as a prudent, cautionary measure."[38] In off-the-record comments, U.S. defense officials said the carrier deployments were meant to reassure U.S. friends and allies in Asia that the United States would not be bullied by China and to demonstrate Washington's determination to protect its interests and credibility in the Western Pacific.[39]

The U.S. naval deployments were not viewed as combat operations, but rather as a political signal of Washington's displeasure over Beijing's intimidation of Taiwan's elections through the use of force. Through its words and actions, the Clinton administration was demonstrating that the security of Taiwan continued to play an important role in U.S. strategic calculations in Asia. The provisions in the 1979 Taiwan Relations Act linking a peaceful resolution of the Taiwan question to U.S. interests in peace and stability in the Western Pacific remained valid. The United States would use force, if necessary, to defend its interests and credibility—despite the obvious desire of President Clinton to preserve his engagement strategy with China.

The administration persistently refused to disclose what it would do in the event of a PRC attack against Taiwan. White House spokesman Mike McCurry told reporters on March 12, "the 1979 Taiwan Relations Act does not answer that question specifically, and indeed there is merit, we believe, in keeping somewhat ambiguous about the answer." Many in Congress, however, criticized this "strategic ambiguity" and argued that the United States should be more specific as to how it would respond if China attacked Taiwan. Several resolutions to that effect were introduced in the Congress during the March 1996 crisis. In a well-timed coincidence, the Pentagon announced during this period that it was awarding a $1.15 billion contract to Lockheed Martin Corporation as part of the sale of 150 F-16s to Taiwan approved by President Bush in 1992. The first planes would be delivered in May or June 1997 and the remainder transferred by the year 2000. The Defense Department explained the long-lead funds were routine and had nothing to do with the on-going missile crisis.[40]

Most Western analysts did not believe the PRC would sacrifice its economic development for a uncertain military confrontation with Taiwan, despite the harsh rhetoric from Beijing and PLA maneuvers.[41] And indeed the economic incentives for peace were considerable. In 1995 the PRC received $27.7 billion in direct foreign investment, up almost 12 percent from 1994. By year's end, Taiwan businessmen alone had invested about $24 billion in the mainland, mostly in 25,000 small- and medium-sized light industrial ventures along China's southern coast. Even though direct trade was not allowed by Taipei, indirect trade across the Taiwan Strait had expanded tremendously. In 1995 China imported $14.8 billion in goods from Taiwan, an increase of nearly 5 percent. Chinese exports to Taiwan totaled $3.1 billion, an increase of over 38 percent. Both foreign investment and investment from Taiwan, as well as trade between China and the rest of the world, including Taiwan, would be severely curtailed in the event of a war in the Taiwan Strait. Since the PRC had placed primary importance on the modernization of its economy, it made little sense—from the point of view of Western analysts—for China to precipitate a conflict with Taiwan at this stage. Generally, this assessment was shared by analysts from Taiwan and other Asian countries.

At the same time, however, the message from Beijing was clear: China considered the Taiwan issue to be of fundamental importance and worth fighting for. The PRC sought to convey the impression that China's sovereignty and territorial integrity were of greater importance than economic modernization in the short-term and worth, if necessary, an armed confrontation with both Taiwan and the United States. Foreign Minister Qian Qichen said on March 11, "It is ridiculous for some people to call for [U.S.] interference in this issue and even more ridiculous for them to call for the protection of Taiwan. These people have forgotten that Taiwan is a part of China and not a protectorate of the United States."[42]

Despite a stated willingness to go to war over Taiwan, China continually assured the Clinton administration that the PRC would not use force against Taiwan. Liu Huaqiu, for example, told U.S. officials during his Washington visit that China did not intend to attack Taiwan. The message China truly wanted understood was that Taiwan authorities were moving too far in the direction of independence. Taiwan needed, in Beijing's view, to be pulled back from the brink of real disaster by a forceful demonstration of PRC resolve. As Joseph Nye described the Chinese view from his meetings in Beijing in November 1995: "They said they understood more missile tests and exercises would have negative effects, but stressed Taiwan was moving toward independence and the situation demanded a remedy."[43]

On this point—the need to warn Taipei not to proceed any further toward independence—there probably was consensus in Beijing. At the same time, however, it was evident that for a period of time (approximately from Lee's visit in June 1995 through the spring of 1996) PRC policy toward Taiwan and the United States slipped from the hands of more moderate elements in the PRC foreign policy bureaucracy to those who felt that China had been too accommodating to Washington and Taipei. These so-called hardliners believed Beijing needed to signal its resolve to use force, if necessary, (1) to prevent Taiwan from slipping away toward independence, (2) to restrain the Lee government from pursuing too aggressively a larger international presence, and (3) to warn foreigners, particularly Americans, not to interfere in Taiwan affairs.

Even as the Taiwan situation was heating up, other issues in Sino-American relations kept emerging. In mid-March, Madame Wu Yi, PRC minister for foreign trade and economic cooperation, offered to announce some $4 billion in orders for commercial jets from Boeing and McDonnell Douglas, but she insisted the orders be linked to a delay in U.S. sanctions against China for software piracy. For the plane order to go forward, Ms. Wu said the United States must not impose trade sanctions on China. U.S. Trade Representative Mickey Kantor responded, "We would never countenance such a linkage." And Treasury Secretary Robert Rubin, on his way to an economic ministers meeting of APEC in Kyoto, Japan, warned that the Clinton administration was prepared to impose trade sanctions if Beijing did not stop the piracy.[44]

Policy Statements on Crisis

During the height of the Taiwan crisis in mid-March, the House Committee on International Relations held a hearing on Taiwan and U.S. policy. Assistant Secretary of State Winston Lord and Deputy Assistant Secretary of Defense Kurt Campbell testified on March 14. In his testimony, Ambassador Lord called the current crisis "one of the United States' most urgent and central issues in Asia," as well as "one of the most difficult."[45]

Lord said the United States had told Beijing that its tough political rhetoric and series of military exercises near Taiwan were "provocative and dangerous." Through private and public messages, consultation with allies, and the deployment of naval units to the region, the United States had underscored its interests as defined in the Taiwan Relations Act, namely, that any use of force against Taiwan would be viewed with "grave concern" by the United States and result in "grave consequences." The administration had "taken a number of prudent precautionary measures—including certain naval deployments in international waters near Taiwan—to underscore our interests, deter the use of force and prevent any miscalculation."

Lord emphasized, "neither Taiwan nor the PRC wants a military confrontation," but there was "a danger that misunderstandings and strong emotions on both sides could lead to a further increase in tensions and even unanticipated conflict." In the U.S. view, the PRC demonstrations of military strength were "designed to send a message to the Taiwan authorities to curb what the PRC regards as efforts to establish an independent Taiwan." The PRC believed that recent Taiwan policies were steps toward independence and were seen as "a challenge to the acceptance of a 'one-China' policy by Taipei." Beijing's leaders were "especially sensitive on this issue, which involves questions of sovereignty and national integrity."

U.S. policy toward the crisis was to urge restraint on the part of both Beijing and Taipei, encouraging the two sides to avoid provocation and to resume their high-level dialogue. "Our fundamental interest on the Taiwan question is that peace and stability be maintained and that the PRC and Taiwan work out their differences peacefully. At the same time, we will strictly avoid interfering as the two sides pursue peaceful resolution of differences." Noting the requirements of the 1979 Taiwan Relations Act, the assistant secretary said: "However serious, the present situation does not constitute a threat to Taiwan of the magnitude contemplated by the drafters of the TRA. The PRC pressure against Taiwan to date does not add up to a 'threat to the security or the social or economic system' of Taiwan."

Lord warned that if "armed conflict were actually to break out in the Taiwan Strait, the impact on Taiwan, the PRC and the region would be devastating." Adversely affected would be the PRC's "positive relationships with the United States and other industrialized countries that have allowed it to carry out the program of reform and opening to the outside world that has propelled the PRC's economic modernization." Taiwan's investment on the mainland would be effected, as would trade between Taiwan and the mainland. The smooth transition in Hong Kong would be placed in jeopardy, as would a whole range of PRC political, diplomatic, and economic interests. "The entire Sino-American relationship would be put at risk. China's ties with Japan and all of its other Asian neighbors would suffer grievously. So would its overall international standing." In addition, the conflict would be costly to the United States and its friends and allies. It would have "a destabilizing effect and constrict the commerce which is the economic life-blood of the region." It would force neighboring countries "to re-evaluate their own defense policies, possibly fueling an arms race with unforeseeable consequences." A conflict would also affect the lives of tens of thousands of Americans living and working in Taiwan and China. Lord then asked rhetorically:

Clinton's Policy: The Military Crisis

What would the U.S. do if commitments to peaceful settlement appeared to weaken, if hostilities appeared likely, if they appeared to be a threat to Taiwan's security or economic and social system? The Administration would immediately meet its obligations under the TRA to consult with the Congress on an appropriate response. The nature of our response would of course depend on the circumstances leading to a breakdown in relations across the Strait. But I hardly need remind this committee that the people of the United States feel strongly about the ability of the people of Taiwan to enjoy a peaceful future. This sentiment must not be underestimated. We have conveyed it to Beijing in unmistakable fashion through our statements and our actions.

Responding to suggestions that the administration spell out in detail its reaction to a use of force in the Taiwan Strait, Lord said, "Providing such details would be very unwise," noting that both the House and the Senate in their reports on the TRA observed that the U.S. response should not be determined beforehand but rather depend on the specific circumstances. "We have stated that grave consequences would flow from a use of force against Taiwan, and we have spelled out our determination to see that the future of Taiwan is worked out in a peaceful manner. We cannot and should not be more precise in advance about hypothetical scenarios. I am confident our message is clear. A resort to force with respect to Taiwan would directly involve American national interests and would carry grave risks. There should be no ambiguity about our posture in Beijing, Taipei or anywhere else." Indicating that the administration was urging restraint not only on Beijing but also Taipei, Lord said: "We have also told the Taiwan authorities that we expect them to avoid any actions that put at risk the interests of all parties concerned," adding, "the United States strongly opposes both aggression and provocation."

The assistant secretary told the committee: "The U.S. does not unilaterally have the capability to impose a solution which would guarantee peace and stability in the Taiwan Strait." The solution had to come from the two sides finding "a common framework for addressing their relationship," avoiding "provocative political or military actions that have the potential to destabilize the situation," and seeking "ways to address their differences peacefully." Lord said, "This is the only long-term guarantee of Taiwan's security. It is also a necessary element in guaranteeing long-term peace and stability in East Asia."

In his testimony during the same March 14 hearing, Kurt Campbell, deputy assistant secretary of defense for Asian and Pacific affairs, said the situation in the Taiwan Strait was being watched closely by the Pentagon, since "the recent series of PRC military exercises—to include the firing of ballistic missiles close to Taiwan—has increased tensions in the cross-Strait relationship."[46] He emphasized, "We have been very clear with our PRC interlocutors and in our public statements, and I want to be very clear today—the Department of Defense and this Administration view the PRC exercises as reckless and irresponsible." Campbell went on to say, however, that the PRC activity, "through highly provocative, and clearly aimed at intimidation, is expected to remain at the exercise level." The Pentagon official said, "the greatest danger to peace in the Taiwan Strait does not come from a PRC attack on Taiwan, or indeed any other direct military action . . . [but] from the potential for an accident or miscalculation."

According to Cambell, the United States could play two key roles "toward achieving [the] longer term goal of peaceful resolution of the dispute: (1) meeting our Taiwan Relations Act obligations, consistent with the Three Communiqués; and (2) continued comprehensive engagement with the PRC." In terms of the first role, Campbell said the Pentagon takes "very seriously" U.S. obligations under the TRA. Specifically, the Department of Defense assesses "the military balance to ascertain Taiwan's defense needs," provides "articles and services necessary to Taiwan to maintain a sufficient self-defense capability," keeps "Congress informed on Taiwan's security requirements," and maintains "the capability of the United States to resist force or coercion against the people of Taiwan." Weapon systems sold to Taiwan included "F-16 fighters, *Knox* Class Frigates, M-60A tanks, and the Modified Air Defense System—a Patriot system derivative."

Campbell said the *Independence* and *Nimitz* aircraft carrier battle groups sent to the Taiwan area during the crisis "are in a position to be helpful if they need be. They will also assist us in monitoring the situation. These forces do not serve to threaten China. . . . These forces serve as a reminder that American strength is solid and enduring, and we are prepared to protect our national interests."

Campbell argued that comprehensive engagement with the PRC continued to be in the U.S. interest, as well as in the interests of China, Taiwan, and the rest of Asia. "We choose to engage China even as tensions rise in the Taiwan Strait. We seek to prevent or minimize conflict through dialogue. As Secretary Perry has stated, engagement does not equate to appeasement, nor does it preclude using whatever means are necessary to protect our key national interests. It is only to say we prefer to protect our national interest through dialogue rather than force." He said, "In the longer term, engagement with China is our best hope for developing a better understanding of the Chinese. It also represents our best hope for influencing China to act as a responsible participant in regional affairs—including with respect to Taiwan."

According to the Pentagon, the U.S. strategy of comprehensive engagement with China related to Taiwan in three important ways: (1) "strategic clarity" with respect to U.S. determination that the Taiwan issue should be settled peacefully; (2) "tactical ambiguity" with respect to the precise U.S. response to a PRC use of force against Taiwan; and (3) close adherence to the basic principles of U.S. China policy followed since 1979 and contained in the three communiqués.[47]

In its own attempt to lower tensions with the mainland, the ROC announced that President Lee Teng-hui would not be making extensive trips overseas in the near future. Foreign Minister Fredrick Chien said on March 15 that Lee "does not foresee any foreign trip" except those required as reciprocal head-of-state visits. Taipei also hinted that it would initiate some sort of compromise in order to get mainland-Taiwan dialogue back on track. Nonetheless, Chien said his government would continue to try to rejoin the United Nations, because 75 percent of the Taiwan people favored such an attempt.[48]

On the same day, China announced yet another series of military exercises in the Taiwan Strait, this time involving live-fire combined forces operations eleven miles from the ROC-occupied islands of Matsu and Wuchiu.[49] Asked whether these exercises were a buildup in preparation for an invasion of Taiwan, Secretary of Defense Perry replied in characteristic fashion:

> I do not believe that the Chinese have any intention of attacking Taiwan. And that what we are seeing is a military exercise. Now, it is a military exercise in which, quite clearly, besides training their own troops, they are trying to intimidate Taiwan. I find that deplorable. I have told my colleagues that I deal with in China that I find it deplorable, [but] the Chinese do not have the capability to launch an invasion of Taiwan. Taiwan is 100 miles away. It is well fortified, well defended, and the Chinese, while they have a formidable army, do not have much amphibious capability. They do not have the power projection capability. . . . Our deployment of two carrier battle groups there is not because we are expecting a military conflict. . . . The message that we are sending is that the United States has a national interest in the security and stability of the western Pacific region. We have a powerful military force there to help us carry out our national interests. And we have complete freedom to move that military force within international waters to make that point.[50]

On March 17, Chinese Premier Li Peng warned the United States not to use its military force to threaten China. He said the deployment of U.S. naval forces around Taiwan would complicate the situation between the two Chinese governments. At the same time, however, he commented that the PRC did not object to the manner in which Taiwan's leader was selected. The critical point, he said, was that Taiwan's leaders must not move Taiwan in the direction of independence. He said, "It is our sincere hope that the people of Taiwan can live their lives in conditions of peace and stability, and I don't think it is difficult to achieve that. . . . What is most important is that the leader of Taiwan, no matter how he is selected, refrain from carrying out actions aimed at creating two Chinas or leading to independence for Taiwan in the future."[51]

These and other PRC comments suggested that much of China's anger was directed at Lee Teng-hui for leading Taiwan down the dangerous path of seeking independence. At the same time, China was clearly angry at the United States for deploying forces near Taiwan. On March 19 the PRC Foreign Ministry condemned Washington for its "brazen show of force" with its aircraft carrier battle groups, saying: "the United States is held accountable for current tensions in the Taiwan Strait area. . . . Taiwan is a part of China and not a U.S. protectorate."[52] To which Secretary Perry replied: "Beijing should know, and [the carrier deployments] will remind them, that while they are a great military power, that the premier, the strongest military power in the western Pacific is the United States. . . . America has the best damned Navy in the world, and no one should ever forget that."[53]

Meanwhile, U.S. and Taiwan military officials met in Washington to discuss arms sales. The Department of Defense emphasized that these were regular annual talks and were not in response to the current crisis. Taiwan's perennial request for submarines was denied, as well as requests for torpedoes, shoulder-fired Stinger air defense missiles, advanced medium-range air-to-air missiles, and laser-guided Maverick missiles. However, vehicle-launched Stinger missiles, an advanced targeting and navigation system for fighters, and electronic warfare devices were approved. Also, Taiwanese officers were given greater opportunities for training at U.S. facilities, and (in the first step toward a missile defense system for Taiwan) it was agreed that a U.S. team would be sent to Taiwan to analyze the PRC missile threat to the island. Together with earlier sales of advanced fighters, frigates, air defense systems, tanks, and other modern equipment, the March 1996 arms approvals helped to upgrade Taiwan's defense capabilities over the longer term.

As a further reflection of American determination to defend Taiwan, both Houses of Congress passed strong resolutions urging U.S. assistance to help Taiwan in the event of a PRC invasion, missile attack, or blockade (in the case of the House), and calling on the administration to review the quality and quantity of defense articles and services sold to Taiwan in view of the heightened military threat to its security.[54] Treasury Secretary Robert Rubin warned in Hong Kong that it would be difficult to renew China's most-favored-nation trading status in 1996 because of a host of issues with China, including Taiwan, proliferation, China's poor human rights record, and trade disagreements over rampant counterfeiting of compact disks, computer software, and other intellectual property.[55]

Taiwan's Elections and Reduced Tensions

On March 23 Taiwan held its first presidential election, with incumbent Lee Teng-hui winning 54 percent of the vote. Over 75 percent of the island's eligible voters went to the polls. The second-place winner was independence advocate Peng Ming-min of the Democratic Progressive Party, who won 21 percent. The two candidates who favored closer relations with mainland China, Lin Yang-kang of the New Party and Chen Li-an, an independent, won 15 percent and 10 percent of the vote respectively. Although not a definitive expression of the people's choice, if a vote for Lee implied favoring the status quo, a vote for Peng implied favoring eventual independence, and a vote for Lin and Chen implied favoring eventual unification, then about 55 percent of Taiwan's electorate favored the status quo, about 20 percent favored Taiwan's eventual independence, and about 25 percent favored eventual unification with China. Many more issues were of course involved in the electorate's choice, but these voting percentages roughly duplicated other polls undertaken on Taiwan to gauge public opinion on policy toward the mainland.

A refusal to be intimidated by the PRC had also become apparent in polls taken on the island before and during the election. For example, a poll taken in February 1995—before the crisis—indicated 23 percent of Taiwan's population supported reunification with China, while 15 percent backed independence. In August 1995, after two rounds of Chinese missile tests, 19 percent favored reunification and 15 percent favored independence. And in March 1996, after several months of military intimidation and verbal abuse from Beijing, 16 percent of those polled said they favored reunification and 17 percent said Taiwan should pursue independence. Some 46 percent of those polled said they favored the status quo in the Taiwan Strait.[56]

After Lee's victory in the elections, the White House issued a congratulatory statement on Taiwan's progress toward democracy: "We congratulate the people of Taiwan on their first [presidential] election. They have made great strides in the past several years toward democracy. We hope to see tensions in the Taiwan Strait greatly reduced in the days to come."[57]

Immediately following the elections, both Chinese sides did work to reduce tensions, although the level of their cooperation prior to Lee's June 1995 visit to the United States was not reached until late 1998 with the resumption of the Koo-Wang talks. Premier Lien Chan, Lee's vice-presidential running mate and heir apparent, said Taiwan "should pursue a policy of detente" with the mainland. The ROC Foreign Ministry hinted that an early summit meeting between Lee and Jiang Zemin could take place. Officials in the Straits Exchange Foundation said a high-ranking delegation could be sent to Beijing to discuss everything, "including very sensitive issues," if the PRC agreed. The ROC Economics Ministry said it would "take a more active approach in economic and trade policies toward the mainland." And the ROC Executive Yuan said it would submit legislation to the Legislative Yuan permitting under certain conditions the "three links" long-sought by Beijing: open trade, open travel, and open communication. For its part, Beijing ended its provocative military exercises and reduced its vituperation against Lee Teng-hui. However, the PRC refused to reopen high-level talks with Taipei, despite repeated entreaties by Taiwan. (By Taipei's count, some 114 public appeals were made by ROC officials until the mainland's favorable reply in February 1998).[58] As overall tensions lowered in the region, the United States quietly withdrew its carrier task forces from the area.[59]

In an interview with *Wall Street Journal* editors on March 26, President Lee Teng-hui emphasized that he was not promoting Taiwan independence, but rather China's unification under a democratic system. He favored expanded cross-Strait relations, but in a gradual manner. At the same time, he wanted the United States to sell more advanced weapons to Taiwan and to assist Taipei to enter the World Trade Organization, without waiting for PRC approval or its admission. According to *Journal* editors, Lee did not seem to favor efforts by Republican congressmen to push for diplomatic recognition nor did he seem eager to discuss congressional efforts to invite him to Washington.[60]

Nonetheless, on March 28 the Senate gave final congressional approval to the Foreign Relations Authorization Act reorganizing the U.S. foreign policy establishment. Included in the bill was an invitation to President Lee to visit the United States, provisions to improve ties with Taiwan, toughen human rights pressure on China, allow a special U.S. envoy to Tibet, and set up Radio Free Asia broadcasts to China. The bill passed the Senate by a vote of 52 to 44 and the House by 226 to 172. The vote was almost exclusively along party lines, and the White House promised it would veto the bill.

With the Taiwan crisis in remission, the Clinton administration turned to other pressing matters in Sino-American relations. One of the most difficult concerned possible sanctions against China for missile and nuclear technology proliferation. During the height of the Taiwan crisis, Deputy Assistant Secretary of State Robert Einhorn went to Beijing to discuss a range of proliferation issues, including the PRC sale of ring magnets to Pakistan, antiship cruise missiles to Iran, chemical weapons equipment to Iran, and Chinese missile and nuclear cooperation with Pakistan. Einhorn found the Chinese polite, but they refused to halt their programs of cooperation with either Iran or Pakistan. PRC officials noted—correctly for the most part—that the individual items sold were not specifically banned by international treaty or agreement. The magnets, for example, did not appear on the list of items subject to controls under the NPT, and the chemical equipment sold to Iran could be used for either military or civilian purposes.[61] Meanwhile, the U.S. Export-Import Bank, which had placed a thirty-day hold on processing loans to China after a request from Secretary Christopher to give the administration time to decide how to respond to China's shipment of the ring magnets, announced that it would resume consideration of some $10 billion in potential loans in mid-April, many involving large American corporations such as Caterpillar and Westinghouse.[62]

In the wake of the crisis over Taiwan, President Clinton resisted growing congressional pressure to impose sanctions on Beijing for its proliferation activities. The administration, for example, avoided having to impose legally mandated sanctions by concluding that Beijing's leadership probably was unaware that the China National Nuclear Corporation—a state-owned firm with government officials on the board of directors—was planning to sell the magnets to a Pakistani nuclear weapons laboratory for centrifuges that produce fissile materials for nuclear weapons. Under this interpretation, the administration was obliged only to bar the corporation from conducting business with the United States, rather than imposing more sweeping sanctions against China as a nation.[63] In mid-April the administration approved the transfer of some $368 million in military equipment to Pakistan and the return of $120 million for weapons and spare parts never delivered. At the same time, the administration decided not to oppose the approval of a $160 million Ex-Im Bank guarantee of a bank loan for the purchase of three Boeing airliners to China. In this way, the White House decided not to punish either China or Pakistan for the ring magnet sale, hoping that further dialogue would enable the United States to advance its nonproliferation interests with both countries.[64]

Conclusion

In spite of the crisis over Taiwan and in spite of persistent problems with China over proliferation, trade, and human rights, the Clinton administration chose to adhere to its strategy of comprehensive engagement with the PRC. Unable to resolve any of these issues—either through dialogue or confrontation—the administration concluded that dialogue was better than confrontation, even though dialogue might be ineffective, at least in the short term. Over the long term, the administration hoped that dialogue would convince Chinese leaders to become more cooperative on global, regional, and bilateral issues.

Still, there were limits as to how far the Clinton administration would go in overlooking objectionable Chinese behavior for the sake of engagement. As seen in the case of the Taiwan Strait crisis, the PRC could push the envelope too far, resulting in a confrontation in which the United States was willing to use all necessary means to protect its interests, even at the cost of engagement. The Taiwan crisis demonstrated that Taiwan had value in U.S. strategic calculations, not the least of which was Taiwan's relationship to peace and stability in the Western Pacific and its symbol of American commitment to oppose hegemony in the region.

Nonetheless, a change in the tone of U.S. relations with Taipei and Beijing seemed to emerge after the Taiwan crisis. There was increased talk in Washington that the Sino-American confrontation in the Taiwan Strait could have been avoided if Taiwan had not pushed its international representation so far. Recognizing that trends on Taiwan pointed to even greater support for independent political status in the future, and that trends on the mainland pointed to a heightened sense of nationalism backed by greater power, a growing number of American analysts became worried that the United States might have difficulty avoiding a future conflict with China over Taiwan. This group of mostly academic specialists, with some sympathy from China experts within the U.S. government, pondered aloud whether the time had come for the United States to use its leverage over Taiwan to foreclose the possibility of Taiwan moving in the direction of independence.

Thus, while the Taiwan crisis resulted in a clear demonstration of U.S. determination to prevent a PRC use of force against Taiwan, the crisis also resulted in increased activity in the United States to find a way to prevent a possible future Sino-American war over Taiwan. As pointed out in the Preface, questions about Taiwan and its future were increasingly asked after March 1996, with conclusions not always in Taiwan's favor. The final chapter will revisit some of these questions and seek to answer many of them in light of the considerations outlined in this book.

Notes

1. Associated Press report from Beijing, January 4, 1996; *Wall Street Journal*, January 5, 1996, p. A6; ibid, January 8, 1996, p. A9; Reuters report from Taipei, January 7, 1996; ibid., report from Beijing, January 9, 1996.

2. Reuters report from Beijing, January 10, 1996.

3. See Associated Press report from New York, January 24, 1996; Reuters report from Beijing, January 24, 1996; Reuters report from New York, January 24, 1996; Reuters report from Taipei, January 24, 1996; UPI report from New York, January 24, 1996.

4. UPI report from Washington, D.C., January 24, 1996.

5. See, for example, James R. Lilley and Chuck Downs, eds., *Crisis in the Taiwan Strait* (Washington, DC: American Enterprise Institute and National Defense University, 1997).

6. Chu Shulong, "The Second PRC-US War: International Involvement in China's Unification," in Greg Austin, ed., *Missile Diplomacy and Taiwan's Future: Innovations in Politics and Military Power* (Canberra: Strategic and Defence Studies Centre, Australian National University, 1997), pp. 227-39.

7. Jiang Minfang and Duan Zhaoxin, "Taiwan zhanlue diwei danxi" (The analysis of Taiwan's strategic position), *The Navy* 8 (1995), p. 9. Cited in You Ji, "Missile Diplomacy and PRC Domestic Politics," in Greg Austin, ed., *Missile Diplomacy and Taiwan's Future: Innovations in Politics and Military Power*, pp. 46-47.

8. Lu Junyuan, "Taiwan's Geostrategic Value Makes Reunification Essential," in *Taiwan Studies* (Beijing), March 20, 1996, in *FBIS-China*, March 20, 1996.

9. Reuters report from Beijing, February 1, 1996; Reuters report from Washington, D.C., February 1, 1996, quoting State Department spokesman Nicholas Burns.

10. *Washington Post*, February 5, 1996, p. A1; Reuters report from Washington, D.C., February 5, 1996; Associated Press report from Washington, D.C., February 5, 1996.

11. "If China Attacks Taiwan," *Washington Post*, February 6, 1996, p. A14.

12. William J. Perry, "Address to the Aspin Institute (Washington Institute for Near East Policy) on U.S. National Strategy in the Middle East," *News Briefing* (Washington, DC: Office of the Assistant Secretary of Defense, Public Affairs, February 6, 1996).

13. "The United States and the Security of Taiwan: Testimony by Ambassador Winston Lord, Assistant Secretary of State for East Asian and Pacific Affairs, before the Subcommittee on East Asia and the Pacific, Senate Foreign Relations Committee, February 7, 1996," ms.

14. "China's Nuclear Exports," *Washington Post*, February 9, 1996, p. A20; UPI report from New York, February 8, 1996.

15. *Washington Post*, February 11, 1996, p. A26.

16. Reuters report from Beijing, February 29, 1996.

17. Reuters report from Beijing, February 9, 1996.

18. *Wall Street Journal*, February 26, 1996, p. A9; Dow Jones report from Washington, D.C., February 28, 1996.

19. "Secretary of Defense William J. Perry, National Defense University, February 13, 1996," *News Release* (Washington, DC: Office of Assistant Secretary of Defense for Public Affairs, February 13, 1996). A more or less carbon copy of his comments on China policy can be found in "Secretary of Defense William J. Perry, Commonwealth Club of California and World Forum of Silicon Valley, February 23, 1996," *News Release* (Washington, DC: Office of Assistant Secretary of Defense for Public Affairs, February 26, 1996).

20. "Worldwide Threat Assessment Brief to the Senate Select Committee on Intelligence, Statement for the Record, 22 February 1996, John Deutch, Director of Central Intelligence," ms.

21. "Statement by Assistant Secretary of State for Intelligence and Research, Toby T. Gati, before the Senate Select Committee on Intelligence, Hearing on Current and Projected National Security Threats to the United States, February 22, 1996," ms.

22. Reuters report from Washington, D.C., February 15, 1996; Associated Press report from Washington, D.C., February 15, 1996.

23. Reuters report from Taipei, February 17, 1996.

24. For a report on the new plan and its background, see *Washington Post*, February 21, 1996, p. A27.

25. *Washington Post*, February 28, 1996, p. A23; *Wall Street Journal*, February 28, 1996, p. A3.

26. Dole's remarks were made on ABC's "This Week With David Brinkley." Associated Press report from Washington, D.C., March 3, 1996.

27. Reuters report from Jacksonville, Florida, March 10, 1996.

28. UPI report from Washington, D.C., March 6, 1996.

29. Reuters report from Beijing, March 4, 1996.

30. *Washington Post*, March 6, 1996, pp. A1, A10.

31. The M-9 is 9.1 meters in length, weighing 6,200 kgs. It has a range of 600 kms, and its 500 kgs warhead can be conventional, chemical, or nuclear. Reuters report from Taipei, March 8, 1996.

32. Reuters report from Washington, D.C., March 5, 1996; UPI report from Beijing, March 5, 1996.

33. Associated Press report from Beijing, March 7, 1996.

34. Quoted in Associated Press report from Washington, D.C., March 6, 1996.

35. *Washington Post*, March 8, 1996, p. A26.

36. "DoD News Briefing, March 8, 1996, Secretary of Defense William J. Perry," *News Briefing* (Washington, DC: Office of the Assistant Secretary of Defense for Public Affairs, March 8, 1996).

37. Reuters report from Washington, D.C., March 14, 1996.

38. Reuters report from Santiago, Chile, March 11, 1996. Perry was visiting Chile at the time of the statement.

39. *Washington Post*, March 12, 1996, p. A10; *Wall Street Journal*, March 12, 1996, p. A14.

40. Reuters report from Washington, D.C., March 13, 1996.

41. For the views of several scholars on the then-current crisis, see Austin, ed., *Missile Diplomacy and Taiwan's Future: Innovations in Politics and Military Power*.

42. Reuters report from Beijing, March 11, 1996.

43. UPI report from Beijing, March 14, 1996.

44. *Wall Street Journal*, March 14, 1996, p. A3; Reuters report from San Francisco, March 14, 1996; Associated Press report from Washington, D.C., March 14, 1996.

45. "The United States and the Security of Taiwan," Testimony by Assistant Secretary of State for East Asian and Pacific Affairs Ambassador Winston Lord, before the House International Relations Committee, Subcommittee on East Asia and the Pacific, March 14, 1996, ms.

46. "Statement by Dr. Kurt M. Campbell, Deputy Assistant Secretary of Defense for Asian and Pacific Affairs, before the House International Relations Committee, Subcommittee on Asia and the Pacific, 14 March 1996," ms.

47. "Strategic clarity" and "tactical ambiguity" were terms used by Kurt Campbell to describe Clinton administration policy toward Taiwan and China in his testimony before Congress on March 14, 1996. See *Washington Post*, March 15, 1996, p. A24.

48. Reuters report from Taipei, March 15, 1996; Associated Press report from Taipei, March 15, 1996.

49. *Washington Post*, March 16, 1995, p. A1.

50. Comments of Secretary of Defense William J. Perry abroad the *USS Carl Vinson* as reported in Department of Defense *News Briefing*, March 16, 1996. For an interesting exchange between reporters and Defense Department spokesmen over the U.S. role in the crisis, see *News Briefing*, March 19, 1996.

51. Quoted in *Washington Post*, March 18, 1996, p. A13.

52. Reuters report from Beijing, March 19, 1996.

53. Reuters report from Washington, D.C., March 19, 1996. See also, *Washington Post*, March 20, 1996, p. A21.

54. *Washington Post*, March 22, 1996, p. A28.

55. *Wall Street Journal*, March 19, 1996, p. A14.

56. Surveys sponsored by Taipei's *United Daily News* as reported by Reuters from Taipei, March 8, 1996.

57. *Washington Post*, March 24, 1996, p. A1. Major American newspapers also congratulated Taiwan. See, for example, *Washington Post*, March 25, 1996, p. A16; *Wall Street Journal*, March 25, 1996, p. A14.

58. "MAC Chairman Dr. Chang King-yuh at the December 31, 1998 Press Conference," *MAC News Briefing* 108 (January 4, 1999), p. 2.

59. *Wall Street Journal*, March 25, 1996, p. A10.

60. See Melanie Kirkpatrick's interview with Lee Teng-hui in *Wall Street Journal*, March 27, 1996, p. A22. Also, *Washington Post*, March 29, 1996, p. A20.

61. *Washington Post*, March 24, 1996, p. A1.

62. *Wall Street Journal*, March 25, 1996, p. A2.

63. *Washington Post*, March 27, 1996, p. A25; *Wall Street Journal*, March 27, 1996, p. A24.

64. *Washington Post*, April 17, 1996, p. A28.

9

Conclusion: The Jiang-Clinton Summits and Beyond

As this study has demonstrated, many elements comprise the Taiwan conundrum in U.S. China policy. When viewed from the perspective of American values such as democracy, free enterprise, freedom, self-determination, individual liberty, and human rights, Taiwan is respected and admired by the American people. This favorable impression is reflected frequently in editorials from newspapers across the nation. There is very little sentiment, from the values point of view, for the United States to sacrifice Taiwan's interests to advance Sino-American relations. Indeed, from this perspective, U.S. interests are served by continued American support for Taiwan.

From the point of view of the Congress, U.S. policy should reflect greater balance and fairness in relations with Beijing and Taipei, as mandated by the Taiwan Relations Act. There is no congressional approval for making additional concessions over Taiwan to further U.S. ties with China. As a body, Congress is very supportive of Taiwan, while at the same time generally in favor of engagement with the PRC. Congress is deeply committed to defending Taiwan against PRC aggression, and it carefully monitors all factors related to Taiwan's security. Many Members support a larger role for Taiwan in the international community, and some sentiment exists in Congress in favor of an independent Taiwan. On many occasions, Congress has shown that if administration policies harm Taiwan's security or treat Taipei in too shabby a fashion, it will write binding legislation to correct these faults. Given the appropriation, oversight, and other powers of Congress, no administration can ignore congressional concerns over Taiwan.

Therefore, from the perspectives of American values and the U.S. Congress, there is not much of a conundrum insofar as Taiwan policy is concerned. On the other hand, the conundrum in U.S. policy toward China is far more evident, with the American public and Congress well aware that engagement has not lived up to its expectations—as evidenced by continued problems in proliferation, trade, espionage, human rights, Taiwan, the South China Sea, regional security issues, and frequently uncooperative attitudes in the U.N. Security Council.

When the Taiwan and China conundrums are viewed from the point of view of U.S. interests, however, assessments become more murky. From the national interest perspective, China is a major power with which the United States must deal on a daily basis. Some way must be found to accommodate the PRC's growth in national power, else a military confrontation between China and the United States might be unavoidable. Engagement seems the only logical choice for U.S. policy, and President Clinton's determination not to allow tension in one area of Sino-American relations to undermine the entire relationship seems valid under present circumstances.

Taiwan, on the other hand, is a worthy U.S. friend and former ally, but its role in world affairs is vastly overshadowed by that of the PRC. In other words, Taiwan is less important than China in most areas of U.S. national interests. This is particularly true in hard national interests such as security and diplomacy; slightly less so in softer national interests such as international finance and trade; and much less true in the more idealist side of American interests such as human rights and support for market democracies. Therefore, from the perspective of national interests, Taiwan is a conundrum in U.S. policy because Beijing often links its cooperation with Washington to U.S. ties with Taiwan.

On the other hand, as China becomes more assertive in exercising its growing national power, China herself has become a conundrum in U.S. policy from the perspective of U.S. national interests. Depending upon which interest takes priority —security, trade, human rights, promotion of democratic values—U.S. policy toward China can be formulated and evaluated quite differently. Moreover, there is not a clear American consensus on the key issue of whether China poses a threat to U.S. interests either now or in the foreseeable future. The various combinations of perspectives on national interests—e.g., which interest takes priority during the post-Cold War era and what is the nature of China's potential threat to U.S. interests—guarantee that few aspects of U.S. policy toward China will escape controversy. What this means is that while arguments can be made that concessions over Taiwan might be in the U.S. interests in its relations with China, counter arguments can be made that such concessions would be premature and perhaps foolhardy. Politically speaking, no single approach can control the China-Taiwan policy agenda.

The U.S. conundrum in its ties with both Taiwan and China becomes even more complex from the perspective of U.S. strategy and policy. As shown in the detailed examination of the 1992-1996 period of the Clinton administration, none of the outstanding issues in Sino-American relations could be solved. In the case of Taiwan, the issue assumed crisis proportions as the people of the island and their government became more determined to gain a respected place in the world, regardless of Beijing's anger or Washington's apprehension.

Despite significant policy differences with the PRC, the Clinton administration worked hard to maintain a cooperative relationship with Beijing. At times, the administration seemed to harden its policy toward China; but mostly it tended, at least publicly, to overlook Chinese affronts. The sensitivity with which the administration approached China could be seen in numerous policy statements and in Clinton's hesitation to confront China or to impose sanctions. At the same time, however, there were an increasing number of Americans becoming convinced that China had moved beyond acceptable behavior in areas of security, trade, and human rights.

Essentially, the problem for the Clinton administration was how to persuade or pressure Beijing to change its objectionable policies. Even when China refused to change, the administration continued to argue in favor of engagement and partnership. These arguments usually were framed in contrast with the straw man of containment; few Americans wanted to contain China and fewer thought it possible to do so. Most Americans wanted to engage China in a comprehensive, cooperative way, but not at the expense of American values or interests. The real question was the type or extent of engagement with China: should China be treated as an ally, a friend, a business partner, a rival, a future threat, or some combination of all of the above? On that question, there was no consensus either in or out of government.

The difficulty, therefore, was not engagement per se with China, but rather that engagement did not produce short-term, positive change in Chinese behavior. China cooperated with the United States when its leaders decided it was in China's (or their own) best interests; Beijing did not cooperate with the United States when it was against China's (or its leaders') best interests. Moreover, there were severe policy differences inside the PRC leadership itself, making definitions of Chinese interests both tenuous and inconsistent. As an instrument for changing PRC behavior—which was the most common justification given for the strategy— engagement often was a short-term failure even while it offered long-term but unproven promise. Nonetheless, the strategy of engagement did serve U.S. interests in maintaining high-level dialogue with Chinese officials and thus preserved the relationship even during the Taiwan crisis—a worthwhile end in itself.

The Clinton administration attempted to build a consensus supporting its China policy, but the failure of engagement to produce anticipated results undermined the credibility of engagement itself. Congress, with both Houses under Republican control after 1994, seized upon the failures of engagement to criticize Clinton and to seek legislative changes in his policies toward China and Taiwan.

The crisis over Taiwan in 1995–1996 revealed a fundamental flaw in the one-China policy of the United States. For most of the postwar period, the United States had strongly supported democratic reform on Taiwan, even while backing the one-China policy of the authoritarian KMT. The KMT's "one China" was the Republic of China, as opposed to the CCP's "one China" which was the People's Republic of China. However, the one-China policy of both Chinese governments helped to sustain peace in the Taiwan Strait from the late 1950s onward.

The successful emergence of democracy on Taiwan in the mid-1980s allowed sentiments of self-determination on the island to come to the surface. These sentiments were powerful both politically and emotionally, fueled by strong Taiwanese resentment over past abuses by KMT mainlanders. After Lee Teng-hui became president in 1988, he increased the role of Taiwanese in determining ROC policies and pressed hard for an expanded autonomous role for Taiwan in international affairs. Beijing saw these efforts as part of a plot to achieve Taiwan independence or "two Chinas." The PRC could accept the status quo in the Taiwan Strait—as long as the eventual goal of unification was agreed upon and some movement in that direction could be seen—and it could promise Taiwan a great deal of autonomy as a special administrative region under its one country, two systems formula; but Beijing could not accept an independent Taiwan, nor was it willing to accept the ROC government as an equal Chinese government.

The imperatives at work in both Chinas, and the broad definition of American interests in both sides of the Taiwan Strait, created a classic contradiction in U.S. foreign policy. Washington supported the democratic process on Taiwan, but that process helped to precipitate a crisis with China, a country with which Washington wanted to maintain strategic cooperation. American foreign policy often has been faced with contradictions between its idealistic impluse and pragmatic interest, but in the case of Taiwan the reconciliation of these values, interests, strategies, and policies has proven extraordinarily difficult.

All three parties—the United States, China, and Taiwan—adhere to fundamental principles on which there is little room for compromise. China must defend its territorial integrity; Taiwan has every right to seek self-determination and international expression; and the United States must support democracy on Taiwan, engage China, and maintain a favorable balance of power in the Western Pacific. These principles brought all sides into a confrontation in 1996 that no one wanted but no one could avoid.

During the first term of the Clinton administration, therefore, very little opportunity existed for resolution of the Taiwan issue. This was mainly because: (1) U.S. concessions over Taiwan would not solve other problems in Sino-American relations; (2) such accommodation to Beijing would not be accepted by the Congress and (probably) not by the American public; (3) Beijing and Taipei were not yet ready to resolve their differences in a mutually acceptable manner; and (4) the Taiwan conundrum in U.S. policy was now inexorably linked to the China conundrum in U.S. policy. This basic conclusion—that the solution to the Taiwan issue was not yet in sight—remained valid through the end of 1998 and indeed through the time of writing in mid-1999.

Conclusion: Summits and Beyond

Continuity of U.S. Policy into Clinton's Second Term

In the November 5, 1996, elections President Bill Clinton retained his office, while the Republicans retained control of the Senate, the House of Representatives, and the majority of state governorships. Clinton won 49.9 percent of the popular vote and 379 electoral votes; the Republican presidential candidate Bob Dole won 41.4 percent of the popular vote and 159 electoral votes; and Ross Perot won 8.6 percent of the vote and no electoral votes. Of the 100 seats in the Senate, Republicans in the 105th Congress held fifty-five and Democrats forty-five. In the new House of Representatives, Republicans held a twenty-seat majority, with 227 seats, compared to 207 seats held by the Democrats, with one seat occupied by an independent. Whereas the GOP added two seats to its majority in the Senate, the GOP lost nine seats to the Democrats in the House. The elections were interpreted by both political parties as reflecting voter comfort in maintaining a balance of power in Washington and a general satisfaction with the way the country was being run.

As is often the case, there were major changes in administration personnel immediately following the election. Virtually the entire top echelon of Clinton's foreign policy and national security team was replaced. New appointees include Madeleine Albright as Secretary of State; William Cohen as Secretary of Defense; Bill Richardson as Ambassador to the United Nations; Sandy Berger as White House national security adviser; Charlene Barshefsky as acting U.S. Trade Representative; and Stanley Roth as Assistant Secretary of State for East Asian and Pacific Affairs. Tony Lake failed to receive Senate support as Director of Central Intelligence, a position that was assumed by George Tenet.

Foreign policy and national security played minor roles in the elections, with most Americans focusing on domestic issues. There was no indication during the election that a new national security strategy would be forthcoming. Engagement and enlargement would continue as the national security strategy of the United States under President Clinton. On the other hand, there were indications that Clinton would like to continue a tradition of second-term presidents by making a mark on foreign policy. In particular, the president wanted to see the expansion of NATO and a more stable relationship with China.

The administration said it would concentrate on Asia early during its second term; however, the basic elements of U.S. strategy and policy toward the region would not change. American goals in Asia continued to focus on security, prosperity, and freedom. The U.S. strategy of comprehensive engagement and enlargement (expressed as a regional strategy of building a new Pacific community) remained in place, including such elements as stability, deterrence, balance of power, peaceful evolution, integration, and the expansion of market democracies. The Clinton administration reaffirmed its commitment to remain engaged in the Asian Pacific over the next four years and promised continuity in its basic strategies and policies.

In terms of China policy, the Clinton administration faced the same outstanding issues with Beijing as it had previously. In economic areas, these included such issues as the terms of China's entrance into the World Trade Organization, trade, investment, IPR protection, legal infrastructure, and technology transfers. In political areas, these issues included human rights and cooperation in the United Nations. In security areas, issues included nuclear technology and missile proliferation, transparency of PRC strategy and PLA capabilities, sea lane and territorial issues in South China Sea, and Taiwan. The issues of illegal Chinese contributions to the Democratic Party and PRC spying at U.S. nuclear weapons laboratories emerged later during the administration.

There was early expectation within the second Clinton administration that Sino-American relations would improve markedly if major controversy could be avoided in the areas of trade, proliferation, human rights, Hong Kong, and Taiwan; if some success in bilateral discussions could be achieved in specific areas of disagreement; if the domestic political environment in both countries remained stable; and if regional or international crises did not arise to derail the relationship. This was an optimistic assessment, but one which seemed possible if Jiang Zemin and the more moderate elements of the CCP power elite could remain in control of Chinese domestic and foreign policies. For the most part, this optimism remained in place through the end of 1998, since Sino-American relations continued to be managed without the tensions generated in the 1995–1996 period. (By mid-1999, this optimism had faded—but that story is beyond the time frame of this book.) At the same time, however, almost none of the problems in the U.S.-PRC relationship had been resolved; and, indeed, the most fundamental dilemma of how the United States could live in harmony with a major rival power in East Asia seemed to intensify as the PLA continued to modernize, the CCP strongly reaffirmed its political dictatorship in China, and the PRC exercised its national power both regionally and globally. As Library of Congress analyst Robert Sutter concluded in one of his books of the period: "there is little agreement in Washington on how the United States should achieve" its national objectives in regards to China.[1]

In terms of Taiwan, the continuity in U.S. policy was perhaps best expressed by Richard Bush, chairman of the American Institute in Taiwan (AIT), in remarks in Los Angeles in January 1998.[2] He said emphatically: "It is unnecessary for Taiwan friends to worry that the United States is going to hurt the interests of the island. The support for people on Taiwan in the Administration, in the Congress, and in our country is too strong for that." Bush said the "fundamental policy approach" of the United States for several decades "has been to strike a balance in our relations with the PRC and with the people of Taiwan, as reflected since 1979 in a framework composed of the Taiwan Relations Act and the US-PRC communiqués." He went to explain that "the thread that runs through US policy toward Taiwan . . . has been to create contexts in which the people and authorities on Taiwan—and the PRC—act. We have not sought to impose our solutions but have attempted to fashion circumstances that will lead the parties involved to act in ways that are in the best interests of all concerned, including the United States." In terms of relations across the Taiwan Strait, Bush stressed three key points:

- Our abiding interest is in a peaceful resolution of the relationship between Taipei and Beijing through the direct interaction of the two parties.
- The United States will continue to foster an environment that facilitates a peaceful resolution and reduces the potential for conflict.
- We continue to emphasize to both sides the need to resume dialogue and to avoid actions that the other could view as provocative.

Although none of the elements of U.S. policy toward Taiwan and China changed through the end of 1998, there was a change in the tone of the U.S. approach to China from one of fairly frequent disagreement over various issues to one of ardent promotion of friendly engagement and strategic partnership. This renewed emphasis on engagement and partnership was seen in the many high-level visits by U.S. and Chinese officials, consummated in President Jiang Zemin's state visit to the United States in the fall of 1997 and President Clinton's reciprocal state visit to China in the summer of 1998.

The Jiang-Clinton Summits

From October 26 through November 3, 1997, President Jiang Zemin became the first Chinese leader in twelve years to come to the United States on an official state visit. In addition to spending several days in Washington, D.C., Jiang visited Hawaii, Colonial Williamsburg, Independence Hall in Philadelphia, Harvard, and the New York Stock Exchange. The trip was heavy on symbolism but light in substance, with Jiang donning a tricorn hat, ringing the opening bell on Wall Street, speaking at prestigious Harvard University, and swimming the breast stroke off Waikiki Beach. Just prior to Jiang's trip, President Clinton once again affirmed U.S. interests in engaging China in a speech at Voice of America in Washington, D.C.[3]

The summits accomplishments were cited in a joint statement issued from the White House on October 29.[4] From the point of view of the United States, the summit's major accomplishments were China's agreement to stop supplying nuclear technology to Iran and China's commitment to stop selling cruise missiles to Iran. Having these nonproliferation promises in hand, the Clinton administration was able to allow U.S. firms like Westinghouse Electric and General Electric to compete for sales of nuclear power reactors to China. Boeing was also pleased with another multibillion Chinese order for some fifty aircraft. Disagreements between Clinton and Jiang were most pointed in the area of human rights, with Jiang saying Chinese actions in Tibet were analogous to Lincoln's freeing of the slaves. Congressional leaders had an opportunity to meet with Jiang and lecture him on forced abortions and the relationship between economic prosperity and political freedom.

In return, Jiang Zemin received renewed American assurances that Washington would not support the independence of Taiwan, a high profile state visit that contrasted sharply with the unofficial trip of Lee Teng-hui in 1995, the rapt attention of corporate America, and a solid political boost at home as China's internationally recognized leader. The establishment of a "hot line" between Washington and Beijing also symbolized U.S. recognition of China as a major power with which it had to maintain the highest possible level of communications in times of crisis, a similar message conveyed by a maritime communications agreement to prevent accidental confrontations at sea between U.S. and Chinese naval forces. At the same time, Jiang made no concessions over the right of China to use force against Taiwan nor did he apologize for the use of force to restore order and stability in Tiananmen Square.

For their part, the Chinese seemed very satisfied with the Jiang-Clinton summit, primarily because it seemed to signal an adjustment in U.S. policy toward more accommodation to China's rising power. *Xinhua*, for example, carried a news analysis on November 9, 1997, in which it stated that Jiang's visit to the United States and Boris Yeltsin's visit to China later in November meant that a new multipolar world was developing in which China, the United States, and Russia cooperated to ensure world peace.[5]

Foreign Minister Qian Qichen expressed a similar view in mid-November 1997, when he observed that the Jiang-Clinton summit moved Sino-American relations into a new phase of cooperation in building toward a constructive strategic partnership. Problems in the relationship remained, he said, the most important of which was Taiwan, and developing bilateral ties will be a long and complicated process; but the framework and orientation for Sino-American relations in the twenty-first century were being laid in a positive fashion.[6]

That the Sino-American constructive strategic partnership was moving forward also was evident in President Clinton's reciprocal state visit to China between June 25 and July 3, 1998. The White House provided a long list of achievements in the summit, including specific progress in nonproliferation and security issues, human rights, economic and commercial ties, energy and environment cooperation, science and technology exchanges, cooperation in the field of law, law enforcement, and people-to-people exchanges.[7] What was most memorable about the trip, however, was the unprecedented opportunity for President Clinton to debate Jiang Zemin publicly over human rights and democracy and to argue openly in favor of individual freedom as being the key ingredient for modernization. In his speech at Beijing University, for example, the president spoke of wanting to build a new relationship with China for the twenty-first century.[8] He argued in a polite yet direct way that freedom was the key to both stability and prosperity, two goals shared by Chinese leaders and the Chinese people. At his best in town meeting-

Conclusion: Summits and Beyond

style settings, the president interacted well with Chinese citizens in question-and-answer sessions after his formal presentations and in radio talk shows.

In his own assessment of the trip in Hong Kong on July 3 before departing for the United States, Clinton emphasized that change was underway in China and expressed his personal conviction that the best way for the United States to handle the restrictions on free speech, assembly, and worship was to deal "directly, forcefully, but respectfully, with the Chinese about our values." The president felt he did this, while at the same time expanding cooperation with the Chinese in areas of importance to U.S. interests.[9]

The most controversial aspect of the president's state visit centered on Taiwan. In Shanghai the president said the United States did not support Taiwan independence, did not support two Chinas or one China and one Taiwan, and did not support Taiwan's participation in international organizations requiring nation-state status for membership. When asked by a journalist whether his "three no's" had changed U.S. policy toward Taiwan, Clinton responded, "I did not announce any change in policy. In fact, the question of independence for Taiwan, for example, has been American policy for a very long time.... So I didn't intend, and I don't believe I did, change the substance of our position in any way by anything that I said. I certainly didn't try to do that."[10] This interpretation was echoed by AIT Chairman Richard Bush in Taipei on July 8.[11] In a news conference just prior to his departure after having briefed Taiwan officials on the Clinton visit to China, Bush said the three-no's did not indicate a shift in U.S. policy toward Taiwan and that the summit meetings between Clinton and Jiang did not harm Taiwan's interests. He said there was a difference between "opposition" and "no support": "'Opposition' is on the negative side of the spectrum, 'support' is on the positive side of the spectrum, while 'no support' belongs to somewhere in the middle." The U.S. position, Bush said, "is that cross-Strait differences should be resolved peacefully and that we don't support Taiwan independence."

The PRC seemed very pleased with the Clinton trip. The Foreign Ministry spokesman said the visit was "crowned with success" and that "new progress has been made toward the goal of establishing Sino-U.S. constructive strategic partnership."[12] Clinton's statement on the three-no's was cited as a reaffirmation of the U.S. commitment to the three joint communiqués and its "proper handling of the Taiwan issue."

The optimism generated by the Jiang-Clinton summits, coupled with U.S. concerns that future Sino-American confrontation over Taiwan had to be avoided if at all possible, contributed to increased efforts by the administration during 1997–1998 to encourage renewed high-level dialogue between Beijing and Taipei. This objective was at least partially achieved by the October 14–19, 1998, trip to the mainland by Straits Exchange Foundation (SEF) Chairman Koo Chen-fu at the invitation of his counterpart Wang Daohan, Chairman of the Association for Relations Across the Taiwan Straits (ARATS).

Second Round of Koo-Wang Talks

It will be recalled that the first meeting between Koo and Wang occurred in Singapore in April 1993. At that meeting, four agreements were signed on the use and verification of certificates of authentication, on inquiries and compensation for lost registered mail, on a system of contacts and meetings between SEF and ARATS officials, and a joint agreement on Koo-Wang talks. A second meeting between Koo and Wang was scheduled to take place in 1995, but it was postponed indefinitely by the PRC after President Lee's visit to the United States. According to Taiwan's Mainland Affairs Council, ROC high-ranking officials made "114 public appeals for an early resumption of negotiations" and at least four SEF letters were sent to ARATS calling for a resumption of normal exchanges between the two sides.[13] The PRC decision to resume dialogue with Taiwan finally came in February 1998, although some thawing of the ice began to occur in late 1997.[14]

Part of the reason for the delay in reestablishing cross-Strait talks was Beijing's conclusion that the principal obstacle to unification was U.S. support for Taiwan, because it emboldened the government of Lee Teng-hui to pursue pragmatic diplomacy and to say "arrogant" things. Consequently, throughout 1996 and the first half of 1997, China focused on relations with the United States and largely ignored cross-Strait dialogue. By mid-1997, however, there were signs that the PRC was willing to reengage Taipei, although not at the level maintained prior to the June 1995 visit of Lee to the United States. Evidence of this change in policy could be seen in several statements and documents emitting from the PRC in 1997, coinciding with improvement in China's relations with the United States noted in the previous section.

Foreign Minister and Vice-Premier Qian Qichen, for example, said in September 1997 that the mainland was willing to discuss suggestions for the unification of China from almost any source. He emphasized that the PRC was directing its anger, not at Taiwan itself, but at a handful of people advocating Taiwan's independence. He said, "The Taiwan compatriots are our blood brothers, and we will continue to protect all their legitimate rights and interests. . . . We are willing to increase contacts with various parties and people from all walks of life in Taiwan, except for the small number of people who stubbornly stick to the stand of 'Taiwan Independence,' and we are willing to hear and discuss any views and suggestions that would benefit the reunification of the motherland." Qian reiterated China's resolute opposition to Taiwan independence, two Chinas, one China and one Taiwan, and said that the Chinese "resolutely oppose the plot to change Taiwan's status as an inseparable part of China through conducting a referendum." Qian emphasized the importance of establishing the three links—direct mail, shipping, and trade services across the Taiwan Strait—and urged the Taiwan authorities "to hold consultations with us in a timely fashion on the procedural arrangements for cross-Strait political talks. The purpose of conducting political talks between the two sides of the Strait is to improve and develop cross-Strait relations and gradually advance the great cause of peaceful reunification."[15]

The Taiwan side was quick to respond, as it had been seeking for some time a resumption of cross-Strait dialogue; however, it shied away from "political talks." The ROC Mainland Affairs Council said it welcomed Qian's remarks and suggested that the two sides resume their talks through the established framework of the Straits Exchange Foundation and the Association for Relations Across the Taiwan Strait, as set up by the 1993 Koo-Wang talks. A day later, Premier Vincent Siew (Hsiao Wan-chang) said, "It is our unswerving stance that the two sides resume institutionalized dialogue without any premises." Specifically, Siew called upon China to shelve the controversial sovereignty issue in order to facilitate the resumption of cross-Strait dialogue.[16]

The crisis in the Taiwan Strait led many Americans to ask Taiwan officials for a better explanation of Taipei's policies toward the mainland: Was Taiwan seeking unification or was it seeking de facto or de jure independence? The answers from the Taiwan government were consistent but still ambiguous and flexible. For example, MAC Vice Chairman Kao Koong-lian stated in December 1996: "The most pragmatic description of the current cross-Straits situation is that Taiwan and the mainland are two parallel political entities in one country."[17]

The position of the ROC government and KMT ruling party was well-summarized by Chang King-yuh, Chairman of the Mainland Affairs Commission, in a news conference in August 1997: "From a legal point of view, the Republic of China's sovereignty and territories cover both sides of the Taiwan Straits. But in terms of the ROC's jurisdiction, since 1949, ours only covers Taiwan, the Pescadores, Quemoy, Matsu and some neighboring islets. So, we treat cross-Strait relations from the viewpoint of 'one country, two equal political entities' in a pragmatic way to deal with the separate jurisdiction."[18] The Straits Exchange Foundation said in September 1997 that the ROC had never denied the "one-China" principle, but rather had maintained that the current political status of China was "shared-sovereignty with separate jurisdiction." The SEF insisted that recognizing the reality of China being ruled by two different political entities did not conflict with there being only "one China."[19]

President Lee Teng-hui further explained his government's view on the key issues of ROC sovereignty, PRC jurisdiction over Taiwan, the ROC's right to engage in diplomatic activity, and China's eventual reunification in a speech to the Panamanian Legislative Assembly in September 1997.[20]

> Ever since 1912, the Republic of China has been a sovereign state enjoying all the rights of a sovereign state, including the right to join all intergovernmental international organizations and [maintaining] normal diplomatic relations with all sovereign states. . . . We have the territory that has a fixed boundary, an elected democratic sovereign government that is exercising effective jurisdiction, a perma-

nent population of twenty-one million people, and the recognition of thirty sovereign countries. . . .

The Chinese communist authorities say that we are not eligible for maintaining normal diplomatic relations with other countries because Taiwan is a province of the "People's Republic of China." This cannot be further from the truth. The Chinese communist regime was established in 1949, thirty-seven years after the founding of the Republic of China; moreover, the Chinese communist regime has never set foot in Taiwan, has never collected a penny of tax there, and has never conscripted our young people for their so-called "People's Liberation Army."

Apparently, the Republic of China is a sovereign democratic state. Thus, in accordance with international law, we are eligible for our normal international status, our participation in international activities, and our cooperation with other countries for mankind's well being.

I am deeply convinced that China will eventually be reunified. As long as the Chinese communist authorities can pragmatically face the fact that the two sides of the Taiwan Strait are under separate rules and are equal international legal entities, and respect the Republic of China's legitimate right to take part in international activities, then the two sides, through interacting with good will, will gradually head for reunification. This is specifically what the "Outline of National Unification" the Republic of China promulgated in 1991 for achieving national reunification in three stages.

In early October 1997 Premier Siew told the ROC Legislative Yuan: "the government will never agree to a hasty reunification or Taiwan independence." Regarding the latter, Siew commented: "Taiwan independence will not do. It will bring disaster to Taiwan."[21]

Also in October, MAC Chairman Chang King-yuh further elaborated on Taiwan's position in an interview with the *Hong Kong Economic Journal*.[22] Chang said the "basic condition" for talks between the two sides was recognition of "the fact that China is still a divided country at the moment." Furthermore, "If the mainland can see things in this way, open the door to cross-Strait consultations, and speed up cross-Strait exchanges, I believe that Taiwan will respond at any time." He explained: "as China is still a divided country ruled by two different governments and has not yet been reunified, the two shores should treat each other with respect, equality, and with goodwill and try to develop good and constructive relations with each other in order to lay a solid foundation for China's peaceful and democratic reunification in the future."

The problem, Chang said, was that the PRC's "one-China principle is nothing but one aimed at negating the ROC's existence. This is why there has not been much space for furthering cross-Strait relations development. The fact is that we often see the mainland trying to suppress the ROC's international status on the pretext of this principle, [and this is] harmful to cross-Strait relations development. We hope that the future CPC collective leadership will see things in a pragmatic way. We will continue to work hard to this end."

Chang then speculated on what type of arrangement might be feasible for a unified China in the future comprising the mainland, Hong Kong, Macau, and Taiwan:

> A country can choose to institute a variety of different political structures, such as a unitary structure, a federal structure, a union structure, and a commonwealth structure . . . . What is important is that all entities concerned should treat each other with equality, goodwill, and mutual respect. . . . No matter how different their respective internal mechanisms are, they should coexist with one another; operate in a basically identical spirit; and be free from intimidation, suppression, or sabotage. . . . It is hard to imagine that a dictatorial mechanism without any democratic experiences in tolerating different views or political parties with different views will suddenly sign a democratic constitution, saying that all people will live together in happiness. Will this work? I don't think that things will be so easy.

Thus, at the end of 1997—and continuing through the end of 1998—the KMT and the ROC government held the following principles in regards to its relations with the mainland: (1) the ROC is a sovereign state, equal to the PRC and legally entitled to take part as a nation-state in the international community; (2) Taiwan is not part of the PRC, and the government of the PRC is not the sole legal government of China; (3) China at present is a divided nation with two separate governments exercising jurisdiction over two separate Chinese territories; (4) the unification of China is a long-term goal, the realization of which can only be achieved when the PRC recognizes the equal status of the ROC and ceases its military and diplomatic threats to Taiwan; (5) unification can be achieved gradually as the two sides narrow their differences politically, economically, and socially; (6) China must be unified under the principles of democracy in which the free will choice of residents of both the mainland and Taiwan are respected; and (7) the "China" referred to in the "one-China" principle refers to the Republic of China, not the People's Republic of China.

In essence, then, the ROC position is that China today is in a state of split jurisdiction. The ROC will not unify Taiwan with the mainland until the PRC changes its socialist system and until the Chinese Communist Party renounces communism, or at least gives up its monopoly of power. Since these conditions run counter to the four cardinal principles enunciated by Deng Xiaoping—i.e., adherence to the leadership of the Chinese Communist Party, to Marxism-Leninism and Mao Zedong thought, to the people's democratic dictatorship, and to the socialist road—and the "one China" referred to by the PRC, it is doubtful Beijing will accept Taipei's terms for unification any time soon.

Not surprising, therefore, the 1998 Koo-Wang talks did not result in any major breakthroughs. But the "ice-thawing" meetings did accomplish several things: an agreement to strengthen cross-Strait dialogue, to reactivate SEF-ARATS consultations, to promote cross-Strait exchange visits at various levels, and to arrange for an exchange visit to Taiwan by Wang Daohan at some appropriate time in the future. Koo's itinerary was impressive in its own right, holding discussions with Wang in Shanghai, then visiting Beijing to meet with Jiang Zemin and other top PRC officials. Koo was able to make the point that Taiwan's democratic model was useful to the mainland's modernization and that unification could occur only when both sides of the Taiwan Strait were on the path to democracy. In the meetings, the two sides continued to disagree over their interpretations of "one China" and whether Taiwan could pursue wider international representation. Nonetheless, the atmosphere of the various discussions was open and friendly, and Koo's meeting with Jiang was described as "exchanging views in a frank yet respectful manner."[23]

The conversations between Koo and Wang indicated that fundamental differences between the two sides remained, with no breakthrough toward unification—or some other resolution—possible in the foreseeable future. However, by the end of 1998, tensions between the two sides had been reduced considerably since 1995–1996, with Taiwan more circumspect in its efforts to gain international recognition, other countries (such as the United States) more sensitive to Beijing's feelings about welcoming official visitors from Taiwan, and the PRC willing to give its policies of peaceful reunification additional time to bear fruit. At the same time, the potential for increased tension in the Taiwan Strait, as well as between Washington and Beijing over the Taiwan issue, was never far from the surface of the triangular relationship. None of the principal parties involved—including the Democratic Progressive Party—seemed willing or able to make the concessions necessary to realize a final resolution of the Taiwan issue. Thus, the Taiwan conundrum in U.S. China policy was alive and well as the countdown to the millennium entered its final year.

U.S. Strategic Assessments of China

One of the most critical factors in evaluating future U.S. policy toward Taiwan and China is American perceptions of the possible Chinese threat to U.S. interests in the Asian Pacific. The ambivalence of U.S. government assessments of this threat during the 1997–1998 period can be seen in the many intelligence estimates made public in reports to Congress and in various Pentagon publications. Despite efforts to maintain dialogue with the PLA and to expand military-to-military contacts through comprehensive engagement, the Department of Defense and the various American intelligence agencies carefully monitored Chinese power projection capabilities and looked for signs as to whether Beijing through military means would seek to expand or exert its influence in the region. In spite of the strategy of engagement, there was very little room in the American global perception of its interests for an emerging great power such as China. And from China's perspective, the United States as a global power was always a potential threat to its growing interests.

One example of the positive but cautious approach taken by Pentagon analysts toward China was the 1997 strategic assessment study published by the National Defense University (NDU).[24] This document, written by NDU's Institute for National Strategic Studies, examined many of the global "flashpoints" that might erupt into conflict over the coming decade. The study divided these flashpoints into four categories: major powers, significant regional contingencies, troubled states, and transnational problems. The NDU report identified China as a potential theater peer which could in the future challenge the United States militarily in the Western Pacific.

As such, China was given considerable attention in the study. "Dealing with China as a rising power is the most compelling of all the many complex challenges facing the United States and its regional allies." According to the report, China's leaders place priority on economic growth; however, there were circumstances under which the PRC leadership could sacrifice economic development. This might occur if Chinese sovereignty were at stake, Taiwan were to declare its independence, or a choice had to be made between internal stability and continued economic development.

According to the study, "Beijing's primary objective is to see China take what it considers its rightful place as a major regional and global power: to set the regional political agenda and determine rather than react to major political and economic currents." The foreign and defense policies of China into the twenty-first century were likely to be based on nationalism rather than communism. However, in these crucial areas of policy Chinese leaders probably would continue to adhere to an essentially statist approach to international relations and narrowly defined national interests, emphasizing the hard as opposed to the soft elements of national power. Chinese leaders would continue to view the world in balance-of-power, zero-sum terms, making only tactical adjustments to multilateral initiatives in the regional security arena.

The NDU study observed that it was in China's national interest that multipolarity exist in the international system, since this diluted the ability of the United States to set global and regional security, political, and economic agendas. In addition to concerns about U.S. global and regional dominance, "China fears that Tokyo will translate its economic power into political and military power that will block or challenge China's great power ambitions and threaten its security." Beijing worried about the U.S.-Japan security alliance, which was seen as an "attempt to establish joint hegemony throughout the Asia Pacific region" and, specifically, as an effort "to contain China."

China's military capabilities were slowly improving. "China's strategic nuclear forces provide a credible deterrent," with the world's third largest nuclear weapons arsenal, more than eighty intermediate-range ballistic missiles, and more than twenty intercontinental ballistic missiles. The PLA Air Force had 180 nuclear-capable bombers, and the Navy deployed one nuclear submarine with twelve ballistic missiles. By the year 2010, Beijing was expected to field ICBMs with multiple independently targeted warheads. Even if China acquired Russian SS-18 related technology, however, limited resources would force Beijing to pursue "a second-strike, counter-value nuclear doctrine" rather than an offensive first-strike capability. China's conventional forces were also slowly improving, the study noted. "The PLA can inflict great damage in limited campaigns against any of its immediate neighbors but is years away from being able to project sustained military force at any distance from China's borders. China lacks the capability either to produce or to purchase new systems in the quantities necessary, and the PLA is 1996 was probably two decades away from challenging or holding its own against a modern military force."

The PLA leadership was concentrating on several key areas of modernization, including developing antisubmarine warfare, ship-borne air defense, sustained naval operations, and amphibious warfare capabilities; developing strategic airlift, aerial refueling, ground-attack capabilities, and a new generation of air-superiority fighters; and improving ground force mobility and logistical support, air defense, all-weather operations, and command-and-control capabilities.

In terms of current capabilities, China had twenty-four Group Armies, all of which had designated rapid-deployment units comprising eighteen to twenty divisions. There were also 5,000 Marines. These forces, equipped with China's most modern weapons, "would be effective in operations in the South China Sea," but their dispersal throughout China, their small size, and the lack of air and sea lift "limit their effectiveness for large-scale operations such as an invasion of Taiwan." The Chinese Air Force had acquired ten Ilyushin heavy-transport aircraft from Russia, as well as one squadron of Su-27 fighters. In 1995 China signed an agreement with Russia for an additional squadron and production rights. "Although the Su-27 provides a clear qualitative gain, limitations on pilot skills and the lack of aerial refueling capability will deny the PLA their full benefit." The PLA Navy "is replacing or improving its old surface combatants and its submarines and has acquired two of the four *Kilo* Class submarines contracted for with Russia. However, these improvements will not address the Navy's fundamental problem: its inability to mount sustained, coordinated operations and to protect itself while doing so."

In assessing China's future capabilities, the report recommended that analysts focus on the following "critical indicators":

- Navy: The number of ships and their associated air defense and antisubmarine warfare systems, new construction of supply and amphibious ships, and development of a carrier-capable aircraft.
- Air Force: Increases in the numbers of lift and ground-attack aircraft, proficiency in aerial refueling, and the deployment of an air-superiority fighter.
- Ground Forces: An increase in the number of rapid reaction units.

Conclusion: Summits and Beyond

- Doctrine and Training: Indicators pointing beyond the upgrading of Navy and Air Force roles and missions in support of ground forces toward superiority and denial missions at some distance from Chinese territorial seas.

NDU pointed to a number of flashpoints around China which might erupt into conflict with adverse consequences for the United States. These included Taiwan; Southeast Asia and the South China Sea, where China had conflicting territorial claims in the Spratly Archipelago with Brunei, Malaysia, the Philippines, and Vietnam; the Korean Peninsula; India, where either a Sino-Indian conflict over territorial disputes in the Himalayas or an Indo-Pakistani conflict might precipitate Chinese or American involvement; and proliferation issues involving ballistic missiles and technology, nuclear weapons technology, and chemical weapons technology.

In January 1998 officials from several U.S. intelligence agencies presented summaries of current and future threats to U.S. interests before the Senate Select Committee on Intelligence.[25] Almost all of their assessments considered China.

In his statement, CIA Director George Tenet noted key challenges to U.S. security in 1998 and beyond.[26] In terms of the challenge of proliferation, Tenet specifically addressed the role of China:

> With regard to China, its defense industries are under increasing pressure to become profit making organizations—an imperative that can put them at odds with US interests. Conventional arms sales have lagged in recent years, encouraging Chinese defense industries to look to WMD [weapons of mass destruction] technology-related sales, primarily to Pakistan and Iran, in order to recoup. There is no question that China has contributed to WMD advances in these countries.
>
> On the positive side, there have recently been signs of improvement in China's proliferation posture. China recently enacted its first comprehensive laws governing nuclear technology exports. It also appears to have tightened down on its most worrisome nuclear transfers, and it recently renewed its pledge to halt sales of anti-ship cruise missiles to Iran.
>
> But China's relations with some proliferant countries are long-standing and deep .... The jury is still out on whether the recent changes are broad enough in scope and whether they will hold over the longer term. As such, Chinese activities in this area will require continued close watching.

Another important challenge to U.S. interests, according to the CIA Director, was Russia and China in transition. In China, Tenet said, "the leadership there has a clear goal: the transformation of their country into East Asia's major power and a leading world economy on a par with the United States by the middle of the 21st Century." He continued, "It is too soon to say what this portends ... whether China in the future will be an aggressive or a benign power. What is clear, though, is that

China will be an increasingly influential player—one that will have the capability to, at a minimum, alter our security calculus in the Far East."

Tenet also discussed regional troublemakers, "states for whom the end of the Cold War did not mean an end to hostility to the United States." Iran, North Korea, and Iraq were mentioned, countries with which China had important relations and thus had the potential either to help or hinder American interests.

In his testimony, Lt. Gen. Patrick Hughes of the DIA addressed the future security environment of the United States, following closely the threat assessments found in the QDR report reviewed in Chapter 4.[27] Hughes observed: "No state has the potential to match the worldwide strength and influence of the United States—in terms of combined political, economic, technological, military, and cultural power—over the next two decades." However, "a select group of states—Russia, China, Japan, Europe (collectively or a coalition of key European states), and India—will likely possess capabilities that are an echelon above other regional powers and nations." In this regard, there were two, but unlikely, developments that would prove most threatening to U.S. interests. First, one or more of the major powers, or a regional alliance led by one of the major powers, could form an anti-U.S. alliance. Second, major power competition could expand from political and economic spheres to the military sphere.

Potential regional threats could arise due to unfavorable developments in virtually any place in the world, but Gen. Hughes spent some time considering China. "China's top priorities will continue to be economic development, modernization, and domestic political stability," he predicted, but China would not likely become "significantly more democratic or pro-Western." Hughes said Beijing would attempt to avoid confrontation with the United States, but "several points of friction will persist, " including:

- The Taiwan issue, which would remain "the major potential flashpoint," with the United States supporting a peaceful evolution in cross-Strait relations, but Beijing believing "US policy encourages the independence movement of Taiwan, deliberately or inadvertently."
- "Beijing believes the US is bent on containing, dividing, and westernizing China and will continue to pursue policies designed to counter perceived US efforts toward that end."
- "China perceives Japan as its principal Asian regional rival, and views US-Japanese defense cooperation as helpful only if it limits the emergence of a long-term Japanese military threat."
- Other regional issues might emerge.
- "China's ethnic separatist movements are another potential point of conflict, especially in Tibet and northwest China."

In terms of China's military strategy and modernization, Gen. Hughes said: "China's military strategy will continue to emphasize the development of a survivable nuclear retaliatory capability as a deterrent against the use of nuclear weapons by the United States, Russia, or India. There is no indication that China will field the much larger number of missiles necessary to shift from a minimalist, retaliation strategy to a first-strike strategy." China's conventional force modernization, "will continue at a measured pace, with emphasis on developing a more credible military threat against Taiwan (though not the large amphibious capability necessary for invasion), and protecting claims in the South China Sea against Southeast Asian rivals. China is not likely to build the capability to project large conventional forces beyond its immediate borders or nearby seas." Since, from China's point of view, the major threat was no longer from a large ground force from Russia but rather air and naval threats from the east [Japan and the United States], "China's top military priority will therefore remain modernizing its air, air defense, and naval forces." The modernization of the PLA Navy included enhanced capability to operate further from shore, with an emphasis "on offensive strike capability against surface ships, including more modern fighters, aerial refueling, and anti-ship cruise missiles launched from surface, sub-surface, and aerial platforms." As part of its military modernization programs, the PRC will continue to actively seek advanced technology from all possible sources, including cooperative nations such as Russia. China also "will proliferate some technical capabilities as it sells selected weapons systems to other countries."

The testimony of Phyllis Oakley of the State Department's Bureau of Intelligence and Research (INR) shared many of the assessments of Tenet and Hughes, with useful definitions of U.S. policy goals and bilateral policy issues with China.[28] Oakley noted that the September 1997 Department of State's International Affairs Strategic Plan listed the following foreign policy goals of the United States:

- secure peace; deter aggression; prevent, defuse, and manage crises; halt the proliferation of weapons of mass destruction; and advance arms control and disarmament
- expand exports, open markets, assist American business, foster economic growth, and promote sustainable development
- protect American citizens abroad and safeguard the borders of the United States
- combat international terrorism, crime, and narcotics trafficking
- support the establishment and consolidation of democracies, and uphold human rights
- provide humanitarian assistance to victims of crisis and disaster
- improve the global environment, stabilize world population growth, and protect human health.

Oakley said that the spread of weapons of mass destruction (WMD) continued to pose a serious threat to U.S. national interests: "Entities in North Korea, China, and Russia are the principal targets of acquisition efforts by countries seeking

WMD capabilities. Entities in these three countries are also the most active purveyors of WMD-related equipment and technology." There were both troubling and hopeful signs in China's WMD activities. In 1997 China took steps "to develop more effective administrative oversight of its nuclear industry by promulgating nuclear export control legislation." It also joined the Nuclear Non-Proliferation Treaty (NPT) exporter committee and "started the process for adoption of comprehensive dual-use export controls." In addition, China "appears to be living up to its commitment—publicly offered in May 1996—not to provide assistance to any unsafeguarded nuclear facilities." Assistance to both Pakistan and Iran had been curtailed. The United States had objected to China's nuclear assistance to Iran, even though it was allowed under the NPT, because such cooperation might "support a nuclear infrastructure and contribute indirectly to Iran's effort to acquire nuclear weapons."

Oakley noted, however: "Unfortunately, China has not made equivalent progress in other areas. At least until mid-1997 Chinese entities have been the main source of supply for Iran's CW [chemical warfare] program. In May 1997, the United States imposed trade sanctions on seven Chinese entities for knowingly and materially contributing to Iran's CW program. Over the past year, China has made some progress in addressing the gaps in its export-control policies, but some key loopholes remain."

In terms of Chinese missile proliferation, Oakley said:

> China has agreed to abide by the "guidelines and parameters" of the Missile Technology Control Regime (MTCR) and has committed not to transfer ground-to-ground MTCR-class missiles. But China does not appear to interpret its responsibilities under the MTCR guidelines as strictly as the US and other MTCR members. By all indications China has taken itself out of the business of exporting complete ballistic missiles. This is an important step—one that has slowed the process of military destabilization in South Asia and the Middle East. But it is not enough. We would like to see China upgrade its commitments to current MTCR levels and implement effective export controls.

Oakley reported that in 1997 the PRC created a separate division within the Ministry of Foreign Affairs "to address all arms control and proliferation issues." Beijing also "agreed to conduct regular dialogues [with the United States] at the senior level on arms control, global security, and nonproliferation." Nonetheless, transfers of modern Chinese antiship missiles to Iran were particularly troubling. "China last fall agreed to end sales of antiship missiles to Iran and reiterated this commitment during Secretary Cohen's recent visit. The administration is reviewing, but has not yet decided, whether the number and type of transfers to date trigger sanctions under the Iran-Iraq Non-Proliferation Act."

Oakley emphasized that "constructive partnership between the US and China is central to the peace and prosperity of the Asia-Pacific region." Although high-level dialogue with Chinese leaders had increased considerably since 1996, "we still have

Conclusion: Summits and Beyond

many unresolved issues and continue to hold sharply different views on important matters, including human rights, religious freedom, political expression, and freedom of association." Nonproliferation also remained an unresolved issue in the relationship.

As the assistant secretary observed, the United States carefully monitors China's military modernization:

> China continues to have the largest standing army in the world and is steadily modernizing its ground, air, and naval weapons and tactics. We must be attentive to China's growing military capabilities, as demonstrated in the 1996 combined-forces exercises in and around the Taiwan Strait.
>
> China's military modernization continues at a steady pace, and Beijing during the past year strengthened its arms-import relationship with Russia. China is replacing its aging naval fleet with new domestically-produced ships and submarines, and recently took delivery of a third *Kilo*-class submarine and finalized a deal to purchase two Russian naval destroyers that could be armed with modern SS-N-22 SUNBURN antiship missiles. While this growth in naval capability bears watching, the gradual pace of Chinese modernization is having only a marginal impact on the current naval balance in the region.

In addition, the PRC "is embarked on a ballistic missile modernization program. Although China's ICBM force will remain considerably smaller and less capable than those of Russia and the United States, Beijing views this modernization effort as essential to maintaining a credible deterrent force."

> China is expected to remain primarily a land-based ballistic missile power, but continues to look at sea-based platforms and land-attack cruise missiles as additional means of delivery. In the next 20 years, the number of Chinese ballistic missiles capable of reaching the continental United States will increase marginally. The greatest growth, both in numbers and capabilities, is expected to be in China's short-range SRBM force—the M-9 and M-11.

Oakley concluded in an optimistic assessment of China's overall direction: "We anticipate that the many transformations under way in China for the past two decades will continue into the next century. The cumulative effect of economic, political, societal, technological, and military change will produce a China that is more powerful and, if we are successful, more tightly integrated into global systems. We are likely to see positive results from the impact of participation in the global economy, exposure to information and ideas from around the world, and the proliferation of shared interests which is intrinsic to modernization everywhere."

As these 1998 threat assessments suggest, China was not viewed by the U.S. intelligence community as an immediate or mid-term threat to the United States. However, the possibility of China emerging as a peer competitor sometime around 2015–2020 was noted. China was seen to be modernizing not only economically but also militarily, with steady progress being made in missile, naval, and air force capabilities. These improvements would give China better ability to project force a greater distance from its shores, but not far enough into the Pacific to be of major concern to the United States. China's strength relative to its neighbors, including Taiwan, was troubling, but PRC strength relative to the United States was a distant problem.

Nonetheless, China's growing power made Beijing much more influential in Asian affairs and better able to resist U.S. pressure when important Chinese interests were at stake. Of the various issues between Washington and Beijing, Taiwan remained the most explosive, an issue on which both China and the United States had strong interests and very little room for maneuver. Thus, two major results of PRC military exercises around Taiwan in 1995-1996 were more focused attention on potential security problems with China and greater effort to find ways to avoid future confrontations in the Taiwan Strait. The next section considers several of the most important policy questions raised during this period of U.S. China-Taiwan policy reassessment.

Critical Questions

By the end of 1998, the Taiwan conundrum in U.S. China policy seemed more complex than ever. By then, the emergence of the PRC as a serious competitor to the United States in Asia made China as much of a conundrum in U.S. policy as Taiwan. The continued balancing of American values, institutional perspectives, national interests, and strategy in U.S. policies toward these two Chinese societies was becoming increasingly difficult as the three societies moved toward the year 2000. Within this evolving context, it is possible to address several fundamental questions about U.S. policy toward Taiwan and China raised earlier in the Preface.

1. *To what extent is China a threat to U.S. interests in Asia?* This is a question that will confront American strategists for years to come, and it centers around the issue of whether the United States and the PRC can accommodate each other as China modernizes and seeks to expand its sphere of influence in Asia, while the United States seeks to maintain its forward presence, its credibility among Asian Pacific allies, and a favorable balance of power, a corollary of which is that the United States will oppose the rise of a rival regional hegemon.

If history is guide, it would be rare for two such countries—one a rising regional power and the other the dominant power sustaining the status quo—not to confront each other in the Western Pacific. The United States and China do not have a common enemy. Russia, Japan, or India are potential, but unlikely candidates. And while the American and Chinese people genuinely seem to like each other, there are vast cultural differences between them. The ideological gulf between the United States and the People's Republic of China is very deep indeed, although it is narrowing at a fast rate, especially outside the circle of the communist elite.

Over the past decade there have been a number of issues between the United States and China which are symptomatic of the tension between the emerging power of the PRC and the status quo power of the United States. Other than Taiwan, these include problems of nuclear weapons and ballistic missile proliferation, imbalanced trade, human rights abuses, the PLA's growing power projection capability, Chinese expansionism in the South China Sea, theft of state secrets, and conflicting visions of the new world order and prescriptions for regional security mechanisms. The fact that China continues to be governed by a communist system at a time when democracy is in ascendency elsewhere around the world continually grates at the American conscience. These differences between the United States and China will not be resolved by settling the Taiwan issue; they are disagreements between two great states.

Some American and Chinese analysts point to these and other difficulties as evidence that the United States and China are on a collision course in East Asia. And indeed there has been much demonizing on both sides. But evidence also exists that such a collision is not inevitable: the majority of leaders in both countries seem committed to maintaining a strategic dialogue, trade and other economic linkages are growing rapidly between the two countries, economic and social trends in China suggest greater political openness in the future, and the United States and China are not natural enemies with common borders. These and similar factors hold out the very real possibility that the two countries will find ways to manage their differences without resort to military conflict. It is certainly in the interests of the United States and China to do so, because the military forces of both countries are powerful in a conventional and nuclear sense and because the costs of such a conflict would be enormous across a wide range of interests for both sides.

Still, in truth, either confrontation or cooperation may characterize future Sino-American relations. Given this reality, a twofold approach for the United States seems most reasonable. Washington should, on the one hand, seek to engage China and increase areas of cooperation; on the other hand, the United States must be prepared to face a possible conflict with China. The United States can do much to ensure that the latter scenario does not occur, but China has responsibilities as well; and the best of intentions may not suffice to overcome the significant tensions that exist in the Sino-American relationship.

Under the circumstances, it would be unwise for the United States to compromise either its values or interests in efforts to maintain friendly relations with China. To the extent that Taiwan has value for the United States and U.S.-Taiwan relations are in the American interest, the United States should not compromise its ties with Taiwan for the sake of engagement or partnership with Beijing; but neither should the United States sacrifice engagement with Beijing for the sake of ties with Taiwan. Taipei is unlikely to force this choice on Washington, but Beijing might; in which case the United States should refuse to play by the PRC rules.

2. *Would U.S. accommodation over Taiwan lead to improved U.S.-PRC ties?* As long as the future of Taiwan remains an unresolved issue between Taipei and Beijing, the Taiwan issue likely will remain an obstacle in Sino-American relations. However, Taiwan is not the only obstacle in Sino-American relations, nor is it the core problem. Even if Taiwan did not exist, there are sufficient differences between the United States and China to cause Sino-American relations to be deeply troubled. Nonetheless, because of the stakes involved, it is worth pondering whether China would change its policies in the areas of security, trade, and democratic and free market values—the traditional American interests in Asia—if Washington changed its policies toward Taiwan, for example, by actively promoting Chinese unification under the one country, two systems formula.

Judging from Beijing's adherence to the four cardinal principles underlying CCP rule, such a tit-for-tat seems unlikely. On the other hand, if China would make significant progress toward becoming more democratic, toward stopping its proliferation of weapons of mass destruction and their delivery systems, toward balancing its trade with the United States and ending unfair trading practices, toward respecting the human rights of its citizens, and toward joining the United States in a true partnership to ensure peace and prosperity in Asia—then perhaps the United States might consider adjusting its policies. However, these conditions are unlikely to be met in the near future, despite Jiang Zemin's willingness to allow Bill Clinton to speak his mind publicly during the U.S. president's state visit.

Because China remains a dictatorship controlled by the communist party, there is no strategic imperative for the United States to make concessions over Taiwan. Furthermore, if the PRC introduces the above policy changes, then the ROC itself has promised to move toward unification with the mainland. This would effectively remove the Taiwan issue from Sino-American relations and be rightfully regarded as a success in U.S. foreign policy, two goals of which have been significant progress toward democratization in China and the peaceful resolution of Taiwan-mainland differences.

Thus, whereas it is true that U.S. concessions over Taiwan probably would lead to short-term improvement in Sino-American relations, it would not lead to substantive change in PRC policies which harm long-term U.S. interests. As long as the United States seeks to maintain a favorable balance of power in the Western Pacific by opposing the rise of a regional hegemon, as long as the PRC seeks to expand its sphere of influence in Asia and to increase its national power, and as long as China is controlled by a communist government and the United States is a democracy, then U.S. and Chinese interests will intersect and sometimes collide in the Western Pacific. Taiwan is a highly visible and sensitive issue in Sino-American relations, but its resolution cannot solve the more fundamental conflict of interests between the United States and China.

3. *Are the forces of independence on Taiwan greater than the forces seeking to preserve the status quo or to unify with the mainland?* There are both centripetal forces drawing Taiwan and the mainland closer together through economic ties and

cultural affiliation and centrifugal forces of self-determination on Taiwan pushing the two sides apart.

Since Taiwan is now a democracy, the KMT or ROC government cannot alone decide Taiwan's future in bilateral negotiations with the mainland. The ROC legislature would have to approve any agreement and, ultimately, the people of Taiwan would have to agree as well. There is at present no clear consensus among the people of Taiwan over their future relationship with the mainland. According to numerous polls taken on Taiwan in recent years, the great majority of residents prefer the status quo with a decision on Taiwan's political relationship with the mainland to be decided later. If given a choice between independence and unification with the communist PRC, most people on Taiwan would almost certainly choose independence. If given a choice between independence and unification under a democratic China, the majority probably would favor unification—or at least not resist it—although a minority of Taiwanese still would prefer independence. Trends point to an increased desire for self-determination on Taiwan, perhaps one day indicated through a referendum; but the preferred choice in such a referendum is difficult to foresee at this time, as are its implications for U.S.-PRC-ROC relations.

Domestic politics on Taiwan have greatly complicated the Taiwan issue in Sino-American relations. The KMT and the ROC government officially adhere to a one-China policy, insisting that Taiwan would become part of a democratic China in the future. KMT and ROC leaders insist that Taiwan will never become part of the PRC, however, specifically saying that the mainland's democratization must precede unification. The DPP holds that Taiwan should be considered a nation-state separate from China, regardless of the form of government on the mainland. Most members of the DPP do not want to antagonize the PRC, however, and many moderate DPP are in favor of cooperative ties with Beijing. Furthermore, DPP leaders have promised that if their party one day becomes the ruling party of Taiwan, they will not formally declare the independence of Taiwan because in their view Taiwan already is independent.

Regardless of whether Taiwan is ruled by the KMT or the DPP, Beijing insists that Taiwan is a part of the People's Republic of China. Virtually everyone on Taiwan rejects that notion. The people of Taiwan, as well as their present KMT-led government and possible future DPP government, are adamantly opposed to unification under any formula with the mainland as long as it is controlled by the communists. On the other hand, the vast majority of Taiwan's population and its political leaders favor closer substantive ties with the PRC, including trade, cultural exchanges, and high-level dialogue. Incremental progress toward eventual unification with the mainland remains a strong possibility as long as China moves toward greater economic and political liberalization, as long as Beijing resists the temptation of trying to resolve the Taiwan issue by force, and as long as the PRC does not push Taiwan into a corner by undermining completely its participation in the international community. If the PRC reverses its policy by curtailing liberalization and threatening to use force against Taiwan, then not only is a peaceful resolution of the Taiwan issue put at risk, the very prospects of unification would seem to fade.

On balance, the forces of long-term integration with the mainland seem stronger than the forces dividing the two sides of the Taiwan Strait. However, the process of integration will take time. It cannot be forced on the people of Taiwan without severe repercussions in terms of their security and their social, economic, and political stability. In this sense, the preservation of the status quo in the Taiwan Strait is the best approach.

4. *Should the United States support a particular outcome of the Taiwan issue?* Despite the Clinton administration's public reaffirmation of the three no's, U.S. policy as of mid-1999 does not support a specific outcome of the Taiwan issue. The policy instead supports the process of peacefully resolving the issue. It is extremely unlikely, for example, that Washington would oppose independence for Taiwan if Beijing and Taipei agreed that Taiwan should be independent, or that Washington would oppose one China, one Taiwan if Beijing and Taipei agreed to that formula, or likewise if they agreed to a two-Chinas solution to the Taiwan issue. The United States probably would support whatever solution was agreed to by the two Chinese sides, whether it be unification, independence, or some other option. U.S. policy toward the Taiwan issue should remain centered around the principle that the future of Taiwan must be resolved peacefully by the two sides of the Taiwan Strait. Washington should not attempt to preempt the process or predetermine its course.

It is not politically possible, morally correct, or sound policy for the United States to try to force the people of Taiwan to unify with a communist-controlled China. Nor is it possible, correct, or wise for Washington to try to force Beijing to accept Taiwan independence. What does seem reasonable is for the United States to continue supporting a peaceful resolution of the Taiwan issue, an important corollary of which is that both sides of the Taiwan Strait must agree to a particular solution. If the two sides cannot agree, however, it is not the responsibility of the United States to compel their agreement, or to find a solution to their problems, or to pressure one side to accept the other's formula. It would remain in the U.S. interest to encourage their continued dialogue.

That being said, the possibility exists that war may break out in the Taiwan Strait if Taipei and Beijing cannot agree on Taiwan's future. Such a war would almost certainly be initiated by the PRC, not Taiwan. Moreover—and this is important—the unwillingness of the ROC government or the people of Taiwan to become part of communist China should not be construed as provoking the PRC into attack. The U.S. policy of urging dialogue between the two sides and insisting that the issue be resolved peacefully contributes to peace and stability in the Taiwan Strait. That policy should be continued, particularly during the next decade when China's military strength is projected to increase substantially and when hardliners within the PRC civilian-military leadership may agitate for increased pressure on Taiwan.

Conclusion: Summits and Beyond

If the people of Taiwan, perhaps under a future DPP government, should elect in a referendum to establish a new country, say the Republic of Taiwan, the PRC may well feel justified to use force to maintain the territorial integrity of China. This would be a nightmare scenario for the United States, and the U.S. reaction would be influenced by enormous surges of emotion in various directions. It would be difficult for the American people and their government to stand aside and watch a communist state attack a democratic society for the express purpose of compelling its absorption into the communist state. However, the United States should not support the division of China. Would it be possible for the United States to ensure that the PRC would be unsuccessful in militarily defeating Taiwan, while at the same time avoiding the diplomatic recognition of an independent Taiwan? It would seem so, but how the U.S. administration in office at the time would respond to this challenge is open to speculation. In truth, no one knows.

Assuming that the resolution of the Taiwan issue can be peaceful, how would the various scenarios for Taiwan's future affect U.S. interests? A great deal depends upon the nature of Sino-American relations.

If China were democratic, market-oriented, non-hegemonic, and wanted cooperative, friendly relations with the United States, then Taiwan's unification with the mainland would not adversely affect U.S. interests. In fact, U.S. relations with the Greater China would probably be quite friendly. If China were communist, socialist-oriented, hegemonic, and considered the United States an enemy, then Taiwan's unification with the mainland could adversely affect U.S. interests—Beijing certainly would be better positioned in the Western Pacific to project power in opposition to the United States. If Taiwan were independent, if there were two Chinas, or if the status quo in the Taiwan Strait were maintained indefinitely, U.S. interests would not be harmed if China were democratic and friendly. If China were hostile, U.S. interests would not be harmed by these scenarios for Taiwan's future since a divided China is a weakened China.

In short, assuming both sides were able to agree upon Taiwan's future relationship with the mainland, only under the circumstance of Taiwan unifying with a China hostile to the United States would American interests be seriously threatened.

If it is assumed that the two sides cannot agree on Taiwan's future, either the status quo would persist or the issue would be settled by military or other pressures exerted on Taiwan. U.S. interests would not be harmed by a continuation of the status quo (although some Americans would add the caveat: except insofar as it hinders better U.S.-PRC relations), but U.S. interests would definitely be harmed if the PRC used force to resolve the Taiwan issue. War between the two sides would disrupt regional peace and stability, and the outcome of the struggle would not be accepted easily by the losing party. Under conditions of forced unification, the government and people of Taiwan would be dissatisfied and possibly agitate for freedom. If the mainland were forced to accept Taiwan independence, two

Chinas, or one China, one Taiwan, then Beijing would be dissatisfied and work to overthrow the arrangement.

Thus, it is clear that U.S. interests are best served by a peaceful resolution of the Taiwan issue—i.e., a resolution agreed to by both sides. Such a resolution is not yet in sight, but until that formula can be found, U.S. interests are served by deterring PRC aggression in the Taiwan Strait, cautioning Taiwan not to be too provocative, and encouraging both sides to continue their dialogue and exchanges.

5. *Is it in the U.S. interest to more actively support Taiwan's unification with China by pressuring Taipei to be more accommodating in cross-Strait negotiations?* The main reason the ROC government and people on Taiwan do not support unification talks is their unwillingness to be part of a China controlled by a central government dominated by the Chinese Communist Party—the essence of Beijing's one country, two systems formula. The residents of Taiwan want to preserve their freedom, self-determination, and new democracy. They have no desire to become a subordinate unit in a China ruled by an authoritarian government.

As long as China is under the control of the CCP, the ROC government and Taiwan people will not accept—absent extreme duress—political unification with the mainland. To do so is to risk their way of life and self-identity in exchange for a PRC promise of non-interference in their internal affairs for a certain period of time. But there is no guarantee the PRC promise will be kept. And if Taiwan already has joined the PRC, then the international community—including the United States—will have no recourse but to accept what Beijing decides in regards to Taiwan.

This is not to say, however, that Taipei is unwilling to negotiate with the PRC on all manner of issues to reduce tensions in the Taiwan Strait, increase mutual understanding, and expand the areas of cooperation so that unification might be possible in the future. Taiwan already is doing this. Moreover, there are indications that greater flexibility may exist in Beijing's negotiating position, as suggested by the renewed Koo-Wang talks and tantalizing comments about accepting different interpretations of "one-China." The difficulty in the wake of Lee Teng-hui's visit to the United States is that Beijing wants to discuss political issues such as terms of unification rather than practical issues of cooperation.

Repeatedly in the past, PRC leaders have concluded that the shortest route to Taipei is not across the Taiwan Strait but through Washington—that is, greater progress toward gaining control of Taiwan can be made by convincing the United States to weaken its support of Taiwan than can be made by negotiating directly with Taipei. After years of dealing with Beijing, the United States should recognize PRC negotiating tactics and not allow itself to be manipulated into supporting unification schemes. As a matter of principle and sound policy, the United States should not pressure—even indirectly—democratic societies to join communist states. Without a serious threat to U.S. security, the likelihood of the Congress and the American people accepting such pressure—even if some administration tried to apply it as a means of furthering strategic partnership with the PRC—is very small.

Conclusion: Summits and Beyond 303

The best U.S. policy is to continue to insist that the two Chinese sides work out their own differences, but that they do so peacefully. President Clinton attempted in Shanghai to deny Taiwan the option of independence and to try to limit Taipei's efforts to be a full-fledged member of the international community. The option of greater international autonomy, however, was one of the most important bargaining chips Taipei possessed to convince the PRC to continue its reforms so as to make the mainland more attractive to the Taiwan people. Clinton's three no's did not further the U.S. goal of a democratic China, but they may have weakened Taiwan's democracy. The lesson should be clear: the United States should avoid taking sides in the Taiwan-China dispute except to insist that the resolution of their differences be peaceful.

6. *What guidelines should govern future U.S. arms sales to Taiwan?* The fundamental U.S. interest in the Taiwan issue is that it be settled peacefully. This implies that Taiwan agree to any settlement with China. Until that occurs, Taiwan should have an adequate self-defense capability. This ensures that Beijing will be deterred from using force under most circumstances and that U.S. forces will not have to be deployed to the Taiwan area except under conditions of extreme provocation by the PRC. These guidelines exist in U.S. law under the Taiwan Relations Act, and the August 17 communiqué must be interpreted in ways consistent with that law since the TRA takes legal precedence over the communiqué. To date, the United States has sold Taiwan generally adequate defensive equipment, including many advanced systems for air, sea, and land defense.

Arms sales to Taiwan are always a sensitive issue in Sino-American relations, in part because Beijing views such sales as encouraging Taiwan to resist PRC unification proposals. There is some truth to this, but to withhold defensive arms to Taiwan would be pressuring Taipei to accept unwanted unification. Of the two options, continued U.S. arms sales to Taiwan is preferable since it serves U.S. interests in a peaceful solution to the Taiwan issue and its corollary that Taiwan must agree to any resolution of its future status with China. It is also the only option that is legally compatible with the TRA and politically viable for the U.S. government.

Future U.S. arms sales should be based on American assessments of the needs of Taiwan for its self-defense, as determined by procedures outlined in the TRA. At present, Taiwan is very weak in the areas of missile defense and countering a submarine-enforced blockade of the island. Arms sales in these areas should be approved fairly quickly by the executive and legislative branches of the U.S. government, despite protests from the PRC.

7. *Should the United States become involved in a war between China and Taiwan, regardless of the circumstances precipitating the conflict?* It is not possible nor wise for the United States to specify under what conditions it would intervene militarily in the Taiwan Strait. The possible conflict scenarios range from a surprise PRC missile attack against key Taiwan installations, to a blockade of the island followed by an amphibious invasion, to a campaign of assassination and

sabotage carried out by PRC special operations forces, to an accidental exchange of fire in the Taiwan Strait during military exercises. Perhaps the key question is whether the United States would intervene if the PRC attacked Taiwan to prevent it from becoming an independent country.

In an era of Sino-American engagement, it is not in the U.S. interest to support or encourage Taiwan to become a separate country, nor is it in the U.S. interest to deny the people of Taiwan their right of self-determination or to compel them to accept a certain status in the world or relationship with China. The key U.S. interest is a peaceful settlement of the Taiwan issue, an interest which requires that the people of Taiwan have a voice in their own destiny.

If a democratically elected government in Taiwan agrees to unify with the mainland, and there is civil disorder on Taiwan caused by those who disagree with that decision, the United States should not intervene to quell that disturbance. Nor should the PRC, unless invited to do so by the Taiwan authorities. If the people of Taiwan decide in a referendum to pursue separate statehood from China, and the democratically elected government of Taiwan seeks to put that decision into effect, there is a strong possibility the PRC will attack Taiwan. Under those circumstances, what should the United States do?

This a policy dilemma of the first order, since the circumstances would pose serious contradictions between U.S. interests in preserving peace in the Taiwan Strait, in avoiding a major conflict with the PRC, in supporting the right of Taiwan's citizens to exercise self-determination, and in protecting market-democracies from communist attack. Without question, there would be strong voices heard in the United States in favor of military intervention, and there would be strong voices opposing involvement. These conditions probably would precipitate a bitter policy debate between an administration reluctant to be drawn into the conflict and a Congress insisting that Taiwan be protected.

The outcome of that debate is impossible to predict with certitude, but U.S. intervention is probable because: (a) the United States has the means of intervening in militarily significant ways without great cost to American personnel; (b) intervention could be confined to the Taiwan area and not be allowed to escalate into a major war with China—although this may be more difficult as the PLA acquires advanced weaponry; (c) enough face-saving measures for the Chinese could be put into place to ensure that Sino-American relations would not be irreparably harmed; (d) the U.S. goal would not necessarily be the defeat of China but rather cessation of hostilities in the Taiwan Strait; and (e) U.S. intervention would not mean U.S. diplomatic recognition of Taiwan as an independent state.

The last two points deserve emphasis: U.S. intervention on Taiwan's behalf and the defeat of the PLA in the Taiwan Strait do not require the United States to recognize an independent Taiwan or to abandon American engagement with Beijing. Again, the key U.S. interest is in the maintenance of peace in the Taiwan Strait, not in support for a particular outcome of the Taiwan issue. Any effort to use nonpeaceful means to resolve the Taiwan issue should be opposed by the United

States as part of its long-standing policy, but that opposition should not be interpreted as U.S. support for a change in Taiwan's status or rejection of cooperative Sino-American relations.

8. *Should the U.S. commitment to defend Taiwan be more explicit?* The U.S. policy of ambiguity toward the defense of Taiwan is designed to deter both Beijing and Taipei from adventurism in the Taiwan Strait: Taiwan cannot be certain of U.S. assistance if it provokes China into an attack, and the PRC cannot be certain the United States would fail to respond to a use of force against Taiwan. From the 1950s, uncertainty as to the U.S. response in case of a PRC threat or use of force against Taiwan was thought necessary because it introduced a high degree of caution in the policies of the PRC and ROC.

Ambiguity worked as long as the two Chinese sides were deterred, but many factors in the 1990s have worked to limit the effectiveness of ambiguity: perceptions of the increased possibility of Taiwan independence have raised the risks of a forceful PRC response; the resolution of the Hong Kong and Macau issues has increased the likelihood of PRC impatience with Taiwan; many Chinese analysts believe U.S. power and resolve to be weakening in the post-Cold War period; advanced arms sales have given Taipei greater confidence that it can defend itself; strong congressional and public support have convinced many in Taiwan that the United States will intervene on their behalf under any circumstance; a modernizing PLA has increased confidence in Beijing of its ability to successfully use force against Taiwan, even if the United States does intervene.

It can be argued that in the mid-1990s ambiguity failed to prevent the Lee Teng-hui government from aggressively pursuing additional overseas representation and that it failed to deter the PRC from using the PLA to threaten Taiwan. To many observers, the events of 1995–1996 signaled the end of ambiguity as an effective strategy. There were calls for a much clearer statement of U.S. intentions to assist Taiwan, and these calls ranged from specific commitments to defend Taiwan to warnings the United States would not support Taiwan if the island declared independence.

By mid-1999, a refined ambiguity characterized U.S. policy. There was "tactical ambiguity" designed to keep Beijing and Taipei guessing as to the specific U.S. response to a Taiwan Strait crisis, and there was "strategic clarity" intended to make clear (through the U.S. military presence in the Pacific and demonstrations such as the March 1996 aircraft carrier deployments) U.S. determination that the Taiwan issue be resolved peacefully. Since it remains in the U.S. interest to have cooperative relations with both Chinese governments while deterring provocative actions by either side in the Taiwan Strait, the U.S. strategy of tactical ambiguity and strategic clarity should continue.

At the same time, however, the utility of ambiguity has weakened as nationalistic forces in both Taiwan and China increasingly exercise a stronger influence over their governments' policies than uncertainty over the American response. PRC leaders, for example, insist that China is willing to fight the United States over

Taiwan; and ROC leaders insist they will not bow to U.S. pressure to limit Taiwan's efforts to increase its overseas presence. Hence, while ambiguity continues to be useful, it has limitations as an instrument of U.S. policy. What should be recognized, however, is that while ambiguity may have become less effective as a method of deterrence, ambiguity continues to be a reflection of political reality in Washington. No one knows how the United States will respond to a future crisis in the Taiwan Strait because circumstances are changing both domestically and internationally.

9. *Is Taiwan defensible without U.S. military intervention?* Most military analysts believe that Taiwan would not be able to withstand a concentrated PRC attack intent on defeating the ROC. On the other hand, the ROC has a formidable defense capability that would make an all-out war extremely expensive for China militarily, economically, and politically. If the United States were to intervene early and purposefully on Taiwan's behalf, the PLA would almost certainly be defeated in its efforts to seize Taiwan.

That being said, however, there are many complicating factors. For example, U.S. intervention could not prevent certain kinds of PRC attack, such as missile strikes or special operations such as terror campaigns on Taiwan. For political reasons, the United States might not want to defeat the PLA but merely cause Beijing to call off the attack and seek a negotiated settlement. The PRC may not deploy sufficient forces against Taiwan, since that would weaken China's defense in other border areas. The Chinese goal may not be heavy destruction on Taiwan but rather the political capitulation of Taipei to accept early unification. Taiwan's armed forces, while perhaps not able to defeat a fully committed PLA attack, could defend against a large array of PRC offensive operations, including amphibious assault and most forms of air and sea strikes against Taiwan island. The use of nuclear weapons by either Chinese side, or other weapons of mass destruction, seems very unlikely. Also, Chinese leaders may not be entirely confident of the PLA's ability to attack Taiwan successfully until 2010 or beyond.

There is also a crucial time factor. Estimates for the duration of a conflict between Taiwan and China range from a few days of high-intensity warfare to several months of protracted struggle. Many analysts believe that a war in the Taiwan Strait would be a short, intensive conflict in which Beijing would have to win to avoid losing Taiwan and the ROC would have to win to avoid losing self-identity. Under these conditions, U.S. intervention would have to be quick if it were to have an impact on the outcome, although—in view of U.S. intelligence gathering capabilities—adequate warning of a pending PLA attack should be received by Washington. While all-or-nothing scenarios must be prepared for by all sides, the use of force in the Taiwan Strait is much more likely to be moderated by the political calculations of Beijing, Taipei, and Washington. Under these circumstances, political will and posturing may be as important as military capabilities.

Hence, there is no definitive answer to this question. Overall, it would seem that U.S. intervention on Taiwan's behalf could guarantee Taipei's overcoming the PRC offensive. Absent U.S. intervention, the critical factors probably are China's intentions in using force against Taiwan, PRC determination to pursue the offensive, and Taipei's will to resist. That the PRC is willing to threaten the use of force was demonstrated once again in 1995 and 1996. The PLA is modernizing fairly rapidly in areas of utility in the Taiwan Strait, and the focus of much of the PLA's planning and training is centered on recovering Taiwan. As long as the United States seeks to maintain a credible deterrence in the Taiwan Strait, it will be necessary to sell Taiwan increasingly more advanced defensive weapons and military "software," to deploy a significant U.S. force in the Western Pacific, and to sustain the perception that U.S. military intervention is likely in case of a PRC-initiated war with Taiwan. These policy guidelines are spelled out in the TRA, and the U.S. Congress has periodically taken steps to ensure that the TRA's provisions are not overshadowed by other considerations.

10. *To what extent should the United States support Taiwan's role in international organizations?* This also is a difficult question since it has many political, legal, and moral dimensions. On the political level, the United States is not seeking to separate Taiwan from China. Washington cannot, therefore, be the champion of Taiwan's drive for wider membership in international organizations. The United States recognizes the PRC as the sole legal government of China. Therefore, Washington cannot support the ROC as a national Chinese government in the United Nations or Taiwan's full membership in organizations limited to nation-states. But there is a difference between not supporting Taipei in these international organizations and opposing Taiwan's participation. China may be opposed to Taiwan's participation, but the United States should be non-supportive. In other words, in consideration of Taiwan's long friendship with the United States, Washington should not oppose Taipei's efforts to gain entry into international political organizations or otherwise to expand its international presence.

Morally speaking—and in recognition of its accomplishments—Taiwan should have a larger role in international non-political organizations, if only as a practical matter benefitting the entire global community. In non-political organizations, therefore, the United States should more actively support Taiwan's membership either by sponsoring Taipei's participation or by approving its application for membership. As a matter of principle, the United States should firmly oppose PRC efforts to deny Taiwan full and equal membership in non-political international organizations as a way of punishing Taipei or of pressuring it to enter into unification talks with the mainland.

Final Comments

For much of the 1990s, the key terms in U.S. China policy were integration, engagement, and enlargement. Integration was the strategy of drawing China more fully into the community of nations, with Beijing accepting both the privileges and responsibilities of being a major power in global politics. Engagement was the policy of expanding contact with China across the complete spectrum of interstate relations. The Clinton administration refined this policy to mean that, from Washington's point of view at least, no single disruptive issue would cause the entire relationship to collapse. Enlargement was the goal of bringing China into the community of market democracies by encouraging those changes in China that one day would lead to democratization and a free market economy. While it was acknowledged that these changes would be slow, with periods of regression, it was widely assumed by Americans that economic reform in the PRC would lead to political reform and that, over time, the Chinese Communist Party would no longer dominate the Chinese political scene but rather compete, if it existed at all, with other political parties in a more democratic system. During the 1997–1998 period, the United States and China also flirted once again with strategic partnership, but by mid-1999 that objective seemed unattainable during the Clinton administration.

The stakes of having China become a cooperative major power were enormous for the United States, if only because by the late 1990s it was clear that China could pose a significant potential threat to the United States as a peer competitor early in the next century. Under the assumption that democracies do not go to war against other democracies, it was in the U.S. interest to encourage China's evolution toward more economic and political openness. Jiang Zemin and other Chinese leaders understood the goal of U.S. engagement and integration, and they frequently promised never to compromise the leading role played by the Communist Party in China. Nonetheless, most Chinese leaders believed it was in China's best interest to modernize and to play a more active role in global affairs—neither of which could be realized easily without cooperative relations with the United States. Thus, for their own reasons, the United States and China agreed on the need for engagement and found many areas of cooperation in the integration of China into the community of nations. On China's membership in an enlarged community of market democracies, however, they was little agreement between Washington and Beijing.

One of the most critical questions facing the United States as it prepared to enter the twenty-first century was the extent to which Sino-American disagreement over China's future would undermine Sino-American cooperation on issues of more immediate concern. The conundrum in U.S. policy toward China centered around this question, made increasingly more urgent by the modernization of the PLA and the rising tide of Chinese nationalism. The conundrum also reflected an historic American ambivalency on the proper balance between realism and idealism in U.S. foreign policy. Few nations presented the United States with more evidence both of the pragmatic need for cooperative relations and moral abhorrence for human rights violations (as well as hope for an enlightened future) than did China.

The Taiwan issue focused American attention on the unavoidable weakness of a U.S. policy of engagement with the PRC, when China's future as friend or foe

Conclusion: Summits and Beyond

had yet to be determined. Unlike China, Taiwan by the 1990s possessed both a thriving market economy and a lively democracy, a leading example of the process by which the United States hoped to expand the global community of market democracies. Taiwan was, in more than a few respects, an embodiment in miniature of what the United States hoped one day to see on mainland China. For these and other reasons, U.S. support for Taiwan and friendly relations between the American and Taiwan people were realities impossible to ignore. But, as China made abundantly clear on repeated occasions, a friendly U.S. relationship with Taiwan was one of the few issues sufficiently sensitive to Beijing to undermine Sino-American relations. In other words, U.S. support of Taiwan—if carried beyond a certain, not clearly defined level—could erode the U.S. policy of engagement with China and set back, if not destroy, the U.S. strategy of integrating a cooperative China into the global community. Part of the conundrum of U.S. policy toward Taiwan, therefore, was finding a proper balance between the twin necessities of continued American support for Taiwan and expanding American engagement with China.

Beijing sought to convey the message that Washington had to choose between friendly relations with the PRC and friendly relations with Taiwan; Taipei tried to convince Washington that it should view U.S. relations with the PRC and with Taiwan separately on their own merits. Although both arguments found sympathetic ears in the United States, U.S. policymakers tried to avoid the black-or-white choice and chose instead a dual-track approach of high-profile engagement with China and quiet but strong support for Taiwan. The parameters of the ambiguous policy were defined broadly in the three communiqués, the Taiwan Relations Act, various pronouncements from different administrations, and legislation passed by the Congress. But—other than the sacrosanct principles that the United States recognizes the government of the PRC as the sole legal government of China, acknowledges the Chinese position on both sides of the Strait that Taiwan is part of China, intends to maintain friendly but unofficial relations with the people of Taiwan, and supports a peaceful resolution of differences between Beijing and Taipei—the specifics of U.S. relations with Beijing and Taipei were subject to changing interpretations, depending on circumstances. And this was to be expected, since China and Taiwan were both evolving, as was the United States itself and indeed the entire international environment in which all three governments and societies functioned.

Thus, the United States faced conundrums both in its policy toward China and in its policy toward Taiwan. Since the conundrum in U.S. policy toward China largely centered around the difficulties of managing superpower-rising power competition, the contradictions in Sino-American relations would exist regardless of whether Taiwan was an issue. But the conundrum in U.S. policy toward Taiwan existed primarily because of China—i.e., the historic connection between Taiwan and China and Beijing's extreme sensitivity to the Taiwan issue in Sino-American relations. In this sense, U.S. policy toward China was a higher-level issue than U.S.

policy toward Taiwan. On the other hand, since the elimination of the Taiwan issue would not resolve other fundamental problems in Sino-American relations, there was no strategic necessity for Washington to resolve the Taiwan issue along lines favored by Beijing—indeed, such a resolution might intensify Sino-American rivalry in the changing East Asian balance of power. Moreover, in a deeply ideological sense, Taiwan represented an American success story in Asia and, to some extent at least, a model of market democracy from which the whole of China might draw lessons.

It was this line of reasoning which ensured that U.S. policy toward Taiwan would remain essentially the same throughout the 1990s, as it had through the 1980s. Furthermore, unless compelling circumstances arise in China, Taiwan, the United States, or the international environment, there is little probability U.S. policy toward Taiwan will change during the first decade of the twenty-first century. That being said, however, complacency on the part of Washington, Beijing, or Taipei would be a mistake, since "compelling circumstances" are not only highly subjective but potentially always around the corner. Dynamic forces are constantly at work which could change strategic and policy calculations.

Examples of such compelling circumstances are not difficult to conceive. For example, Taiwan may issue a formal declaration of independence; the DPP may emerge as the ruling party of Taiwan and act on its inclination to hold a referendum on Taiwan's future; the ROC may become more active in its efforts to undermine the CCP; Taipei may decide to enter into formal political talks with Beijing; violent confrontations might occur on Taiwan between mainlanders and Taiwanese; Taiwan might deliberately provoke Beijing into military action; the PRC may attack Taiwan or threaten to use force in ways compelling a tough American response; Beijing may attempt to undermine Taiwan's social stability, economic prosperity, or political cohesion; it might declare or institute a blockade of Taiwan; the CCP might adopt political reforms to match its remarkable economic reforms; Beijing might offer Taiwan extremely generous terms as a largely autonomous region in a China defined in ways acceptable to all Chinese; the PRC might openly identify the United States as an enemy; Beijing might pursue hegemony around its borders; the PLA might modernize in ways posing a significant threat to U.S. security; China might change its military posture from one oriented toward defense to one oriented toward offense; the current modernization program on the mainland might fail or be abandoned, signaling a return to repressive political, economic, and social policies; the central government in Beijing might collapse and the country splinter into several parts; China might become involved in a war on the Korean Peninsula, in the South China Sea, or between India and Pakistan; a PRC leadership might emerge that was unfriendly toward the United States; U.S. congressional support for Taiwan might weaken; an administration might come to office decidedly unsupportive of Taiwan; the American people might waver in their support for Taiwan; high-level administration officials might try to resolve the

Conclusion: Summits and Beyond

Taiwan issue by forcing a change in U.S. policy; domestic U.S. opposition to engagement might lead to some less friendly approach to China.

These are circumstances which could occur, but hopefully they will not. And barring these or other compelling circumstances, existing U.S. policy toward Taiwan and China will likely remain in place.

In sum, there is a conundrum in the Taiwan issue, as well as in the China issue, conundrums that exist because of uncertainty about the future and because of seemingly intractable differences between Washington, Beijing, and Taipei. However, unless circumstances compel a change in U.S. policy, there is no need to pressure Taiwan or disengage from China. Just as it is difficult to maintain a relative military balance in the Taiwan Strait, so it is difficult to maintain a political balance in U.S. policy toward Beijing and Taipei. But these balances must be sought—however imperfectly—if the broad range of U.S. values and interests in Taiwan and China are to be served. There is, in other words, no current solution to the Taiwan conundrum in U.S. China policy. And a premature effort to solve the conundrum would likely result in a situation far more harmful to the United States than the conundrum itself.

Notes

1. Robert G. Sutter, *Shaping China's Future in World Affairs: The Role of the United States* (Boulder, CO: Westview, 1998), quoted and reviewed by Richard Halloran in *Far Eastern Economic Review*, February 12, 1998, p. 43.

2. "Speech by Richard C. Bush to the Taiwanese-American Chamber of Commerce of Greater Los Angeles, January 24, 1998," ms.

3. "Remarks by the President in Address on China and the National Interests to Voice of America, Washington, D.C." (White House: Office of the Press Secretary, October 24, 1997).

4. "Joint U.S.-China Statement" (White House: Office of the Press Secretary, October 29, 1997).

5. Lu Jin and Liu Yunfei, "Major Powers Reshape Their Relations," *Xinhua*, November 9, 1997, in *FBIS-China*, November 9, 1997.

6. Qian's report to departments under the CCP Central Committee, November 19, 1997, as reported in *Xinhua*, November 19, 1997, in *FBIS-China*, November 19, 1997.

7. "Fact Sheet: Achievements of U.S.-China Summit" (Beijing: White House Office of the Press Secretary, June 27, 1998).

8. "Remarks by the President to Students and Community of Beijing University" (Beijing: White House Office of the Press Secretary, June 29, 1998).

9. "Press Conference by the President, Grand Hyatt, Hong Kong Special Administrative Region" (Hong Kong Special Administration Region: White House Office of the Press Secretary, July 3, 1998).

10. Ibid.

11. Taiwan Central News Agency, July 8, 1998, in *FBIS-China*, July 8, 1998.

12. *Xinhua*, June 30, 1998, in *FBIS-China*, June 30, 1998.

13. "MAC Vice Chairman, Spokesman Sheu Ke-sheng at the October 6, 1998, News Conference," *MAC New Briefing* 96 (October 12, 1998), p. 1.

14. For a discussion of cross-Strait relations through 1997 and implications for U.S. policy, see Ralph N. Clough, *Cooperation or Conflict in the Taiwan Strait?* (New York: Rowman & Littlefield, 1999).

15. Speech to the PRC State Council's Office of Overseas Chinese Affairs, Office of Hong Kong and Macao Affairs, and Taiwan Affairs Office, as reported in *Xinhua*, September 29, 1997, in *FBIS-China*, September 29, 1997. For further elaboration of Qian's speech, see *Zongguo Xinwen She*, September 29, 1997, in *FBIS-China*, September 30, 1997.

16. Taiwan Central News Agency, September 30, 1997, in *FBIS-China*, September 30, 1997.

17. Quoted in *Free China Journal*, December 13, 1996, p. 1. Also, see Kao's report in *MAC News Briefing* 8 (January 6, 1997).

18. *MAC News Briefing* 37 (August 18, 1997).

19. Taiwan Central News Agency, September 19, 1997, in *FBIS-China*, September 22, 1997.

20. "Text of President Lee Teng-hui's Speech at Panama's Legislative Assembly," *Taipei Chung-Yang Jih-Pao*, September 10, 1997, in *FBIS-China*, September 10, 1997.

21. Wang Yuen-hua, "The Government Will Never Agree to Hasty Reunification or Taiwan Independence," *Chung-Yang Jih-Pao*, October 4, 1997, in *FBIS-China*, October 8, 1997.

22. Chang Wei-kuo, "Look Forward to New Pattern of Cross-Strait Relations—Interviewing Chang King-yu, Taiwan's Mainland Affairs Commission Chairman," *Hong Kong Hsin Pao*, October 9, 1997, in *FBIS-China*, October 9, 1997.

23. For a full report on the Koo visit from Taipei's point of view, see *Free China Journal*, October 23, 1998, p. 1.

24. *Strategic Assessments 1997: Flashpoints and Force Structure* (Washington, DC: Institute for National Strategic Studies, National Defense University, 1997). The sections on China were mainly written by Ronald Montaperto of INSS.

25. The public hearings on "Current and Projected National Security Threats to the United States," were held on January 28, 1998, before the Senate Select Committee on Intelligence, chaired by Senator Richard C. Shelby. Written statements for the record were presented by George J. Tenet, Director of Central Intelligence; Lt. Gen. Patrick M. Hughes, Director of the Defense Intelligence Agency; Phyllis E. Oakley, Assistant Secretary of State for Intelligence and Research; and Louis J. Freeh, Director of the Federal Bureau of Investigation.

26. "Statement by Director of Central Intelligence George J. Tenet before the Senate Select Committee on Intelligence Hearing on Current and Projected National Security Threats, 28 January 1998," ms.

27. Lt. Gen. Patrick M. Hughes, USA, Director, Defense Intelligence Agency, "Global Threats and Challenges: The Decades Ahead," statement for the Senate Select Committee on Intelligence, 28 January 1998, ms.

28. "Statement by Assistant Secretary of State for Intelligence and Research, Phyllis E. Oakley, before the Senate Select Committee on Intelligence Hearing on Current and Projected National Security Threats to the United States, January 28, 1998," ms.

Bibliography

Accinelli, Robert. *Crisis and Commitment: United States Policy toward Taiwan, 1950-1955*. Chapel Hill: University of North Carolina Press, 1996.
Aspin, Les. *Report on the Bottom-Up Review*. Washington, DC: Department of Defense, October 1993.
Austin, Greg, ed. *Missile Diplomacy and Taiwan's Future: Innovations in Politics and Military Power*. Canberra: Australian National University Press, 1998.
Bader, William B., and Jeffrey T. Bergner, eds. *The Taiwan Relations Act: A Decade of Implementation*. Indianapolis, IN: Hudson Institute, 1989.
Baldwin, Robert E. *Political Economy of U.S.-Taiwan Trade*. Ann Arbor: University of Michigan Press, 1995.
Bernstein, Richard, and Ross H. Munro. *The Coming Conflict with China*. New York: Knopf, 1997.
Borthwick, Mark. *Pacific Century: The Emergence of Modern Pacific Asia*. Boulder, CO: Westview, 1992.
Bullock, Mary Brown, and Robert S. Litwak, eds. *The United States and the Pacific Basin: Changing Economic and Security Relationships*. Washington, DC: Woodrow Wilson Center, 1991.
Carter, Jimmy. *Keeping Faith: Memoirs of a President*. New York: Bantam Books, 1982.
Chang Jaw-Ling, Joanne, ed. *ROC-US Relations, 1979-1989*. Taipei: Academia Sinica, 1991.
Chang, Parris H., and Martin L Lasater, eds. *If China Crosses the Taiwan Strait: The International Response*. Lanham, MD: University Press of America, 1993.
China: U.S. Policy Since 1945. Washington, DC: Congressional Quarterly, 1980.
Chiu, Hungdah. *Koo-Wang Talks and the Prospect of Building Constructive and Stable Relations Across the Taiwan Straits*. Baltimore: University of Maryland School of Law, 1993.
Clough, Ralph N. *Island China*. Cambridge, MA: Harvard University Press, 1978.
———. *Reaching Across the Taiwan Strait: People-to-People Diplomacy*. Boulder, CO: Westview, 1993.
———. *Cooperation or Conflict in the Taiwan Strait?* New York: Rowman & Littlefield, 1999.
Cohen, William S. *Report of the Quadrennial Defense Review*. Washington, DC: Department of Defense, May 1997.
Copper, John F. *Taiwan: Nation-State or Province?* Boulder, CO: Westview, 1990.
Downen, Robert L. *The Taiwan Pawn in the China Game: Congress to the Rescue*. Washington, DC: Georgetown University Press, 1979.
A Draft Agreement between the Government of the United Kingdom of Great Britain and Northern Ireland and the Government of the People's Republic of China on the Future of Hong Kong. London: Her Majesty's Government, September 26, 1984.
Garver, John W. *Face off: China, the United States, and Taiwan's Democratization*. Seattle: University of Washington Press, 1997.

Gertz, Bill. *Betrayal: How the Clinton Administration Undermined American Security.* Washington, DC: Regnery, 1999.

Gibert, Stephen P., and William M. Carpenter, eds. *America and Island China: A Documentary History.* Lanham, MD: University Press of America, 1989

Green, Marshall, John H. Holdridge, and William N. Stokes. *War and Peace with China: First-hand Experiences in the Foreign Service of the United States.* Bethesda, MD: Dacor, 1994.

"Guidelines for National Unification." Taipei: National Unification Council, 1991.

Harding, Harry. *A Fragile Relationship: The United States and China Since 1972.* Washington, DC: Brookings Institution, 1992.

Harding, Harry, and Yuan Ming, eds. *Sino-American Relations, 1945–1955: A Joint Reassessment of a Critical Decade.* Wilmington, DE: Scholarly Resources, 1989.

Hickey, Dennis Van Vranken. *United States-Taiwan Security Ties: From Cold War to Beyond Containment.* Westport, CT: Praeger, 1994.

Hood, Steven J. *The KMT and the Democratization of Taiwan.* Boulder, CO: Westview, 1997.

Institute for National Strategic Studies. *Strategic Assessments 1997: Flashpoints and Force Structure.* Washington, DC: National Defense University Press, 1997.

Jackson, Karl D., ed. *Asian Contagion: The Causes and Consequences of a Financial Crisis.* Boulder, CO: Westview, 1999.

Kissinger, Henry A. *White House Years.* Boston: Little, Brown and Co., 1979.

Klintworth, Gary, ed. *Asia-Pacific Security: Less Uncertainty, New Opportunities.* New York: St. Martin's, 1996.

Koenig, Louis W., ed. *Congress, the Presidency, and the Taiwan Relations Act.* New York: Praeger, 1985.

Lasater, Martin L. *The Taiwan Issue in Sino-American Strategic Cooperation.* Boulder, CO: Westview, 1984.

———. *Policy in Evolution: The U.S. Role in China's Reunification.* Boulder, CO: Westview, 1989.

———. *U.S. Interests in the New Taiwan.* Boulder, CO: Westview, 1993.

———. *The Changing of the Guard: President Clinton and the Security of Taiwan.* Boulder, CO: Westview, 1995.

Lee Teng-hui. *Taiwan's Viewpoint.* Taipei: Liou Publishing Company, 1999.

Lilley, James R., and Chuck Downs, eds. *Crisis in the Taiwan Strait.* Washington, DC: American Enterprise Institute and National Defense University Press, 1997.

Mandelbaum, Michael, ed. *The Strategic Quadrangle: Russia, China, Japan, and the United States in East Asia.* New York: Council on Foreign Relations, 1994.

Mann, James. *About Face: A History of America's Curious Relationship with China, from Nixon to Clinton.* New York: Knopf, 1999.

Metzger, Thomas A., and Ramon H. Myers, eds. *Greater China and U.S. Foreign Policy: The Choice between Confrontation and Mutual Respect.* Stanford: Hoover Institution, 1996.

Mosher, Steven W. *China Misperceived: American Illusions and Chinese Reality.* New York: Basic Books, 1990.

Myers, Ramon H., ed. *A Unique Relationship: The United States and the Republic of China under the Taiwan Relations Act.* Stanford, CA: Hoover Institution, 1989.

Bibliography

Nathan, Andrew J., and Robert Ross. *The Great Wall and the Empty Fortress: China's Search for Security.* New York: Norton, 1997.

A National Security Strategy of Engagement and Enlargement. Washington, DC: The White House, July 1994.

A National Security Strategy for a New Century. Washington, DC: The White House, May 1997.

Nixon, Richard M. *RN: The Memoirs of Richard Nixon.* New York: Grosset and Dunlap, 1978.

Pillsbury, Michael, ed. *Chinese Views of Future Warfare.* Washington, DC: National Defense University Press, 1997.

Shambaugh, David. *Beautiful Imperialist: China Perceives America, 1972-1990.* Princeton: Princeton University Press, 1992.

Solomon, Richard H. *Chinese Political Negotiating Behavior, 1967-1984.* Santa Monica, CA: RAND, 1985.

Spence, Jonathan. *To Change China: Western Advisers in China, 1620-1960.* New York: Penguin Books, 1980.

Sutter, Robert G. *Shaping China's Future in World Affairs: The Role of the United States.* Boulder, CO: Westview, 1998.

———. *U.S. Policy toward China: An Introduction to the Role of Interest Groups.* Lanham, MD: Rowman & Littlefield, 1998.

"The Taiwan Question and the Reunification of China." Beijing: Taiwan Affairs Office and Information Office, State Council, August 1993.

Tow, William T. *Encountering the Dominant Player: U.S. Extended Deterrence Strategy in the Asia-Pacific.* New York: Columbia University Press, 1991.

Tucker, Nancy Bernkopf. *Taiwan, Hong Kong, & the United States.* New York: Maxwell Macmillan International, 1994.

U.S. Congress, House of Representatives. *House Report 105-851: Report of the Select Committee on U.S. National Security and Military/Commercial Concerns with the People's Republic of China.* Washington, DC: GPO, 1999.

———. House of Representatives, Committee on Foreign Affairs. *China-Taiwan: United States Policy.* Washington, DC: GPO, 1982.

———. Senate, Committee on Foreign Relations. *Taiwan: Hearings on S. 245.* Washington, DC: GPO, 1979.

U.S. Department of Defense. *A Strategic Framework for the Asian Pacific Rim: Looking Toward the 21st Century.* Washington, DC: Department of Defense, April 1990.

———. *A Strategic Framework for the Asian Pacific Rim: Looking Toward the 21st Century: A Report to Congress.* Washington, DC: Department of Defense, February 28, 1991.

———. *A Strategic Framework for the Asian Pacific Rim: Report to Congress 1992.* Washington, DC: Department of Defense, 1992.

———. *1992 Joint Military Net Assessment.* Washington, DC: Joint Chiefs of Staff, August 1992.

———. *United States Security Strategy for the East Asia-Pacific Region.* Washington, DC: Department of Defense, February 1995.

———. *United States Security Strategy for the East Asia-Pacific Region.* Washington, DC: Department of Defense, November 1998.

———. "The Security Situation in the Taiwan Strait: Report to Congress Pursuant to the FY99 Appropriations Bill." Washington, DC: Department of Defense, March 1999.

———. "Report to Congress on Theater Missile Defense Architecture Options for the Asia-Pacific Region." Washington, DC: Department of Defense, 1999.

White, Lynn T. "Taiwan's China Problem: After a Decade or Two, Can There Be a Solution?" Washington, DC: SAIS Policy Forum Series, December 1998.

Wilhelm, Alfred D., Jr. *The Chinese at the Negotiating Table.* Washington, DC: National Defense University Press, 1994.

Wolff, Lester L., and David L. Simon. *Legislative History of the Taiwan Relations Act: An Analytic Compilation with Documents on Subsequent Developments.* Jamaica, NY: American Association for Chinese Studies, 1982.

Yang, Maysing H., ed. *Taiwan's Expanding Role in the International Arena.* Armonk, NY: M.E. Sharpe, 1997.

Yu, Peter Kien-hong, ed. *The Chinese PLA's Perception of an Invasion of Taiwan.* New York: Contemporary U.S.-Asia Research Institute, 1996.

About the Book and the Author

The Taiwan issue in Sino-American relations remains one of the most complex, controversial, and even dangerous policy dilemmas facing the United States in the post-Cold War period. In an era of growing nationalism on mainland China and Taiwan, tremendous strain is being placed on relations across the Taiwan Strait. As demonstrated by the 1996 Taiwan missile crisis, conflict between the two Chinese sides is a growing possibility, with important implications for U.S. security interests in peace and stability in the Western Pacific. *The Taiwan Conundrum* explains the complex policy interaction between Washington, Taipei, and Beijing in the context of their respective values, politics, strategies, and interests.

Martin L. Lasater is a Non-Resident Scholar at the Atlantic Council of the United States in Washington, D.C. A specialist on Asia-Pacific security issues, he has written several books on Taiwan and China, the most recent being *The Changing of the Guard: President Clinton and the Security of Taiwan* (Westview, 1995).

Index

Acheson, Dean, 115
Ackerman, Gary, 35
Activists, Chinese, 24
　See also Political prisoners
Adams, Gerry, 39
Agreement on Peaceful Nuclear
　Cooperation, 173
Airline services, international, 58, 132, 179, 183
Air supremacy, 147
Albright, Madeleine K., 83, 279
Ambiguity, ix, 33, 131, 262, 305–306
American Institute in Taiwan (AIT), 34, 174, 177, 280, 283
Amnesty International, 201
APEC. See Asian Pacific Economic Cooperation (APEC)
Appeasement, 231
Arafat, Yasser, 39
ARATS. See Association for Relations Across theTaiwan Strait (ARATS)
Arms Control and Disarmament Agency (ACDA), 219, 222
Arms Export Control Act, 1990, 170
Arms race, 58
Arms sales, xii, 15, 255, 259, 266, 303
　during 1993–1994, 175
　August 17 communiqué, 127–130
　ceilings on, 131–132
　Murkowski Amendment, 30–34
　during Strait crisis, 262, 268
　TRA implementation, 125–127
　white paper stance, 183–184
　See also Proliferation, arms; Taiwan Relations Act (TRA)
ASEAN. See Association of Southeast Asian Nations (ASEAN)
ASEAN Regional Forum (ARF), 105–106, 222

Asia, 50, 51–52, 58
　Bush administration policy, 63–74
　Reagan administration policy, 62–63
　sources of instability, 72
　U.S. strategy and policy towards, 60–61,95–97, 105–106, 215
Asian Pacific Economic Cooperation (APEC), 37, 68, 100–101, 105, 164, 177, 228, 229
Asian strategic triangle, 64
Association for Relations Across the Taiwan Strait (ARATS), 136, 178–179, 199, 283, 284, 285, 287
Association of Southeast Asian Nations (ASEAN), 47, 99, 169, 202
August 17, 1982, Sino-American joint communiqué, 30–33, 63, 127–130, 147, 151, 251, 303

Baker, James
　1991 visit, 146–147
　collective engagement, 65–66
　U.S. engagement in the Pacific, 68–69
Balance, in policy, 13, 22, 30, 34, 177
Balance wheel of Asia, 69–74
　See also Power, balance of
Bao Tong, 165
Barshefsky, Charlene, 200, 228, 279
Base Force, 67, 91
Beijing. See China
Beijing Central People's Radio, 209
Beijing University, 282
Belgrade, 1999 missile attack, 172
Bellocchi, Natale, 34, 174, 175
Bentsen, Lloyd, 164
Berger, Sandy, 279
Bernstein, Richard, 52
Bilateral relations, 102, 105–106

Index

Bills and resolutions, U.S., 23–29
  See also Congress
Biological and Chemical Weapons
  Conventions, 149
Biological and Toxin Weapons Convention,
  1972, 219
Biological warfare program, 169, 219
Blockade, 243, 245–247, 259–260
Brown, Hank, 37
Brown, Ronald, 168
Brzezinski, Zbigniew, 121
Bush, George, 242
  sale of F–16s to Taiwan, 31, 147–148
Bush, Richard, 280–281, 283
Bush administration
  Asian strategy and policy, 63–77
  Base Force, 67, 91
  policy toward China and Taiwan,
    140–149
  troop strength at end of, 73

Cambodian peace process, 69
Campbell, Kurt, 263, 265–266
Carter, Ashton, 16
Carter, Jimmy, 62
  normalization, 121–123
  TRA implementation, 23, 125–126
Cassidy & Associates, 39
CCP. *See* Chinese Communist Party (CCP)
Chang King-yuh, 285, 286–287
Check-and-balance system, 21, 29, 44
Chemical Weapons Convention, 89, 168,
  170, 172, 260
Chen Li-an, 268
Chen Shui-bian, 17, 52
Chen Ziming, 214
Chiang Ching-kuo, 147
  death and accomplishments of, 2–3
Chiang Kai-Shek, 113, 114, 117, 118
Chiang Kai-Shek, Madame, 220
Chien, Fredrick, 266–267
Chi Haotian, 41, 208, 232
China
  recalls Ambassador to United States,
    207, 211, 215
  American values toward, 3–5
  ARATS, 178–179
  arms sales, 168–173, 254–255, 258, 260
  description of, 55
  diplomatic recognition with U.S.,
    121–123
  emergence in global affairs, 106, 226
  as growing power, 47, 94–95, 194, 226,
    258, 282
  human rights, views on, 143, 162–163
  improvement of relations, 157
  independent foreign policy, 130–131
  leadership, 120–121, 193, 194, 207, 211,
    234, 257
  Lee's U.S. visit, reaction to, 38–43, 205,
    207–210, 234, 244, 247, 284
  MFN status, response to, 162, 165–167
  military, 104–105, 144, 232, 256–257, 258,
    288–296
  nuclear weapons arsenal, 289–290
  peaceful reunification, adoption of,
    124–125
  as peer competitor, 295–296, 308
  policy adjustments, post-Lee visit,
    210–213
  as rightful leader, 139
  role in Clinton's Asian Pacific strategy,
    99–101
  Soviet Union, relations with, 115, 118,
    130–131, 290
  state visits, cancellation of, 208, 215
  Strait military exercises, 221–229, 248,
    257, 259–260, 261, 267, 269
  as strategic partner, 87–88
  Summer Olympic Games 2000, 163–164,
    244
  suspicions of U.S. divisive strategy,
    244–245
  Taiwan, recovery of, ix
  "The Taiwan Question and the
    Reunification of
  China", 179–184
  Taiwan's influence on policies, 51
  Taiwan's international presence, 42,
    194
  Taiwan policy review, 178
  Taiwan's strategic value to, 48–49,
    243–247
  in transition, 291–292
  U.S. bilateral security relations, 102–103
  U.S. interests in, 54–57
  warning to Taipei, 263
  WTO, entrance to, 200–201, 204, 228
  Ye Jianying's "nine-point" proposal,
    132–137
  See also Jiang Zemin
China National Nuclear Corporation, 270
China Policy Act, 220
Chinese Academy of Social Sciences, 208

Index

Chinese Communist Party (CCP), 143, 280, 302, 308
  hardliners, 42, 130, 207, 210, 211–212, 263
  "One China", 278
Ching, Frank, 228
Christopher, Warren, 33, 34, 99, 168, 173, 270
  1993 MFN, 159–160
  engagement objectives, 82
  human rights violations, 165–166
  Lee's visit, 40, 221, 227
  meetings with Qian, 164, 202, 222, 224, 228–229
  policy interpretation, 169
  U.S. leadership, 83
  warning to China, 260, 261
Christopher-Qian talks, 164, 202, 222, 224, 228–229
Chu Shulong, 243–245
Clinton, Bill, 66
  address to Korean National Assembly, 98–99
  "bottom-up review", 67, 88
  integration strategy, 109–110
  Lee's visit, 40–41, 207
  MFN status linked with human rights, 156–157
  Murkowski amendment, 32–33
  sale of F-16s, 148, 156, 173
  sanctions avoided, 270–271
  state visits, 5, 9–12, 224, 225, 227–228, 281, 282–283, 298
  "three-no's" policy, xii, 9, 12, 17, 50, 283, 300, 303
  Waseda University speech, 97–98, 174
  See also Clinton administration
Clinton, Hillary Rodham, 223–224
Clinton administration, 81–82
  adoption of Bush policies, 66, 69
  APEC forum, 100–101
  Asian Pacific strategy, 74–77, 95–99
  "bottom-up review", 67, 88
  China's role in Pacific community, 99–101
  comprehensive engagement, 202–203
  definition of China policy, 155–159
  engagement and enlargement strategy, 82–88
  human rights policy, revised, 167–168
  military strategies, 88–95
  policy statements, 203–205, 249–253

proliferation issues, 168–173
public criticism of missile tests, 223
"reengagement", 164, 171
regional security policy, 101–109
second term, 279–281
security strategy, 85–87
Taiwan policies, 173–178
Taiwan Policy Review, 36–38
trade and human rights, 159–168
Cohen, William, 279
Cold War, 61, 83
Cold War, post-, 81
  new world order, 141–143
  U.S. strategies, 64–74
Communications, back channel of, 17
Communications satellites, 172
Communiqués, joint, 30, 118–119, 122, 127–130, 147, 164, 224, 229, 251, 266, 309
Communist government, 139, 186, 205, 297, 299
Comprehensive engagement, 202–205, 226, 230, 233–234, 266, 277, 279
Comprehensive Test Ban Treaty, 172, 223, 225
Compromise, 278
Concessions, U.S., 297, 298
Conference on Security and Cooperation in Europe (CSCE), 96
Conflict, armed, 241, 300
  avoidance, 13, 271
  cross-Strait, 252–253
  U.S. response to, 58–59
  See also Military conflict
Confrontation, 234–235, 248, 271, 297
Congress, U.S.
  influence on policy, 22–30, 123–124, 269–270, 275
  Lee's visit, 39, 43–44
  meeting with Jiang, 281–282
  Murkowski Amendment, 30–34
  Taiwan policy review, 34–38, 177–178
Consensus, U.S., 13, 21, 59
Containment strategy, 61, 64–65, 83, 116, 117, 214, 220, 256, 277
Cooperative engagement strategy, 102–109
Coordination Council for North American Affairs, 173
Copyrights, violation of, 175
  See also Intellectual Property Rights (IPR)

Cornell University, Lee's visit to, 38–43, 205
Cox report, 171
Crane, Philip, 35
Cray supercomputer, sale of, 172
Cross-Strait relations, 178–186, 206, 281
   China, accommodation of, 302–303
   conflict in, 57–60
   eight-point and six-point proposals, 195–199
   trade, 262
   See also Koo-Wang talks; Reunification, peaceful

Dalai Lama, 161, 164, 168, 224
D'Amato, Alfonse, 35
Democracy, promotion of, 52, 68, 87, 96, 99, 158, 176–177
Democracy Wall Movement, 157, 160
Democratic Party, 155–156
Democratic Progressive Party (DPP), xii, 17, 52, 206, 268, 288, 299, 301
Deng Xiaoping, 193, 234
   as leader, 120, 121, 130, 212
   death and accomplishments of, 3–5
   Hong Kong Agreement, 59
   "one country, two systems", 134, 207, 227
   reforms of, 125, 140, 287
Department of Defense
   engagement policy, 255–256
   role in China-Taiwan policy, 229–233
   during Strait crisis, 262, 268
Deutch, John, 256–257
Dialogue
   Christopher-Qian, 164, 202, 222, 224, 228–229
   GATT, 68, 98
   Koo-Wang, 38, 179, 199, 210, 212, 269, 284–288, 302, 309
   military-to-military, 171–172, 202, 232–233, 248
   See also Cross-Strait relations; State visits
Diplomatic relations, 18, 34, 36–37, 42–43, 121–123, 177, 206, 207, 211, 215
Dobrynin, Anatoly, 118
Dole, Robert, 258–259, 279
Donovan, Hedley, 125
DPP. *See* Democratic Progressive Party (DPP)
"Dual-track" approach, ix, 30, 53, 54, 150, 175, 211, 309
Duan Zhaoxian, 245

Dulles, John Foster, 117
Dutch government, sale of submarines by, 126–127

East Asia Strategic Initiative (EASI) reports, 70, 71–74, 75, 103–104
Economic interests, 56, 58, 96, 97–98, 100–101
   post-Cold War, 67–69
   Taiwan in China, 51, 262
   U.S. in Taiwan, 51–52
   See also Trade
Editorial views, U.S.
   Chiang, passing of, 2–3
   Clinton state visit, 9–12
   Deng, passing of, 3–5
   Jiang state visit, 5–8
Einhorn, Robert, 270
Eisenhower, Dwight D., 116
Enemy, common, 296
Engagement strategy, 48, 53, 57, 75, 82–84, 100, 150, 194, 215–217, 279, 308
   achievements of, 217–218
   collective, 65–66
   military, 88–89, 92–93
   as only logical choice, 276–277
   Reagan administration, 63
Enlargement strategy, 84–85, 76, 279, 308
Environmental issues, Asian, 97, 158
Espy, Mike, 164
Executive branch, 21–22, 34, 44
Export-Import Bank, 254, 258, 270

F–16s, sale of, 31, 140, 147–148, 150–152, 156, 170, 173, 175, 211, 244, 262
   See also Arms sales
Far Eastern Economic Review, 228
Financial crisis, 1997, 108
"Flashpoints", global, 72, 289, 291
Force, use of, 15, 55, 179, 181, 198, 205, 241, 242, 259, 262, 265, 300, 301
Ford, Gerald, 120
Formosa. *See* Taiwan
Formosa Resolution, 117
Foundation for Exchanges Across the Taiwan Strait, 178–179
"Four little dragons", 51–52
"Four tigers", 51–52
France, sale of Mirage fighters, 147–148, 252
Franklin, Barbara, 149
Freeman, Charles, 15, 164, 171–172, 242

Index

Free passage, right of, 202, 245–247, 259–260

Gang of Four, 120, 121
Gao Shan, 157
Gati, Toby, 257
GATT, 37, 200
   China seeks entry to, 157
   Taiwan seeks entry to, 175–176
   Uruguay Round of talks, 68, 98
   See also World Trade Organization (WTO)
Geostrategic value, of Taiwan, 53, 245–247
Gephardt, Richard, 258
Gingrich, Newt, 39, 220, 260
Global leadership, 64, 66, 83, 142, 288
Goldwater, Barry, 130
Gorbachev, Mikhail, 151
Gore, Al, 224, 228

Haig, Alexander, 130
Hardliners, 42, 130, 207, 210, 211–212, 263
Havel, Vaclav, 42
Hay, John, 60
Hayakawa, S.I., 131
Hills, Carla A., 149
Historical overview, Taiwan, 113–118
Holbrooke, Richard, 13
Hong Kong, 24, 51, 264, 268, 287
   Agreement, 59, 134–136
   "one country, two systems", 138
Hong Kong Economic Journal, 286
Hsiao Wan-chang, 285
Hsu Hsin-liang, 17
Hu, Jason, 42
Hua Guofeng, 120, 121, 124
Huang Hua-Leonard Woodcock talks, 121
Huang-Middleton-Wood controversy, 14
Huan Xiang, 131
Hughes, Patrick, 292–293
Human rights, 48, 56, 69, 77, 158, 201, 204, 260, 281
   Chinese views on, 143, 162–163
   MFN status and, 156–157, 159–161, 162, 165–167
Hu Yaobang, 130

Independence, 261, 266
Instability, sources of, 68, 72, 289, 291
Integration strategy, 64–65, 95, 105, 109–110, 169, 307–308

Intellectual Property Rights (IPR), 145, 159, 161, 165, 175–176, 199, 200, 255, 263
Intelligence and Research (INR), 257, 293
Interests, national, 48, 86–87, 276
   China as conflict to, 76–77, 296–297
   in Taiwan, 50–54, 301–302
International Olympic Committee (IOC), 163
Iran, arms proliferation of, 170, 172, 202, 213–214, 248, 254, 260, 270, 281
Iraq, 90
Iraq-Iran Arms Non-Proliferation Act, 1992, 254
Isolationism, 61, 93, 94
Issues, controversial, 57, 280
   Clinton's stand on, 158–159
   resolution of, 276–277, 278

Japan, x, 47, 50, 97, 114
   security alliance, 73, 90, 102, 105, 146, 289
Jiang Minfang, 245
Jiang Zemin, 269, 288
   APEC forum, 101, 164
   criticism of West, 164
   Eight-Point proposal, 195–197, 212
   as leader, 193, 210, 213, 234, 280
   Lee's visit to U.S., 207
   role of communism, 308
   sensitivity of Taiwan, 227, 242
   Sino-American relations, 14, 157
   state visits, 5–8, 38, 50, 51, 224, 225, 227–228, 281–282, 298
   See also China
Joint Military Net Assessment (JMNA), 66–67, 73

Kantor, Mickey, 165, 176, 199, 200, 255, 263
Kao Koong-lian, 285
Kearney, Jude, 221
Keizo Obuchi, 50
Kinmen (Quemoy), 117, 243
Kissinger, Henry, 118, 120–121
Klaus, Vaclav, 42
KMT. *See* Kuomintang (KMT)
Koo Chen-fu, 179, 210, 283, 288
Koo-Wang talks, 38, 179, 199, 210, 212, 269, 284–288, 302
Korea, 108
   See also North Korea; South Korea
Korean War, 115–117

Kuomintang (KMT), xii, 2, 48, 52, 114, 206, 277–278, 287, 299

Lake, Anthony, 83–85, 168, 260, 279
Lantos, Tom, 35
Lardy, Nicholas, 228
Larson, Charles R., 102
Law of the Sea Treaty, 1982, 202
Lee Teng-hui, 266
    APEC, 101, 177
    Hawaii, humiliation in, 34–35, 37, 177
    international presence, x-xi, 278
    Lee Doctrine, 42–43
    "pragmatic diplomacy", 39, 81
    on reunification, 285–286
    Six-Point Proposal, 195, 197–198
    as successor to Chiang, 2–3, 268
    Taiwan independence, 14, 267
    unification plan by, 136–137
    unofficial visit to U.S., x-xi, 5, 38–43, 172, 205–210, 234, 244, 259, 284
    See also Taiwan
Lewis, John, 242
Liao Chengzhi, 125
Liaowang, 210
Li Daoyu, 211, 223
Lieberman, Joseph, 35
Lien Chan, 34, 42, 213, 269
Lien Ho Pao, 207
Li Guixian, 41, 208
Lin Chong-pin, 135–136
Lin Yang-kang, 268
Li Peng, 157, 234, 259, 267
Liu Huaqiu, 170, 178, 260, 262
Li Xiannian, 124
Li Xilin, 223
Li Yuan-zu, 242, 248
Li Zhaoxing, 248
Lord, Winston, 228
    Asian policy, 95–97, 105–106, 215
    China policy, 157–158, 161–162, 225–226
    Strait crisis, 263–265
    Taiwan policy, 41, 174, 229, 249–253
Lu Junyuan, 53, 246–247

MacArthur, Douglas, 116
Macau, 135, 207, 287
McCain, John, 219
McCarthy, Joseph R., 115
McCurry, Mike, 262
Macke, Richard C., 203–204

Mainland Affairs Council, ROC, 184–185, 285
Mainlanders, x, 2, 114, 120, 278
Mao Zedong, 3, 113, 115, 117, 120, 212, 287
Market democracies, 36, 52, 64–65, 67–69, 74, 310
Matsu, 117, 243
Memorandum of Understanding, 159
Military, Chinese, 104–105, 144, 232, 242–243, 249, 256–257, 258
    assessment of strength, 288–296
    Strait exercises, 213, 221–229, 248, 257, 259–260,261, 267, 269
Military, U.S., 71–74, 90, 93–94
Military conflict
    between China and U.S., xi, 241
    cross-Strait, 57–60, 213, 221–229, 248, 252–253, 257, 259–260, 261, 267, 269
Military strategy, U.S., 107
    Clinton administration, 88–95
    military-to-military talks, 171–172, 202, 232–233, 248
    regional contingencies, 66–67, 101–109
Missiles, sale of, 146, 147, 169–170, 213, 219, 222, 254, 270
    See also Arms sales; Proliferation, arms
Missile Technology Control Regime (MTCR), 89, 146, 147, 149, 168, 169–170, 172
Missile tests, Chinese. *See* Military, Chinese, Strait exercises
Model Business Principles, 201
Morality, state, 12–18, 19
Most-favored-nation (MFN) trading status, 23, 24, 145–146, 201, 214–215, 258
    conflict with, 48, 268
    human rights and, 156–157, 159–161, 162, 165–167
Multilateralism, 69, 83
Munro, Ross, 52
Murkowski, Frank, 30, 31, 37, 38, 132, 177, 258
Murkowski Amendment to the TRA, 30–34
Mutual Defense Treaty, 117, 122

Narcotics, traffic in, 97, 158
Nathan, Andrew, 53
National Defense University (NDU), 289
National interests. *See* Interests, national
Nationalists, 113, 114, 116, 193

Index

Naval
 blockade, 243
 deployments, U.S., xii, 261, 266, 267
New partnership in Asia, 67–69
New Party, 52, 268
Newsweek, 227
New World Order, 64–65, 141–143
New Year's Day Letter to Taiwan Compatriots, 125
Nimitz, 233, 261, 266
Nixon, Richard, 118, 121
Nonproliferation. *See* Proliferation, arms
Normalization
 Sino-American relations, 118–131
 Vietnam, 219–220
North Korea, 72, 90, 98, 106–107, 115, 169, 172, 214
NPT Exporters Committee, 172
Nuclear Non-Proliferation Treaty (NPT), 89, 149, 168, 172, 202, 254, 294
Nuclear Proliferation Prevention Act, 1994, 254
Nuclear weapons, detonation of, 171, 223
Nunn, Sam, 125
Nye, Joseph, 106, 249, 263
 engagement, 215–217
 policy clarification, 15–16
 role in China-Taiwan policy, 230, 232–233

Oakley, Phyllis, 293–295
Okinawa, 90, 114
O'Leary, Hazel R., 199–200
Olympic Games, Summer 2000, 163–164, 244
"One China, one Taiwan" policy, 128, 182, 196, 208
"One China" policy, 120, 150, 194, 211, 256
 fundamental flaw in, 277–278
"One country, two systems" policy, 49, 134, 137, 138, 180–181, 186, 207, 227
105th Congress, 26–29, 279
104th Congress, 25–26
103rd Congress, 24–25

Pacific Fleet, U.S., 261
Pakistan, 146
 missile sales to, 169, 170, 213, 219, 222, 254, 270
 nuclear-related technology sale to, 254, 258, 270
Partisan politics, U.S., 29

Pell, Claiborne, 33, 35
Peng Ming-min, 268
Peng Zhen, 133
People's Daily, 221, 223, 259
People's Liberation Army (PLA), xii, 16, 140, 171–172
 military capability, 144, 242–243
 Taiwan Strait crisis, 31, 258, 261
People's Republic of China (PRC)
 as sole government of China, 122
 See also China; Chinese Communist Party (CCP)
Perot, Ross, 279
Perry, William J., 201, 249
 delegation to China, 16–17
 engagement strategy, 106–107, 255–256
 role in China-Taiwan policy, 229–232
 on Strait crisis, 260, 267
 warning to China, 260–261
Perry delegation, 16–17
Persian Gulf, 248
 War, 143–144
Perspectives, 12, 275–278
Philippines, 50
Policeman, world's, 93, 170
Policy, Chinese, 130–131, 210–213
 See also China
Policy, U.S., ix
 balanced, 13, 22, 30, 34, 177
 Bush administration, 140–149
 Clinton administration, 15–16, 82–84, 95–97, 157–159, 249–253, 277
 congressional influence on, 22–30
 critical questions for, xi–xiii, 296–307
 economic, 96, 97–98, 100–101
 influences on, xiii, 21–22
 Reagan administration, 131–140
 Strait crisis statements, 263–268
 Taiwan, 280–281, 305–306, 310
 See also specific topics
Political interests, U.S., 55–56
Political prisoners, 157, 163, 164, 165, 214
Population growth, Asian, 97
Power, balance of, 18, 47, 54–55
 emerging vs. status quo, 296–297
 Reagan, 62–63
 regional, 59–60, 298
 at turn of century, 60–61
 U.S. role in, 50, 69–74, 94–95, 96, 104, 143, 194
PRC. *See* People's Republic of China (PRC)
Presidential politics, U.S., 258–259, 279

Principles, Taiwan issue, 118–119
  arms sales, 125–127
  August 17 communiqué, 127–130
  normalization agreement, 120–123
  peaceful reunification, 124–125
  PRC independent foreign policy, 130–131
  Shanghai Communiqué, 119–120
  Taiwan Relations Act, 123–124
Prison labor, exports made with, 156, 157, 159, 161, 166
Proliferation, arms, 97, 149, 293–294
  Chinese practices, 76, 146, 204–205, 219, 248, 255, 270, 291
  Clinton administration issues, 168–173, 202
  nuclear, 89, 98–99
Prosperity, promotion of, 87
Protectionist barriers, 145
Public opinion
  engagement, 22
  Lee's visit, 39–40
  PLA buildup, 248–249
  sanctions, 254–255
  in Taiwan, 268–269
  Taiwan, support of, 51, 150
  Tiananmen Square, 140–141

QDR. *See Report of the Quadrennial Defense Review* (QDR)
Qian Qichen, 225
  meetings with Christopher, 164, 202, 222, 224, 228–229
  peaceful unification, 284–285
  sensitivity of Taiwan, 262
  on strategic partnership, 282
  trade, 166, 170–171
Quemoy (Kinmen), 117, 243

Radio Free Asia, 168, 270
Reagan, Ronald. *See* Reagan administration
Reagan administration, 54
  arms sales, 126–127, 147
  Asian strategy and policy, 62–63
  August 17 communiqué, 30–33, 128–129, 130
  Taiwan policy precedents, 131–140
Realpolitik, xiii, 19, 44
  in U.S. foreign policy, 12–18
Red Cross, 166
Refugee migration, 97

Regional security, 59, 66–67, 90–91
  Clinton policy, 95–99, 101–109
  concerns regarding China, 225–226
Renmin Ribao, 208–209
Report of the Quadrennial Defense Review (QDR), 91
Report on the Bottom-up Review, 88
Republic of China (ROC)
  termination of diplomatic relations, 34
  See also Nationalists; Taiwan
Republic of Taiwan. *See* Taiwan
Reunification, peaceful, 109, 124–125, 179–181, 259
  Chinese and Taiwanese attitudes toward, 48–49
  eight-point and six-point proposals, 195–199
  international presence of Taiwan, 207
  Taiwan's conditions, 136, 205
  U.S. policy toward, 137–140
  Ye Jianying's "nine-point" proposal, 132–137
  See also Cross-Strait relations
Richardson, Bill, 279
Ring magnets, 254
Robinson, Davis R., 31
ROC. *See* Republic of China (ROC)
Ross, Robert, 53
Roth, Stanley, 108–109, 279
Roy, J. Stapleton, 178, 211
Rubin, Robert, 263, 268
Russia, 105, 121
  as challenge, 63, 127, 291
  collapse of, 64, 66, 75, 140
  relations with China, 115, 118, 130–131, 290

Sanctions, imposition of
  arms sales, 149, 169, 170, 172, 213, 219, 222, 254, 270–271
  Tiananmen Square, 141, 143–144, 225
  trade, 199, 255, 263
Sasser, James, 211, 226–227
Schultz, George, 137–138
Scowcroft, Brent, 16, 156
Second World War, 52, 61, 113
Security, Taiwan, 30–34, 51
Security, U.S.
  challenges to, 91–94, 291–292
  Clinton strategy, 85–87, 107–108, 169, 201–202

Index

engagement and, 216–217, 230–231
during Taiwan Strait crisis, 254–257
SEF. *See* Straits Exchange Foundation (SEF)
Seiroku Kajiyama, 50
Seventh Fleet, U.S., 90, 115–116
Shalikashvili, John, 16, 17, 232, 257–258
Shanghai Communiqué, 119–120
Shattuck, John, 164, 201
Shipping lanes, 50, 58, 202, 245–247, 259–260
Siew, Vincent, 177, 285, 286
Sigur, Gaston, 137, 138
Simon, Paul, 35, 37
Singapore, 52
Sino-American relations, 51, 150
  Clinton administration, 199–203, 217–219
  joint communiqués, 118–123, 127–130, 164, 224, 229, 251, 266, 309
  normalization, 118–131
  Persian Gulf War and, 143–144
Sino-British agreement, Hong Kong, 134–136
Sino-Soviet split, 118
Smith, Adam, 4
Solomon, Gerald, 35
Solomon, Richard, 70
South China Sea, 202
Southeast Asian Treaty Organization, 117
South Korea, 51, 102
Soviet Union, 105, 121
  as challenge, 63, 127, 291
  collapse of, 64, 66, 75, 140
  relations with China, 115, 118, 130–131, 290
Spanish-American War, 1898, 60
Spratly Islands, 72, 202
State Department Authorization Bill, 31–32
State visits, 164
  canceled by Chinese, 208, 215
  dialogue resumed, 222
  Jiang, 50
  Jiang-Clinton, 5–12, 24, 38, 51, 224, 225, 281–283
  between Taiwan and U.S., 33, 35, 36–37
Straits Exchange Foundation (SEF), 136, 178–179, 199, 269, 283, 284, 285, 287
Strategic considerations, 14, 47–48, 52–53, 55
  assessment of China, 81, 288–296

EASI reports, 70, 71–74, 75, 103–104
Taiwan, 48–49, 245–247
Strategic Framework for the Asian Pacific Rim, A, 70, 71
Strategic partnership, 22, 41, 87–88, 282
Summer Olympic Games 2000, 163–164, 244
Summits. *See* State visits
Superpowers, 92–94, 139, 245, 267, 288, 291–292
Sutter, Robert, 280
Symington Amendment, 1976, 254

Taipai. *See* Taiwan
Taipei Economic and Cultural Representative Office in the United States, 178
Taiwan
  American values and, 2–3, 22
  Clinton policies, 173–178
  copyright violation, 175–176
  cross-Strait relations, 42, 51, 178–179, 266–267, 269, 285
  democratization of, 2–3, 176–177, 193, 278, 299, 309
  demographics, x
  description of, 50–51
  diplomatic isolation, 42–43, 206
  "dollar diplomacy", 194
  future scenarios, 310–311
  geostrategic value, 53, 245–247
  independence, 14, 15, 263, 267, 298–300
  Indigenous Defense Fighter program, 147, 251–252
  international presence, 14, 42, 173, 177–178, 182, 183, 206, 307
  Japanese rule, x, 114
  Lee's U.S. visit, 38–43
  as market democracy, 36, 52, 310
  military equipment, acquisition of, 147–148
  "nine-point" proposal rejection, 133
  as obstacle, 87, 95
  "pragmatic diplomacy", 182, 193–194, 207
  presidential election, 248, 268–269
  reunification with China, 48–49
  self-determination, x, 16, 241
  strategic value assessment by China, 243–247
  support in U.S., 18, 23, 43–44, 81, 150, 211

"There Is No 'Taiwan Question'; There Is Only a 'China Question'", 184–185
U.S. interests in, 50–54
U.S. military support, xii–xiii, 17, 306–307
"vacation diplomacy", 194, 206
See also Lee Teng-hui
"Taiwan bucket", 31, 132
"Taiwan card", 211, 245
Taiwan Conundrum in U.S. China Policy, The (Lasater), organization of, xiii–xiv
Taiwanese, x, 114, 120, 176–177, 193, 206, 221, 278, 299
Taiwan Independence Party, 52
Taiwan issue, 5–8, 300–302
principles governing, 118–131
Taiwan Policy Review, 34–38, 177–178, 242
"Taiwan Question and the Reunification of China, The", 179–184
Taiwan Relations Act (TRA), 1979, 14, 23, 118, 173, 250–251, 264, 303, 309
Murkowski Amendment to, 30–34
as reaction to Carter normalization, 123–124
use of force and, 261–262
Taiwan Strait crisis, x, 14, 19, 242–243, 277
Chinese assessment of Taiwan's strategic value, 243–247
escalation of, 259–263
policy statements on, 263–268
other security issues, 254–257
Taiwan issue heats up, 248–254
Taiwan's elections and reduced tensions, 268–271
tensions increase, 257–259
See also Cross-Strait relations
Talbott, Strobe, 33
Tarnoff, Peter, 222, 223
Technology, military, 132, 146–147, 158, 173, 202
See also Arms sales; Proliferation, arms
Tenet, George, 279, 291–292
Textiles, illegally labeled, 161, 165
"There Is No 'Taiwan Question'; There Is Only a 'China Question'", 184–185
Third World, technology transfers to, 146
Threats, categories of, 86
See also Military conflict
Tiananmen Square, 4, 9, 63, 145, 160
effects of, 64, 69, 81, 140–141
sanctions after, 141, 143–144, 225

Tibet, 160, 161, 168, 270, 281
See also Dalai Lama
Time magazine, 223
Tong Zhiguang, 157
Torricelli, Robert, 35
TRA. See Taiwan Relations Act (TRA), 1979
Trade, 149, 199
Clinton administration, 159–168
cross-Strait, 262
deficit, 56, 158, 204, 255
surplus, 145, 156, 159, 228
Trade Act, 1974, 145, 161
Trademark Law, 176
See also Intellectual Property Rights (IPR)
Trading partners, 50, 52, 76, 174
Truman administration, 114–116
"Two Chinas" policy, 14, 118, 128, 182, 196, 208, 278
Two-track approach, 258
See also A Dual-track approach

Unification, 139
See also Reunification, peaceful
United Nations, 55, 83, 225
China denounces U.S., 170–171
cooperation of China, 145, 158
Fourth World Conference on Women, 223–224
Taiwan seeks entry to, 35, 37, 183, 206, 222, 267, 307
United States
accomodation over Taiwan, 298
after Lee's visit, 213–221
See also specific topics
U.S. News and World Report, 227
U.S. Pacific Forces (USCINCPAC), 102
USPACOM, 203
USS Bunker Hill, 202
USS Fort McHenry, 248

Values, American, 1–2, 13, 22, 44, 69, 275
in assessment of U.S. policy, 9–12
toward China, 3–5
influence on U.S. foreign policy, 8, 17–19
related to Taiwan, 2–3
Vietnam, 105, 117, 121, 219–220
Visas, 34, 242, 248
Lee's visit to U.S., 38–43
Voice of America, 161, 166, 168

Wall Street Journal, 269
Wang Dan, 157
Wang Daohan, 179, 210, 283, 287
Wang Jisi, 144
Wang Juntao, 165
Wang-Koo talks, 38, 179, 199, 210, 212, 269, 284–288, 302
Wang Xizhe, 157
Wang Zhen, 157
War, in Taiwan Strait, 300–301, 303–305
  See also Military conflict
Warner, Ted, 202
Warning, by U.S., 17, 260–261
Washington Post, 248–249, 254
Weapons of mass destruction (WMD), 76, 89, 293–294
Wei Jingsheng, 24, 163, 165
Wen Guangchun, 248
White, Lynn, 16
White paper, the, 180–184
Wiedemann, Kent, 204–205, 217–219
Wilson, Woodrow, 61
Wolfowitz, Paul, 63

World Trade Organization (WTO)
  China seeks entrance to, 24, 200–201, 204, 228
  Taiwan seeks entrance to, 269
World War II, 52, 61, 113
Wu, Harry, 24, 214, 220, 222, 223
Wu Yi, 200, 263

Xinhua, 209, 212, 282
Xiong Guankai, 202
Xu Wenli, 157

Yang Shangkun, 157
Yan Xuetong, 259
Ye Jianying's "nine-point" proposal, 132–137
Yeltsin, Boris, 282
Yinghe incident, 170, 244
Yu Zhenwu, 41

Zhang Yebai, 208
Zhao Ziyang, 126
Zhou Enlai, 118, 142